MEANTONE TEMPERAMENTS ON LUTES AND VIOLS

PUBLICATIONS OF THE EARLY MUSIC INSTITUTE

Paul Elliott, editor

MEANTONE TEMPERAMENTS ON LUTES AND VIOLS

David Dolata

INDIANA UNIVERSITY PRESS
Bloomington and Indianapolis

This book is a publication of

Indiana University Press
Office of Scholarly Publishing
Herman B Wells Library 350
1320 East 10th Street
Bloomington, Indiana 47405 USA

iupress.indiana.edu

The paper used in this publication meets the minimum requirements of the American National Standard for Information Sciences—Permanence of Paper for Printed Library Materials, ANSI Z39.48-1992.

Manufactured in the United States of America

Library of Congress Cataloging-in-Publication Data

Names: Dolata, David, author.
Title: Meantone temperaments on lutes and viols / David Dolata.
Other titles: Publications of the Early Music Institute.
Description: Bloomington ; Indianapolis : Indiana University Press, 2016. | ?2016 | Series: Publications of the Early Music Institute | Includes bibliographical references and index.
Identifiers: LCCN 2016002164 | ISBN 9780253021236 (cloth : alkaline paper) | ISBN 9780253021465 (ebook)
Subjects: LCSH: Lute—Tuning. | Viols—Tuning. | Musical temperament.
Classification: LCC MT165 .D65 2016 | DDC 787.8/1928—dc23
LC record available at http://lccn.loc.gov/2016002164

1 2 3 4 5 21 20 19 18 17 16

For my wife, Mary

Before one plays of the lute he must have his lute well strung and well tuned as it behoveth to get good ink, good paper and a good pen before one undertakes to write well. Therefore to follow good order we shall begin by this discourse, since that it is impossible to play well unless the lute be well strung and set in tune.

—Burwell Lute Tutor

Contents

Diagrams

Tables

Audio Files

Audio files can be accessed via the book's Indiana University Press web page, www.iupress.indiana.edu.

4.1. Pure major third C–E (386c.) [treble viol]

4.2. 1/6-comma meantone temperament major third C–E (393c.) [treble viol]

4.3. Equal temperament major third C–E (400c.) [treble viol]

4.4. Pythagorean major third C–E (408c.) [treble viol]

4.5.1. Pure perfect fifth between C (262 Hz) and G (393 Hz) [MaxMSP]

4.5.2. Pure perfect fifth between C (524 Hz) and G (786 Hz) [MaxMSP]

4.6.1. Equal temperament fifth between C (262 Hz) and G (391.7 Hz) [MaxMSP]

4.6.2. Equal temperament fifth between C (524 Hz) and G (783.4 Hz) [MaxMSP]

4.7.1. Pure major third between C (262 Hz) and E (327.5 Hz) [MaxMSP]

4.7.2. Pure major third between C (524 Hz) and E (655 Hz) [MaxMSP]

4.8.1. Equal temperament major third between C (262 Hz) and E (330.2 Hz) [MaxMSP]

4.8.2. Equal temperament major third between C (524 Hz) and E (660.4 Hz) [MaxMSP]

4.9.1. Pythagorean comma between C (262 Hz) and B♯ (265.6 Hz) played melodically [MaxMSP]

4.9.2. Pythagorean comma between C (524 Hz) and B♯ (531.2 Hz) played melodically [MaxMSP]

4.10.1. Pythagorean comma between C (262 Hz) and B♯ (265.6 Hz) played harmonically [MaxMSP]

4.10.2. Pythagorean comma between C (524 Hz) and B♯ (531.2 Hz) played harmonically [MaxMSP]

4.11.1. Pythagorean major third between C (262 Hz) and E (331.6 Hz) [MaxMSP]

4.11.2. Pythagorean major third between C (524 Hz) and E (663.2 Hz) [MaxMSP]

4.12. Syntonic comma between the first and sixth courses [lute]

5.1. Equal temperament triad [lute]

5.2. 1/4-comma meantone triad [lute]

5.3. V–I cadence in G Major in 1/4-comma meantone temperament [lute]

5.4. I–IV–V–I progression in B♭ Major in 1/4-comma meantone temperament [lute]

5.5. i–iv–V–I progression in G Minor in 1/4-comma meantone temperament [lute]

5.6. I–IV–V–I progression in B♭ Major in 1/5-comma meantone temperament [lute]

5.7. i–iv–V–I progression in G Minor in 1/5-comma meantone temperament [lute]

5.8. I–IV–V–I progression in B♭ Major in 1/6-comma meantone temperament [lute]

5.9. i–iv–V–I progression in G Minor in 1/6-comma meantone temperament [lute]

5.10. I–IV–V–I progression in B♭ Major in 1/8-comma meantone temperament [lute]

5.11. i–iv–V–I progression in G Minor in 1/8-comma meantone temperament [lute]

5.12. B Major chord in Vallotti temperament [harpsichord]

5.13. E Major chord in Vallotti temperament [harpsichord]

7.1. John Dowland, "Tarleton's Riserrectione" in 1/4-comma meantone temperament [lute]

7.2. John Dowland, "Tarleton's Riserrectione" in 1/6-comma meantone temperament [lute]

7.3. John Dowland, "Tarleton's Riserrectione" in 1/8-comma meantone temperament [lute]

7.4. John Dowland, "Tarleton's Riserrectione" in equal temperament [lute]

7.5. Denis Gaultier, "La Coquette virtuose" in 1/5-comma meantone temperament [baroque lute]

7.6. Girolamo Giovanni Kapsberger, "Toccata arpeggiata" in 1/6-comma meantone temperament [theorbo]

Acoustic audio files were performed by David Dolata. Artificially generated files were created by Federico Bonacossa. The audio files were recorded at the Herbert and Nicole Wertheim Performing Arts Center Concert Hall at the Florida International University School of Music in Miami, Florida, using the following instruments:

Eight-course Renaissance lute after V. Venere I (Padova, 1592) by Paolo Busato

Thirteen-course Baroque lute after M. Dieffopruchar/J. J. Edlinger by Paolo Busato

Fourteen-course theorbo after M. Tieffenbrucker by Paolo Busato

Treble viol by the Charlie Ogle Workshop

Double manual Flemish harpsichord by Carl Fudge

Acknowledgments

One of the great pleasures of writing a book such as this is that it has brought me into varying degrees of contact with a wide range of thoughtful artists, luthiers, scholars, and others whose generosity and enthusiasm for this project has been truly moving. These include lutenists Kenneth Bé, Richard Stone, Pascale Bouquet of the Société Française de Luth, Gian Luca Lastraioli of the Società del Liuto, Christopher Goodwin of the Lute Society, Matthias Spaeter, and Andreas Schlegel; luthiers Paolo Busato, Ray Nurse, Alexis Anderson, Maurice Ottiger, John Pringle, Daniel Larson, and Stephen Barber; gambists Alison Crum, Suzanne Ferguson, Kathleen Merfeld, Mikaho Somekawa, and José Vázquez; guitarists Clare Callahan, Neil Haverstick, Monica Hall, John Schneider, and Tolgahan Çoğulu; vihuelist John Griffiths; art collector George Kremer and curators Ture Bergstrøm and Margaret Downie Banks; Patricia Sidlinger, David Chatfield, the late Kathy Gaubatz and the Miami Bach Society, Andrew Hartig, Arthur Ness, Aldo Abreu, Darryl Martin, Joshua Rifkin, Joel Galand, Federico Bonacossa, Daniel Russo-Batterham, Nuria Torres, Stewart Carter, Margaret Murata, Kerala Snyder, and Philippe Canguilhem. I owe a particular debt of gratitude to Victor Coelho, my partner in so many musical activities, for all his helpful suggestions.

Much of this book was written during a one-semester sabbatical provided by Florida International University, for which I am most grateful. The FIU graduate students who have participated in my seminars on tunings and temperaments have been a constant source of practical knowledge and inspiration, and their kind critiques have made this a better book. I am also pleased to thank the Society for Music Theory for its generous subvention in support of the book's musical examples, diagrams, and figures.

Librarians from Boston to Italy, but especially Daniel Hardin at FIU, delighted in hunting down sources for me, and others whose names I either never knew or have long since forgotten include the student assistants at the Case Western Reserve University engineering computer lab who relentlessly helped me derive the correct formula for converting fretting ratios into cents and vice versa and furthermore insisted on furnishing me with that information in spreadsheet form so that I would always have access to it long after our paths had parted. Without their foresight and dedication and that of many others, this book would have been less helpful than I hope it is.

Ross Duffin and Paul O'Dette have been involved in this project from its very inception. Their ardent support, probing criticisms, and insightful advice have shaped much of this book's content. Most of the material in part 2, I learned directly from Ross Duffin. He also kindly read a draft of chapter 1, suggesting numerous improvements to the historical narrative that require a perspective on the topic that few possess. In addition to creating the MaxMSP audio files, Federico Bonacossa also checked my hertz math, gently pointed out instances where I had gone astray, and provided invaluable guidance in the creation of all the audio files. Peter Forrester lent his extensive knowledge and expertise on fixed metal-fret wire instruments to chapter 2, which benefited greatly from his input. Tim Watson turned his sharp eye to the murky issue of iconography in chapter 3 as it pertains to lutes and viols; I hope his work inspires others to enlist objective scientific method in the service of aesthetic beauty. Over the years, Olav Chris Henriksen has taught me a good deal of what I know about strings, frets, pegs, and atmospheric conditions as they pertain to tuning. His perspective and close reading of early drafts and patient explanation of many of the concepts described in chapter 6 helped me better understand the interplay among the various physical factors that affect our capacity to tune well. As a result, I tune more effectively and easily since I incorporated his advice into that chapter. As an amateur viola da gamba player, I have had to rely on greater assistance from others in chapter 9 more than any other. That aid has chiefly come from Richard Carter, Johanna Valencia, Mary Springfels, and Michael Twyford, who have guided me into the glorious world of the viol, for which I will always be grateful. Richard Carter has pored over the entire manuscript with his eagle eye and thankfully left no stone unturned. His perspective, insights, and constructive criticism have made this book immeasurably better and considerably more nuanced than it would have been without his acuity. To him I owe my deepest thanks.

It has been an honor and joy to be in regular communication with each of these brilliant scholars and musicians in the advancement of our shared interest in improving how players of our instruments tune. Errors of commission and omission inevitably creep into any book. I can confidently claim that any in the book you are about to read are of my own making, notwithstanding the efforts of all whom I thank here.

For the better part of my life, I have profited from the wisdom and common sense of my wife, Mary. Indeed, she has made our time together the best part of my life, and a considerable portion of it has been spent discussing Bellerofonte Castaldi and tunings and temperaments. Whether they know it or not, she and I are on a first-name basis with Bellerofonte, Pythagoras, and Vincenzo Galilei, often discussing their accomplishments and foibles as if they were family members. Mary is my finest editor, always my first, last, and best counselor, my dearest friend, and closest confidant. For these reasons and many more, I dedicate this book to her.

MEANTONE TEMPERAMENTS ON LUTES AND VIOLS

Introduction

Tuning can be among the most vexing, frustrating, and time-consuming aspects of playing the lute or viol. The old French expression "to swear like a lute tuner" is not without some merit. Yet there are few adjustments a fretted instrument player can make that require so little effort but return such dramatic rewards, including more stable consonances, colorful dissonances, and better resonance. Contemporary players of instruments with movable frets who set their frets in equal temperament usually do so by default, since they are unaware that there are other temperaments that might work better for their purposes.

What is the point of having movable frets if you don't move them? It's like owning a Ferrari but only driving it five city blocks to work and never taking it out on an isolated, arcing highway in the countryside or on a straightaway in the middle of nowhere; all its handling capacity and power under the hood are reduced to nothing but unrealized potential. Without exploiting the full measure of lutes' and viols' sonic resources by failing to take advantage of the benefits of movable frets, like the Ferrari, you are left with something that looks good but remains only a shadow of what it could be.

Throughout the course of music history, our concept of consonance and dissonance has changed significantly. For instance, centuries ago the perfect fourth was considered a dissonance that required resolution by a major third in a 4–3 suspension. Prior to that, the tritone was referred to as the *diablo in musica,* yet today we don't even notice it in the dominant V7 chord or in jazz, its shock value long faded into the recesses of music history. Dissonance has become so relative and constant that it has largely lost its impact, not unlike violence or vulgarity in movies. Like the boy who cried wolf, we cry dissonance and receive no response. As children of the twentieth and twenty-first centuries, Westerners have been conditioned to hear equal temperament as acceptable because we've known nothing else. But just as easily as we learn to appreciate finer food after being brought up on a diet of fast food, where the latter becomes no longer acceptable, we can move beyond tolerating the excessively wide and stringent equal-tempered third in favor of a more euphonious narrower third that is pure or nearly so. And we can return to a place where consonances are consonances and dissonances are dissonances.

Fretted instruments tuned predominantly in fourths rather than fifths are especially suitable for chordal music because the fourths allow the chord tones on the fretboard to be physically close enough to enable the fingers to form chords, which is also facilitated by the frets, particularly on the viol, where they mimic the open string resonance. Frets and instruments tuned in fourths go together. We must recognize that they favor verticalities, that is, harmonic over melodic beauty. It is their nature. In the transition from meantone temperaments to equal temperament, we sacrificed the beauty of the thirds to gain total key flexibility. Meantone temperaments, that is, those with narrower thirds than in equal temperament, can give you a more satisfying experience, and the vast majority of the lute, theorbo, guitar, vihuela, and viol repertoire can be performed in 1/6-comma meantone temperament to good effect. Remember that most of the music we play on these instruments features the major third prominently. Although I use equal temperament when circumstances beyond my control dictate that I must, I much prefer the sound of meantone temperaments and refer to it throughout the book as if it were a given that it sounds better than equal temperament. By the end of this book, I hope you'll agree.

On the other hand, some do not believe that the effort required to learn to tune in unequal temperaments is justified because they have simply never heard the difference. I hope that your own experience as you work your way through this book and the audio files that accompany it will convince you otherwise. There are those who prove their fundamental misunderstanding of the most basic precepts of unequal temperaments by contending that they cannot work on fretted instruments because the octaves are necessarily out of tune. You will soon learn the simple fallacy of such statements. To these arguments, we must add the hastily produced trump card, the refuge of the historically unaware, that proclaims that the historical use of meantone temperaments on fretted instruments is unsubstantiated by evidence. Several chapters will dispel this pervasive myth.

Others disparagingly assert that the plucked sound decays so quickly that one temperament is as good as another or that even at full volume the lute and theorbo are so quiet compared with other instruments that it really doesn't matter how they're tuned in ensemble situations. But is that really the case? When the theorbo is paired with a chamber organ, the theorbo's strong attack is easily heard against the organ's sustained tones. As the theory goes, following the lute's initial attack, any dissonance quickly dissipates with the lute's sound. But again, the notes on a good theorbo, particularly those struck on the longer bass strings attached to the second pegbox, sustain long enough when played with a chamber organ to allow any tuning inconsistency to be heard. To my knowledge no one has had the temerity to use this specious argument with regard to the viol, which can certainly hold its own against any harpsichord or chamber organ.

Lutes are often minimized by the statement that they appear in the ensemble mix solely to provide local color, the plucked sound, or to bind the various instruments together in the ensemble sound wash. While plucked instruments do indeed provide those services, such statements ignore the myriad situations in which players of fretted instruments play with just one other musician, for example, when a lutenist accompanies a singer or a gambist performs an Ortiz *recercada* accompanied by a harpsichord. In large ensembles, it can be difficult to pick any one individual continuo instrument out of the mix, but the texture often thins enough at some point or another to allow the plucked instrument to be heard.

Over the years I have heard critics argue that tuning infelicities involving fretted instruments are easily ignored. You may have noticed that "easily ignored" is in the passive voice; that is, the agent is not expressed and with good reason. Rare is the musician who would admit: "I hear that the tuning is poor, but I choose to ignore it." Ignoring a problem is not the same as not noticing it. The former involves a conscious decision to act in one way or another. You cannot ignore something that you do not notice in the first place; you can only ignore something of which you are aware. Who wants to admit to ignoring a problem? Ignoring a problem tacitly acknowledges that there is indeed a problem. The point of this book, however, is that there isn't a problem because in most circumstances, fretted instruments can accommodate themselves to virtually any tuning system.

At the other end of the spectrum regarding volume, a common but misguided saw is that since citterns were used primarily for "crash and bang" rhythm guitar–type accompaniments, the temperament doesn't really matter. This view, of course, neglects consideration of the cittern's solo repertoire and that it can be used for less raucous music. Ironically, as we will discover, the construction of citterns and orpharions conclusively proves that their makers were obsessively scrupulous about euphonious tuning.

As you reflect on the preceding paragraphs and will see throughout this book, the arguments against using any temperament but equal quickly dissolve under the least bit of scrutiny. The fact that many of today's finest fretted instrument players arrange their frets in unequal temperaments to enhance the beauty of the music they play every day is sufficient evidence that unequal temperaments merit your attention. That it is an easily attainable goal is demonstrated by the fact that from an early age, French children learn to play the lute in meantone temperaments, as do Cuban viol players.[1] Those who reject unequal temperaments implicitly ask you to limit yourself, to stay within your comfort zone. I ask that you open yourself to the possibility that there might be another way and, for you, perhaps a better way.

Three figures loom largely over this book. No discussion of tunings and temperaments would be complete without considering their work, and it is safe to say that for one reason or another, this book could or would not have been written without their influence. The first is Ross Duffin, whom you've already met. His syndicated NPR program, *Micrologus: Exploring the World of Early Music,* his articles and book chapters on tuning, and, most recently, his *How Equal Temperament Ruined Harmony (and Why You Should Care)* have introduced an entire generation to historically informed performance practice and in particular historical tunings and temperaments.

Nothing can replace Mark Lindley's pivotal *Lutes, Viols and Temperaments* (1984). It is, of course, the groundbreaking work in tunings and temperaments on fretted instruments and is one of my most treasured tomes.[2] As the most extensive treatment of historical information to date concerning historical temperaments on fretted instruments, Lindley's book serves as one of our main sources of information. While *Lutes, Viols and Temperaments* provides a comprehensive tour through the historical writings on various tunings and temperaments, its aim was not to provide practical advice that can be used on a daily basis. That, however, is the goal of this book, and, in that sense, they complement each other. Although I take the facts, historical information, and translations Lindley provides at face value, my assessment of the evidence occasionally leads me to form opinions divergent from his. This in no means diminishes my admiration and gratitude to him, for without his work, I wouldn't have been able to form any opinion whatsoever. I advise you to read this book as well as his other works, including his nuanced article on temperaments in *Grove Music Online.*

Finally, we come to lutenist and theorist Vincenzo Galilei, the most outspoken proponent of equal temperament and father of the famous astronomer Galileo. He will appear throughout these pages on a regular basis. An irascible, bold iconoclast and contrarian, Galilei is one of the most vexing figures I suspect you and I will ever encounter. As inconsistent as he was brilliant, Galilei's energetic and exhaustive publications still await a thorough untangling.

Other useful sources are listed in the extensive bibliography and cited in the text. Our brief overview of the state of research would be incomplete without mention of Eugen Dombois's influential articles in the 1970s. They sparked the first interest in meantone temperaments among lutenists, in particular his 1974 article "Varieties of Meantone Temperament Realized on the Lute," in the *Journal of the Lute Society of America.* Unfortunately, the excitement this article generated in the lute world was short-lived because of a single fatal flaw that undermined Dombois's attempt to convince lutenists that meantone temperaments can work on the lute: the printer inverted the denominator and numerator of the formula Dombois gave for converting cents into length to set the frets accurately along the fretboard. The correction in the subsequent Lute Society of America journal was marred by yet another typo, and by the time the correct formula appeared in the next issue, the damage was irreversible.[3]

Meantone Temperaments on Lutes and Viols is designed to serve as a practical guide consisting of parts and chapters that can be read as a continuing narrative or excerpted as needed. The book is divided into three large parts, "Precedent," "Theory," and "Practice," reflecting the historical progression of the reclassification of music from a science to an art and, more specifically, science's evolving focus from theory to practice, manifested in the art of manipulating theoretical information to serve practical purposes in the sixteenth and seventeenth centuries.[4]

Part 1 consists of several chapters surveying the evidence supporting the use of unequal temperaments on fretted instruments. It does not pretend to be a complete treatment of the subject, which merits its own dedicated book. As an integrated whole, it can be considered separately. If you are unfamiliar with temperaments in general, and meantone temperaments in particular, you may profit from reading part 2 prior to part 1.

Split into two chapters, part 2 begins with an explanation of why temperaments are necessary and how they work, followed by a chapter that describes a variety of temperaments with which fretted instrument players should be familiar. This information is fundamental to your understanding of how to control temperaments so they don't control you. My aim here is to demystify tuning systems by providing only what is necessary to accomplish that end. Accordingly, I round off numbers to simplify life for us both. For instance, we spend some time with a discrepancy known as the "syntonic" comma. Its precise size is slightly larger than 21.5 cents, "cents" being the unit used to measure the width of intervals that will be explained in due course. For our purposes, however, I use 22c.; in the large scheme of things, the difference is negligible.[5] In other instances where figures need to add up to a particular sum, it will be necessary to include one or two decimal places. Musical examples will be given primarily in G tuning since it is commonly used on both viol and lute. General tablature examples of intervals are provided in French tablature, but extracts from intabulated compositions appear in the original national tablature style.

Part 3 provides you with the practical guidance required to try unequal temperaments on your instrument. Chapter 6 addresses the physical and environmental factors that can affect tuning, in particular, sharpening. Additional chapters are dedicated to the tuning process, continuo playing in unequal temperaments, and special issues that pertain to the viol and related instruments. The continuo information in chapter 8 devoted to the archlute and theorbo can be easily applied to less common instruments such as the arch-cittern, ceterone, and gittern.

Finally, I give you advance notice that while this book concerns fretted instruments writ large, since I am a lutenist, you might find the text somewhat lute-centric. With a great deal of help from several well-known viol virtuosi and pedagogues, duly noted in the acknowledgments and notes, chapter 9 attempts to redress this predisposition. The audio files referred to in the text can be accessed through the book's Indiana University Press web page, www.iupress.indiana.edu.

Because of our repertoires, lute players tend to be somewhat insular. Many of us in large countries such as the United States, Canada, and Australia may be the only lutenist or viol player for hundreds of miles around. So it's entirely understandable that fretted instrument players might not often be exposed to other players who tune in unequal temperaments. But as the interest in earlier musics continues to expand, fretted instrument players are increasingly mingling with keyboard and other instrumentalists who use meantone and related temperaments as a matter of course. To many of them, meantone temperaments are second nature. They can easily become so for us, too.

During the course of writing this book, the evidence has challenged me to reexamine and ultimately revise many of my previously held assumptions. I entered into this project presuming that the issues were black and white, but soon realized that they were really just so many shades of gray, which eventually melted into a beautiful palette of color. I hope you too can share this experience. At the very least, I ask that you welcome the prospect that the ideas in this book might be of some benefit to you. But if you are reading these words right now, I suspect you're already there.

PART ONE

Precedent

PART ONE INTRODUCTION

Myth's stronghold on history is not easily weakened.

—Victor Coelho, *Music and Science in the Age of Galileo*

AND NOWHERE MORE THAN on the issue of temperaments on fretted instruments. The myth, of course, is that fretted instruments have always been restricted to equal temperament. One temperament and one temperament only, not even an "either/or." But even "either/or" is antithetical to art, which welcomes multiple solutions to its challenges and diverse interpretations of its subject matter. In the Renaissance and Baroque eras as now, equal and unequal systems traveled together along parallel tracks, occasionally intersecting, but coexisting more or less peacefully outside the contentious realm of the professional theorists who oftentimes drew lines in the wet concrete, appropriating tuning systems as metaphors for a variety of worldviews regarding Nature and Art, God and Man, and so on, issues that went far beyond the concern of practical everyday musicians who were simply interested in making music sound as well as it could. It seems most likely that players of fretted instruments chose meantone or equal temperament according to their needs and abilities depending on the circumstances at hand.

That many of today's finest players of fretted instruments arrange their frets in meantone temperaments whenever possible is indisputable. The following chapters aim to demonstrate that the same was true of our musical ancestors, particularly professional players and those who regularly performed with other instrumentalists, especially keyboard players, whom we know with certainty chose unequal temperaments for their instruments.[1] While the ability to tune in unequal temperaments may have been restricted to advanced players and professionals, as lutenist Paul O'Dette has suggested on many occasions, shouldn't these be the players we emulate?[2] After all, who hopes to follow in the footsteps of a mediocre player? My purpose here is not to convince you that all our predecessors on fretted instruments set their frets in a meantone arrangement, but rather that enough of them did so to warrant our pursuit of this subject.

The array of evidence pointing to the use of unequal temperaments on fretted instruments in the sixteenth through eighteenth centuries is multifaceted. It includes reports of countless well-known ensemble situations where lutenists or viol players joined keyboard players who presumably favored meantone temperaments, as well as scores specifying such ensembles. Historical treatises and commentaries offer bountiful evidence that fretted instruments were set in unequal temperaments. Lutes and viols also performed in prescribed consorts with wire-strung instruments whose metal frets were set in meantone and related temperaments; these instruments survive today. And, finally, there is iconography, a nascent field overflowing with promise and offering a great deal of fodder for future study.

Despite all this evidence, nothing, however, is more compelling than the fact that many of us use meantone temperaments on lutes and viols on a daily basis with very little effort. Just like our predecessors.

CHAPTER ONE

Historical Performance, Thought, and Perspective

Historical Performance Situations Involving Fretted Instruments

FOLLOWING THE BAROQUE PENCHANT for categorization, in 1600 the noted music critic Giovanni Maria Artusi classified instruments into three orders:

1. Keyboard instruments tuned in unequal temperaments
2. Those such as the human voice, trombones, recorders, and so on, that could accommodate themselves to any temperament, equal or un
3. Fretted instruments that are restricted to equal temperament

He furthermore claimed that instruments of the first and third orders cannot play with each other and that those of the second can play with any of them, views that echo those stated by Nicola Vicentino in 1555 and Ercole Bottrigari in 1594.[1] Since we know that fretted instruments regularly appeared with instruments from the other two orders in professional ensemble settings, it is both obvious and fortunate that professional lutenists and gambists either did not get the memo or, if they did, disregarded it. Innumerable paintings illustrating ensembles with both a keyboard and one or more lutes or viols hang in museums all over the world, but, more important, the finest composers continued to specify lutes and viols together with keyboards in their scores long before and after the period of Artusi's writings.[2]

In the 1570s Don Girolamo Merenda described a scene at the Ferrarese court where composer and harpsichordist Luzzasco Luzzaschi was joined by a lutenist in the accompaniment of three singers, who also accompanied themselves on lute, viol, and harp. Theorbists, for instance, are fond of citing Cavalieri's singling out the pairing of the organ and theorbo for the "buonissimo effetto" they make together, a clear contradiction of Artusi's injunction. The Dutch-born Roman engraver and printer Simone Verovio, best known for his publications of Luzzaschi's *Madrigali* (1601) and two books of Merulo's toccata intabulations in 1598 and 1604, even published two collections, *Diletto spirituale* (1586) and *Lodi della musica* (1595), containing a vocal part accompanied by both a keyboard score and Italian lute tablature. As late as 1669, Giovanni Pittoni's two-volume *Intavolatura di tiorba* includes twelve sonatas da chiesa with a clearly marked "organo" basso continuo part and twelve sonatas da camera with a clavicembalo part, each presented below the theorbo tablature.

Giovanni Battista Doni reported how theorbos, lutes, and harpsichords played together in Cavalieri's *Rappresentazione di anima, et di corpo* and in Monteverdi's *Orfeo,* where the composer specified particular combinations of instruments to accompany various scenes—the theorbo appears with both the harpsichord and organ together and in more than one scene with the organ alone. The viola da gamba is also paired with keyboard instruments as well. Following *Orfeo,* Monteverdi continued to pair the theorbo and viol with keyboard instruments as a matter of course; indeed, the combination of lutes, keyboards, and sometimes guitar formed the core of the opera continuo section throughout most of Europe for the rest of the Baroque era.[3]

Theorbo and keyboard together also continued to be regularly specified in the performance of accompanied madrigals and arias by Monteverdi, Carlo Milanuzzi, Bartolomeo Barbarino, and many others.[4] In the introduction to his third book of madrigals (1619) Francesco Turini wrote:

> The madrigals presented here may be played with a keyboard instrument alone, without the *chitarrone;* or with a *chitarrone,* or other similar instrument, without the keyboard instrument; nevertheless, they will turn out much better with one and the other. . . . Hence to remedy this a supplicated basso continuo part has been given here that can be used not only by the *chitarrone* but by a *bassetto da braccio,* a *viola da gamba,* a bassoon and, as well, other such instruments, all of which go well with the violins but do not have quite the same effect as the *chitarrone* when played throughout.[5]

In the preface to his *Pièces de viole* (1689) Marin Marais specified that his viol pieces could be accompanied by the harpsichord or theorbo, the latter of which "ce qui fait très bien avec la Viole."[6] The harpsichord would certainly have been set in some variety of meantone or a closely related temperament. It follows that Marais assumed that the theorbo player would be able to field a suitable version of the same temperament, for a theorbo tuned in equal temperament would hardly sound "très bien" with a gamba tuned otherwise.

We must keep in mind that the theorists cited above and elsewhere did not claim that players of fretted instruments did not play with instruments known to have arranged their tuning systems in unequal temperaments, but rather that they should not play together. It is curious that these theorists simply dismissed the theoretical possibility of what they must have known regularly occurred in real life rather than attempting to discover the methods practical musicians used to accommodate themselves to each other. Perhaps they lacked the practical experience to do so. While these and countless other examples confirm that

Artusi's recommendations were either unknown or rejected, the longer such seemingly authoritative statements remain unchallenged, the greater the sense of legitimacy they tend to gain with each reprint or citation, a potency as uncanny as it is unearned.

Sixteenth- to Eighteenth-Century Discourses on Fretted Instruments

Despite the popularity of fretted instruments and the fundamental nature of arranging frets into patterns that produce workable tunings or temperaments, from ca. 1520 to 1760 only around forty players and theorists addressed the arrangement of frets on lutes and viols, divided almost evenly between Italian and non-Italian sources.[7] Many of these sources are manuscripts, and quite a few of them do not actually confront how to position the frets. This unexpected dearth of practical advice in historical writings addressing such an elemental chore could easily lead one to believe that setting and maintaining frets is not something lutenists and viol players must attend to every day. And yet we must. Our predecessors certainly set and maintained their frets just as assuredly as they tied their shoes, but, like tying their shoes, it was not something they chose to write about all that much, obviously considering it to be "craft knowledge," that is, "professional knowledge gained by experience . . . but which is rarely articulated in any conscious manner."[8] Professional musicians who made their reputations primarily as performers were particularly reluctant to reveal their secrets for reasons we discuss below.

Motivation to Publish or Refrain from Publishing

Players are naturally much more interested in what the best players do than what nonplaying theorists write they should do. After all, it is *Guitar Player* not *Guitar Theory* magazine that has been so popular since 1967. Published instruction of this nature that can now be found at any bookstand or online, however, has not always been quite so available. Diana Poulton and Tim Crawford begin the "Technique" section of the Grove entry on lute with: "Several writers of instruction books for the lute have remarked that many masters of the art were, as Mace put it, 'extreme Shie in revealing the Occult and Hidden Secrets of the Lute.'" Further on Mace laments that when great masters die, their secrets die with them. This, Mace tells us, is one of the primary reasons that, up until his book's publication, the lute was so difficult to learn.[9]

Alluding to craft secrets, Modenese lutenist Bellerofonte Castaldi (1580–1649) plainly enunciated his thoughts on the matter in the advice to performers in his *Capricci a due stromenti* (1622), containing theorbo music of a level that would be inaccessible to all but the most advanced players: "Advice on . . . the tuning of the instrument . . . is not given here, because he who can securely play this tablature will already know these things."[10] Although as an aristocrat Castaldi did not expect to derive income from his musical activities, his attitude toward providing pedagogical information was somewhat typical. Virtuosi whose fame was founded exclusively on their performance ability felt no obligation to provide lesser players with the tools required to join their ranks, fearing that revealing their closely guarded professional secrets would somehow diminish their status or marketability. Why increase your competition?

Even worse, how dare you reveal trade secrets? Following the publication of his *Prattica di musica* (1592/1622), contemporary professionals accused Ludovico Zacconi of "having dared to expose the innermost secrets of music, and thus undermining and devaluing the importance of the personal transmission of an art that, by tacit consensus, no one had ever fully revealed."[11] The subtext is clear: if you disseminate practical musical knowledge in a readily accessible form, you run the risk of reducing the need for private tutelage. Few things provoke more outrage than threatening one's livelihood.

On the other hand, there were those with a wider view, such as Mace and Bermudo, who lamented: "What a pity it is (and those who have Christian understanding must weep for it) that the great secrets of music die in a moment with the person of the musician, for lack of having communicated them to others." According to Poulton and Crawford, "The training of professional players was almost certainly carried on through some system of apprenticeship, and this may well be one of the reasons why comparatively few books give really informative instructions on all aspects of playing technique."[12] Penelope Gouk furthermore suggests, "The knowledge possessed by artisans was usually transmitted orally, comprising a body of secrets kept within the crafts."[13]

The practice of providing elementary playing instructions for fretted instruments began with Petrucci's publication of Spinacino's lute music in 1507, yet these and those that followed for all manner of fretted instruments with increasing frequency throughout the next two centuries include very little useful or coherent information regarding how to arrange frets. Perhaps they considered such information too basic, or, on the other hand, they may have just assumed, as many did, that the frets must be set by ear.

John Dowland's inexplicably unworkable fretting instructions that appear in his son Robert's *Varietie of Lute Lessons* (1610), loosely based on Gerle's instructions of some eighty years prior (1532), are so garbled that they cannot be taken seriously, resulting in an irregular utilitarian temperament that is not so utilitarian. They begin with a historical précis of sorts on tuning replete with references to Pythagoras, hammers, Babylon, and God, and do nothing to dispel the impression that his instructions were intended more to impress than inform. An additional clue to Dowland's motivation may be gleaned from the fact that twice in the same paragraph he mentions how skillful lutenists and violists set their frets by ear; for the rest of you, here are some instructions. In a most entertaining description of the chaos, Mark Lindley attributes the cascading errors in Dowland's instructions to the work of gremlins.[14]

As we have seen with regard to Dowland's instructions, it is wise to interpret the essays on tuning and temperament found in early treatises contextually by evaluating the writers' motivations for including these virtually obligatory exegeses. Tracts such as Dowland's can often be properly considered erudite displays designed to demonstrate either the author's mastery of classical theoretical musical concepts or his membership in the vanguard of the latest musical fashion rather than practical advice. The former generally advocate Pythagorean tuning or Just intonation, the latter, equal temperament. Each of these systems also linked theorists with a greater authority with whom or which the contemporary theorist could be associated: Pythagorean tuning of course to Pythagoras, Just intonation to Nature, and equal temperament to Aristoxenus or Art.[15] Theorists and those who fancied themselves as such concentrated their attention on the science of temperament, whereas practicing musicians focused on the art of temperament. The former often obsessed about describing a perfect world, while the latter confronted the real world.

General Approaches to Setting Frets

In his chapter regarding how "To Fret the Common Vihuela," from his *Declaración de instrumentos musicales* (1555) Juan Bermudo wrote, "You will rarely find this instrument well fretted, except the ones used by those exceptional players, who place them by good ear."[16] John Dowland asserted that skillful musicians can set their frets by ear, but that the less skillful require instructions.[17] As Bermudo did fifty-five years earlier, Dowland then went on to explain a method for placing the frets for nonprofessional players who are unable to set them by ear. Artusi reported that the lute maker Venere told him that he positioned the frets by ear as did other fine makers.[18] Much earlier, Juan de Espinosa (1520) suggested that players tune by ear to create their own personalized systems. Craft knowledge.

The most consistent tuning advice found in sixteenth- and seventeenth-century lute and viol publications is to adjust the frets up or down by checking unisons and octaves after tuning by ear or by referring to some sort of measuring guide derived by formula or provided by the lute or viol maker. Among the notable composers, theorists, and performers to recommend this approach are Luis Milán (1536), Sylvestro Ganassi (1542–1543), Pietro Aron (1545), Martin Agricola (1545), Alonso Mudarra (1546), Vincenzo Galilei (1581), Gioseffo Zarlino (1588), Ercole Bottrigari (1599), John Dowland (1610), Michael Praetorius (1619), Mary Burwell's lute tutor (ca. 1660–1672), Thomas Mace (1676), Jean Rousseau (1687), and Le Sieur Danoville (1687).

Real-Time Refinements

Aron (1545) and Bermudo (1555) wrote that lutenists can adjust the pitch by reducing or increasing the left-hand pressure.[19] After explaining how lutenists and viol players set their frets with equal semitones compared with the unequal semitones that prevail on keyboards, Bottrigari (1599) then asked the very reasonable question: How then can these instruments play together if they are tuned differently? He responded by explaining that good players are able to match another instrument's pitches "with diligent application . . . helping himself by placing the finger a little higher or a little lower on the fingerboard when he feels the need"—clearly a real-time adjustment.[20] Praetorius (1619) wrote that even though their instruments are tuned in equal temperament, lutenists and violists can aid intonation with the left-hand fingers.[21] He made it clear that the goal is to emulate a keyboard with split black keys, which provide both the *mi* and *fa* (sharp or flat) version of the note. Praetorius goes on to give this ability to alter the ostensibly equal-tempered notes as the reason that an equal temperament fretting pattern on lutes and viols is therefore not disturbing.

Prior to the invention of wooden body frets by Matthias Mason as described by Dowland in his son Robert's *Varietie of Lute Lessons,* lute music required stopped notes where the frets would have been had they existed, the execution of which Le Roy's *Brief Instruction* (1574) refers to in the Seventh Rule.[22] Indeed, Ganassi describes having heard Alfonso da Ferrara, Giovannbattista Ciciliano, Francesco da Milano, and Rubertino da Mantova play beyond the frets "with such good skill and to such good effect that one would have thought that there were frets there."[23] Surely, lutenists and viol players who were accustomed to playing beyond the frets would not feel put upon to adjust the tuning of individual fretted notes.

It is best, of course, to set the frets as close as possible to the required pitches and to reserve pulling and pushing for those rare situations that cannot be addressed by clever fret arrangements. To be sure, pulling and pushing are advanced techniques, but they can be effective arrows in the virtuoso player's quiver, especially on single-course instruments such as viols and the theorbo.

Pythagorean Tuning

Theorists like Bermudo who did not themselves play or in some cases even understand fretted instruments often received their information secondhand by copying from another theorist or relying on the authority of someone else who may or may not have been reliable or knowledgeable. For example, nonplayer theorists who often treated topics other than music as well, such as Oronce Fine (1530), suggested Pythagorean fretting schemes based on monochords that owe more to theory than practice. (For a detailed description of Pythagorean tuning, see chapters 4 and 5.) A monochord with one string is one thing; a six-course lute with eleven strings is another. Recommendations such as Fine's are totally impractical for virtually the entire solo lute repertoire, although they may be of some limited use in ensemble music that features predominant fourths and fifths. By 1530, were he a player, Fine would most likely have encountered Petrucci's publication of the lute tablatures of Spinacino, Dalza, and others, which are replete with major thirds that preclude the use of Pythagorean tuning.

Why would otherwise reputable theorists advocate a theoretical system with major thirds so wide and minor thirds so narrow as to render it impractical to serve as a default fretting arrangement for repertoires whose very tonalities are defined by the character and quality of the third? First, as we have seen, a demonstration of the ability to describe a system first identified by an ancient Greek philosopher, scientist, and mathematician of Pythagoras's enduring mythical stature associates the theorist with the classical learning that Renaissance writers were so keen to emulate.[24] Fretted instruments are also particularly suitable for such erudite demonstrations because, unlike keyboard instruments, strings subdivided by frets both duplicate Pythagoras's monochord and provide an immediate visual realization of the principles because one can actually see and physically measure the distances that Pythagoras's ratios represent that on other instruments one can only hear. Furthermore, there is a certain elegant simplicity to Pythagorean tuning that must have attracted those who were not burdened with having to actually listen to the unacceptably wide harmonic thirds it generally produced.[25]

Although Bermudo revered the learning of the ancients and devoted a great deal of space in his *Declaración* to the discussion of Pythagorean fretting arrangements, he admits that theory is one thing and practice something else entirely; he was obviously torn between the two.[26] As John Griffiths so succinctly puts it: "Theoretical and practical differences are irreconcilable."[27] As we will see later, freeing themselves from the strictures of traditional theory, instrument makers were able to concoct customized fretting arrangements that broke all the rules and sounded much better than either Pythagorean tuning or equal temperament, while at the same time removing the guilt from the pleasure.

Keeping in mind that lutes and guitars are chordophones that emphasize harmonic rather than melodic intervals, it is reasonable to wonder if any of these theorists actually used Pythagorean tuning on fretted instruments to any good effect. Its pure fourths and fifths may be useful for Medieval or extremely early Renaissance repertoire in situations where a drone of a fifth is called for or for simple polyphony such as found in the Faenza Codex (ca. 1430). But even in that case, it is likely that lutenists would have adjusted the frets to accommodate the tonality should major thirds be more than just passing.

Since its pure fifths make Pythagorean tuning so easy to set by ear, John Reeve proposes the plausible theory that Pythagorean tuning may have served as a "starting point" from which one could arrive at equal or other temperaments with adjustments by ear. Reeve's proposition is supported by historical precedent. In the first comprehensive method book devoted to lute playing and intabulation, Bartolomeo Lieto's *Dialogo quarto di musica* (Naples, 1559),

Lieto explains that while one begins tuning the lute by setting it in Pythagorean tuning, since it produces many false intervals, it is necessary to adjust the fret locations to make the intervals more perfect.[28]

The fact that so many theorists advocated arrangements featuring unequal fret sizes, albeit those of Pythagorean tuning, suggests that the concept of equally spaced frets was neither as universal nor as timeless as we may have been led to believe. We tend to forget that the long documented history of musicians using unequal systems extends as far back as Islamic theorists such as Al-Kindi (ca. 790–874) who advocated their use on the ud or lute.[29]

Much later, Mersenne claimed that instruments with movable frets are superior to those with fixed frets because they can be adjusted to compensate for defects in the string, to adjust the pitch one way or the other in isolated instances, and so that one can play in a variety of temperaments.[30] With all these factors in mind, I think we can safely contextualize theorists' descriptions of an unfiltered Pythagorean tuning on fretted instruments as in no way suggesting its use as a practical system in most of the music we play. At best, it was a place to begin.

Just Intonation

Just intonation is a theoretical tuning system in which each and every interval is mathematically pure at all times in all situations. Its attraction extends beyond the intrinsic beauty of its intervals; the pursuit of a systematic Just intonation scheme for fixed pitch instruments is akin to the search for a musical Holy Grail, a glorious quest that is, in the end, as futile as it is worthy.[31] This futility arises from the fact that without significant concessions, that is, the acceptance of certain considerably impure intervals, thus negating the very definition of Just intonation, the pitch level begins to rise rather quickly, which is, of course, unacceptable. But not chasing rainbows does not mean that we cannot do our best to approximate Just intonation, which in a sense is what this book is about.

While attempts to devise a workable Just intonation scheme were largely restricted to a cappella choral applications, such as that proposed by Zarlino in his *Le Istitutioni harmoniche* (1588), fretted instrument players and makers also sought to create such systems for their instruments and still do.[32] Vincenzo Galilei seemed to go back and forth regarding his opinion of the viability of Just intonation and announced that he intended to explain how to overcome its challenges in a later volume that never materialized, although he did continue his research on Just intonation.[33] A number of other theoretical schemes aspiring to Just intonation that cannot work in practice other than in isolated circumstances, include those proposed by Marin Mersenne (1636–1637), Giovanni Battista Doni (1640), Joseph Sauveur (1697), Thomas Salmon (1705), Benedetto Bresciani (1719), and Thomas Perronet Thompson (1829).[34]

The elusive dream of a workable Just intonation system on fretted instruments represents our unattainable desire to have it all. Fretted instrument players can, however, choose a system that serves the music we are playing within limits practical enough to be employed by on a day-to-day basis. Meantone temperaments were created for that very purpose.

Meantone Temperaments

By 1482, according to Bartolomé Ramos de Pareja, keyboard players were already using the temperament known today as 1/4-comma meantone, which Pietro Aron first described in his *Toscanello de la musica* of 1523.[35] In the liner notes to his recording of the music of Marco dall'Aquila (ca. 1480–1544), lutenist Paul O'Dette points out that Marco's correspondence with Aron "suggests that the lutenist may have been involved in experimenting with a new temperament for the lute that better suited the fuller textures of the new compositional styles."[36]

In his *Musica instrumentalis deudsch* (1545) Martin Agricola wrote:

> The fact that the majority of the brotherhood of lutenists and fiddlers make all of their frets the same [distance] from each other is truly a telling indication of their great inexperience—of the fact that they have no knowledge of the science that noble Music proclaims. Thus they too go astray, for they understand nothing at all about how the division of the whole-tone is accomplished. They also do not know that a fret that produces a minor semitone should stand somewhat farther [back] from the following [higher] fret, for the closest fret [i.e., the one for the lower pitch of the minor semitone, placed at the back of the first fret in question] takes precedence. Thus the major semitone is indeed somewhat larger than the minor semitone, for the major has five commas [*Commata*] and the minor only four, as the monochord displays; there one perceives how a comparison is made.[37]

Agricola's statement that most lutenists and fiddlers set their frets equally means, of course, that there were those who did set them unequally. According to Agricola, those who do set their frets equally demonstrate their inexperience by doing so. In other words, he is referring to the ubiquitous amateur who is content to find a quick and easy way to arrange the frets in a functional pattern, basically anything that works. Then, in an attempt to show the relationship between what one hears and what one sees, Agricola explains how the whole tone is divided into major and minor semitones and that the former is wider than the latter. The matter-of-fact tenor of this explanation demonstrates that Agricola did not consider unequal semitones on fretted instruments to be a problem whatsoever.

On page 43 of Adriano Banchieri's *L'Organo suonarino* (1611) we find "Regola per Accordare Stromenti da Corde Budellate Insieme con l'organo over' Arpicordo," a chart with instructions for tuning the open strings of gut-strung instruments such as violins, viols, the chitarrone, and lute to the organ and harpsichord, which were presumably tuned in a meantone temperament.[38] Effective today as it was four hundred years ago, this method of tuning an ensemble could result in nothing other than meantone temperaments on the fretted instruments. Two years later in 1613, Pedro Cerone described a meantone system for viola da gamba, and Pietro Della Valle (ca. 1640–1641) claimed that it is untrue that fretted instruments have equal semitones.[39]

One of the most convincing and articulate writers on the lute was the Roman theorist Pier Francesco Valentini (ca. 1642–1645), who titled his manuscript treatise devoted to the lute *Il Leuto anatomizzato* (The dissected lute).[40] Begun in 1636 and revised, condensed, and then expanded with additional material from another now lost treatise around 1650, Valentini describes the visual appearance of meantone temperaments on the lute, cittern, and "similar instruments" as follows: "One can clearly see that the third fret is wider than the second, which shows that there is a larger semitone on the third fret than on the second. One also sees that the first fret greatly exceeds the second [in width]." He steadfastly refutes the notion that lutes are tuned in equal temperament: "I realized that the way [the lute] has been used up to the present day, is not [tuned] entirely with equal tones and semitones . . . in this, not only the common folk, but also the most serious authors have erred, writing that on the said instrument there is equality in the tones and semitones." Note that he specifies "common folk" (amateur players) and "authors" (theorists) as those who have erroneously perpetuated the myth that lutes are tuned in equal temperament. Valentini's statement, coupled with evidence provided in this and later chapters, also contradicts the assertions of those who hold that while the lute may have been tuned in meantone temperaments for a brief period during the sixteenth century, it conclusively turned to equal temperament in the seventeenth century.

Music theorist, classicist, and sometimes lutenist Giovanni Battista Doni (1595–1647), was loath to even admit the possibility of the existence of equal temperament, referring to it as "a mere chimera and a non-existent, impossible thing." Citing Ercole Bottrigari's *Il Desiderio* (1599) as his source, Doni explains that on fretted instruments the fourths and fifths were more pure and the thirds and sixths less so than on keyboards. In fact, Doni goes on to express astonishment that "so many theorists had believed that fretted instruments had equal semitones,"[41] and then challenges the reader to explain to him how any fretted instrument you care to choose can produce equal temperament when the frets are set unequally, clearly indicating that frets are not characteristically set in equal temperament and further insinuating that other theorists were unthinkingly following the party line.[42] In light of this, a reasonable interpretation of Doni's remarks would be that both keyboards and fretted instruments were tuned in unequal temperaments, but that fretted instruments favored a more ecumenical version of the meantone, such as 1/6 comma.

Solo lute and viol tablatures can offer additional evidence that music for fretted instruments may have been intended for instruments set in unequal temperaments. In fact, most of the solo repertoire for these instruments sounds much better when set in meantone temperaments with little or no adjustment, than it does in equal temperament.

Mark Lindley points out that Luis Milán's tablatures in *El Maestro* (1536) indicate that he considered the 1st fret a *fa* because while he employed it regularly for flat accidentals, only occasionally did he allow a *fa* (A♭, for instance) to stand in for a *mi* (G♯), and when he did, with one exception, the *mi* is always alone, functioning as the 3 in a 4–3 suspension on E. Similarly, with one isolated exception, Arnolt Schlick uses the 1st fret as a *fa* in his fifteen lute pieces (1512).[43] At the beginning of a couple pieces that feature the 4th fret prominently to produce a major third, Milán advises that the 4th fret be moved slightly toward the tuning pegs to provide a better sound, that is, to ensure that the 4th fret functions as a *mi* rather than as a *fa.*[44] Conversely, there are occasions when the 4th fret must function as a *fa,* particularly when the instrument is tuned in A, as we will see in chapter 8. In his *Silva de sirenas* (1547), Enriquez de Valderrabano suggested raising the 4th fret toward the rose when its notes function as *fas.*[45]

We must linger here for a moment to explore exactly what happens when only one fret is relocated and the open strings are not retuned. To use an extreme example for the sake of illustration, let's say that a lute or viol in G has its open strings and frets set in 1/4-comma meantone temperament, and only the 4th fret is moved, as Milán and others have suggested. The major third from the open third course A to the 4th fret when it is set to a *mi* (C♯) is 386c., a pure major third.[46] The difference between a *mi* and *fa* in 1/4 comma is 42c. Moving the 4th fret toward the bridge by 42c. into the *fa* position changes the C♯ into a D♭, transforming the major third (A–C♯) of 386c. into a diminished fourth (A–D♭) of 428c. (386c. + 42c.). Easy enough. But instead of moving the fret 42c., let's move it halfway (21c.) as in the example above. The interval between the open A and the 4th fret, A–C♯/D♭ is now 407c. (386c. + 21c.). Yet unless the open strings between F and A are retuned, they are still tuned as a pure major third, and, therefore, the A–C♯ at the 4th fret between the fourth and third courses is still a pure major third.[47] See diagram 1.1.[48] But, remember that the relocation of the 4th fret to the compromise position has raised the A at the 4th fret of the fourth course by 21c., so that "A" is 21c. higher than the A produced by the open third course. Yet the A–C♯ on the first course between the 2nd and 6th frets, for instance, remains unaffected—it is still a pure major third of 386c. We already have two different interval sizes and two different starting pitches for the "A–C♯," and we've only just begun. From this brief exercise you can see that this is only the beginning of a cascade of alterations that can ultimately affect every interval, which, as we will see in chapter 2, was not necessarily considered a bad thing and perhaps quite the contrary.

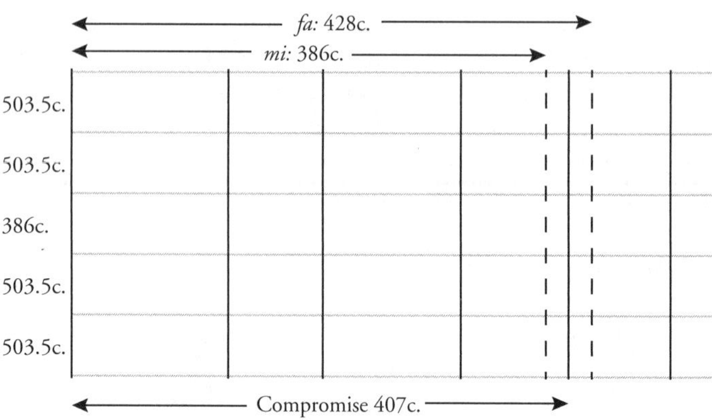

Diagram 1.1. 4th fret in compromise position.

A word of caution is in order here with regard to Milán: we are not in a position to determine what temperament raising the 4th fret toward the nut would result in because we don't know with what temperament Milán began. While Bermudo's fondness for Pythagorean tuning could possibly incline us to think that Milán's default temperament might have been the same, it's difficult to conceive that music as third laden as Milán's would be tolerable to anyone in Pythagorean tuning. Raising the 4th fret a tad would do little to make it palatable. If Milán's default arrangement were equal temperament, moving the 4th fret toward the nut would create a utilitarian temperament as described below, softening the rather prominent thirds that appear at the 4th fret but do nothing for other equally prominent thirds located elsewhere. Were his vihuela set in a meantone temperament, the direction could be taken to indicate the *mi* rather than *fa* position for the famously variable 4th fret, the ramifications of which Antonio Corona-Alcalde explores in detail in his article "'You Will Raise a Little Your 4th Fret': An Equivocal Instruction by Luis Milan?" Later on, Doni also claimed that the 4th fret's location varied more than the other frets.[49] As we will see in following chapters, there are compromises that can be made to accommodate the occasional instances where a tablature requires a *mi* and *fa* at the same fret on adjacent strings.

According to Lindley, Milán's music sounds better in meantone than in equal temperament: "To my ear, Milán's music displays in meantone temperament a certain blend of poise and expressive opulence which equal temperament particularly disrupts at those moments."[50] Indeed it does. In the end, Corona-Alcalde proposes that Milán most likely set his frets around halfway between equal temperament and 1/4-comma meantone. In other words, 1/6-comma meantone temperament. I agree.

The main technical difficulty in using unequal temperaments is that enharmonic chromatic notes are not equivalent as they are in equal temperament, for example, E♭ differs noticeably from D♯. Much of chapters 7–9 revolve around overcoming this obstacle on fretted instruments. Some early keyboards met this challenge by providing split keys, the first of which appeared in the late sixteenth century. A black key was split horizontally or vertically into two segments, following the example above, one segment providing the E♭, the other the D♯. While most keyboards equipped with split keys are now housed in museums, some are still in use; for example, here in the United States, the organs at Oberlin College's Fairchild and Yale's Marquand Chapels have split keys, both tuned in extended 1/4-comma meantone temperament.

Among the strategies available to players of fretted instruments are split frets and so-called tastini (little frets). Split frets refer to either the division of the two strands of a double fret into two separate frets or simply the use of two frets to provide both *mi* and *fa* at a particular fret location. Such was recommended by Bermudo in chapter 83 of his "On Playing the Vihuela" of his *Declaración* (1555) although since he simply says to add another 1st fret, it is not clear what type of special fret he intended.[51] He implies that the extra fret should be placed between the nut and the 1st fret, and we can infer that this was his intention from several other pieces of information that he does supply. Shortly after Bermudo, Lieto as well mentioned "tasti geminate" (twin frets) as a way to produce smaller intervals.[52]

Barbieri reports that the Dutch singer in the Papal Chapel, Ghiselin Danckerts, wrote in the 1550s that fretted instruments are arranged in major and minor semitones.[53] Danckerts served as one of the judges in the famous debate between Vicentino and the Portuguese theorist and composer Vicente Lusitano regarding diatonic, chromatic, and enharmonic genres. In the final section of the second and third editions of his *Introduttione facilissima, et novissima, di canto fermo, figurato, contraponto semplice, et in concerto, con regole generali per far fughe differenti sopra il canto fermo, a 2, 3, et 4 voci, et compositioni, proportioni, generi. s. diatonico, cromatico, enarmonico* (1553, 1558, and 1561), Lusitano discusses the three genres. After describing several intervals, Lusitano concludes his book with the following paragraph:

> These [intervals of the enharmonic genre, that is, involving quartertones] are demonstrated by the lute when it is fitted with another fret between those that it ordinarily has, rather than keyboard instruments in which such intervals can be tuned until the consonance, whereas the lute naturally shows the dissonance. Hence, instruments built to produce the enharmonic genre show themselves to have been made in vain.[54]

Lusitano would have only cited a lute with split frets or tastini as his example of an instrument capable of producing intervals differing from one another by small degrees such as quartertones if split frets or tastini were commonly known to have been used on the lute. As we will soon discuss, the purpose of split frets and tastini is to provide *mis* at a *fa* fret in meantone temperaments.[55] Here, he furthermore distinguishes between keyboard instruments in which the temperament is limited by the tuning of the twelve notes within the octave in contrast to the lute, which can extend the temperament beyond the normal twelve semitones of the octave through the use of split frets or tastini, as we will see in later chapters.

Special frets had a role in Doni's set of prepared viols, and, according to Martin Kirnbauer: "Additional frets permitted the execution of pure chords as well as the 'correct' disposition of melodic steps, which in treatises tend to be mentioned in the context of chromatic and enharmonic music (for example, Ghiselin Danckerts 1555/6, Girolamo Cardanus 1574, Vincenzo Galilei 1584, Marin Mersenne 1636 and Christopher Simpson 1667)."[56] To be sure, "chromatic and enharmonic" refers to complicated music, what we might consider experimental music. Nevertheless, the use of special frets in this context further confirms their use for the purpose of more precise tuning in numerous circumstances.

Tastini are short portions of fret made out of gut or ivory that were glued onto the fingerboard to provide an alternate chromatic note, that is, a *mi* at a *fa* fret or vice versa. They were first mentioned in Galilei's *Il Fronimo* (1584) albeit disparagingly, a topic that is expanded on below.[57] Doni wrote that tastini were most commonly used at the 1st fret to provide the *mi* enharmonic, although he fretted about the added difficulties tastini caused players and the inconsistent sharpening of octave courses.[58] Intonation problems due to sharpening are, of course, certainly not restricted to tastini. Barbieri makes the salient point that the 1st fret is the best candidate for a special fret because the physical distance between the *mi* and *fa* locations is the greatest, as we will discover when we discuss the harmonic diesis in chapter 5.[59] The only known historical depiction of double or split frets appears in Antonio Domenico Gabbiani's (1652–1726) painting *The Prince Ferdinando de' Medici and the Musicians of the Court* (ca. 1684), hanging in the Palazzo Pitti in Florence, where double or split frets are visible on a *lirone enarmonico,* a type of viola da gamba invented by Pietro Salvetti (see plate 1).[60] The only other instrument to specifically call for double or split frets is Doni's own *violone panarmonico.*

Harpsichord maker Jean Denis wrote in 1650 that rather than harpsichords accommodating themselves to lutes and gambas by tuning in equal temperament, lutes and gambas should accommodate themselves to the unequal temperaments favored by harpsichords through the means of "ivory" frets, which would accomplish the same thing as staggering the frets, which is, of course impossible with tied-on frets.[61] With regard to fretted instruments fielding unequal temperaments, Denis questioned not the ability but the will.

In his *A Compendium of Practical Music in Five Parts* (1667), Christopher Simpson nonchalantly wrote:

> I do not deny but that the slitting of the keys in harpsichords and organs, as also the placing of a middle fret near the top or nut of a viol or theorbo where the space is wide, may be useful in some cases for the sweetening of such dissonances as may happen in those places; but I do not conceive that the enharmonic scale is therein concerned, seeing those dissonances are sometimes more, sometimes less, and seldom that any of them do hit precisely the quarter of a note.[62]

This demonstrates that some viol or theorbo players used special frets, and some did not.

We must keep in mind that Simpson is not advocating the use of tastini, but rather simply reporting what he has seen others do. Following his comments on tastini, Simpson goes on to furnish a lucid explanation on how to set frets in Pythagorean tuning, allowing for the fact that others prefer meantone temperaments, which he describes without naming. In his instructions, he repeatedly makes allowances for sharpening and also goes to great lengths to describe how it is impossible to divide a whole tone into two equal semitones: "Thus you see a tone or note divided into a greater and lesser half, but how to divide it into two equal halves I never see determined."[63] To summarize, while not recommending meantone temperaments or tastini, Simpson describes their use by others and for his own part, provides a method for setting Pythagorean tuning and rejects equal temperament out of hand.

Claude-François Millet de Chales's *Cursus seu mundus mathematicus* (1674, reprinted in 1682 and 1690) illustrates the "common" viola da gamba fretting pattern including tastini at the 1st fret. See figure 1.1. De Chales then passes on to lute and guitar makers, whom he says "commonly" set their frets in equal temperament following the 18:17 method espoused by Galilei. "Commonly," of course, implies most but not all. Barbieri points out that the viola da gamba's often being accompanied by basso continuo performed on keyboards that were assuredly tuned in meantone temperaments makes it all the more likely that gambas were also tuned in meantone temperaments to match their accompanying instruments. Mersenne's representation that the lute and viol are always tuned in equal temperament was contradicted by Gabriel de la Charlonie in a 1632 letter to Mersenne, Jean Rousseau in his *Traité de la viole* (1687), Joseph Sauveur's *Traité de la théorie de la musique* (1697), and indirectly by Jean-Philippe Rameau in his *Génération harmonique* (1737).[64] These sources refute the notion that equal temperament was universally applied to lutes and viols by end of the seventeenth century.

While many eighteenth-century authors wrote about narrowing the violin's open fifths to accommodate keyboard tuning, some were even more specific or

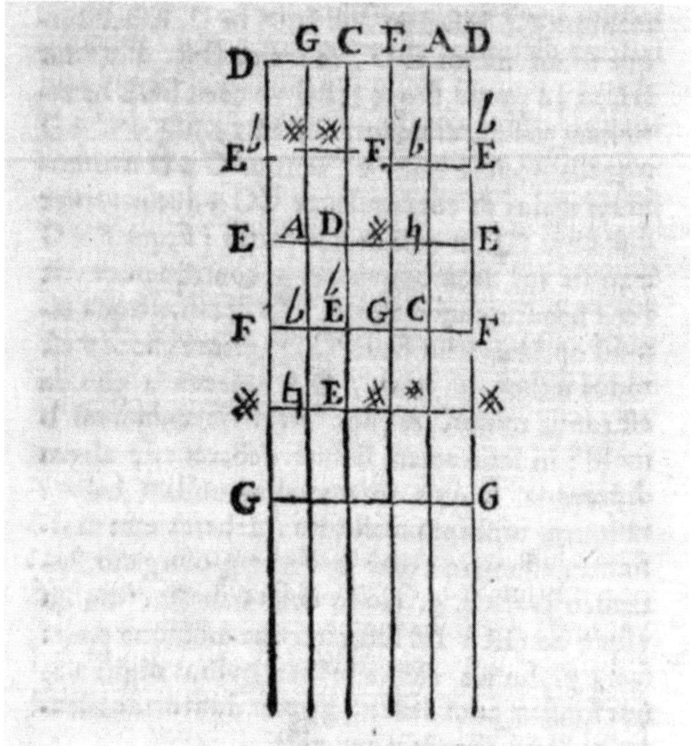

Figure 1.1. "Common fretting" for viola da gamba in Claude-François Millet de Chales's *Cursus seu mundus mathematicus* (1674), 38.

provided fingering charts that clearly illustrate meantone fingering such as Peter Prelleur in *The Modern Musick-Master* (1730–1731) and Francesco Geminiani in his *The Art of Playing the Violin* (1751), who went so far as to caution his readers, "Note also that as G♯ and A♭, or A♯ and B♭, or also D♯ and E♭, etc., are not the same notes, you must not stop them with the same finger."[65] Geminiani also clearly describes the difference between major and minor semitones. Surely the theorbo and archlute players who played in ensembles with professional bowed string and keyboard players of Geminiani's caliber and discernment did their best to accommodate themselves to the prevailing temperament, if only for a matter of professional pride.

It seems reasonable to assume that the use of split frets and tastini was restricted to the most astute fretted instrument players as was the appreciation of meantone temperaments to reduce the harshness of the major thirds that dominated the music they played. The examples cited above demonstrate that such players believed that the practical and aesthetic advantages unequal temperaments offered far outweighed any inconveniencies associated with special frets or having to keep track of which frets were *mi* and which were *fa,* granting us yet another glimpse into the values and craft knowledge of professional lutenists and gambists. Now, thanks to the extraordinary technological advances of the past few years that have generated a plethora of multitemperament tuners and computer, tablet, and smartphone tuning applications, players at any level can enjoy the benefits of meantone temperaments.

Utilitarian Temperaments

Hans Gerle was more concerned with providing a workable fretting arrangement so that his readers could play his music than demonstrating his erudition. His fretting instructions of 1532 crafted with a ruler and compass combine features of Pythagorean tuning, 1/6-comma meantone, and equal temperament. Gerle's directions for positioning frets 4, 6, and 8 are sufficiently vague to facilitate the flexibility necessary for frets that are sometimes called upon to serve as a *mi* and sometimes as a *fa* in meantone temperaments or something in between. All of this qualifies Gerle's temperament as utilitarian.

A proposed solution to the problem of where to place the chromatic frets that may need to serve both *mi* and *fa* positions articulated in sources around 1700 is to set the frets in a meantone temperament, but to relocate the chromatic frets in compromise positions, often halfway between the *mi* and *fa* positions, essentially dividing the whole tone between the diatonic frets into two equal semitones. Some years earlier, Vincenzo Galilei appears to have alluded to such a system in an unpublished manuscript, Joseph Sauveur (1697) proposed the same for the viola da gamba, and Benedetto Bresciani quite precisely described such an arrangement for lute in his *Trattato del sistema armonico* (1719).[66] The principle of inserting equal semitones between diatonic whole tones may have also been applied to other unequal systems such as Pythagorean tuning.

As we have seen, on fretted instruments, relocating only one fret without making any other adjustment results in more than one interval size for any nominal interval between two specific notes if either of them falls on the relocated fret. In chapter 2, we will learn that instrument makers and players did not worry so much about everything lining up perfectly and consistently, having thrown over theory for practicality.[67] And, just as musicians in the Renaissance and Baroque eras preferred to cultivate the varied colors of melodies positioned across the strings rather than along them in Romantic fashion, they also seemed to enjoy the kaleidoscopic tonal colors provided by the variety of sizes for the same interval typically found in irregular temperaments.

Equal Temperament

Still in the throes of the Platonic ideal that theoretical musical understanding is superior to performing ability, many early authors were enchanted primarily by the thrill of equal temperament's mathematical elegance, relegating how it actually sounds to secondary importance.[68] Equal temperament trumps all other temperaments in practicality, serviceability, and facility. Galilei and Bottrigari, for instance, celebrated the ability of lutes and viols tuned in equal temperament to transpose in any direction, up or down.[69] The few references to temperament on guitar are typified by Nicolas Doisi de Velasco's statement in 1640 that "the arrangement of its frets according to equal division makes all its tones and semitones equal."[70] Since the guitar was so prominently used to accompany song, guitarists were practically obsessed with the ability to transpose to any key on a moment's notice to accommodate the voice's range. For many, equal temperament's conveniences more than compensated for the harshness of its thirds and sixths. Furthermore, like Pythagorean tuning, equal temperament was also able to claim ancient authority in the person of Aristoxenus (fourth century BC).

In his *Libro de música para vihuela intitulado Orphenica lyra* (1554) Miguel di Fuenllana described in general terms a fretting system that can be nothing other than equal temperament.[71] This represents one of the earliest associations of equal temperament with fretted instruments. According to Lindley, equal-tempered fretting schemes became accepted by *theorists* as the norm for fretted instruments after ca. 1550.[72] These included Vicentino, Zarlino, Salinas, Artusi, Praetorius, and Mersenne. This may very well be the case though we have seen plenty of evidence that *players* continued to try to mitigate the harshness of equal temperament's thirds.

Vincenzo Galilei was, of course, equal temperament's greatest champion. His so-called 18:17 method for determining fret locations was by far the most popular for its accuracy and ease of use. Introduced in his *Dialogo* of 1581, Galilei's explanation is a paradigm of simplicity and clarity buried within a book that is as complicated as its scope is vast:

> Therefore, I divide the line AB into eighteen parts, and toward the high end [starting from the low end], where the first segment ends, I place the first fret. Then I divide the entire remainder of the line again in eighteen parts, and at the end of the first segment I locate the second fret. By this method, I go on to divide the distance that the frets leave empty until I reach the twelfth step. This takes me to the point where half the string ends, and I find that I have divided the first and lowest octave into twelve so-called Aristoxenian equal semitones and six tones. To do this, the only number you need is eighteen.[73]

Galilei then explains how nineteen or more divisions would generate too many frets, and less than eighteen, too few. His method also has the advantage that it compensates somewhat for sharpening, although as Galilei himself advised, the locations that the 18:17 rule generate should be double-checked for accuracy, presumably by ear. Nevertheless, as you can easily determine for yourself on your own instrument, Galilei's method is both easy to use and surprisingly accurate.[74]

There is no doubt that the facility of Galilei's method further cemented the relationship between fretted instruments and equal temperament. Despite its simplicity, its precision compared with the recommendations of Gerle and Dowland certainly made it an attractive default temperament for amateurs who looked for an authority to tell them how to set their frets. If somewhat more advanced players used his method as a quick and easy way to generate a workable fretboard pattern with the intention of then adjusting it toward a more euphonious meantone temperament, it is not difficult to surmise that many players simply didn't get around to the final step while in the meantime becoming accustomed to the sound and ease of equal temperament. We will explore Galilei's relationship with equal temperament in a little more depth down below. Bermudo, Ganassi, Salinas, Zarlino, and others also devised equal-tempered fretting formulas or patterns with varying degrees of success. None, however, had the lasting popularity of Galilei's formula, which was often subsequently described by Mersenne and other theorists well into the nineteenth century.

In his monumental *Harmonie universelle* (1637) Marin Mersenne condemned the lute as the "charlatan of music" because it passes off as good that which is bad on good instruments, echoing Vicentino, who many years earlier asserted that the lute and viol's being tuned in equal temperament was one of their "defects," although he immediately follows this criticism with a description of how to properly arrange the frets in the alternating wide and narrow frets that characterize meantone temperaments.[75] It's ironic that what was originally perceived as a vice would later come to be considered a virtue. Mersenne suggested the following remedy: "If the organ and harpsichord were tempered according to the fretting of lutes and viols, performances in which they are combined would seem more in tune because their tuning would agree."[76] Strangely, and perhaps no more than an oversight, although he asserts that equal temperament rather than meantone temperament is the defect, he recommends that the organ and harpsichord should be tuned as the lute and not the other way around. Note that a few years later the harpsichord maker Denis would bring up the same conflict but suggest the opposite solution.

David Chua writes, "[Max] Weber claims that modern tuning has desensitized modern ears with a 'dulling effect' and has shackled music in 'dragging chains'"[77] and that, according to Weber, it is all our fault: "Weber explains the disenchantment by isolating equal temperament as the most modern mode of musical rationalism. Music, by bowing to the regulations demanded by the technology of fretted instruments, forfeits its power to enchant."[78] There's no getting around the fact that right or wrong, accurate or not, equal temperament has come to be associated with fretted instruments, and, indeed, there are those examples of complicated lute music such as Molinaro's Fantasia XII and

Dowland's chromatic fantasias that are nearly impossible in anything but equal temperament or a very broad meantone temperament with clever adjustments, but they are rare. For Lindley, the real question is "the extent to which players [since ca. 1550] may have used their instruments' resources of flexibility to depart from the theoretical norm of equal temperament, for the sake, perhaps, of more euphonious 3rds."[79] Ross Duffin suggests they did indeed and that good players likely shaded frets 1, 4, and 6 toward a meantone configuration, which as we have seen actually creates an ultra-irregular temperament if the open strings and other frets are not adjusted as well.[80] But it is an ultra-irregular temperament with meantone features, whose inconsistencies were quite well tolerated for the benefits they provide over equal temperament, as we will see in chapter 2, devoted to fixed fret instruments.

Vincenzo Galilei

Some of our best evidence for meantone temperaments on fretted instruments comes from the least likely sources. Among them is the chief proponent of equal temperament on lutes, the theorist and lutenist Vincenzo Galilei (1520–1591), father of the lutenist Michelangelo Galilei (1575–1631) and astronomer Galileo Galilei (1564–1642), who was also purportedly a splendid lutenist.[81] Galilei, more than any other music theorist before him, established the link between theory and practice, recognizing that the purpose of theory is to serve practice. Related to this, he was also the first music theorist to emphasize the role physical experimentation and empirical experience plays in the formation of theoretical concepts, a practice he certainly passed on to his son Galileo.[82] Brilliant, but contentious, Galilei's credibility occasionally suffers from lapses in consistency and the impression that his objectivity was at times overwhelmed by his vitriol toward Gioseffo Zarlino (1517–1590) in a relentless campaign to humiliate his former teacher in recompense for slights either real or perceived.[83]

While he may have reversed himself on other issues, throughout his career Galilei consistently advocated for equal temperament on lutes and viols. He acknowledged that equal temperament's wide thirds were offensive, but he countered that the nature of gut strings softened the effect of the sharp major thirds that on the steel strings of the harpsichord were intolerable, although he conceded that this in itself does not justify using equal temperament when meantone temperaments are available.[84] To further bolster his campaign to legitimize equal temperament, Galilei echoed Girolamo Cardano's statement in his *De subtilitate* (1559) that the mind attempts to "classify" a slightly impure interval as "the closest correct one," an argument, however, that could be appropriated to mitigate the impurity of intervals in any tuning or temperament.[85] Galilei didn't seem to have any issue with meantone temperaments per se, only with their use on lutes.

In *Il Fronimo* (1584), Galilei has his interlocutor Eumatius ask Fronimo (Galilei) why he does not use unequal temperaments and tastini "as I have seen used by some universally known, skillful men, from whom I understand that both are exceedingly necessary and useful."[86] Fronimo does not respond that meantone temperaments and tastini do not work on the lute, but rather that lutenists do not know how to use them properly. Furthermore, in his zeal to prove that lutenists do not know how to set their frets properly, Galilei provides mensural notation and tablature demonstrating the "common" arrangement of frets in a meantone temperament, complete with indication of major (*fa*) and minor (*mi*) frets![87] See figure 1.2. Game, set, and match!

Galilei has the same problem with tastini. It's not that they don't work, but that lutenists do not know how to use them properly. After several pages of cogent examples of how tastini can be used to produce euphonious thirds in this or that octave or tonality, in the end, Galilei concludes that they are just not worth the trouble. Galilei also accurately describes the challenges with irregular schemes that occur when only one fret is adjusted. All of this he rejects for its lack of uniformity.

We have seen that Galilei valued uniformity and had little faith in the average lutenist's ability to understand meantone temperaments well enough to use them. But why would he have so assiduously lobbied for equal temperament when he readily acknowledged its flaws? Equal temperament is unquestionably uniform and easy to use, but more than anything, for Galilei's purposes, equal temperament is versatile. Included among the thirty new pages that appear in the 1584 *Il Fronimo* are twenty-four brief ricercars in every major and minor mode, following a similar model introduced by Giacomo Gorzanis for a series of passamezzos and saltarellos in his *Libro de intabulatura de liuto* (1567) and the manuscript Galilei intended to become his *Libro d'intavolatura di liuto* (1584), which includes two separate dance cycles containing sets of dances arranged in a similar fashion. Although not impossible in meantone temperaments, many

Figure 1.2. Score and tablature detail in Vincenzo Galilei's *Il Fronimo* (1584), 103.

of these pieces are much more easily played in equal temperament, particularly if performed in sequence, which undoubtedly explains one of Galilei's primary motivations for pursuing the standardization of equal-tempered lute tuning. There can be little doubt that his theoretical and compositional agendas supported each other.[88]

To summarize, although Galilei provides us with some of the best evidence we have that well-admired lutenists set their frets unequally, he preferred equal temperament because it is uniform, easy to use, versatile, and supported his own compositional agenda, thus becoming an end unto itself.

What Did Giovanni Bardi Really See and Hear?

Nothing has done more to lend credence to the notion that lutes and viols were tuned in equal temperament than Count Giovanni de' Bardi's widely disseminated "Discourse on Ancient Music and Good Singing" (1578), addressed to Giulio Caccini. Bardi (1534–1612) was the prime mover of the Florentine musical intelligentsia's campaign to revive ancient Greek musical principles. In that capacity he hosted the gatherings of the famous Camerata in his home and generously supported and encouraged musicians such as Galilei and Caccini. Galilei's energetic development and application of Girolamo Mei's interpretation of most everything the ancient Greeks had written about music, to a large extent, drove the Camerata's agenda under Bardi's leadership and patronage. Galilei and Bardi proved to be a formidable team; Galilei provided the theoretical, technical, and practical know-how, while Bardi supplied the political, organizational, and financial support.

The letter in question provides a succinct but elegant overview memorializing the guiding principles that informed the Camerata's work.[89] Although the letter is addressed to Caccini, its broad sweep implies that Bardi's intended audience was not limited to Caccini. Galilei and the other members of his circle must have been aware of its content. Strunk suggests that Galilei or some other member of Bardi's circle might have written the letter on his behalf, but Palisca correctly rejects this claim on several grounds.[90] This view is also supported by a comparison of Galilei's and Bardi's writing styles. Galilei's is rough around the edges, revealing itself in its forced artifice, as if in an effort to emulate a style with which he is not entirely comfortable.[91] Bardi's letter, on the other hand, is flowing and natural, demonstrating the author's good breeding and cultivation. Its credibility, alas, does not always rise to the level of its eloquence.

Regarding fretted instruments and keyboards playing together Bardi writes:

> Besides this, it is necessary to take great care in combining these instruments [string instruments], for not all of them are tuned according to the same tuning, the viol and lute being tuned according to the tuning of Aristoxenus, the harp and *gravicembalo* make their modulations with

> other intervals. And more than once I have felt like laughing when I saw musicians struggling to put a lute or viol into proper tune with a keyboard instrument, for aside from the octave these instruments have few strings in common that are in unison,[92] a circumstance that may detract from their usefulness, since until now this highly important matter has gone unnoticed or, if noticed, unremedied. In your consorts, then, you will as far as possible avoid combining lutes or viols with keyboard instruments or harps or other instruments not tuned in unison, but in various ways.[93]

Unfortunately, this mocking bell cannot be unrung, its witty toll of ridicule eclipsing any reasonably objective appraisal of its content.

Without any evidence to support his claim, Bardi ascribes the pre-performance tuning activities to the fretted instrument players in equal temperament finding it difficult to match a keyboard in meantone temperament. Such a proposition is quite unlikely because any minimally competent musician would immediately recognize that in such a situation the fretted instruments must be able to match the keyboard as a condition of playing together and would indeed be able accomplish this task. Even if they happen to be in the same temperament, this can still take some time to accomplish as the fretted players must check their open strings and frets with the keyboard and one another, as Banchieri would later describe. Further tuning-related negotiation and planning may have to take place depending on the tonalities of the pieces to be performed, such as who plays which accidentals or in which keys, where to insert tuning breaks to retune bass courses, and so on. What might seem like "struggling" to the layperson was probably nothing more than the normal pre-performance routine to a professional musician. This practice could include determining the pitch level, who plays where and in what kind of texture, determining sightlines, cues, tempi, and a dozen other things that have nothing to do with tuning.

Doni, in his "Trattato della musica scenica" in *De' trattati di musica* (written in 1640, but published in 1763) provides a colorful and much more accurate description of the troubles that beset the ensemble musician while preparing for a concert:

> The pains, the distastefulness, the anxieties and the sorrows that the poor musicians feel in arranging together so many players and sounds in so narrow a place, would scarcely be believed. For, with much loss of time and confusion, they must arrange the instruments, distribute the lamps, order the seats, set up the music stands, and tune the instruments. And God knows if, after tuning them well, they don't often have to do the whole thing again from the beginning, because of the multiplicity of the strings and their slackening on account of [the heat of] the lamps, as well as they can be readjusted while the others are playing. To say nothing of the

> trouble and time it takes to make so many copies of the *intavolatura* of the bass, and of other problems which result from the miscellany, introduced without any grounds.[94]

Doni's characterization of the typical pre-performance chaos is certainly familiar to any of us who have performed in ensemble situations. What is most striking is how little things have changed in over 350-plus years.

To his credit, Bardi essentially says that because fretted instrument and keyboard players haven't learned to play together nicely, they must play separately, that is, until they find a way to play together in harmony, as it were. Although he may have misattributed normal preconcert tuning challenges that he didn't have the practical experience to understand to fretted and keyboard instruments being tuned in different temperaments, the heart and soul of his complaint is legitimate: instruments must be tuned in the same temperament when playing together.

The theorists who addressed the topic of fretting on lutes and viols in the sixteenth through eighteenth centuries, many with little or no practical experience, seem to be in some general agreement that most fretted instrument players tended to set their frets in something like equal temperament, but that good players adjusted fret locations by ear to provide better consonances. Clearly fretted instrument players felt responsible for playing in tune with others and adjusted their open strings and frets accordingly. Arranging frets in a systematic fashion can easily produce a perfectly workable meantone arrangement, but players of fretted instruments also seemed comfortable adjusting isolated frets (1st, 4th, and 6th most commonly), resulting in pragmatic utilitarian temperaments that allow for a variety of sizes for the same nominal interval, E–G♯, for instance. Several of the instructions we surveyed also result in pragmatic utilitarian temperaments combining features of Pythagorean, meantone, and equal tuning systems.

For a number of reasons, however, most professional players were silent on the subject, and discussion of tunings and temperaments on fretted instruments eventually disappeared from theoretical works altogether. Viewing music more as an art than a science, when theory fell short, practical musicians improvised, as they always do. But they rarely wrote about it. Craft knowledge.

We have seen that despite the naysayers, composers continued to create music that paired fretted and keyboard instruments together in ensemble settings. Obviously, practicing musicians found a way to make it work. From the overview of the literature addressing the tuning of fretted instruments, we have also seen that associating fretted instruments with equal temperament exclusively is a gross oversimplification of the day-to-day circumstances. As usual, with both history and art, the reality is inconveniently often much more subtle than it first appears to be. Until a thorough and comprehensive study of all fretted instrument tuning instructions has been made, our understanding of our predecessors' attitudes toward temperaments will necessarily be limited.

Leaving theory, opinion, and conjecture behind, chapter 2 examines tangible measurable artifacts where there is little if any room for ambiguity: fixed fret wire-strung instruments where a luthier was compelled to permanently and conclusively claim a temperament for his instrument by embedding metal into wood for all the world to see . . . and hear.

CHAPTER TWO

Surviving Fixed Metal-Fret Instruments

One of the standard ensembles to emerge during the Renaissance was the popular Elizabethan "broken" consort, sometimes also referred to as a "mixed" consort, "lessons for the consort," or, as Praetorius referred to it, an "English consort."[1] In the 1960s, the ensemble was resurrected in performances and recordings by the Julian Bream Consort and then later by the Musicians of Swanne Alley and the Baltimore Consort.[2] It concerns us here because the instruments that constitute this standard ensemble are the violin or treble viol, recorder or transverse flute, lute, viola da gamba, cittern, and bandora (or pandora), sometimes with the addition of the voice. Segerman suggests that there is evidence that the orpharion was considered a suitable alternative to the bandora.[3] The cittern and the lower-pitched bandora or orpharion combined to form a broad spectrum of wire-strung sound comparable to that of a virginal.[4] In such a transparent texture, as a matter of practicality, the temperament of the two fixed metal-fret instruments that functioned as a unit must have determined the ensemble's temperament to which the lute and viol, as well as the violin, flute, and voice, would be obliged to adhere as best they could.[5]

The Cittern

Comprehensive studies of surviving historical instruments and paintings by Peter Forrester and Ephraim Segerman have determined conclusively that citterns were tuned very nearly to some variety or other of meantone temperament between 1/4-comma meantone and equal temperament or in a utilitarian combination of several varieties of meantone temperament. Forrester concludes that 1/6-comma meantone is a good average, while some Italian citterns are closer to 1/5-comma meantone.[6] According to Forrester, the fret positions were marked on a rule and transferred to the fingerboard, which, of course, introduces an additional step during which errors could appear. That they were then checked by ear is confirmed by the fact that "there is considerable deviation from theoretical positions on most citterns."[7] A close-up view of the fretboard of the four-course

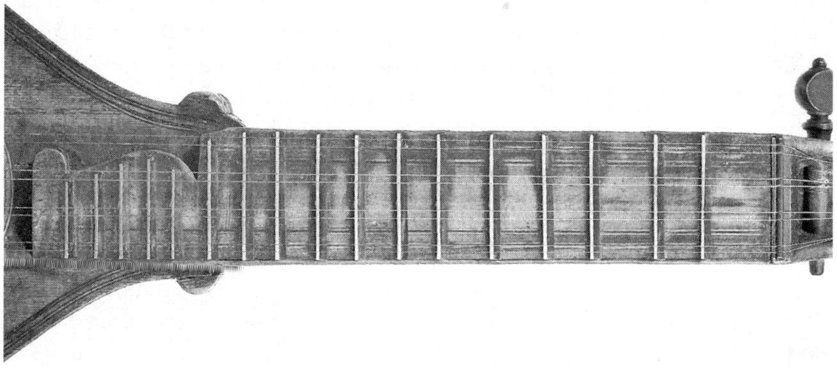

Figure 2.1. Fretboard of English cittern. National Music Museum, University of South Dakota, Bill Willroth Sr., Photographer.

English cittern enshrined at the National Music Museum in Vermillion, South Dakota, in figure 2.1 clearly shows the typical and easily identifiable meantone temperament pattern of generally alternating wide and narrow frets.[8] Cittern makers clearly chose to arrange the frets of their instruments to provide stable chords in the relatively narrow range of keys that citterns generally play in near the top of the Circle of Fifths at the expense of the complete serviceability offered by equal temperament, a service that was not needed at that time. Of necessity, the lute and viola da gamba in the consort would have been tuned with the cittern's and bandora's temperament as their point of reference.

Citterns, which for several reasons can be notoriously difficult to tune and play in tune, were conscientiously constructed with regard to temperament.[9] And as we all know, since luthiers build instruments at the behest of players, the players themselves must have required this level of care. Citterns were commonly equipped with scalloped frets to allow the left-hand fingers to depress the strings deeper than a normal flat fingerboard surface would allow, providing greater ability to raise the pitch.[10] Although this is not much of a weapon in the cittern player's arsenal, it does provide further evidence that the players themselves were not only concerned about their instruments' ability to produce accurate pitches but moreover viewed it as their responsibility to do what they could to play in tune, in spite of not having the flexibility of repositioning or slanting frets, as players of the lute and viol did. Nevertheless, as we will see, the artisans who crafted fixed metal-fret wire-strung instruments elevated practicality to a constructive principle.

While makers' choices of temperament may have been an attempt to give players a predetermined advantage to compensate for the difficulties associated with tuning the instrument, I suspect that three additional factors related to both the instrument's features and the way it is played contributed to this fastidiousness: volume, timbre, and tessitura. The cittern's vivid presence has the ability to overwhelm other instruments in an ensemble setting in terms of all three. Since it is usually strummed in ensemble situations, it projects whatever harmony it produces in a simple and direct fashion. If it is out of tune, everyone can hear it, and there's not much to be done about it. On the other hand, a lutenist or viol player performing on an instrument set in equal temperament has the ability to shade the temperament enough toward meantone temperaments to at least diminish equal temperament's deficiencies with well-chosen adjustments before playing and occasionally even on the fly. And, more often than not, lutes and viols are not strumming full chords, warts and all. The uniformity of surviving citterns set in some variety or other of meantone temperament testifies to makers' trying to stack the deck in favor of sweeter thirds.

Timbre is the tonal quality or tone color that differentiates one instrument or voice from another. It is the instantly recognizable quality that distinguishes Luciano Pavarotti's voice from that of any other tenor singing the same aria in the same key. On instruments capable of producing harmonic intervals, that is, two or more notes at a time, the more brilliant the instrument's timbre, the more offensive it is when it is out of tune. This is because brighter-timbred instruments have more prominent upper partials, which, as we will see, tend to be more out of tune than lower partials. For instance, to the casual listener, equal temperament's infelicities tend to be somewhat muted on the classical guitar compared with the lute thanks to the guitar's rounder timbre resulting from fewer upper partials than on the lute. Listeners attuned to subtle tuning differences, on the other hand, note that tuning problems are more noticeable on classical guitars with brighter sounding spruce soundboards compared with those with darker sounding cedar tops. The cittern's crystalline timbre that favors higher harmonics actually accentuates intonation problems. One of its prime virtues is one of its worst defects. Additionally, playing with a plectrum, as is the custom with the cittern, produces a greater number of high partials than were it played with the fingers.[11]

A third culprit is the cittern's high pitch. Think of the orchestra. Egregious errors aside, intonation issues are most evident in the upper strings, higher woodwind, and brass instruments since our ears are better able to discern minute pitch differences in higher than lower registers. How often do we ever read a concert review claiming that the performance was marred by consistently poor intonation in the basses, low brass, or contrabassoon?

The Orpharion and Bandora

Citterns were more commonplace in a variety of performance situations than orpharions or bandoras, a fact reflected in the dearth of extant orpharions compared with numerous surviving examples of citterns and the possible complete absence of surviving bandoras. In the past and present, the terms *orpharion* and *bandora* have often been used interchangeably, as have *tiorba, chitarrone,* and *archlute.* Although there is still some difference of opinion regarding how to label the specific instruments that appear to be either orpharions or bandoras, experts seem to have come to some sort of agreement that the bandora is a slightly larger and lower-pitched instrument than the orpharion and that the former instrument was used primarily for ensemble music, for instance, in the aforementioned broken consort, while its smaller, higher-pitched relative was preferred for solo music. The bandora and orpharion are tuned differently, the bandora as *C D G c e a* or *G′ C D G c e a* with the addition of the alternative *C D G c f a d′* provided by Praetorius, whereas the orpharion is tuned like a lute in G.[12] Lyle Nordstrom, however, refers to the orpharion as a treble bandora.[13] Orpharions were played with the fingers rather than a plectrum, as indicated by their tablatures and the wear pattern where the little finger would have been planted on the soundboard, which can be clearly seen on the orpharion constructed by Francis Palmer in 1617 in London and now held at the Musikmuseet, Musikhistorisk Museum and Carl Claudius's Samling in Copenhagen, whose fretting pattern we will examine in detail below.[14] See figure 2.2. Two other orpharions survive as well. Segerman reports that the fingerboard of the instrument conserved at the Historisches Museum in Frankfurt am Main has been re-fretted to produce equal temperament.[15] From this we can draw the logical conclusion that its original frets were set in something other than equal temperament. The frets on the orpharion housed at the Städtisches Museum in Brunswick are arranged in what appears to be a meantone or meantone-based pattern; however, whether the fretboard is original is yet to be determined. Information provided by a detailed study of this relatively unknown instrument has the potential to further contribute to our tunings and temperament knowledge base.[16]

One other instrument, the glorious bandora or orpharion built by John Rose in 1580, according to the label inside, has drawn considerable discussion and some controversy. See figure 2.3. Donald Gill and Lyle Nordstrom suggest that the Rose instrument might be thought of as an orpharion, while Francis Galpin, Ian Harwood, Ephraim Segerman, Djilda Abbott, and Darryl Martin consider it a small bandora. In any event, what concerns us here is that the constructive principles of the two instruments are closely related.[17]

According to Forrester, the Rose is a small bandora in a meantone temperament, but closer to equal temperament than the Palmer orpharion, which he describes as being in the vicinity of 1/6-comma meantone.[18] Significantly, the dozen or so books of tablatures for solo music for lute or orpharion meant that the music must have been conceived with meantone temperaments in mind for it to have worked on the orpharion, since there is no evidence that original orpharion fretboards were ever set in equal temperament. The same music would therefore be well suited for a lute set in a meantone temperament.

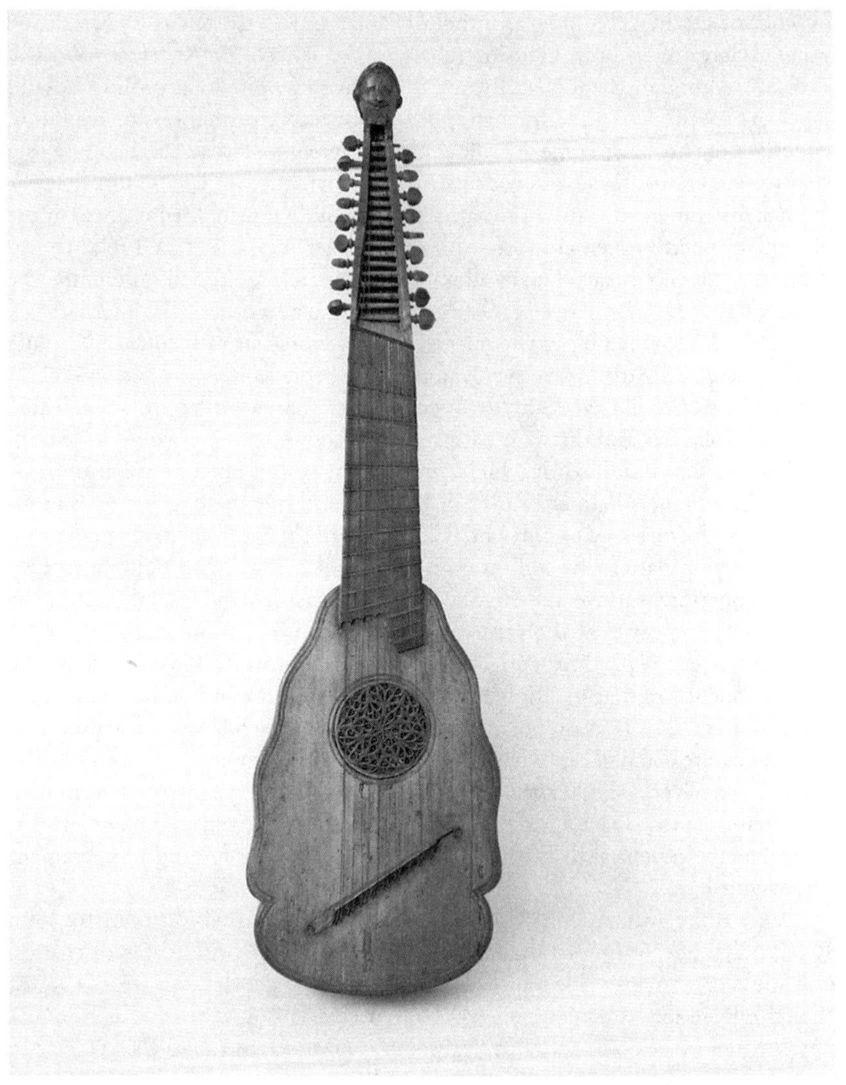

Figure 2.2. Palmer orpharion. Photo by Ture Bergstrøm, courtesy of the Danish Music Museum.

My research indicates that both instruments, the Palmer and Rose, are set in utilitarian temperaments combining elements of several varieties of meantone temperament but also incorporating some features of equal temperament in a shrewdly pragmatic arrangement that favors the keys these instruments normally play in while disregarding those that they do not. Frozen improvisations

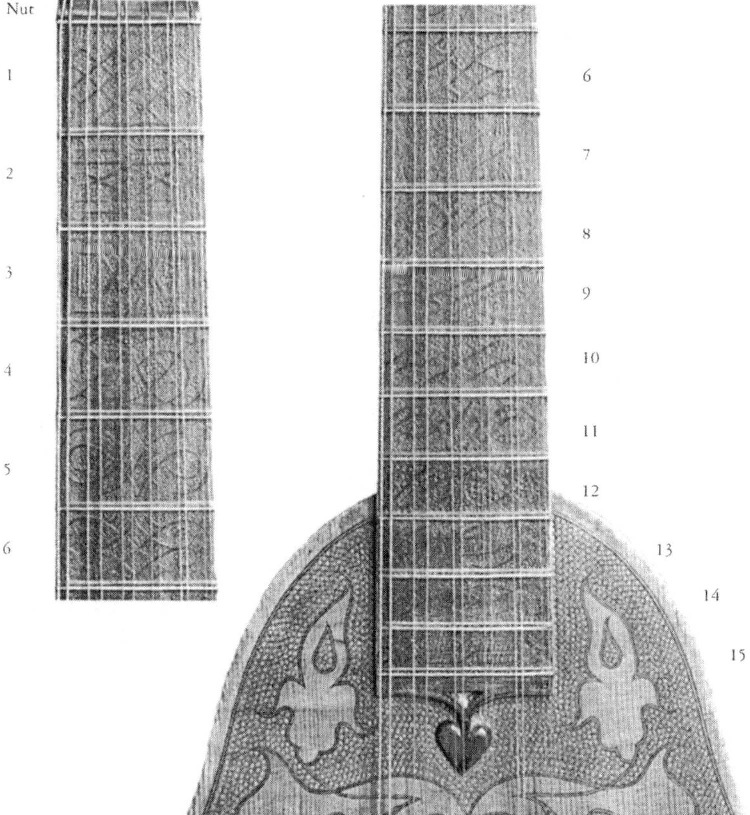

Figure 2.3. Rose bandora or orpharion. Courtesy of the Lute Society.

that epitomize the triumph of practicality over science, the Palmer and Rose fretboard patterns demonstrate that their players and makers were more concerned with what sounded good to them than following a theoretical model that adhered to the dictates of a regular system. We now examine their fretboard patterns in some detail.

The Palmer Orpharion

In the absence of actually playing it, the identification of the temperament that would have been produced by the Palmer orpharion in its original playing condition is complicated by several factors, including that, as Darryl Martin has reported, the bridge and saddle are not original and that the saddle is not in its original position. Additionally, the saddle is set excessively high, and the entire instrument is bowed from end to end, the front of the instrument concave.[19]

That the original saddle must have been set farther away from the nut than it is currently situated is confirmed by the location of the 12th fret. The current vibrating length at the first course is 518.5 mm, but yet the 12th fret is located 261 mm from the nut and 257.5 mm from the saddle, roughly the opposite of the expected relationship.[20] To account for sharpening, the 12th fret should be approximately 1.5 mm closer to the nut than the saddle to lengthen the string beyond its actual midpoint to compensate for the increase in pitch caused when the course is depressed with the goal of producing a precise octave. Yet the 12th fret is 2.5 mm farther away from the nut than it should be: at 518.5 mm, a reasonable relationship would be 258.5 mm from the nut to the 12th fret and 260 mm from the 12th fret to the saddle.[21] Since there's no evidence that the fret positions have been altered, we must assume that the 12th fret is precisely placed. The actual length of 261 mm between the nut and 12th fret suggests an original vibrating length of approximately 523.5 mm, 5 mm longer than it is in its current state, with a length of 262.5 mm between the 12th fret and the saddle.

Wire-strung instruments generally include a color-coded "wedge" on the nut side of each fret. The wedge is simply a distinctly colored piece of wood inserted into the fingerboard that is flush with the fingerboard surface designed to provide a visual guide to the type of note found at that fret, a more sophisticated version of the dots on modern guitar fingerboards or bass side neck purflings that serve as fret location guideposts.[22] On the Palmer orpharion, the ebony wedges at frets 2, 3, 5, 7, 9, 10, 12, and 14 identify natural notes while the maple wedges at frets 1, 4, 6, 8, 11, 13, and 15 represent accidentals, that is, sharp or flat notes. Peter Forrester points out that the Palmer's color-coding follows that of citterns.[23]

Table 2.1 presents the distances from frets 1 to 12 to the nut on what I imagine the original string length to be from the saddle to the nut on first course based on Martin's report and Nurse's tracing and generates the cents those fret positions would theoretically produce. Remember that because of sharpening, while the fret positions as they relate to the nut are precise, the pitches they would generate may not be. This is immediately evident at the 12th fret, with a cents figure of 1195.1c. Table 2.1 also provides the width of each fret space in cents.

Several features that table 2.1 reveals merit comment. The numbers confirm the instrument's visual appearance: the first seven frets are obviously arranged in some sort of meantone temperament scheme, but while frets 8–12 continue that trend, they somewhat flatten out into something that is much closer to equal temperament. This makes perfect sense since most of the music played on an orpharion is restricted to the first seven frets. Most notable is that the 2nd and 4th frets are almost indistinguishable from a 1/4-comma whole tone of 193c. and major third of 386c. The tritone at the 6th fret is just .3c. shy of pure, and the 8th fret is only .6c. wider than pure. In several forums, Ross Duffin has commented on the importance of 1/6 comma's pure

Table 2.1.
Palmer orpharion first course fret distances to nut, in millimeters and cents, and fret space widths in cents

Fret	Millimeters to nut	Cents	Fret width
1	30.5	103.9	103.9
2	55.5	194.0	90.1
3	83.3	300.0	106.0
4	104.5	385.5	85.5
5	129.9	493.8	108.3
6	151.3	590.5	96.7
7	173.7	698.0	107.5
8	192.7	794.7	96.7
9	210.9	892.6	97.9
10	228.9	995.3	102.7
11	245.3	1094.5	99.2
12	261.0	1195.1	100.6

augmented fourth.[24] Palmer's perfect fifth comes in at 698c., a compromise between 1/5- and 1/6-comma fifths. The semitone between the 4th and 5th frets is essentially a 1/6-comma major semitone, and the 1st fret corresponds to a 1/8-comma semitone. The minor third between the open string and the 3rd fret produces an equal-tempered minor third. Remember that although these figures are close, they may not be precise. Because of the repositioning of the bridge, we cannot be absolutely certain what temperament Palmer intended, although we can confidently claim that it veered toward 1/6-comma meantone temperament, with some tendencies toward both 1/4-comma and 1/8-comma meantone temperaments. It is not so much the individual details that concern us, but rather what they tell us collectively about Palmer's pragmatic approach to temperament.

As we broaden our view to consider how such a temperament might have actually sounded, we need to consider the names of the pitches produced and how they might interact in the real world of a fingerboard that is used primarily across the strings rather than along them. Table 2.2 outlines the pitch names of the notes for the first twelve frets. It also includes three additional columns indicating whether the fret should be considered a *mi* or a *fa,* fret width in cents, and Palmer's designation of the fret as natural or accidental where *N* indicates natural and ♯ or ♭ for my choice of accidental based on fret width for frets Palmer designated as accidentals. Keep in mind that frets 9–12 are so close to equal temperament that in most cases they could serve as a *mi* or a *fa* depending on the context.

Because players of fixed fret instruments such as the cittern, orpharion, and bandora do not have the luxury of altering the frets to accommodate the tonality of the piece being played at the time, what we see is what we get. We must

Table 2.2.
Palmer orpharion pitch names, *mi/fa* designation, fret widths in cents, and Palmer's natural/accidental designation

Fret	G	C	F	A	D	G	*mi/fa*	Fret width	Natural/ accidental
1	A♭	D♭	G♭	B♭	E♭	A♭	*fa*	103.9	♭
2	A	D	G	B	E	A	*mi*	90.1	N
3	B♭	E♭	A♭	C	F	B♭	*fa*	106.0	N
4	B	E	A	C♯	F♯	B	*mi*	85.5	♯
5	C	F	B♭	D	G	C	*fa*	108.3	N
6	C♯	F♯	B	D♯	G♯	C♯	*mi*	96.7	♯
7	D	G	C	E	A	D	*fa*	107.5	N
8	D♯	G♯	C♯	E♯	A♯	D♯	*mi*	96.7	♯
9	E	A	D	F♯	B	E	*mi*	97.9	N
10	F	B♭	E♭	G	C	F	*fa*	102.7	N
11	F♯	B	E	G♯	C♯	F♯	*mi*	99.2	♯
12	G	C	F	A	D	G	*fa*	100.6	N

therefore accommodate our chord shapes to the pitches as they are.[25] As we saw in chapter 1 with regard to relocating the 4th fret in isolation without altering the location of any other fret, ultra-irregular temperaments such as those created in those circumstances or when the features of a variety of temperaments are combined to create a customized temperament, such as we find with the Palmer orpharion, or utilitarian temperaments, such as Gerle's, all intervals between the same two nominal pitches, the major third A–C♯, for instance, are not necessarily of the same size. The important thing to bear in mind when choosing chord shapes, a topic that will be dealt with in some detail in later chapters, is to choose locations that favor the third, whether major or minor, because that is what determines the quality of the chord. Here's where Palmer's color-coded fret wedges come in handy. Referring to table 2.2, notice that each ebony wedge that is not one of a pair of consecutive ebony wedges designates a *fa* fret; these would be frets 5, 7, and 12. A pair of consecutive ebony wedges such as found at frets 2 and 3 and frets 9 and 10 indicate a *mi/fa* pair.[26] Except for the easily remembered 1st fret, all the maple wedges indicate *mi* frets. Such a system serves no purpose if you are reading tablature, but if you are short-scoring or providing continuo, Palmer's system provides a convenient guide to the best places to form euphonious chords. As long as you place the third at a *mi* fret for major chords and at a *fa* fret for minor chords, the chord will be most pleasing. For instance, the D Major chord shape in musical example 2.1 sounds a little out-of-tune because it includes the fourth course 1st fret, a G♭ that strains to stand in for an F♯, whereas the D Major chord shape in musical example 2.2 sounds fine because the third is placed on the 4th fret, which is a *mi.* Similarly, the C Minor chord in musical example 2.3 sounds great because

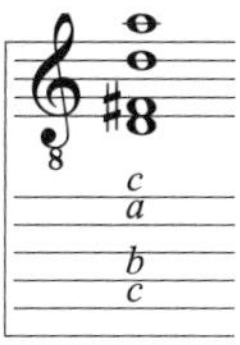

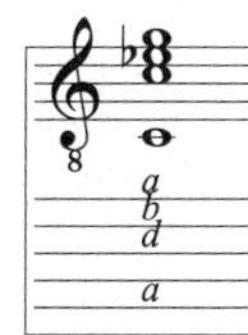

Musical Example 2.1. D Major on orpharion.

Musical Example 2.2. Alternate D Major on orpharion.

Musical Example 2.3. C Minor on orpharion.

Musical Example 2.4. Alternate C Minor on orpharion.

its third, the E♭, is placed at the first fret, which is a *fa;* however, when placed at the 6th fret (*mi*) as in musical example 2.4, it doesn't sound quite so good. So, it's a matter of choosing appropriate chord locations. Clearly then, Palmer presumed that the player of his instrument would be concerned enough with the location of *mi* and *fa* frets to wish to be able to choose chord shapes that provide the best sound.

To confirm all this, I arranged the frets on my lute to conform to the Palmer's configuration.[27] I played a progression of I–IV–V–I chords in each major key and i–iv–V–i chords in each minor key and noted what worked and what didn't. As expected, the quality of the chords varies quite dramatically depending on the chord shape choice and location, but in short order, thinking in terms of *mi* and *fa* frets, I found it quite easy to find chords that worked well in most keys. Restricting my experiment to the first five frets, I found that the major keys of E♭, B♭, F, C, G, and D and the minor keys of C, G, D, and A sounded lovely. By expanding my range to include the 7th fret, thereby admitting the 6th fret, *mi,* I was able to add four more keys, A and E Major and Minor, to the pantheon of keys that work well on the Palmer orpharion. By pushing and pulling strings with the left-hand fingers, advanced players would be able to expand the available tonal palette even further.

So how did Palmer set the frets? He must have first set the distances on the first course because since the sharpening effect is the least there, he could assure himself that his customized temperament would be truest on that course. From there he assuredly experimented to slant the frets to match octaves with the most commonly used chord positions. He could have accomplished this with metal frets whose length was wider than the fingerboard and whose bass and treble ends were tied together on the back of the instruments. This would have allowed him to adjust the frets while he listened. The frets on the Palmer's bass side do not progress in the same proportion as they do on the treble side, but while it's impossible to calculate their locations theoretically, I found it surprisingly easy to accomplish by ear.

Perhaps Palmer set out to create a meantone temperament, and this is the best he could come up with. On the other hand, he may have intended to create his own temperament by ear that works well in the tonalities commonly found in the orpharion repertoire. He certainly did accomplish that without slavishly following the dictates of musical theory, and yet he created a temperament that represents a triumph of art and practicality over science and theory.

The Rose Orpharion (or Bandora)

Compared with the Palmer orpharion, John Rose's magnificent instrument is much more straightforward. Its bridge, nut, and frets are perpendicular rather than fan shaped, the bridge and saddle are original, the action is normal, and it is not bowed. Table 2.3 reproduces the fret distances from the nut as measured by Peter Forrester and reported by Ian Harwood based on a vibrating string length of 599.1 mm.[28]

Several features of table 2.3 immediately attract our attention. Most noticeable is that Rose's temperament is a much gentler meantone variant, with many

Table 2.3.
Rose orpharion (or bandora) fret distances to nut, in millimeters and cents, and fret space widths in cents

Fret	Distance	Cents	Fret width
1	35.0	104.2	104.2
2	64.2	196.2	92.0
3	94.0	295.5	99.3
4	122.2	394.9	99.4
5	150.2	499.7	104.8
6	175.0	598.1	98.4
7	199.1	699.4	101.3
8	222.3	802.8	103.4
9	242.6	898.7	95.9
10	261.5	993.0	94.3
11	280.7	1094.3	101.3
12	298.7	1195.1	100.8

of the frets deviating only slightly from equal temperament. The Rose's meantone tendencies are most evident at the first three frets. Overall, the temperament seems to favor 1/8 comma with a tip of the hat to 1/6 comma and a bow to equal temperament. The 3rd and 4th frets are strikingly similar in terms of cents; the 3rd seems too narrow and the 4th too wide, perhaps intended as compromise positions within a meantone context. Several of the major (diatonic) semitones are close to 1/8 comma's 103.75c., with the *mi* semitone between the 1st and 2nd frets matching 1/7 comma's chromatic semitone. The perfect fourth between the open course and the 5th fret is virtually an equal-tempered (ET) fourth with the fifth between the open course and the 7th fret practically identical to 1/8 comma's perfect fifth of 699.25 just shy of an ET fifth. At 898.7c., the major sixth at the 9th fret is very close to 1/8 comma's 897.75c., and the major seventh at the 11th fret matches a 1/7-comma 11th fret precisely. Just short of 1/6 comma's 196.6c., the whole tone at the 2nd fret comes in at 196.2c., and the all-important major third at the 4th fret is close to 1/7 comma's 395.44c. The Rose's 12th fret compensation produces a theoretical cents figure of 1195.1c. It bears repeating that because the Rose seems to be well constructed in terms of action, these cents figures are close but probably not precise because of sharpening. Nevertheless, they allow us to draw the following conclusions.

Similar to the Palmer orpharion, Rose's instrument adheres to no standard pattern but instead favors a subtle meantone arrangement consisting of components of several meantone varieties mixed in with equal temperament. Compared with the Palmer, Rose's temperament is tolerable in a wider range of keys approaching the versatility of well temperaments. One physical difference between the two instruments, however, may provide a clue as to their makers' approaches to temperament. Palmer's frets are flat, whereas Rose's are scalloped.[29] The apparent chromatic blandness in the Rose could be mitigated somewhat by pushing and pulling with the left-hand fingers facilitated by the scalloped frets, particularly since the alteration in pitch required to change a pitch from a *mi* to a *fa* is much less in broader temperaments such as that fielded on the Rose than in temperaments that favor fewer tonalities such as that on the Palmer. And this in a nutshell is the conundrum that musicians faced during this period: whether to favor serviceability in a greater number of tonalities or better quality in fewer tonalities.

The degree to which practicality governs fretboard arrangements on wire-strung instruments is nothing less than striking. As we have seen, the standard temperament for fixed fret instruments was either some variety or meantone or a utilitarian temperament with predominantly meantone features. Lutes and viols that played with them obviously tuned to their fixed fret brethren just as assuredly as they tuned to the keyboards that anchored the other ensembles in which they played. To add yet another dimension to our overview of historical precedent, we now turn our attention to iconographical representations of fretted instruments for the documentary evidence they can provide that the fretting arrangements on lutes, viols, and guitars were anything but uniform. Or necessarily equal.

CHAPTER THREE

Fretting Pattern Iconography

General Introduction to the Use of Iconography

At its simplest, "applied" iconography is "the study of historical depictions for their documentary content and value," according to guitarist, university librarian, and iconographer Thomas Heck.[1] M. A. Katritzky refines this definition even further: "performing-arts iconography focuses on effective ways in which information of significance to the history of the performing arts can be gained from visual material, in order to facilitate investigation of the history of the performing arts from a visual perspective."[2] For instruments with movable frets, the only visual evidence we have that shows rather than tells us how the frets were arranged is iconography such as paintings, drawings, and book illustrations.

Musical instruments appear in the fine art of earlier eras much more frequently than they do in our own for a number of reasons, not the least of which is that, in the absence of the entertainments facilitated by the stunning array of technology we enjoy today, playing musical instruments was much more a part of the daily lives of our ancestors than our own. Instruments also symbolized the sense of hearing, but also sensibility and sensuality in all their guises, and depending how they were depicted, musical instruments could represent a lively present, pleasures past, or even death itself as in the countless works in the *vanitas* tradition. The lute, for instance, is so ubiquitous in the iconography of the sixteenth and seventeenth centuries not only because it was the most widespread instrument of its time but also for its iconic value as a symbol of sophistication and culture. It stood in for the ancient Greek lyre as the ideal instrument for the accompaniment of poetry and was associated with the privileged classes and the court. The lute's high cost and the level of skill required to master its complexities further enhanced its value as a status symbol.[3]

The following paragraphs seek to begin the discussion by broadly identifying fretboard patterns that can generate a practical temperament and describing those that actually do appear in iconography with intersections noted. We consider some factors that can impede the artist's power to render fretboard patterns precisely and the viewer's ability to recognize them. And because so many of the fret patterns on lutes and viols in paintings and drawings would produce no workable temperament whatsoever, we examine some of the practical causes for this phenomenon, which, coupled with clues that indicate greater fealty to reality, can aid us in separating artworks that merit further research from those that do not.

What Functional Fretboard Patterns Look Like

A fretboard arranged in equal temperament yields frets that incrementally decrease in width from the 1st fret to the 12th, and so on, a pattern that can be seen on any modern guitar. Meantone temperaments, on the other hand, generally require a pattern of fret widths that alternate between the wide *fa* and narrow *mi* frets, each also decreasing incrementally from the 1st to 12th frets—the 1st fret will be the widest, the 2nd will be narrower, the 3rd wide, but not as wide as the 1st. The 4th fret is narrower than the 2nd fret, and the 5th narrower than the 3rd, but wider than the 4th. In other words, each successive *fa* or *mi* fret will be narrower than its predecessor of the same class. Occasionally there will be two adjacent *fa* frets, for instance, when a theorbo or lute tuned in A raises the 4th fret to produce an E♭ on the third course. In that circumstance, both the 3rd and 4th frets would be wide *fa* frets, though often the 4th fret would be slanted to yield *fas* on the highest courses and *mis* on lowest courses, a procedure that we examine in greater detail in subsequent chapters. The differences between the widths of the *fa* and *mi* frets are the greatest in 1/4-comma meantone and decrease as the tempering of the fifth decreases from 1/5- to 1/6-comma meantone temperaments, and so forth. Finally, the difference in width between *fa* and *mi* frets also increases with the size of the instrument. For example, it is much easier to estimate a temperament on a bass viol or a theorbo than on a treble viol or a small six-course lute of Francesco's era, the differences between *fa* and *mi* frets visually more subtle and difficult to discern on the smaller instruments.

Fretboard patterns suggesting Pythagorean tuning with fret relationships that are the exact opposite pattern as in meantone temperaments appear from time to time. Similar to meantone temperaments, in the Pythagorean fret pattern, each successive *mi* or *fa* fret is narrower than the previous one. Refer to diagrams 3.1 and 3.2, which show characteristic fret patterns for Pythagorean tuning; 1/4-, 1/5-, 1/6-, and 1/8-comma meantone temperaments; and equal temperament.[4] These are what most practical fretting patterns actually look like; how they appear in paintings and drawings can be another thing entirely.

A number of other factors, some of which will be discussed in considerable detail later in this and other chapters, can impact the arrangements of the frets. These primarily fall under the categories of loose frets, sharpening, and pitch choice, the last two of which often involve slanted frets.

As frets age and become loose, players tend to slide them up toward the 12th fret, where the neck gradually widens to tighten them so that they stay put

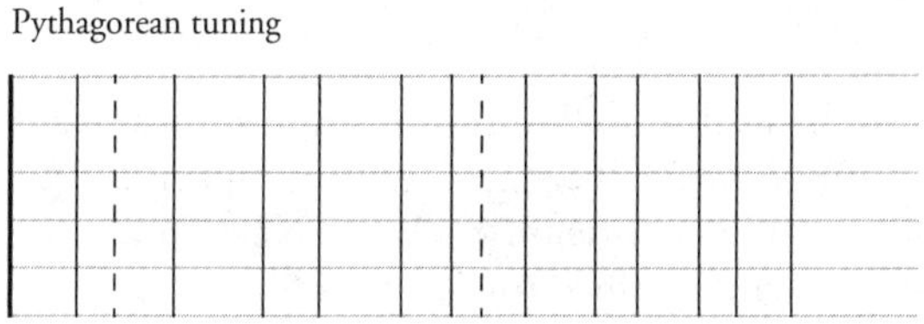

Pythagorean tuning

Diagram 3.1. Pythagorean tuning fretboard in G.

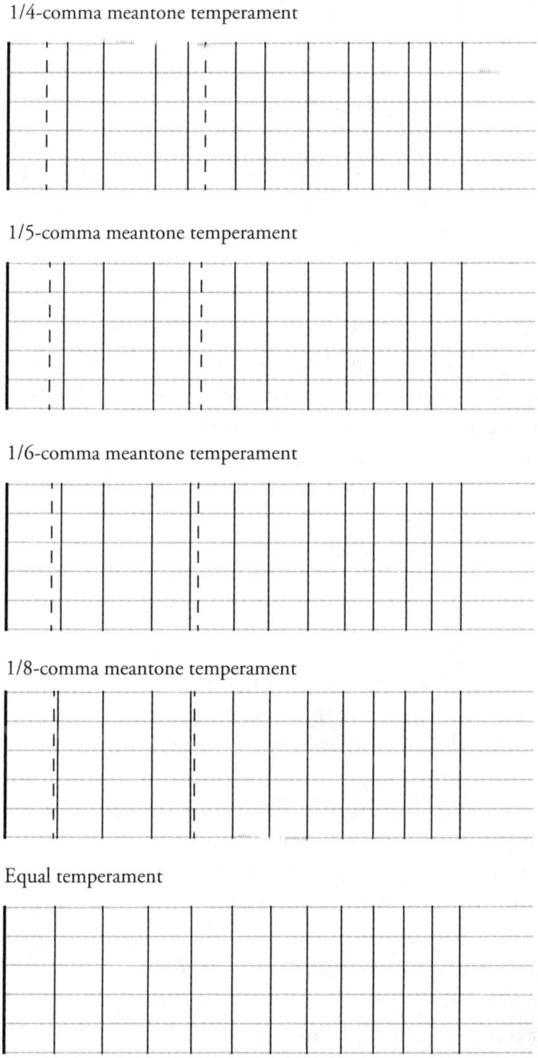

1/4-comma meantone temperament

1/5-comma meantone temperament

1/6-comma meantone temperament

1/8-comma meantone temperament

Equal temperament

Diagram 3.2. Fretboard patterns for 1/4-, 1/5-, 1/6-, and 1/8-comma meantone and equal temperaments.

until they can be changed. A well-known example of this phenomenon can be seen in *The Musicians* by Michelangelo Merisi, known as Caravaggio (1573–1610), at the Metropolitan Museum of Art in New York; the 5th and higher frets all seem to be slightly pushed toward the 12th fret, as if to tighten them.[5]

Successive frets approaching the 12th fret are narrower than the previous fret in equal temperament or the previous *mi* or *fa* fret in unequal temperaments to account for sharpening, the physical factor that causes the string to produce a pitch sharper than the desired pitch when the fret is positioned at its theoretically correct position. To compensate for this phenomenon, the fret is placed slightly closer to the nut so that the correct pitch is sounded. The physical factors that impact sharpening are discussed in greater detail below and in chapter 6.

Frets are usually slanted to either account for sharpening particularly on the bass courses, which are more susceptible to it, or for the purpose of accessing pitches unavailable when the fret is perfectly perpendicular. As the frets age, become worn and flattened with use, their decrease in height and profile causes the sharpening effect to intensify since greater left-hand finger pressure is required for the note to speak clearly. The increased finger pressure that lets the note speak clearly also increases the longitudinal tension on the string, raising its pitch and thereby requiring an increasingly greater compensatory slant of the fret. Thicker strings tend to sharpen more extremely than thinner strings do. For this reason, frets are almost always slanted toward the nut on the bass side to increase the length of the stopped string to compensate for the sharpening. Slanting accommodates sharpening on the bass courses while allowing the thinner strings at the same fret to stay reasonably close to their desired positions. In humid conditions, strings absorb excess moisture, thereby increasing their density, particularly the bass strings, magnifying the sharpening effect and the concomitant requirement for compensation.[6] In general, the amount of slanting required to compensate for sharpening increases toward the 12th fret, particularly on gut strings, often resulting in very slanted frets in the upper positions.

As Doni pointed out in 1640, octave stringing is especially problematic because the thicker fundamental string requires much more compensation than its octave partner, which may need none at all, a difficulty that can be somewhat mitigated by double frets since they support a lower action.[7] I suspect that these tuning issues are among the reasons that many repertoires avoid the upper positions on the lower courses. A final word of caution: when frets are slanted, the entire fret tends to eventually migrate toward the nut, which can, of course, skew our visual perception of an affected fretboard.

We began this section by asking what functional fretboard patterns look like. Art can be messy, but its transformative moments make it quite easy to tolerate a little chaos now and then. And so too with fret arrangements. Figure 3.1 shows a treble viol after a concert. It demonstrates how a professional musician's tuning goals can be facilitated by a particular fret arrangement given the

Figure 3.1. Treble viol with split double and sloped frets after a concert. Courtesy of Richard Carter.

circumstances of the moment. Here we see an ad hoc fretting arrangement in some sort of meantone arrangement with split double and sloped frets to provide more precise tuning. As we will see below, sometimes art does imitate life.

What Fretboard Patterns Depicted in Artwork Look Like

In paintings such as Nicholas Tournier's (1590–ca. 1639) *Le Concert,* Carlo Saraceni's (1585–1620) depiction of Saint Cecilia tuning her lute, reproduced here as plates 2 and 3, and the viola da gamba player among the musical company in a painting by Johannes Voorhout (1647–1723) best known for including the only known portrait of Dieterich Buxtehude, the arrangement of the first five frets form an instantly recognizable typical meantone temperament pattern of *fa, mi, fa, mi, fa.*[8]

Ironically, however, many paintings depicting fretted instruments space the frets in such a fashion that they could not possibly yield any usable tuning or temperament—Pythagorean, meantone, equal, or ad hoc—reducing such paintings' evidentiary value significantly. For instance, a fretboard pattern found in an uncomfortably large number of paintings positions the frets precisely evenly up the neck in an equidistant fretting arrangement. It is understandable that in the interests of symmetry, a painter might desire to regularize what appears to be an irregular or unequal fretting arrangement.[9] Sometimes spacings inexplicably increase toward the 12th fret. Another widespread category of fret arrangements portrays portions of the fretboard in either equal temperament or precisely equidistant fretting coupled with another portion of the frets arranged unequally. Although the unequal portion can appear anywhere along the fretboard, it is most commonly found in the frets closest to the nut, for reasons discussed in chapter 1 and below. The famous woodcuts of the viols, violone, and large Paduan theorbo in Praetorius's *Syntagma musicum* appear to be of this sort, that is, partially meantone and partially not. Sometimes the fretting arrangement appears to be in some sort of meantone temperament with the 1st, 4th, or 6th frets in a compromise position between the *mi* and *fa* position.

Conversely, there are paintings such as John Michael Wright's (ca. 1617–1700) *Lady with a Theorbo* that show the 1st and 4th frets in their customary *fa* and *mi* positions, while the other frets seem to be spaced equally. See plate 4. The illustrations of fretted instruments that amplify the text in the second part of Mersenne's *Harmonie universelle* (1637) are somewhat less inconsistent but still unreliable: notwithstanding Mersenne's discussion of Just intonation on lutes, the lute illustrations (page 46) show lutes in equal temperament or something very close to it; all the citterns (97v–98v) are in an extreme form of meantone temperament. However, the frets on the four-course guitar on page 95 are arranged in a subtle but clear meantone temperament, whereas the frets on the five-course guitar on the following page seem to be arranged somewhat randomly. The fret arrangement of the bass viola da gamba on page 192 makes no sense whatsoever. Occasionally artworks show instruments with one or more frets missing.[10] Frets are frequently slanted every which way, and a great number of fret patterns depicted in paintings and drawings seem to be totally unruly and haphazard.[11]

The majority of depictions of the viola da gamba that display fret formations based on reality appear to be set in equal temperament or something like it. Yet we know from Praetorius and others that viol players in particular who set their frets in equal temperament were accustomed to adjusting pitches on the fly with a combination of left-hand pushing and pulling, variations in bow pressure, and ad hoc fret adjustments, topics we explore in greater depth in subsequent chapters. This makes perfect sense because these techniques are quite easy on the viol, whereas on the lute they reside primarily in the domain of advanced players. Therefore, evidence derived from lute fretting arrangements depicted in historical paintings is more likely to indicate the actual temperament in use at the time of the painting than that derived from paintings of viols. So even a painting of an instrument, particularly a viol, in equal temperament does not unequivocally prove that equal temperament was the tuning system actually produced when that instrument was played.

Finally and unfortunately, to my knowledge, there is no iconographical evidence of tastini, but as it is said: "Absence of evidence is not necessarily evidence of absence." Refer to plate 1 for the only known painting to depict double or split frets.[12] We will discuss this technique further in later chapters.

Impediments to Identifying Temperaments from Paintings: The Artist

Now that we have compared what fretboard patterns should look like with those that actually do appear in artwork, let us survey some of the factors that may impede the production or perception of a viable fretboard pattern. Production, of course, is restricted to the artist's purview, whereas perception issues can impact both the artist's ability to accurately represent a fretboard pattern and the viewer's ability to comprehend what the artist has rendered.

In the Renaissance, painters were often more interested in representing idealized scenes than providing photographic reproductions. In the Baroque era the perfect world of imaginary settings began to expand to include depictions of the lute in real-life situations, such as in the hands of drunkards and prostitutes in taverns. The seventeenth-century artist's newfound concern with situational verisimilitude did not, regrettably, necessarily extend to the depictions of the lutes themselves. Nevertheless, regarding what works of art can teach us about music, Howard Mayer Brown and Joan Lascelle wrote that despite the inherent limitations in using iconography, such as the artist's skill level, ignorance of the significance of certain details, or goals that could prevent an accurate representation of the instrument, "works of art are still our best source of information on the history, construction and playing techniques of early instruments."[13] Indeed, in some cases, they are our only source.

We must acknowledge that without some sort of measurement tool or device such as depicted in Albrecht Dürer's (1471–1528) "The Draughtsman with Lute," a woodcut that appears in his *Treatise on Mensuration with the Compass and Ruler in Lines, Planes, and Whole Bodies* (1525) (see plate 5), it would be extraordinarily difficult to faithfully reproduce relative distances between frets that at the actual fretboard are measured in millimeters, a measurement that becomes even more infinitesimal with every meter the artist is removed from the subject. Although there is no evidence that any of the painters we discuss here used such an aid, that Dürer chose the lute over every other instrument to illustrate his technique implies that such aids were likely to have been used to depict the lute because the many varied and interacting geometrical elements that converge to give the instrument its shape make it a particularly challenging object to draw accurately. According to Tim Watson, the ability to render a lute in its precise proportions and details such as the spacing and color of the strings, the tuning pegs, the frets, and even the representation of such basic structural elements as perfectly straight strings, exceeds the capacity of many painters' ability or interest.[14] Yet, like moths to flames, artists were probably attracted by the challenge of depicting these instruments, a factor that may have contributed in some part to their ubiquity in early paintings. Fretting patterns, though, are perhaps among the most complicated organological details to challenge an artist's dedication to faithful representation with each of the aforementioned limitations intertwined and acting on the others.

Since the ability to accurately reproduce an object on canvas is more a matter of the eye than the hand, the desire to precisely represent a feature as subtly elusive as the relative distances between frets flows from sensitivity to the fact that frets are never evenly spaced in real life. After all, if painters were not aware of the significance of such details, they may not have had any reason to aspire to accuracy.[15] And, as mentioned above, it is not uncommon for artists to regularize the spacing deliberately for the sake of symmetry, a motivation that also raises the possibility that some artists were uninterested in verisimilitude, as is their prerogative. Other factors such as the medium, target audience, or stage in which the artistic work is found can also impact the accuracy of a rendering.[16] Perhaps if painters knew that four hundred years later, we'd be looking to them for photographic depictions of fret arrangements, they might have approached their work differently, but how were they to know?

Impediments to Identifying Temperaments from Paintings: The Viewer

Assuming that the artist has rendered the fretboard as accurately as possible, there are several perception issues that can prevent the viewer from clearly identifying the temperament: distance, perspective, and angle.

The farther the viewer is from the painting, the less noticeable are differences of the widths between frets, just as individual trees in a row of poplars viewed from a distance may appear to be equidistant from each other when in reality they are not. Quite often, close scrutiny of a portrayal of a lute or viol reveals that what at a cursory glance appears to an equidistant or equal-tempered arrangement actually presents a subtly unequal fret arrangement; for instance, the visual difference between equal temperament and 1/6-comma or subtler meantone shadings can escape detection by an inexperienced eye particularly on small instruments or miniature depictions of such.

Another factor to consider is that the correct rendering of perspective dictates that objects are drawn gradually smaller when the painter wants to give the impression that they are receding into the distance. In those cases where the lute player is turned away from the painter toward the fingerboard with the lute angled back to the player's left, the tendency would be for the painter to reduce the size of the frets as they approach the nut to give the appearance of receding perspective. In such circumstances, this desire to provide the viewer with depth perception counteracts the frets' becoming larger as they approach the nut. The opposite phenomenon takes place when viewing the lute from the direction of the pegbox. Again, the dictates of perspective would intensify the expected diminution in fret width as the frets recede into the distance toward the 12th fret. When depicting a lute angled in either fashion in 1/4-comma meantone, for instance, perspective reduces the contrasting differences in width between the frets as the fretboard recedes from view, a visual parallel of softening 1/4-comma meantone temperament into a division of the comma with a greater number of smaller slices.

The 1st Fret

Let's assume for a moment that the artist's rendering is spot-on precise. Enough paintings present an image of lutes or viols with excessively wide 1st frets that may or may not continue in a meantone pattern up the neck to warrant further exploration. Wide 1st frets are easiest to spot when the fingerboard and nut are in sharply contrasting colors, that is, the fingerboard black and the nut white as in the painting by Wright.

Like so many other aspects of lute and viol maintenance, tying tight frets that don't slip is a matter of technique, physical strength, and experience. It is by no means easy. Because the neck narrows as it approaches the nut, a fret is normally tied one or two fret distances closer to the nut from where it will ultimately reside. From that location, it is slid toward the 12th fret into its assigned position. As the fret moves up the widening neck, it becomes tighter. This is an easy matter with all the frets except for the 1st. Since it does not have the benefit of being tied at a narrower fret and slid up the neck, it is the most difficult fret to attach snugly. The back of the neck behind the 1st fret also suffers from the intrusion of angled pegboxes or the beginning of the neck extension on a long-necked lute, which further limits the distance from the 1st fret's final position that the fret can be tied on to the neck. Consequently, the 1st fret is always the loosest of all, tending to be the first to start to slip away toward the nut as the fret loses its elasticity and expands.

To counteract this, as a practical matter, until they have the opportunity replace the 1st fret or tighten it with matchsticks or little paper or cardboard shims inserted between the fret and back of the neck, players of instruments with movable frets tend to slide the 1st fret up toward the bridge a little, where the increased width of the neck permits a fit tight enough to keep the fret from slipping and sliding while playing. The result of this practical necessity is that regardless of the temperament, the 1st fret is sometimes wider than desirable to be in proper tune. If the 1st fret is wider, the 2nd fret will, of course, be narrower, inadvertently misleading the viewer to conclude a meantone fretting scheme where there may be none. To further complicate matters, keep in mind that the "loose fret" phenomenon can occur at any fret, although it is most common at the 1st. The depiction of an excessively wide 1st fret and the consequently narrow 2nd fret followed by the remaining frets in equal temperament is common, particularly in paintings of the viola da gamba, the most famous example of which is André Bouys's (1656–1740) well-known depiction of Marin Marais holding his viol as if it were a lute or guitar (see plate 6), although the same situation probably pertains to the lute depicted in Gerrit van Honthorst's (1592–1656) *The Concert* (1623) hanging at the National Gallery of Art in Washington, DC (*The Concert* is also shown at the top of this book's cover).

Taking 1st fret slippage into account as we examine fretting patterns found in historical paintings, when the 1st fret appears to be excessively wide and the 2nd fret narrow, perhaps due to the practical concerns outlined above, we must pay particular attention to the disposition of the 3rd, 4th, and 5th frets, which can unfortunately appear less than definitive owing to fading perspective in paintings such as Caravaggio's *The Musicians.* See plate 7. Not surprisingly, as is the case with a great many portraits of lutenists, the player is tuning rather than playing. In this painting, close examination reveals that the 1st fret is clearly disproportionately wider than any of the other frets, and the 4th fret is noticeably narrower than both the 3rd and 5th frets, possibly suggesting features of a meantone temperament, although the 2nd and 3rd frets seem to be of approximately equal widths as in the Wright painting. The perception of all of the preceding is, of course, complicated by the angle of the lute to the viewer. Alas, we can only wonder how the lute would have appeared straight on.

The other two Caravaggio paintings depicting the same lute player, both carrying the title *The Lute Player,* one also at the Metropolitan Museum of Art in New York and the other at the Hermitage in Saint Petersburg, show the lute from a relatively similar angle; however, the lutes in these portraits are not as tilted upward, but angled longitudinally away from the viewer such that they display less of the fingerboard. Furthermore, in these paintings, because of the viewer's perspective from the lutenist's left side, the player's left hand covers much of the fingerboard.[17]

Additionally, many paintings suggest meantone properties restricted to the lower frets. After all, since we spend more time playing in the lower than the upper positions, particularly when playing with others or accompanying singers, functionality is more important on the lower than higher fret positions. All of this, of course, pertains only when the lute or viol depicted is actually used for playing rather than as a prop or symbol of culture, good taste, erudition, or something else. In the latter cases, all bets are off.

Despite these obstacles, close scrutiny of such depictions may still offer us some useful information. Although "excessively wide" from a visual point of view is subjective, it is useful to distinguish among five basic categories of wide 1st frets:

1. The normal width of the 1st fret in equal, and any other temperament as the first in a series of frets that becomes relatively smaller as they approach the 12th fret to compensate for sharpening

2. The normal width of the 1st fret in any one of the standard meantone temperaments, 1/4 comma generally being the widest
3. Excessive width as a result of a loose fret slid up the neck to tighten it
4. A combination of either or both of the first two categories exacerbated by the third
5. The appearance of excessive width due to perspective

Signposts to Realism: Anatolian Rugs and Slanted Frets

For a painter's depiction of a fretting scheme to serve as evidence of any particular class of temperament, we must assess both the entire painting's overall level of detail as well as the precision with which the lute's proportions and physical details are represented. Noting the level of detail of other complicated objects presented in the same paintings, such the Anatolian rugs that often cover the tables on which the instruments are placed, drapery, books, sheet music, and other instruments such as those found in the series of paintings depicting lutes by Baschenis and in Holbein's *The Ambassadors,* is a first step toward determining whether the rendering of the lute or viol might be fairly accurate, but that alone is not nearly enough. A painting such as the Holbein may be astonishingly representational in many ways, down to a precise depiction of such details as the wood grain on the lute's ribs, but still misrepresent the lute's proportions as demonstrated by Tim Watson's in his article "Dei pericoli nell'avere fiducia nell'iconografia, ovvero: Possiamo consolarci che, se il liuto è così difficile da suonare è ancora difficile da dipingere: Un viaggio attraverso i comuni errori geometrici nelle raffigurazioni pittoriche del liuto," in which he superimposed three-dimensional (3D) computer model grids of typical lutes of the period over the lutes in numerous well-known paintings, including the Holbein, to illustrate defects in proportion. In several cases, he used the same technology with the assistance of Photoshop to reconstruct the lutes in the paintings in proper proportion.[18] Additionally, portraits of musicians employing realistic playing techniques can also provide evidence of faithful representation.

Another clue indicating that the painter provided a conscientious rendering of a fretting pattern is the treatment of the 3rd and, to a lesser extent, the 1st fret. As any experienced lutenist knows, the sharpening affect can be rather pronounced at the 3rd fret of the sixth course, a location frequently employed for the B♭ in the very common B♭ Major chord on a lute or viol tuned in G or C in the C Major chord on a theorbo, lute, or vihuela tuned in A where the 3rd fret is slanted toward the nut to keep the sixth course B♭ or C in tune primarily with the octave on the third course and the double octave on the first course. The lute in the painting by Theodor Rombouts (1597–1637) depicted in plate 8 is quite true to life in many respects. As in other paintings by the same artist, whose close attention to many details identify him as a rather reliable source, the lute player is frozen in time while tuning a lute. The 1st fret, already rather close to the nut in the *mi* position, is even closer on the bass side, clearly to compensate for sharpening since it cannot be slanted for the purpose of achieving a *mi* since the fret is already set to *mi.*

Other frets may be slanted as well, while still others remain perpendicular to the neck. For instance, a close examination of Giovanni di Jacopo (known as Rosso) Fiorentino's (1494–1540) beloved portrait of an angel playing a lute that hangs in the Uffizi Gallery in Florence reveals that most of the frets are ever so slightly slanted toward the nut on the bass side, particularly the 1st fret as can be expected. See plate 9. A 1st fret may be slanted to compensate for sharpening, but it can also be slanted on the bass side toward the nut to produce a sharp note rather than the flat note that would normally prevail at the 1st fret. On a G lute, with the 1st fret placed in its customary *fa* position, the pitch at the 1st fret of the sixth course would be A♭. A lute composer would know well enough to avoid placing a G♯ in that position, but improvising an accompaniment from a score, there are many occasions where that particular G♯ would be useful, for example, in the tonality of A Minor. The G♯ is easily attainable by slanting the bass side of the 1st fret toward the nut. Perhaps that is the situation represented by the detail from the familiar painting by Hendrick ter Brugghen (1588–1629) *The Singing Lute Player.*[19] See plate 10.

In conclusion, a painting that depicts a 3rd or other frets slanted toward the nut on the bass side bears increased reliability as a measure of temperament, since it is not something of which a painter or any "civilian" would necessarily be aware. We can therefore be certain that a painter who depicted slanted frets was conscientious about realism and conclude that he was as meticulous as his skill or the circumstances permitted. Fortunately, such examples are common in the iconography of instruments with movable frets, particularly lutes. Finally, we must, however, keep in mind that a depiction of a lute or viol with a perfectly perpendicular 3rd fret does not invalidate it for the reason that a freshly tied 3rd fret initially functions adequately in the perpendicular position until it begins to wear down or become adversely affected by environmental conditions.

Lombard Realism: Campi, Caravaggio, and Baschenis

The well-known painting attributed to Giulio Campi (1502–1572), which some fancy as portraying Francesco da Milano, that hangs in Como's Pinacoteca Civica exhibits many characteristics that indicate reality, but it also demonstrates some of the difficulties associated with interpreting artworks for the purposes of determining temperaments.[20] See plate 11. Giulio and his two younger brothers, like their father before them, became painters and were noted for applying Venetian color to their native Lombard realism, the school of painting that also produced Caravaggio and later Baschenis.[21] Giulio Campi also worked as an architect, a profession requiring the sort of exacting precision that serves our purposes here particularly well. His painting of a lutenist easily crosses the threshold described above for its generally accurate depiction of both player and instrument: the lutenist's hands are appropriately situated, and the six-course lute appears to be proportionate and precise.[22] For instance, the rose pattern is clearly visible, the relative diameters of the individual strings of the octave courses show significant attention to detail, the 3rd fret is typically slanted toward the nut on the bass side, and the entire instrument is in a characteristic playing position tilted ever so slightly back so that the lower edge of the body and neck are closer to the viewer than the top edge.

Now to the fret arrangement. Here we run into some problems. In his attempt to portray the lute in a typical playing position, Campi has tilted the body of the lute farther back than the neck, resulting in a gently torqued lute. The curve of the upper frets also gives the impression that the fingerboard itself is curved. Watson points out that there are eight frets in the space of ten and that the 11th and 12th fret positions (played during this era without frets as on the viol) would normally fall within the area of the body darkened by the varnish applied to protect the soundboard from the fingers. Unfortunately, however, the halfway point of the string length, which should correspond to the 12th fret, is well beyond the varnished area. Even more troubling is that were we to continue following the pattern Campi began with the frets tied to the neck, the 12th fret would land even farther beyond the string's halfway point.[23] See the discussion of plate 13 below.

We must be careful to not allow the slanting of the frets to distract us from identifying the relative distances between the frets, which should be considered from the treble side of the neck even though they are partially obscured by the lutenist's left-hand fingers, rather than the more easily viewed bass side that is not since the first string requires little if any compensation for sharpening. The spacing among the frets clearly does not reveal a pattern of progressive diminution from the nut to the highest fret. This fret arrangement could not have yielded equal temperament without excessive pushing and pulling of the left-hand fingers. The 1st fret is very wide, followed by a narrower 2nd fret and a 3rd fret that is about 10 percent wider than the 2nd, but not as wide as we would expect were the instrument to be set in a meantone temperament. Keep in mind, however, that the bass side of a slanted fret can sometimes drag the entire fret toward the nut, reducing the intended size of the fret, which is what appears to be happening here. This pattern of *fa, mi, fa* frets could correspond to a subtle variety of meantone temperament or an ad hoc irregular temperament. The 4th fret, however, appears to be in the less common *fa* position. A lute tuned in A or a lutenist thinking in A would occasionally have reason to use the 4th fret as a *fa,* as we will see when we discuss meantone temperaments on theorbo in subsequent chapters. Finally, as mentioned above, it is not uncommon for lutenists to limit themselves to arranging only the frets they are using at the moment, which in many circumstances could be restricted to the first three frets.

When it came to depicting lutes and guitars, both Caravaggio and Baschenis enjoyed a distinct advantage over other painters: they both owned and played fretted instruments. Caravaggio wrote to a friend that he played the guitar in Spanish Milan, and he certainly had wide exposure to musical activities, both cultivated and otherwise, in Rome, Naples, and Malta. That Caravaggio knew his way around the instrument is confirmed by his landlady's reference to his guitar playing in a 1605 lawsuit against him and the fact that a violin and a guitar were found among his possessions at the time of his death.[24] According to Ferraris, Caravaggio rendered lutes with "objective precision" and "extreme realism."[25] Watson concurs that Caravaggio was scrupulous in his observations of precise details, citing the realism of the Metropolitan Museum of Art *Lute Player,* which even shows a double 1st fret and excess string issuing from the tuning pegs in the pegbox. He points out, however, that while the instruments may be precise in their details, their postural relationship with their players may not be.[26] Nor are the performance situations, which, according to Camiz, were intended to portray idealized settings, a typical conceit of the age.[27] And, as we have seen, unlike the Campi portrait, in which the lute is viewed from the front, all the previously mentioned Caravaggio paintings depicting lutes show them from such an angle that some sort of 3D modeling would be necessary to determine their temperaments with any degree of certainty.

It all comes together in Evaristo Baschenis (1617–1677), who depicted instruments with "absolute precision in all details," including correct playing posture and realistic performance settings.[28] According to Victor Coelho, his paintings are "a rich source of information about lute and guitar construction, instrumentation, and musical aesthetics" rendered in such detail that in the Agliardi Triptych the maker's label: "Giorgio Sellas a la Stela in Venetia," is clearly visible on the front of a baroque guitar.[29] In contrast to Caravaggio, the musical scores Baschenis depicted "are not identifiable in terms of titles, authors, editions, or musical notes," although they are recognizable as mensural notation or Italian lute or guitar tablature.[30]

Baschenis owned and played fourteen musical instruments, including spinets, lutes, guitars, violins, and a theorbo, and in one of the Agliardi Triptych panels, he even portrays himself playing the spinet with Ottavio Agliardi, the son of the portrait's commissioner, playing archlute.[31] See plate 12. The archlute faces the viewer straight on. From a distance, the archlute appears to be set up in equal temperament, but on closer examination, the first three frets are clearly in a subtle form of meantone temperament or a utilitarian irregular temperament. Sadly, most of Baschenis's paintings inconveniently depict lutes with their faces down and backs up, the symbolic meaning of which is explored extensively by both Coelho and Ferraris.

Are these paintings smoking guns? Do they suggest that meantone temperaments or ad hoc irregular temperaments were typical? No, but they do demonstrate that the temperament in use on these lutes at the moment they were painted was probably not equal.

The preceding pages may seem like an excessive amount of attention devoted to a potentially futile endeavor with little hope of producing anything conclusive or of value. Research is like that. Yet even at this nascent stage, there are enough depictions of workable fret patterns such as Saraceni's *St. Cecilia* to inspire further study by scholars with the requisite skills. For instance, Thomas Gainsborough's portrait of his friend Carl Friedrich Abel with his viol at the National Portrait Gallery in London inspired Brian Capleton to undertake a detailed analysis of the viol's fretting pattern in relationship to *The Pure Method of Tuning the Harpsichord, According to Abel* contained in a manuscript preserved at the British Library.

Research involving keen visual analysis and 3D modeling such as that taken on by Watson with regard to the representation of lute proportion in paintings can certainly be applied to fretboard patterns in a systematic fashion. With plate 13, Watson gives us some sense of how such a representation might look applied to Campi's lute player. Grids in various colors represent the frets as they appear in the painting as well as in different divisions of the fretboard. These grids can be manipulated to represent theoretical fret positions that can then be compared with the actual fret positions. As always, we must keep in mind that theoretical fret positions cannot factor in sharpening relative to the idiosyncrasies of every individual instrument setup.

Complex research of this type can easily lose its validity without guiding principles. In this chapter we have isolated at least three such guidelines for future research:[32]

1. Through several of the methods described above, we should assess whether the artist represents his subjects precisely enough to suggest further investigation.
2. Because the first string is generally not subject to much sharpening, frets should be measured at their locations on that string.
3. We should generally restrict our assessment to the first several frets given the multiplicity of extraneous factors that impact the location and perception of location of the upper frets.

Although the inherent constraints imposed by the artistic process from production to perception as described above limit the information we can derive from artistic renderings of fretboard patterns, objective research of this sort can, to some extent, mitigate the subjectivity and wishful thinking that can lead me to see a meantone temperament pattern where you see an equal temperament pattern, and so on. As we have seen above, the identification of a fretboard pattern as representing a particular class of tuning or temperament (Pythagorean, meantone, equal, utilitarian, and so forth) does not necessarily always correlate precisely to the tuning system that a superb player produces on that instrument, a point that can be easily verified by attending a concert performed by any number of today's finest lute or viol virtuosi. Yet a fretboard pattern on a lute that appears to be in a certain temperament most likely does produce that temperament. Viols, as we have seen, however, may be a different matter. I suspect that in the end, we will discover that for our musical ancestors, tunings and temperaments began as a science but developed into an art of a level of subtlety that has, in recent centuries, been eclipsed by other more seemingly pressing concerns.

At the moment, then, we must make the best of the bits, pieces, and clues that we do have. For instance, a cursory survey of iconographical depictions of fretboard patters demonstrates that the use of slanted frets to compensate for sharpening or to locate both *mis* and *fas* on the same fret was widespread, and as Grijp has pointed out, even nonsense fret patterns can tell us something.[33] Armed with the preceding information you are now equipped to begin judging for yourself whether a particular fret pattern depicted in a painting or drawing might mean nothing, something, or everything.

PART ONE CONCLUSION

Choosing a tuning or temperament has always been a matter of compromise. Even in the best of circumstances, tuning was fluid and often determined by the player's knowledge, experience, and the situation at hand. In large part, it seems that the player's ability level was the main determinant. Professional players who regularly performed in ensembles with keyboards and other instruments that were typically tuned in meantone temperaments almost certainly accommodated their frets to the keyboard, especially in the case of intimate settings where differences between temperaments would have been most audible.

Historical sources cast doubt on the widespread assumption that players of fretted instruments necessarily arranged their frets in equal temperament, although it seems likely that less refined players did resort to it. Players of fixed metal-fret wire-strung instruments, who participated in established ensembles with movable fret instruments, had their luthiers permanently set their frets either in meantone temperaments or utilitarian systems based on meantone temperaments that adjusted the size of particularly prominent thirds through the creation of customized fret arrangements, even though it meant that certain nominal intervals would field a variety of sizes and some pitches would be inconsistent with instruments tuned in regular systems. Although at an inchoate stage of its development, research into the iconographical representations of fretted instruments offers some promise of helping us discern which temperaments were in use during the fifteenth through the eighteenth centuries. Untangling and classifying the thicket of fretboard patterns illustrated in period paintings will likely require skills in 3D imaging, the perspective of an artist, the experience of a player, the contextual awareness of a musicologist, the organizational ability of a field general, and the patience of Job. It will be a tall but rewarding task for someone.

In sum, the evidence supports the view that, while amateurs probably used equal temperament, the best players most likely set their frets unequally. Three common practices prevailed among players of fretted instruments:

1. Equal temperament or something like it for amateurs.
2. Customized fretting schemes involving the relocation of one or more frets in isolation, most commonly the 4th fret, in an attempt to address

the most audible infelicities resulting in ultra-irregular utilitarian temperaments. While players of fretted instruments may have aspired to regular temperaments, they easily tolerated temperaments that feature various sizes of the same interval.

3. Meantone temperaments for professionals, particularly those who played in ensembles.

I recommend that we follow the example of the very best players of yesterday and today. With the availability of easy-to-use electronic digital tuners, we can all set our frets in meantone temperaments and aspire to a more Just intonation. How to accomplish this is the subject of the remaining chapters.

PART TWO

Theory

PART TWO INTRODUCTION

Nothing is so firmly believed as that which is least known.
—Michel de Montaigne (*Apology for Raymond Sebond*)

For more than two thousand years, theorists and musicians have sought to discover or create a tuning system in which all the intervals contained within an octave are rendered pure. Until that Holy Grail is found, we must do our best to manipulate natural acoustical discrepancies into workable systems that best suit our needs. Every tuning system is a compromise between practicality and beauty; more of one results in less of the other. While theorists theorized, practicing musicians began to arrange the notes within their octaves empirically to suit their needs.

Our threshold for theory in the next two chapters is my assessment of what is minimally necessary for you to understand temperaments well enough to use them to your advantage; the bibliography lists many superb books on tuning systems should you wish to explore the theoretical foundations of tunings systems in greater depth.[1]

In order to manipulate temperaments to our benefit, we must understand how they work, especially on fretted instruments because theoretical principles inform how we arrange our frets. After these concepts are internalized, it is a relatively easy thing to marshal them to our advantage. Finally, as tedious as it may be, I strongly encourage you to redo and check the math I present here, for it is the only way to truly own this material for yourself.

CHAPTER FOUR

Inside the Numbers: How Tuning Systems Work and Why We Need Them

WHAT IF YOU WERE TOLD that you had to fit thirteen full inches into one foot? In other words, you couldn't simply divide 12 by 13 to arrive at .923 because 92.3 percent of an inch is less than a full inch. Nor could you fit ten full inches and then divide the remaining units by three: 2 ÷ 3 = .666 because again, you'd have three units less than a full inch. Thirteen inches simply cannot be jammed into one foot unless we are discussing shoe size. You can only fit thirteen inches into one foot if you redefine what constitutes an inch. If we pretend that an inch is now 92.3 percent of the size of the previous definition of an inch, we could do it. Or we could agree to preserve some units as full inches while reducing others to a smaller percentage of its true size as in the second example above. But we still cannot fit thirteen full inches into one foot. This is pretty much the situation with the musical scale. It is impossible to fit twelve semitones into an octave in such a manner that they or any other resulting intervals are all pure.

Tunings and temperaments are the tools we use to fit thirteen musical inches into the octave foot, striking a compromise between varying degrees of interval purity and serviceability over a broad range of keys. The many thousands of pages written about tuning systems come down to determining which system works best given the circumstances, that is, how to arrange the size of the various intervals that must fit within the octave (semitones, thirds, fifths, and so on) so that they best serve our purposes. Different repertoires and performance situations tend to favor certain arrangements of the notes within an octave. Tenth-century parallel organum, for instance, emphasizes perfect fifths and fourths, while most repertoires from the early Renaissance to the Classical era favor major and minor thirds. The notes are arranged within the octave so that the prominent intervals are pure or relatively pure, while the less prominent intervals are impure. We also sacrifice the quality of intervals in some tonal areas to preserve the purity of the intervals in the tonal areas we deem most important. Nowadays, the priority is to be able to play in all the keys, which means that we sacrifice the purity of all of the intervals except the octave to be able to function in every key. It's important to remember that relatively speaking, this is a recent approach and that most music prior to the nineteenth century did not venture into the nether regions of the bottom of the Circle of Fifths, a helpful device that we now briefly examine.

Most of the remaining diagrams in this chapter and the next use the Circle of Fifths to demonstrate the relationship between fifths and the tonal areas they represent. It is a circle that resembles a clock with notes replacing hours. Traditionally, C is placed where the 12 on a clock appears, G at 1 o'clock, D at 2 o'clock, and so on, progressing by fifths. At some point, the sharp notes convert to flat notes. Where this border is placed is up to you. It most commonly occurs at F♯/G♭ (6 o'clock), C♯/D♭ (7 o'clock), or G♯/A♭ (8 o'clock). In a perfect world, 11 o'clock, the F, progresses another fifth to C at noon or midnight, depending on your disposition. We can think of the Circle of Fifths moving clockwise by fifth or counterclockwise by fourth; both are useful to our study. Since the Circle of Fifths is also used to represent the key areas whose letter names are its tonic, it can also be used to represent the progression of minor keys in which case, the relative minor tonality replaces its major relation—A Minor replaces C Major, E Minor replaces G Major, and so on. Diagram 4.1 shows a standard version of the Circle of Fifths.

Throughout the history of music, as instruments adapted and evolved in response to musical requirements, so have tuning systems. With its many pure fourths and fifths, Pythagorean tuning served tenth-century parallel organum well, but as the previously dissonant major thirds became much more common as a by-product of polyphony's evolution from a predominantly two- to

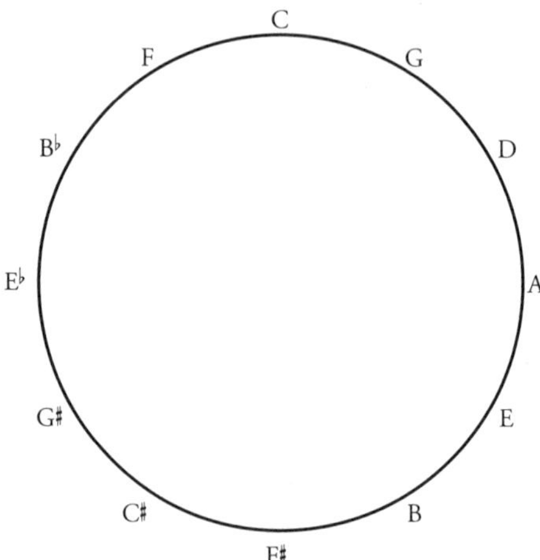

Diagram 4.1. Standard Circle of Fifths.

a three-voice texture in the thirteenth century, the major third was necessarily transformed from a dissonance into a consonance. Concurrent with this development was late Medieval and early Renaissance singers' discovery of the pleasures of singing in parallel thirds and sixths rather than the parallel fourths and fifths that prevailed centuries before. In response, instrumentalists and theorists were compelled to create or discover tuning systems that accentuated the sweetness of thirds and sixths, that is, meantone temperaments. In these configurations, the third replaced the fifth as the privileged interval. Pythagorean tuning's excruciatingly wide thirds made it intolerable for increasingly triadic music, banishing it largely to theoretical treatises and ostentatious displays of erudition with the exception of its utility for the occasional music that favored open fourths or fifths. Meantone temperaments placed the best thirds in the keys at the top of the Circle of Fifths at the expense of the seldom-used keys at the bottom of the circle. In the Baroque era, musicians and theorists such as Kirnberger, Vallotti, and Werckmeister, among others, managed to manipulate interval size in even more complex fashions to create modifications of meantone temperaments specifically designed for keyboard instruments that pinpointed the location of the "good keys" even more precisely. These circulating temperaments, that is, temperaments that are functional in every key, though to varying degrees, mirrored the Baroque fascination with color by imbuing each key area with its own distinct character.

As modulation increased and the use of keys expanded down toward the bottom of the Circle of Fifths, a narrowly focused band of beautifully tuned keys was sacrificed for serviceability in a variety of keys, which ultimately led to these circulating temperaments. Equal temperament is the only circulating temperament that is equally serviceable in every key. But that serviceability comes with a heavy price in the form of major thirds so wide that they were deemed unacceptable throughout most of music history. Since the majority of the pre-Classical music we play restricts itself to the top of the Circle of Fifths and does not require the catholicity that equal temperament offers, we need not accept its deficiencies when other more suitable options are available. Because we have grown up in an era during which equal temperament is the only tuning system most of us ever encountered, we have lost sight of the historical perspective that empowers us to realize that we can still choose whatever tuning system works best for our purposes. If you play early music, most of the time, that system will not be equal temperament.

Interval Purity and Pitch Designation

Each named interval such as a perfect fifth or major third, and so on, encompasses a variety of interval sizes within a range that we recognize as being that interval, but only one size is actually pure. An interval is acoustically pure when there are no beats, which are the alternating increases and decreases in volume that are heard as rhythmic pulsations when an interval is nearly, but not quite, in tune. A fifth may be perfect, but it is not necessarily pure. Although a perfect fifth that is slightly narrower or wider than an acoustically pure fifth may be recognized as a perfect fifth, it will beat, introducing dissonance and friction into the interval, reducing its resonance and bell-like clarity. We will spend more time on beats later in this chapter.

Also known as Just intervals, pure intervals are the result of whole number ratios between the frequencies of the component pitches. For instance, the ratio for the octave is 2:1. On your instrument, this simply means that dividing the vibrating length of your string into two portions and stopping it halfway produces an octave. The ratio for a perfect fifth is 3:2. If you divide your string into three portions and fret it at the intersection between the second and third portions from the saddle, that is, two-thirds of the string's length, which corresponds to your 7th fret, you will produce a perfect fifth. If you look at your instrument, you will see that your 7th fret does indeed divide your string into approximately two thirds between the saddle or bridge and the 7th fret and one third between the 7th fret and the nut. Throughout history, the ratios with the smaller numbers have been considered more consonant than ratios containing larger numbers. This you can see from table 4.1, which lists the primary intervals we will discuss in this book. Its columns list the ratio that produces the Just interval, the size of the Just or pure interval in cents,[1] its size in equal temperament, and, for comparison, how equal temperament differs from Just.[2]

You will immediately notice how significantly the ET values differ from Just. The most egregious discrepancies are in the thirds and sixths and in the minor whole tone and the greater minor seventh. Shortly, you will hear how noticeable those differences are. For the moment, though, it suffices to notice

Table 4.1.
Table of intervals, in ratios and cents

Interval	Example	Ratio	Just	ET	Difference
Minor semitone	C–C♯	135:128	92	100	+8
Major semitone	C–D♭	16:15	112	100	-12
Minor whole tone	C–D	10:9	182	200	+18
Major whole tone	C–D	9:8	204	200	-4
Minor third	C–E♭	6:5	316	300	-16
Major third	C–E	5:4	386	400	+14
Perfect fourth	C–F	4:3	498	500	+2
Augmented fourth	C–F♯	45:32	590	600	+10
Perfect fifth	C–G	3:2	702	700	-2
Minor sixth	C–A♭	8:5	814	800	-14
Major sixth	C–A	5:3	884	900	+16
Minor seventh (lesser)	C–B♭	16:9	996	1000	+4
Minor seventh (greater)	C–B♭	9:5	1018	1000	-18
Major seventh	C–B	15:8	1088	1100	+12
Octave	C–C	2:1	1200	1200	±0

that equal temperament's only pure interval is the octave. You will have also noticed that an equal-tempered interval's inversion diverges from its pure form in the same amount of cents, but in the opposite direction. For instance, an ET major third is a noticeable 14c. wider than a Just major third; accordingly, its inversion, the ET minor sixth, is 14c. narrower than a Just minor sixth.

Turning your attention now to the ratios, you'll see that the smaller number ratio intervals are those we consider most consonant in the following order: octave (2:1), perfect fifth (3:2), perfect fourth (4:3), major third (5:4), minor third (6:5), and so forth. When we get to the harmonic series, you'll see that it's no coincidence that our perception of degrees of consonance as represented by these ratios progresses in this orderly fashion. Nowadays, the only interval among these that is inviolable, that is, that must always be pure no matter what, is the octave. The divergences between the Just and ET cents values illustrates the fact that intervals within in a wide range of sizes are perceived as that interval even though only one size is actually pure. As you have probably already inferred, throughout history, theorists and musicians have not always agreed on how wide the range of admissible sizes for a given interval should be. Since most of our subsequent discussions revolve around the perception of the quality of the major third, audio files 4.1–4.4 present C–E as pure, 1/6-comma meantone temperament, equal temperament, and Pythagorean major thirds of 386c., 393c., 400c., and 408c., respectively, played on a treble viol. Notice how stable the pure third sounds compared with the others. The 1/6-comma major third is less stable but still much more consonant than the ET and Pythagorean thirds. After hearing no beats in audio file 4.1, the speed of the beats in audio files 4.2–4.4 increases noticeably as you progress through the examples; the faster the beats, the more out of tune the interval is. Initially, the pure major third may sound flat or rather narrow to you because most of us have become accustomed to the very wide ET major third. Much ink has been spilled over the validity of these various sizes of major third, and this book will do its part to continue that tradition.

Now it's your turn to experiment. On your lute, viol, or guitar, play the F–A major third in musical example 4.1.[3] Play the interval melodically and harmonically several times listening carefully to the quality of the sound, measuring in your mind its width, stability, and general character.[4] Now, nudge your 2nd fret a little bit closer to the nut, and notice how different the interval sounds. Again, play the interval both melodically and harmonically several times. By nudging the fret toward the nut, you have lowered the pitch of the upper note, thereby reducing the width of the interval. It's still a major third, but a major third of a different flavor. Now slide the fret toward the nut a little more and notice how that sounds. Try to find the place where the interval sounds most stable, clean, and resonant. Notice again that it still sounds like a major third, but again, of a slightly different variety. Now push your fret back the other way toward the bridge a little past your fret's original

Musical Example 4.1. F–A major third.

Musical Example 4.2. C–E major third.

location. Play and listen. You can tell that it's still a major third, but now after having listened to the previous thirds, this third will probably sound rather sketchy to you. You might characterize it as nervous, agitated, or unstable. Try the same exercise with the major third between C and E in musical example 4.2.[5]

Assuming that your frets were originally set in equal temperament, with this exercise, you first narrowed the width of your major third to something closer to pure or even pure by sliding your 2nd fret toward the nut, and then you widened it beyond the already wide ET major third to something approaching a Pythagorean third. Don't worry if this seems confusing right now. Later on, you will learn how to position your frets so that they produce precisely the size of major third or any other interval you desire. The important thing right now is that you've proven to yourself that there are several different sizes of interval that can all be classified as a major third. Incidentally, you've also just experienced how players of fretted instruments in earlier times experimented to find fret locations by ear to produce beautiful intervals in the chord shapes they played most frequently. As you have seen, sometimes players relocated only one fret as you just did, but more often, once they found a sound they liked, they continued to adjust the rest of the frets by comparing octaves and unisons.

You've seen how several intervals of varying widths within a range can be classified as the same interval, a phenomenon known as "categorical perception." Since intervals are composed of two distinct named pitches, it stands to reason that the frequencies of the named pitches are also variable. In other words, just as several intervals of differing widths can be classified as the same interval, several different frequencies can be classified with the same note name. Each time you relocated your 2nd fret in our first experiment above, you thought of the top pitch as A (F♯ on guitar and E on viol in D) no matter where you relocated your fret. Although your 2nd fret produced four different pitches, you considered them all to be A. The common thread between our contemplation of the interval and its component pitches is that we choose to name the various interval sizes and component pitches the same despite their measurable differences. Another way of thinking about it is that while the pitches and the intervals they combine to produce are absolute and precisely measurable, how we name them is relative and variable. It is very important that you keep this distinction firmly in mind as we now turn our attention to how to measure pitch in absolute terms.

On our journey toward understanding how temperaments work, we will need to think of pitch in both absolute and relative terms; at the beginning of our study, more in absolute terms, and then later increasingly in relative terms. The pitch, that is, the frequency of a musical tone, is absolute no matter how we choose to name that pitch. It is what it is. And so is the size of an interval between two absolute pitches, no matter how we chose to name that interval. The art of tuning revolves around manipulating the size of the various intervals to best suit our needs. As you have seen, there is not just one size of perfect fifth or major third but a range of sizes that we accept as perfect fifths or major thirds. Nevertheless, as you have also seen, there is only one size of each of these intervals that is acoustically pure.

At this point, it will serve us well to pause for a moment to consider hertz (Hz), a measurement named in honor of the German physicist Heinrich Hertz (1857–1894). In the current discussion we will find it useful because it is an absolute rather than relative measurement. Hertz measure the frequency of a pitch in terms of cycles per second. One complete cycle, that is, the vibrating body completing a phase and then returning to its original position, is the equivalent of 1 Hz. The faster the vibration, the higher the hertz. For instance, the familiar tuning pitch A vibrates at 440 cycles per second and is therefore referred to as A = 440 Hz. In spoken musical parlance the "=" and "Hz" are often dropped: most of the time we just say "A 440" even though we write A = 440 Hz. The A one octave below A = 440 Hz is A = 220 Hz, that is, it vibrates half as fast as A = 440 Hz, and, as a result, we perceive it as the pitch an octave lower. Frequency is inversely proportional to string length: as the length of the string is reduced, the frequency rises and vice versa.

Assuming that our reference pitch is A = 440 Hz, A = 220 Hz corresponds to the open third course or string of a lute or viol in G, the open second string of a bass viol in D, or the first string on a theorbo. Stopping the string at the 12th fret on a lute, that is, reducing the string's length in half, increases the frequency by the same proportion to yield A = 440 Hz. On a viol and lute, playing the harmonic exactly halfway along the string's length produces the same A = 440 Hz.[6] Although some orchestras use a higher A, most Westerners consider A = 440 Hz to be the tuning standard tuning pitch. That then sets the relationship between all the rest of the named pitches and their hertz equivalents. The hertz and the pitch it represents are constant, but how we name that pitch is not. For instance, in the past, depending on the country, the tuning standard was lower or higher, A = 415 Hz or A = 460 Hz, for instance. A = 415 Hz is roughly the equivalent of our modern G♯. It is easiest to think of hertz as a fixed scale and the letter names as a sliding scale. In this example, we've slid the letter name scale to the left by a semitone. If A is now 415 Hz, the equivalent of the previous G♯, then B♭ = 440 Hz is now the equivalent of the former A. Regardless, of what we call it, that pitch still vibrates at 440 Hz. If you have Cleartune or some other tuning app, you can easily demonstrate this for yourself by following the instructions in appendix 1.[7]

Harmonic Series and Beats

Each sounded note is composed of its fundamental frequency as well as other higher frequencies sometimes referred to as partials or overtones in a pattern known as the harmonic series.[8] The relative strengths of these constituent frequencies, which vary from instrument to instrument and voice to voice, endow the note with its unique tone color. Because each string on your instrument has its own individual set of audible partials depending on whether it is played open or stopped at a particular fret, the same pitch produced on one string will have a different timbre when produced on another string.[9] Most of the time, the fundamental dominates with varying degrees of participation from the other frequencies, but other frequencies can occasionally overwhelm the fundamental frequency. You may have experienced this phenomenon when tuning very low notes with an electronic tuner; instead of perceiving the fundamental note, an electronic tuning meter will occasionally register the twelfth (octave + fifth) above of the fundamental note instead. The harmonic series interval pattern is exactly the same for every fundamental pitch: an octave, followed by a perfect fifth,

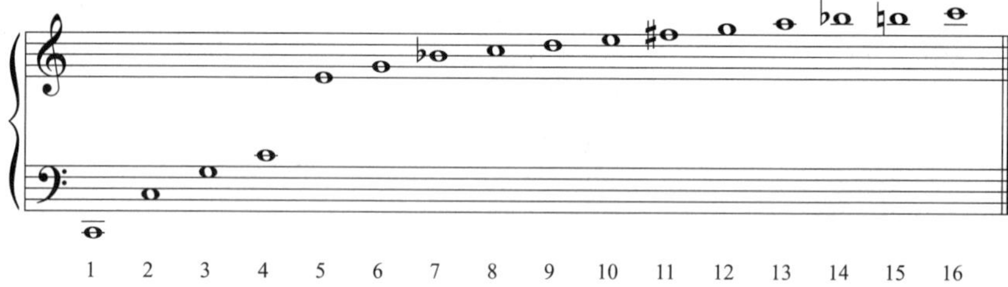

Musical Example 4.3. Harmonic series on C.

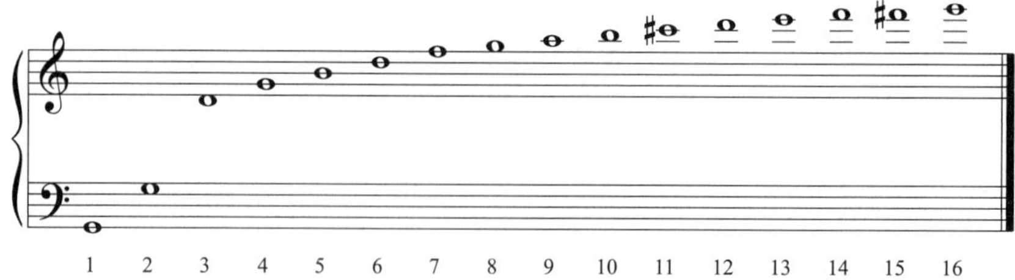

Musical Example 4.4. Harmonic series on G.

perfect fourth, major third, two minor thirds, followed by a series of whole tones and semitones. This you can see clearly from musical examples 4.3 and 4.4, the harmonic series for C and G.

Sound waves and strings vibrate in several wave patterns simultaneously. Each of these patterns is represented by one of the frequencies along the harmonic series. For instance, in addition to vibrating in one wave back and forth to produce the fundamental note, a string also simultaneously divides itself into two, each half vibrating in opposite phase to one another. A node at half the string's length, the 12th fret on lutes, where the string is motionless, divides the two loops. You can produce a harmonic at the location of half your string's length or your 12th fret because that location is a node. If your 12th fret is set properly, the harmonic at the 12th fret should produce exactly the same pitch as the fretted note, an octave above the open string. The third frequency in the harmonic series, which you can see is a 12th above the fundamental note, divides the string into three sections or waves. As you may recall, a string fretted two-thirds along its length from the saddle produces a perfect fifth. That location corresponds roughly to your 7th fret and the equivalent distance, two-thirds the length of the string from your saddle. See diagram 4.2. The fretted note is a 5th above the open string in whatever temperament your frets are set, but the harmonic produced there is a pure 12th above the open string or fundamental frequency, that is, approximately an octave higher than the note produced at your 7th fret. Unless your 7th fret is set to produce a pure perfect fifth, which is unlikely, adjusted for the octave, the harmonic will sound slightly higher than an octave higher than the fretted 7th fret. An even easier way to check this is to compare the 7th fret harmonic on the sixth course octave string, if you have

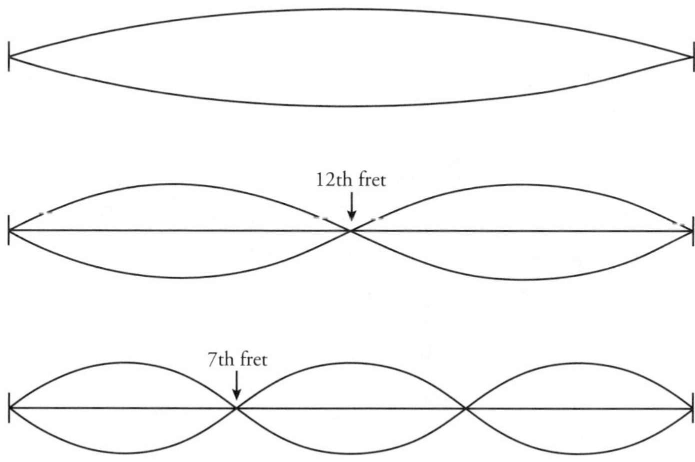

Diagram 4.2. String wave patterns.

one, with the fretted note at the 7th fret on the first course, which although the same basic pitch, should sound noticeably flatter. Again, this is because the frequencies above the fundamental note in the harmonic series produce pure intervals in relation to the fundamental frequency, whereas the fretted notes are tempered intervals with the exception of the octave. This knowledge will serve you well in understanding how temperaments work but also how to tune and how not to tune, a subject addressed in chapter 7.

For our purposes, we will examine only the first six pitches in the harmonic series, which are generally the easiest to hear. Let's consider the harmonic series of C and G, a pure perfect fifth higher as verticalities side by side. See musical example 4.5. As you can see, they share two pitches in common: the third and sixth frequencies in the harmonic series on C and the second and fourth on G. Table 4.2 presents the frequencies of the component pitches side by side in hertz.[10] From table 4.2 you can see that the pitches shared by each harmonic series are exactly the same in terms of absolute pitch measured in hertz. These pitches shared by each harmonic series are referred to as "coinciding harmonic frequencies."

Table 4.3 compares the relative pitch of the intervals between the fundamental frequency and those above it in each harmonic series in cents. Because we are comparing the harmonic series of two pitches a pure perfect fifth in width, the G begins with a value of 702c. above the C. You can see that the

Musical Example 4.5. Harmonic series of the first six notes of the harmonic series on C and G side by side.

Table 4.2.
Harmonic frequencies of the first six notes of the harmonic series on C and a pure perfect fifth higher on G, in hertz

Frequency number	C	G
6	**786.0**	1179.0
5	655.0	982.5
4	524.0	**786.0**
3	**393.0**	589.5
2	262.0	**393.0**
1	131.0	196.5

Table 4.3.
Intervals between the first six notes of the harmonic series on C and a pure perfect fifth higher on G, in cents

Frequency number	C	G
6	**3102**	3804
5	2786	3488
4	2400	**3102**
3	**1902**	2604
2	1200	**1902**
1		702

intervals that were identical in terms of the absolute value as represented by hertz are also identical in terms of cents.

Now, what happens when we compare the harmonic series of two fundamental frequencies separated by an ET perfect fifth? Here's where it gets interesting. Remember that regardless of the relationship between the fundamental frequencies of the component pitches of our perfect fifth, the upper frequencies or partials are still pure in relation to each respective fundamental frequency, in this case, C and G. Table 4.4 provides the frequencies of the component pitches of the first six notes of each harmonic series of ET perfect fifth between C and G.

As you know, an ET fifth is slightly narrower than a pure fifth, which is demonstrated by the fact that the starting pitch is 0.7 Hz lower. It might not seem like much of a difference, but from comparing the coinciding harmonic frequencies, you can see that the discrepancies compound as the series progresses: the first coinciding frequencies differ by 1.3 Hz and the second by 2.6 Hz, and so forth, on up the series. We hear the difference in phase between the vibrations between the pure interval and impure interval as beats where the number of beats or pulsations per second is a product of the difference between

Table 4.4.
Harmonic frequencies of the first six notes of the harmonic series on C and an ET fifth higher on G, in hertz

Frequency number	C	G
6	**786.0**	1175.0
5	655.0	979.2
4	524.0	**783.4**
3	**393.0**	587.5
2	262.0	**391.7**
1	131.0	195.8

the two frequencies. Charles Padgham describes beats as "a periodic throbbing sound or fluttering unstable sound when rapid. The number of beats heard per second is equal to the frequency difference of the two notes."[11] Gerald Klickstein provides a clear and precise explanation of how beats occur:

> Beats are caused by the sound waves of two slightly differing pitches interacting in the eardrum. Though the two waves are of differing frequencies, periodically the wave crests or troughs will exactly coincide. When this occurs, the waves interact in two respects: 1) when the crest of one wave coincides with the trough of another, volume *decreases* because the two waves are trying to move the eardrum in opposite directions and these forces cancel each other out causing the eardrum to move less; 2) when either two crests coincide or two troughs coincide, volume *increases* because the waves support each other and move the eardrum more. As these two interactions alternate, a regular, pulsating change in volume and timbre is heard.[12]

The rate of beating slows down the closer an interval approaches purity at which point the beats disappear. Some auditors characterize this process as "locking in" because there can be a sense of arrival as an interval progresses from being very out of tune to slightly out of tune to pure. Whether or not you are able to hear beats at this point, it is useful to try to develop a perception of intervals' relative sourness or purity. In addition to an absence of beats, a pure interval projects an almost ethereal sense of resonance that rings without any sonic friction. It is that ethereal sense that seems to lock in. Nevertheless, because the concept of beating is so integral to understanding interval purity, later in this chapter we discuss some strategies to help identify beats on lutes and viols. For the moment, however, we resort to the artificial production of intervals so that you can clearly hear the beats.

Audio file 4.5.1 is a pure perfect fifth between C (262 Hz) and G (393 Hz); audio file 4.5.2 is a pure perfect fifth an octave higher between C (524 Hz) and G (786 Hz).[13] Note how stable and pure they sound. Previously we noted that an ET fifth beats at a rate of 1.3 and 2.6 beats per second, which you can hear in audio files 4.6.1 and 4.6.2, an ET fifth between C (262 Hz) and G (391.7 Hz) and an ET fifth between C (524 Hz) and G (783.4 Hz). Here, while the beating is evident, it is so slow as to be relatively inoffensive. If this is the first time you have listened for beats, you may have to listen to the examples a few times to hear them. Sometimes it helps to wag your index finger with the pulsations, in a sense, linking your finger with your ears and bypassing your mind. Since beat rates are measured in hertz, we have already arrived at the salient discrepancies; however, to complete the exercise, table 4.5 provides the corresponding interval sizes in cents. From table 4.5 you can see that the difference between a pure and ET perfect fifth is not all that significant in and of itself; however, as you see shortly, that 2c. snowflake becomes an insurmountable snow bank when compounded.

Table 4.5.
Intervals between the first six notes of the harmonic series on C and an ET fifth higher on G, in cents

Frequency number	C	G
6	**3102**	3802
5	2786	3486
4	2400	**3100**
3	**1902**	2602
2	1200	**1900**
1		700

Since we will spend so much time discussing the size of the major third, let's see what happens when we compare a pure major third with an ET major third so that we can observe a little of that compounding in action. Before beginning, you should realize that the size of the perfect fifth determines the size of the major third. We spend a great deal of time on that concept later in this and the next chapter, but for now, I ask that you simply accept that fact on faith. First, to get our bearings, let's examine table 4.6, which compares the harmonic series for the component pitches of a pure major third, one beginning on C and the other on E. As you can see, there is one coinciding harmonic frequency at 655 Hz. Keep in mind that the only thing that has changed is the fundamental frequency of the upper note in the interval, E. All the notes above E in the harmonic series are pure intervals in relation to E.

That information is easier to digest when examined in cents. The interval between the first and second frequencies is still 1200c., 702c. between the second and third frequencies, and so forth, for both C and E. See table 4.7. Audio files 4.7.1 and 4.7.2 demonstrate the sound of a pure major third. There are no beats whatsoever.

Table 4.6.
Harmonic frequencies of the first six notes of the harmonic series on C and a pure major third higher on E, in hertz

Frequency number	C	E
6	786.0	982.5
5	**655.0**	818.8
4	524.0	**655.0**
3	393.0	491.3
2	262.0	327.5
1	131.0	163.8

Table 4.7.
Intervals between the first six notes of the harmonic series on C and a pure major third higher on E, in cents

Frequency number	C	E
6	3102	3488
5	**2786**	3172
4	2400	**2786**
3	1902	2288
2	1200	1586
1		386

Table 4.8.
Harmonic frequencies of the first six notes of the harmonic series on C and an ET major third higher on E, in hertz

Frequency number	C	E
6	786.0	990.6
5	**655.0**	825.4
4	524.0	**660.4**
3	393.0	495.3
2	262.0	330.2
1	131.0	165.1

Here's where it gets even more interesting. Table 4.8 shows the same information as table 4.6, but with an ET instead of pure third separating the starting pitches. As you can see, the coinciding harmonic frequency beats at a rate of 5.4 pulsations per second. That's twice the rate of the most egregious of the ET perfect fifth beat rates we encountered in table 4.4. Audio files 4.8.1 and 4.8.2 demonstrate that an ET major third produced by C and E beats noticeably.

The next time you find yourself near a piano, play middle C and the E to its right to easily verify how much an ET major third beats. Try to disregard the attack; beats are much easier to hear after the attack has died away. And while you are there, notice how the fifth from C to G also beats, but much less violently. To complete our exercise, table 4.9 provides the corresponding information in cents. As you can see, the ET major third is a rather significant 14c. wider than pure. That's a 3.6 percent divergence from pure as opposed to the ET fifth's .28 percent difference, which makes sense because the major third is a smaller interval with a discrepancy greater than that of the ET perfect fifth.

How disagreeable we find an impure interval to be depends on a number of factors.[14] In general, beating is much easier to discern in the first few partials, so whatever beating is there will be more prominent, and the faster the

Table 4.9.
Intervals between the first six notes of the harmonic series on C and an ET major third higher on E, in cents

Frequency number	C	E
6	3102	3502
5	**2786**	3186
4	2400	**2800**
3	1902	2302
2	1200	1600
1		400

note beats, the more out of tune it is, and the more annoying we find it to be. Beating introduces a sense of unease, agitation, and nervousness to an interval, as well as an element of friction that constrains resonance. To reiterate, the rate of beating decreases as the interval approaches acoustic purity. When the beats disappear, the interval is acoustically pure. Conversely, as the beat rate increases, the interval becomes more out of tune. Consider also the fact that certain instruments emphasize or de-emphasize particular partials; for instance, the Renaissance lute emphasizes higher partials to a greater extent than does the classical guitar, which in part accounts for each of these instrument's characteristic tonal qualities, which can also ultimately impact our temperament choice, as discussed previously.

On keyboards, after you become accustomed to listening for beats, with practice, you can actually hear various beat rates simultaneously. It is often helpful to visualize the beating in a vertical sense, the slower beats lower, the faster beats higher. Before the advent of electronic tuners, professional tuners counted and compared beat rates to tune instruments, a method that truly enters into the realm of the Zen of tuning.

Hearing beats is much more difficult on lutes and viols, although it is a little easier on the larger and more resonant members of their families. Because their sound dissipates rather quickly, whether they are plucked or bowed, it is frequently difficult to identify the beats at first—we often hear them not so much as regular pulsations but as a general sense of discomfort that eases as the interval becomes more in tune. Nevertheless, with practice you can learn to identify beats on your fretted instrument.

Beats are the most noticeable on unisons and octaves. No matter how much various experts may disagree on the virtues of various tunings and temperaments, the one thing everyone agrees on is that unisons and octaves must be in tune. Mistuned unisons and octaves are offensive to even the most casual listeners because they are so obvious.

On instruments with double courses, the easiest way to hear beats is to mistune one of the individual strings that comprises a unison course. Martin

Shepherd suggests the fourth course on the lute because the beats are easiest to hear in that pitch range.[15] On the cittern either of the two highest courses will do. Simply lower the pitch of one of the strings about one-fourth of a tone and listen carefully as the two strings are struck at the same time. You should hear a somewhat rapid beating. We are often distracted by the attack of the note, so try to focus your attention on the sound of the interval just after you have plucked the strings. If you can, block out the sound of the attack. Now gradually tune the string back up to the unison, and you will hear that the beats will start to slow down and then disappear completely as the pitches unite to form a pure unison. Don't be discouraged if you have to try it several times before hearing it. On extended neck lutes with double courses and Baroque lutes, it is also quite easy to hear beats between the fundamental and octave strings of the bass courses.

If yours is a single-course instrument, such as a theorbo or a viol, you can perform the same experiment at the double octave between your sixth and first strings. With viols, it is easiest to pluck the viol while holding it like a lute or guitar, as did Marais when he sat for André Bouys in the portrait shown in plate 6. This allows your ears to be closer to the sound holes, making the beats much easier to hear. Applying Martin Shepherd's suggestion to the viol, comparing the unisons between the 5th fret fifth string to the open F on the tenor, the 4th fret fourth string to the open E on the bass, and the 5th fret sixth course with the open G on the treble puts you at or near the pitch level where it is easiest to hear beats. I have also found beats relatively easy to hear by simply comparing the 5th fret of the second string with the open first string on any viol. Again, don't despair if you have trouble hearing beats at first. Try to get to a piano where beats are very easy to hear. Once you know what they sound like, it's much easier to then identify them on your own instrument.

The unfortunate fact of the matter is that there is no practical tuning system in which all intervals are acoustically pure. We have seen how isolated pitches and intervals within a range can be classified as a particular named pitch or interval, but we have not yet considered how pitches and intervals work together collectively to create a functional tuning system. To do so, we must first identify the excess inch that must be accounted for to fit our metaphorical thirteen inches into a foot.

Two Commas

There are two structural discrepancies or commas that temperaments address: the Pythagorean (or ditonic) comma and the syntonic comma. The Pythagorean comma of 24c. can be considered a systematic excess, while the syntonic comma of 22c. can be thought of as an internal excess. Both commas are intertwined, each in its own way reflecting the irreconcilable relationships among pure intervals.

PYTHAGOREAN COMMA

In a perfect world, twelve pure fifths (C–G–D–A–E–B–F♯–C♯–G♯–D♯–A♯–E♯–B♯)[16] would arrive at the same exact pitch as seven successive octaves (C–C–C, and so on) do, but, alas, they do not. The twelve pure fifths arrive slightly past the location of the starting C, adjusted for octaves, of course. In diagram 4.3, following the E♯, the B♯ would land slightly to the right of the location of the starting C. The math makes it easy to understand. Seven successive octaves (7 × 1200c.) close the circle at 8400c., but twelve pure fifths (12 × 702c.) close it at 8424c. as demonstrated in table 4.10. The difference between the two,

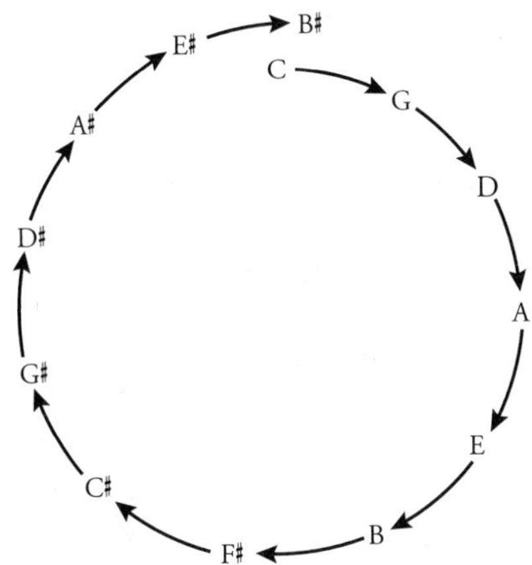

Diagram 4.3. Derivation of the Pythagorean comma.

Table 4.10.
Octaves versus pure perfect fifths, in cents

Octaves		Pure perfect fifths	
C–C	1200	C–G	702
C–C	2400	G–D	1404
C–C	3600	D–A	2106
C–C	4800	A–E	2808
C–C	6000	E–B	3510
C–C	7200	B–F♯	4212
C–C	8400	F♯–C♯	4914
		C♯–G♯	5616
		G♯–D♯	6318
		D♯–A♯	7020
		A♯–E♯	7722
		E♯–B♯	8424

a very noticeable 24c., is the Pythagorean comma. This B♯ twelve pure fifths from the starting pitch is distinctly higher than the C seven octaves from the starting note, adjusted to be within the same octave, of course. Audio files 4.9.1 and 4.9.2 present the C and B♯ melodically and audio files 4.10.1 and 4.10.2 harmonically. As you can hear from this example, the B♯ is so much higher than the C that it cannot possibly substitute for it under any circumstance.[17]

Twelve pure fifths do not fit into seven octaves no matter how tightly they are squeezed. They are simply 24c. too wide. It is the same thing as trying to make 7.02 ft. (rather than 7.00 ft.) fit into 84 in. The total of 84.24 in. (7.02 ft. × 12 in.) is almost 1/4 in. too long. If you were measuring the length of a door for a 7 ft. opening, the door would be too tall to fit in the opening. Later we will see how temperaments plane the door to make it fit.[18]

Another way to arrive at the same conclusion is to sail through the Circle of Fifths by tacking right and left by adding perfect fifths and then subtracting perfect fourths as illustrated in musical example 4.6. Each fifth up adds 702c., but each fourth down subtracts 498c. for a net gain of 204c. every two notes. As you may have noticed, 204c. is a Just whole tone. Remember that at this point we are discussing the pure intervals that nature has given us. We have yet to interfere. Table 4.11 provides the fruits of this labor. As you can see, from the starting C to the final B♯, the pitch has risen to 1224c.: an octave + the

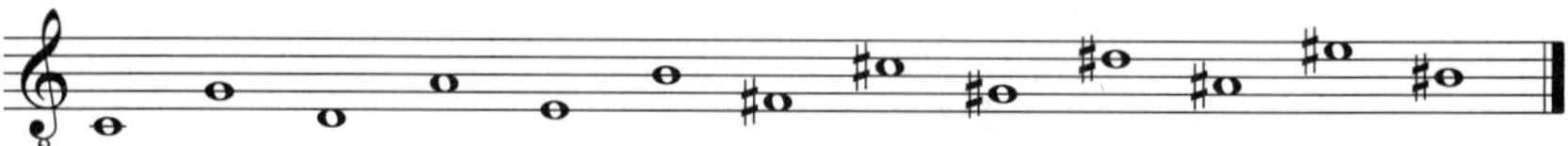

Musical Example 4.6. Journey to Pythagorean comma by alternating pure fifths and fourths.

Table 4.11.
Journey through Circle of Fifths by adding fifths and subtracting fourths, in cents

Interval + or –	Interval size	Cumulative result
C + G	+702c.	
G – D	–498c.	204c.
D + A	+702c.	
A – E	–498c.	408c.
E + B	+702c.	
B – F♯	–498c.	612c.
F♯ + C♯	+702c.	
C♯ – G♯	–498c.	816c.
G♯ + D♯	+702c.	
D♯ – A♯	–498c.	1020c.
A♯ + E♯	+702c.	
E♯ – B♯	–498c.	1224c.

Pythagorean comma (1200c. + 24c.) Any way you look at it, we are going to have to account for those 24c.

You have seen that the 24c. of the Pythagorean comma is the difference between twelve acoustically pure perfect fifths and seven acoustically pure octaves. The Pythagorean comma also manifests itself as the amount by which six pure whole tones (6 × 204c. = 1224c.) exceed an octave, but there are also other discrepancies beyond the Pythagorean comma, such as the inability of three pure major thirds (C–E–G♯ [A♭]–C) to fill an octave (386c. × 3 = 1158c.) that you can read about in books dedicated to the theoretical aspects of tuning. By now, however, you're getting familiar enough with the issues to recognize that the last interval G♯–C is not really a major third, but a diminished fourth. If it were a true major third G♯–B♯ instead, you can see that the three pure major thirds would fall short of the octave by 42c. And so on, but you get the point. Our focus so far has revolved around the systemic relationship between fifths and octaves. We will now turn our attention to the internal relationship between perfect fifths and major thirds as the size of the former determines the dimensions of the latter.

SYNTONIC COMMA

The syntonic comma measures the discrepancy between a pure third and a Pythagorean third (408c. – 386c. = 22c.). Thus, it is particularly germane to the increasingly triadic music that began to appear by the early Renaissance. By referring to the Circle of Fifths in diagram 4.4, you can see that the size of the major third between C and E is determined by adding four successive fifths (C–G–D–A–E) and subtracting two octaves from the total to keep the result in

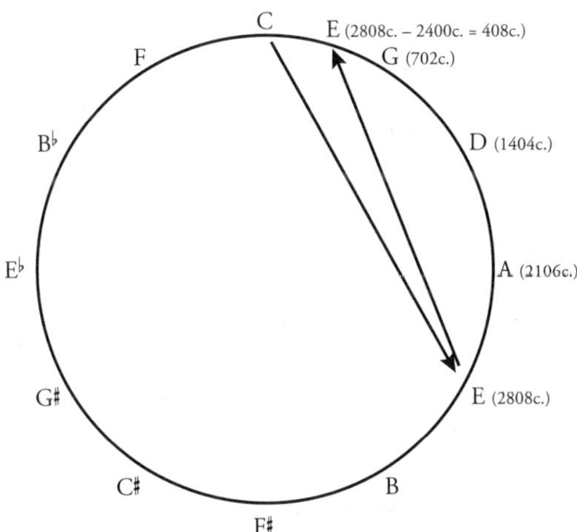

Diagram 4.4. Derivation of the Pythagorean major third.

the same octave: 702c. × 4 = 2808c. - 2400c. = 408c. Notice that the size of the third was derived by adding pure fifths of 702c. The result is what is known as a Pythagorean third of 408c. A third of 408c. beats wildly and is unacceptable by any standard as demonstrated in audio files 4.4, 4.11.1, and 4.11.2.

Another and perhaps easier way to think about the syntonic comma for fretted instrument players is to realize that it is the amount by which four pure fourths and a pure major third, for example, G–C–F–A–D–G (4 × 498c. = 1992c. + 386c. = 2378c.), fall short of two octaves: 2400c. - 2378c. = 22c. You can attempt to reproduce this on your own lute, guitar, or viol or listen to audio file 4.12, which presents the result harmonically and melodically. To try it yourself, do your best to tune your open fourths and the third such that they are absolutely pure with no beating whatsoever. If you have managed to do this accurately, you'll notice that when you compare your first and sixth courses, the double octave will be too narrow because you've fallen short by the 22c. of the syntonic comma. It may take you a many attempts to be able to accomplish this experiment since we are unaccustomed to tuning in this fashion. From this experiment, you can see that the syntonic comma is clearly a discrepancy that has a significant impact on how we tune.

The syntonic comma causes a dilemma that is essentially the same as with the Pythagorean comma only on a different scale: the projected fifths contain too many cents to fit within the bounds of the desired interval, in this case a pure major third of 386c. As we will see in chapter 5, since a Pythagorean third is intolerably wide by any measure, musicians learned to narrow its width by reducing the size of the perfect fifths from which it was derived.

Like the Pythagorean comma, the syntonic comma is simply another way of expressing the mathematical and aural discrepancies inherent in our musical system. There are a number of other incongruities that can be cited, but they all reach the same conclusion: it is impossible to arrange the notes within an octave so that every interval is pure. It is the unique way that each temperament accounts for these extra cents that endows it with its own distinctive sonic characteristics.

Making Cents

A cents chart lists the size of the interval between the starting pitch and each half step up to the octave. Once a cents chart is created, it is an easy matter to extrapolate the size of any interval within the particular tuning system the chart represents. The ability to construct a cents chart is indispensable toward gaining an understanding of tunings and temperaments. It also has a very practical application in that it is the first step toward creating an ET offset chart that we can input into our electronic tuners to create our own temperaments or better versions than those that come preloaded.

Since we've spent so much time discussing pure perfect fifths, let's construct a cents chart based on pure fifths. In diagram 4.3 our purpose was to

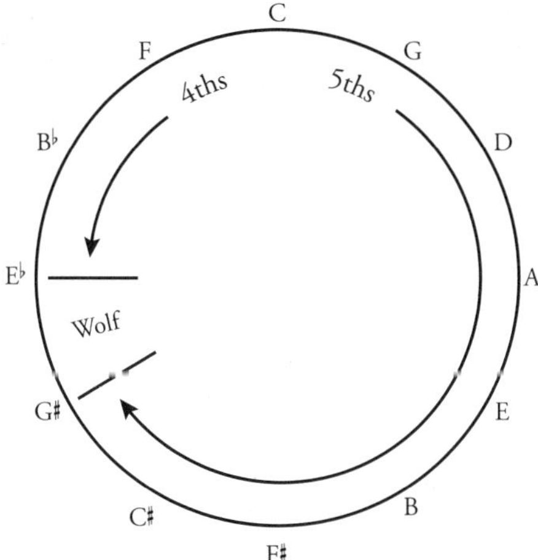

Diagram 4.5. Cents chart construction.

construct a cycle of pure fifths from C to B♯, each fifth progressing to the next in clockwise order. For this reason, we wrote all the keys that we normally think of as flat keys as sharp keys, but, for everyday use, the key of A♯ is only so useful to us. Now we're going to create a cents chart based on a clockwise progression through the Circle of Fifths from C to G to D to A to E to B to F♯ to C♯ to G♯. Once we reach G♯, we're going to return to C and fill in the rest of the fifths from E♭ to B♭ to F to C in counterclockwise motion. The choice of where to place the border between the sharp and flat keys is totally arbitrary. If you find yourself protesting that C–F–B♭–E♭ are really fourths rather than fifths, you are correct; it's all a matter of the direction you're going. Clockwise motion adds fifths or subtracts fourths. Counterclockwise motion adds fourths or subtracts fifths. We have the option of adding perfect fourths rather than subtracting perfect fifths to make the math easier for the E♭–C chain of fifths (or fourths). Both work. The choice is entirely yours. I prefer to add fourths. See diagram 4.5. Don't worry about the "wolf." We introduce it later in this chapter and discuss it in detail in the next. For now, just recognize that it represents the border between sharps and flats.

To begin, write out the chromatic scale starting on C, choosing the enharmonics indicated above.[19] Enter 1200c. for the final C because we know that octaves are always pure. Since we're going to be compounding pure perfect fifths, begin by entering 702c. for the G:

C	C♯	D	E♭	E	F	F♯	G	G♯	A	B♭	B	C
							702					1200

The next fifth is G–D. Add 702c. to the C–G 702c. to arrive at 1404c. (702c. + 702c.). To keep the cents figure for D within the octave, subtract 1200c. from 1404c. to arrive at 204c.:

C	C♯	D	E♭	E	F	F♯	G	G♯	A	B♭	B	C
		204					702					1200

You are now well on your way. Let's pause for a moment on E:

C	C♯	D	E♭	E	F	F♯	G	G♯	A	B♭	B	C
		204		408			702		906			1200

As you can see, you derived the size of the major third from C to E by compounding fifths and subtracting octaves as you went along to keep the third within the same octave. From the Renaissance on, or perhaps even earlier, theorists and musicians isolated this part of the process to generate the defining quality of the temperament, measured predominantly by the size of the major third. If you compounded fifths that were narrower than 702c., the resultant major third would have been narrower as well. In chapter 5, you will see that this very specific process is the primary method by which musicians manipulated the system to create the temperament's defining characteristics according to their needs. The size of every major third is determined in the same fashion, for instance, G–B is constructed by compounding the fifths G–D–A–E–B and subtracting two octaves.

Now, continue all the way to G♯, making sure that you subtract 1200c. from every amount above 1200c. to keep it within one octave. At this point, your chart should look like:

C	C♯	D	E♭	E	F	F♯	G	G♯	A	B♭	B	C
	114	204		408		612	702	816	906		1110	1200

Now that we've reached G♯, we must return to C and start over again. Here's where you have a choice. The next pitch we're concerned with is F. There are two ways to get there. First, continuing along in fifths, we can subtract 702c. from the C at 1200c. to arrive at 498c. for F. From there we can arrive at the figure for B♭ by subtracting 702c. from 498c. to get –204c. To this figure we must add 1200c. to keep it within the octave, which yields 996c. Knowing ahead of time that the sum of 498c. – 702c. is going to be a negative number, it's easier to add the 1200c. up front: 498c. + 1200c. = 1698c. – 702c. = 996c. This method has the advantage of maintaining the consistency of 702c., but I find it much simpler to start adding fourths to C. Since we know that the pure fourth is 498c. (1200c. – 702c.), we just add 498c. to the starting C to get the F and continue adding 498c. to B♭ and E♭, always subtracting 1200c. whenever the sum exceeds that amount, to arrive at the finished product, which looks like:

C	C♯	D	E♭	E	F	F♯	G	G♯	A	B♭	B	C
	114	204	294	408	498	612	702	816	906	996	1110	1200

From the completed cents chart you can determine the size of any interval. For instance, to calculate the size of the major sixth between B♭ and G, you can either extend the cents chart with an additional octave:

C	C♯	D	E♭	E	F	F♯	G	G♯	A	B♭	B	C
1200	1314	1404	1494	1608	1698	1812	1902	2016	2106	2196	2310	2400

and subtract 996c. from 1902c. to get 906c. or simply add 1200c. to 702c. and subtract 996c. (1200c. + 702c. = 1902c. – 996c. = 906c.).

Let's take this opportunity to make a few observations about this tuning. You can see that all the perfect fifths are a pure 702c., except for G♯–E♭. G♯–E♭ isn't really a fifth, but rather a diminished sixth occupying the space we would expect a fifth to reside. At 678c., G♯–E♭ is so narrow and out of tune that it is referred to as a "wolf" because it beats so wildly that it resembles the howling of a wolf. You might be interested to know that you can also derive the size of the wolf in this tuning by subtracting the entire Pythagorean comma from this one "fifth" (702c. – 24c. = 678c.). You'll notice that the major third from C to E is very wide, but that some of the diminished fourths such as C♯–F actually yield a rather sweet 384c. that can substitute for a major third, not that there's much opportunity for a C♯–E♯ major third in early music.

Perhaps the most striking feature of this tuning is that there are two sizes of semitone: a diatonic semitone (for example, D–E♭) at 90c. and a chromatic semitone (for example, C–C♯) of 114c. From this information, you can see that what we think of as enharmonics (for example, D♯ and E♭) are completely different pitches. Since a chromatic semitone is 114c., D♯ comes in at 318c. (1404c. + 114c. = 1518c. – 1200c. = 318c.). Not surprisingly, the difference between the sharp and flat versions of an accidental is 24c. Within the class of a particular interval, there may be more than one specific size of interval that is still recognizable as a member of that class, for example, the two sizes of semitone just described; it is the rule to which equal temperament is the exception.[20]

Finally, just to check ourselves, and to gain some notion of how theorists thought of intervals and temperaments before the advent of cents, it's a good idea to go through creating a ratio chart rather than a cents chart based on pure fifths.[21] Because the accidental notes quickly get into such complicated fractions as 729/512 for F♯ and 2187/2048 for C♯, for instance, we will limit our exercise to the natural notes beginning on C. Instead of adding and subtracting cents, we'll be multiplying and dividing fractions, beginning with the 3/2 for the C–G fifth:

C	D	E	F	G	A	B	C
1/1				3/2			2/1

Continuing on to derive the size of the G–D fifth, we add fifths and subtract an octave to keep the results within the same octave: 3/2 × 3/2 = 9/4 ÷ 2/1 (9/4 × 1/2) = 9/8:

C	D	E	F	G	A	B	C
1/1	9/8			3/2			2/1

In the same fashion we keep adding fifths until we must return to C to calculate the F, we find ourselves with:

C	D	E	F	G	A	B	C
1/1	9/8	81/64		3/2	27/16	243/128	2/1

There are a number of ways to derive the ratio of the pure fourth between C and F; however, the simplest is to subtract a fifth from the octave: 2/1 ÷ 3/2 (2/1 × 2/3) = 4/3, which completes our chart:

C	D	E	F	G	A	B	C
1/1	9/8	81/64	4/3	3/2	27/16	243/128	2/1

You might find it constructive to compare these ratios with the corresponding pure ratios in table 4.1.

Congratulations! You have just created the cents and white-note ratio charts for Pythagorean tuning, Western music's dominant tuning system until the Renaissance and the first tuning system we will examine in chapter 5. Recalculate the Pythagorean tuning cents chart a number of times on a variety of starting pitches until you can do it quickly. This skill is basic to comprehending the intricacies of the tunings and temperaments we examine throughout this book. The only way to truly master this material is to do the math yourself. Only then will it make cents.

As you have seen in this chapter, because it is impossible to create a tuning system in which all the intervals are acoustically pure, we must choose which intervals to make pure and which to make less than pure.[22] By now you have certainly guessed that something is going to have to give to be able to create any functional tuning system whatsoever. Each tuning system is a compromise, and, like any compromise, we agree to have less of this so we can have more of that or give up this so we can have that—a metaphor for life if ever there was one.

Plate 1. Antonio Domenico Gabbiani (1652–1726): Lirone enarmonico in detail of *The Prince Ferdinando de' Medici and the Musicians of the Court* (ca. 1684). Galaria Palatina, Palazzo Pitti, Florence. Scala / Art Resource, NY.

Plate 2. Nicholas Tournier (1590–ca. 1639): Detail of *Le Concert.* Louvre, Paris. © RMN-Grand Palais / Art Resource, NY.

Plate 3. Carlo Saraceni (1585–1620): Detail of *St. Cecilia.* Galleria Nazionale d'Arte Antica, Rome. Scala / Art Resource, NY.

Plate 4. John Michael Wright (ca. 1617–1700): *Lady with a Theorbo* (ca. 1675). Columbus Museum of Art, Ohio. Schumacher Fund Purchase 1963.033.

Plate 5. Albrecht Dürer (1471–1528): "The Draughtsman with Lute," from his *Treatise on Mensuration with the Compass and Ruler in Lines, Planes, and Whole Bodies* (1525). Kupferstichkabinett, Staatliche Museen, Berlin. Volker-h. Schneider / Art Resource, NY.

Plate 6. André Bouys (1656–1740): *Portrait of the Composer and Musician Marin Marais (1656–1728).* Bibliotheque Nationale de l'Opera, Paris. © RMN Grand Palais / Art Resource, NY.

Plate 7. Michelangelo Merisi known as Caravaggio (1573–1610): *The Musicians.* Metropolitan Museum of Art, New York. Art Resource, NY.

Plate 8. Theodor Rombouts (1597–1637): Detail of *Musical Company with Bacchus.* The Kremer Collection (www.thekremercollection.com).

Plate 9. Giovanni di Jacopo Rosso Fiorentino (1494–1541): *Angelo che suona il liuto* (ca. 1520). Galeria degli Uffizi, Florence. Gianni Dagli Orti / The Art Archive at Art Resource, NY.

Plate 10. Detail of Hendrick ter Brugghen (1588–1629): *The Singing Lute Player.* The Kremer Collection (www.thekremercollection.com).

Plate 11. Giulio Campi (1502–1572): *Portrait of a Lutenist.* Pinacoteca Civica, Como.

Plate 12. Evaristo Baschenis (1617–1677): *Self-Portrait with the Count Alessandro Agliardi with Instruments* (ca. 1637–1677). Painting belonging to the Count Agliardi Collection of Bergamo, Bergamo, Italy. Alinari / Art Resource, NY.

Plate 13. Giulio Campi (1502–1572): Overlay of 3D fretting grid on detail of *Portrait of a Lutenist.* Pinacoteca Civica, Como. Courtesy of Tim Watson.

CHAPTER FIVE

Tour through Tuning Systems

Pythagorean Tuning

Associated with Pythagoras (570–504 BC) by tradition if not by fact, Pythagorean tuning was the first major tuning system to achieve widespread use in Western music. Since the fifths in the Pythagorean system are not narrowed or tempered, it is a tuning rather than a temperament.[1] Its perfect fourths and fifths are acoustically pure, and its major thirds are an excruciatingly wide 408c., except for four compressed diminished fourths on B, F♯, C♯, and G♯ narrow enough to measure nearly a pure major third at 384c., which we discuss further below. The wolf is a narrow 678c. See diagram 5.1, the Pythagorean tuning Circle of Fifths. Diagram 5.2 illustrates how the systemic 24c. excess of the Pythagorean comma is absorbed by the wolf. There are also two sizes of semitone, the narrow diatonic at 90c. and the wider chromatic at 114c., as you discovered from the cents chart we constructed in chapter 4.[2] The slimmer semitones are sometimes referred to as minor semitones, while the wider

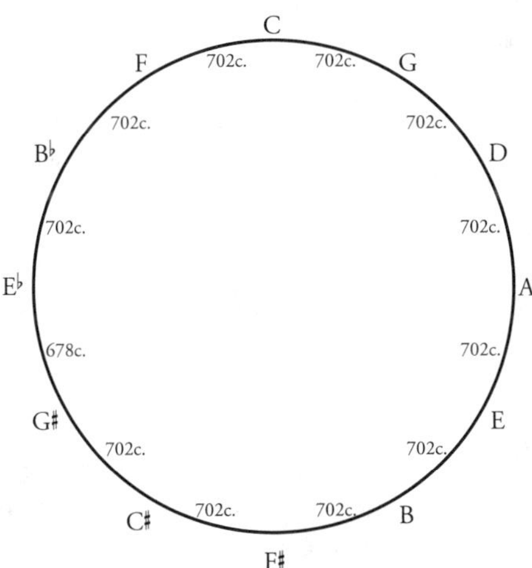

Diagram 5.1. Pythagorean tuning Circle of Fifths.

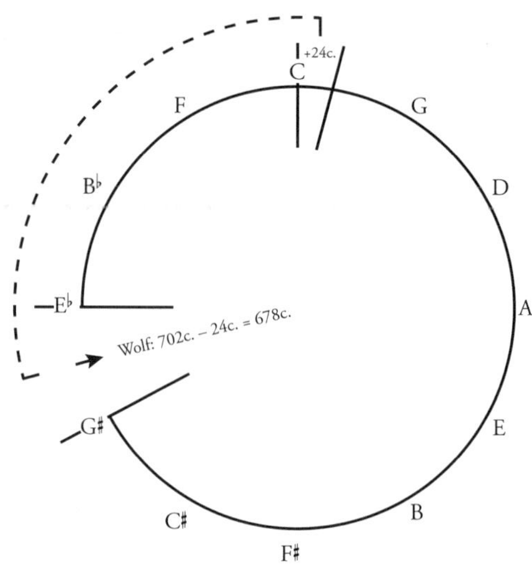

Diagram 5.2. Absorption of the Pythagorean comma into the wolf.

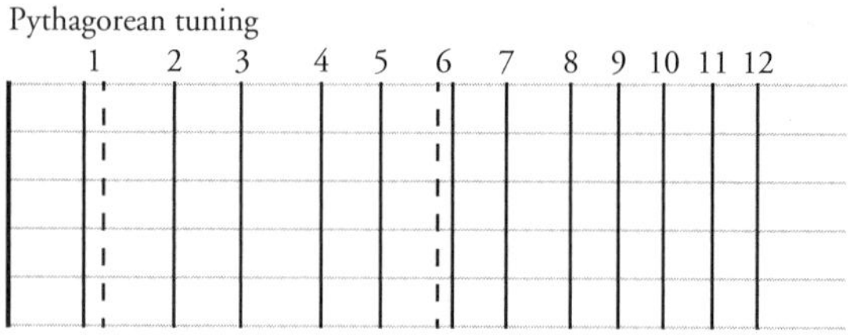

Pythagorean tuning
1 2 3 4 5 6 7 8 9 10 11 12

Diagram 5.3. Pythagorean tuning fretboard in G.

ones are thought of as major. Because the semitones differ in size, Pythagorean tuning is an "unequal" system, as you can see from diagram 5.3, which shows a fretboard configured in Pythagorean tuning. The 1st fret is set to *fa* with the wider alternate *mi* position indicated by the dashed-line fret, whereas the 6th fret is set in the *mi* position with the narrower alternate *fa* position indicated by the dashed-line fret according to the pitches most commonly used on an instrument tuned in G.

Before the advent of free organum in the twelfth century, polyphony generally involved parallel fourths or fifths or a melody against a drone, textures ideally suited for Pythagorean tuning. In those circumstances, the more important relationships were between successive or melodic notes where such infelicities as the extremely wide major third were much less obvious. Yet, when three- and occasional four-voice organum and three-part conductus arrived on the scene in the thirteenth century, harmonic major thirds became much more commonplace. Coupled with the appearance of *fauxbourdon* and the English penchant for thirds and sixths in the early fifteenth century and before, it is inconceivable that the wide Pythagorean third would have been tolerated in those situations, particularly since the sweetness of the pure fifth does nothing to mitigate the harshness of the wide major third when the two are played together as in a major triad.[3]

In standard Pythagorean tuning, the four diminished fourths that can stand in for nearly pure major thirds are marooned where they can be of little use. Around 1440 at the dawn of the Renaissance, Henri Arnaut de Zwolle, whom lutenists know from his publication of the first known set of builder's drawings for the lute, proposed a solution that kept the good "major third" of B–D♯ (E♭), while relocating the others to E–G♯ (A♭), A–C♯ (D♭), and D–F♯ (G♭) with the wolf placed between B and G♭.[4] Its cents chart:

C	D♭/C♯	D	E♭/D♯	E	F	G♭/F♯	G	A♭/G♯	A	B♭	B	C
	90	204	294	408	498	588	702	792	906	996	1110	1200

is derived from the Circle of Fifths illustrated in diagram 5.4: you'll notice that the narrow wolf fifth of 678c. is always one of the fifths that compound to generate the better "thirds"; Arnaut appropriated the wolf's reduced width to narrow the intervals he would then use as thirds. As you will realize after we've discussed meantone temperaments, rotating the circle in this fashion and thinking of the F♯, C♯, G♯, and D♯ as G♭, D♭, A♭, and E♭ essentially endows a portion of the tuning with meantone characteristics. Note that Pythagorean tuning's iconic status had waned enough to give Arnaut the leave to manipulate

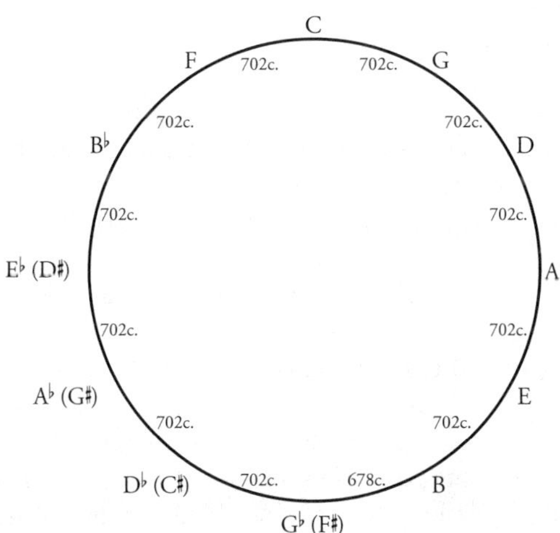

Diagram 5.4. Arnaut's transposed Pythagorean tuning Circle of Fifths.

it by relocating the wolf to a location that better suited his purposes, or perhaps he was a renegade. Either way, he may have provided the impetus that ultimately led to the development of meantone temperaments.[5]

We must keep in mind that until the twentieth century, most theoretical treatises lagged far behind current conditions, often describing musical practices that had long since passed out of fashion. Furthermore, as we will later see, since the thousand-year tradition of valuing theoretical musical contemplations over those with practical applications finally started to reverse itself in the Renaissance, we must attempt to discern which writings or portions of writings were primarily theoretical and which were practical, a judgment that is usually clear from the context. The ubiquitous discussion of Pythagorean tuning in Renaissance theoretical treatises can lead to the mistaken assumption that it was still in common use in the fifteenth and sixteenth centuries when, in fact, it had long outlived its usefulness. An explanation of Pythagorean tuning had become an almost obligatory intellectual exercise designed to illustrate the author's erudition rather than a recommendation for its use.

Temperaments, that is, tuning systems that narrow or temper certain intervals to absorb the Pythagorean comma and influence the size of other intervals, can be classified as regular or irregular. In regular temperaments, all the fifths except for the wolf are tempered by the same amount and are therefore the same size. As a result, there is only one size of diatonic and one size of chromatic semitone. Irregular temperaments, on the other hand, eliminate the wolf completely by fielding fifths of various sizes, which results in more than one size of diatonic and chromatic semitone. These temperaments focus the good-sounding keys in an even more narrowly circumscribed region than regular meantone temperaments do.

Regular Temperaments: Meantone

A more radical response than Arnaut's to the increasing importance of thirds and sixths was meantone temperament. Meantone temperament narrows the size of the perfect fifth by 1/4 of the syntonic comma for the express purpose of reducing the size of eight major thirds near the top of the Circle of Fifths to pure, leaving four others too wide to be of any use in remote areas at the bottom of the Circle of Fifths where they can do little harm. The pleasure gained from the pure thirds more than compensates for the narrowness of the fifths. In general this temperament is arranged so that the concentration of keys near the top of the Circle of Fifths sounds quite good while the keys farther away from the top of the circle become progressively more dissonant.[6]

As you may have noticed, this arrangement inverts the distribution of the good major thirds in Pythagorean tuning. In other details as well, meantone temperament is the opposite of Pythagorean tuning. Like Pythagorean tuning, meantone temperament also features two sizes of semitone; however, the diatonic semitone is wider and the chromatic semitone narrower, again in exact opposition to Pythagorean tuning. And rather than a narrower wolf fifth as in Pythagorean tuning, the meantone wolf is wider than pure, for reasons we examine shortly.

Meantone temperament is especially useful in music from the fifteenth and sixteenth centuries and following where the third is the preponderant interval, tonal centers tend to congregate around the top of the Circle of Fifths, temporary tonal centers do not tend to stray too far afield, and no more than one of a note's enharmonic forms is called for, although fretted instruments can often supply both forms in some fashion or other.[7] In other words, meantone temperament and its derivatives work splendidly for most Renaissance and Baroque music for fretted instruments. Meantone temperament for keyboards was first mentioned within the context of reporting what practicing musicians were already doing. Since one of the primary reasons to tune the open strings of fretted instrument in fourths and a third is to facilitate chord shapes for the left hand and the fact that their role as accompanying instruments from their inception is unchallenged, I suspect that lutenists and guitarists were already experimenting with meantone temperament or something like it well before written notice of its existence first appeared in 1482.

Strictly speaking, there is only one "meantone" temperament, 1/4-syntonic-comma meantone, sometimes referred to as "standard meantone temperament." Musicians, and particularly fretted instrument players, however, found that they could diminish each fifth by other usually smaller fractions of the comma such as 1/5 or 1/6, and so on, resulting in thirds that, while not quite pure, are closer to pure than in equal temperament, which in turns allowed them to function in a wider range of keys than in 1/4-comma meantone.[8] Their "bad" major thirds are not quite as poor as in 1/4-comma meantone, and the "wolf" is smaller. These temperaments are sometimes referred to as "attenuated," an appellation that is particularly appropriate because both of its meanings accurately describe characteristics of these temperaments. "Attenuated" primarily means to weaken something, in this case, the purity of the major thirds. It can also indicate making something thinner. In the context of our discussion, this refers to the slice of the comma deducted from each fifth, except for the wolf, of course. In 1/5-comma meantone temperament, for instance, the comma is sliced into five pieces, each one thinner or narrower than each of the four slices in 1/4-comma meantone temperament, and so on. Since the temperaments that divide the comma into more than four slices are already attenuated when compared with standard meantone temperament, the term "1/6 SC—Attenuated," that is, 1/6 syntonic comma, attenuated, that you can find on electronic tuners is a well intentioned but confusing redundancy.

Moving past terminology, depending on the variety of meantone, the thirds are pure or nearly pure, the fifths are narrower, and the fourths are wider than pure to a relatively small degree. In any case, musicians felt that the sweetness of the thirds more than compensated for the narrow fifths and wide fourths. As we will see, the real balancing act is between the purity of the major thirds and the range of usable keys. The more Just the third, the fewer usable keys; the wider the third, the greater number of usable keys. When confined to a tight range of tonal areas, 1/4-comma meantone temperament's pure thirds make it a most attractive choice, but as the range of keys to be performed expands, we must sacrifice a little third purity in exchange for wider tonal area serviceability. This will all become clear when we delve into the construction of meantone temperaments.

Before doing so, a pleasant word of caution is in order. When we speak of temperaments, cents charts and Circles of Fifths give the impression that once the enharmonic choices are made, that is, D♯ rather than E♭, the temperament is set and the serviceable tonal areas defined. This is largely the case with keyboard instruments unless the keyboard has split keys or the player retunes the D♯ to E♭, for example, for pieces that require E♭, which is much more of a production on keyboards than fretted instruments. For us, it is simply a matter of either arranging our frets so that the D♯ is placed in one location and the E♭ in another since we can play the same note in several difference locations or by quickly nudging a fret one way or another.[9] This means that on fretted instruments we can make temperaments much more serviceable by extending the good keys through the use of tastini, slanted or repositioned frets, and a number of other strategies particularly in temperaments that divide the comma into a larger number of smaller slices. We discuss these techniques in later chapters. Because of this, the charts or circles provide an incomplete picture, and you can safely assume that fretted instruments are able extend the good chords somewhat beyond the wolf in either direction, sharp or flat. In this case, the temperament becomes "extended" as in "extended 1/6-comma meantone temperament."

1/4-SYNTONIC-COMMA MEANTONE TEMPERAMENT

The defining feature in 1/4-syntonic-comma meantone temperament is its pure third of 386c.[10] Remember that the size of the third is a function of the size of the fifth. Pure fifths of 702c. result in a third of 408c.: 702c. × 4 = 2808c. – 2400c. = 408c. This Pythagorean third is a syntonic comma (22c.) wider than the pure third of 386c. We can also subtract those 22c. and two octaves from the 2808c., arriving at a pure 5:4 third of 386c.: 2808c. – 22c. = 2786c. – 2400c. = 386c. But from where and how are those 22c. taken?

Recalling our method for deriving the size of the third by adding four fifths and subtracting 2400c. to keep the resultant third within the proper octave, it follows that the smaller the size of the fifths, the smaller the size of the third. The syntonic comma of 22c. divided by four yields 5.5c. Subtracting this amount from a pure fifth of 702c. results in a fifth of 696.5c. Plugging this

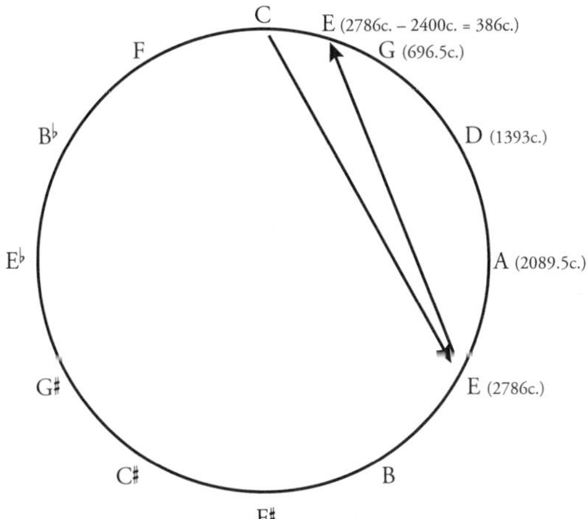

Diagram 5.5. Derivation of the 1/4-comma third.

number into the above formula gives us a pure third of 386c.: 696.5c. × 4 = 2786c. – 2400c. = 386c. See diagram 5.5.

1/4 COMMA AND THE BIG BAD "WOLF"

Recall that in Pythagorean tuning, all of the fifths, except for the wolf, are the same size. So too in meantone temperament. As in Pythagorean tuning, the 24c. of the Pythagorean comma is subtracted from the wolf; however, in meantone temperament the 1/4 of a syntonic comma (5.5c.) subtracted from each of eleven fifths (60.5c.) is also deposited into the wolf. Diagram 5.6 shows how much each fifth differs from a pure fifth of 702c. So the 1/4-comma meantone wolf is derived as follows: 702c. – 24c. + 60.5c. = 738.5c. See diagram 5.7. This results in the Circle of Fifths as shown in diagram 5.8 and the following cents chart:

C	C♯	D	E♭	E	F	F♯	G	G♯	A	B♭	B	C
	75.5	193	310.5	386	503.5	579	696.5	772	889.5	1007	1082.5	1200

To review, 1/4 of a syntonic comma (5.5c.) is subtracted from each of *eleven* fifths, rendering them each 1 percent narrower than pure. One percent is not a lot, but since we hear even slight beating more easily in perfect fifths than thirds, it is noticeable, albeit fortunately for us, much more so on keyboards than on lutes and viols. The fact that beating in thirds is less easily perceived than beating in fifths is trumped by the fact that, for instance, in equal temperament, the major third is 3.6 percent wider than pure. In an ET triad, the major third beats so rapidly that it obscures the relatively placid fifth. In a 1/4-comma

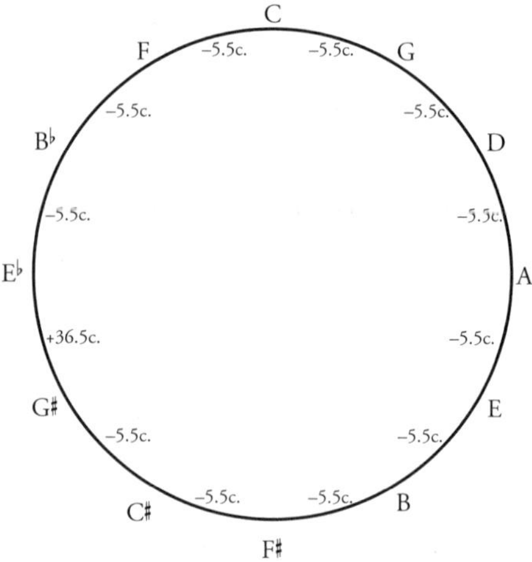

Diagram 5.6. Adjustment of fifths in 1/4-comma meantone temperament Circle of Fifths.

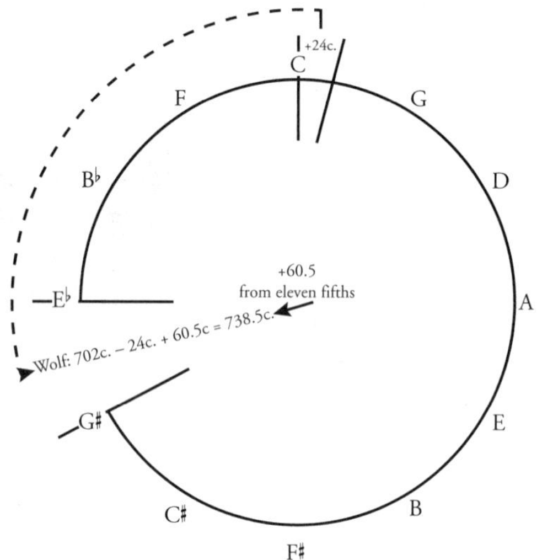

Diagram 5.7. Absorption of Pythagorean and syntonic commas into wolf.

triad, on the other hand, the ear is drawn to the sweetness of the pure third, which tends to absorb the slight narrowness of the fifth. See if you can hear it in audio files 5.1 and 5.2, ET and 1/4-comma versions of musical example 5.1. Note the sense of agitation or tightness in audio file 5.1 versus the tranquility and resonance of audio file 5.2.

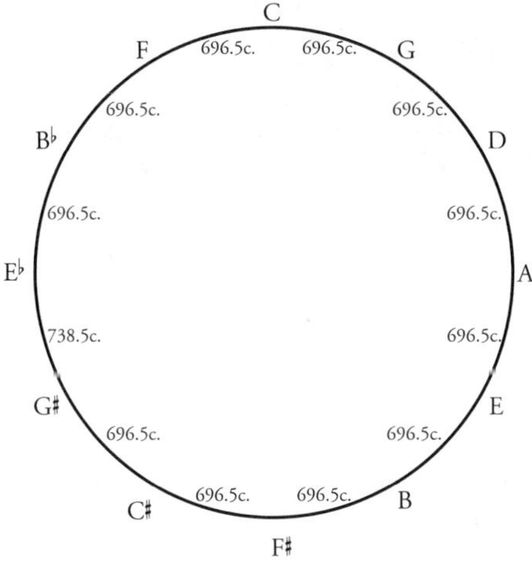

Diagram 5.8. 1/4-comma meantone temperament Circle of Fifths.

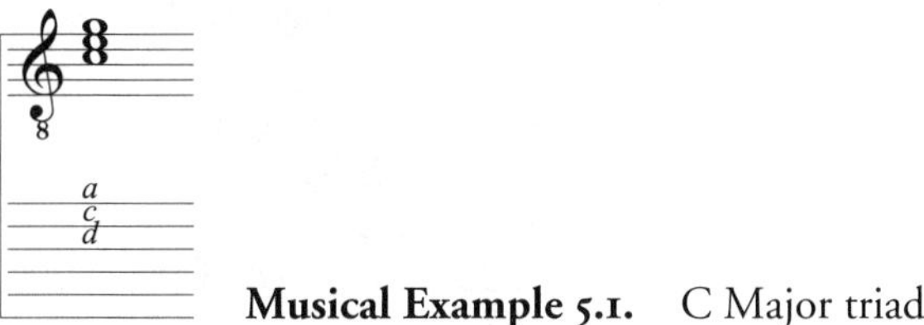

Musical Example 5.1. C Major triad.

Returning to the wolf, those 60.5c. subtracted from the eleven fifths that are then deposited into the wolf render it so wide as to be unusable. Note again that in 1/4 comma the wolf is larger than a pure fifth, whereas in Pythagorean tuning it is smaller than a pure fifth. Here we will mention just two of the several systemic methods used to calculate the size of the wolf. First, eleven pure fifths, 7722c. (11 × 702c.), minus the total amount removed from those eleven fifths, 60.5c. (11 × 5.5c.), equals 7661.5c. (7722c. – 60.5c.). Subtracting 7661.5c. from seven octaves, 8400c., equals 738.5c., the size of the wolf fifth in 1/4 comma. It also works to think in terms of eleven 1/4-comma fifths, 7661.5c. (11 × 696.5c.), subtracted from 8400c. leaving 738.5c. The wolf is usually placed in a fifth that is used infrequently such as A♭ (G♯)–E♭ or D♭ (C♯)–A♭; however, where in the forest it lurks is entirely up to you. Returning to the cents charts, you can also derive the size of the wolf fifth the same way you calculate any other interval: G♯–E♭ (1510.5c. [310.5c. + 1200c.] – 772c. = 738.5c.).

All this attention to the wolf may seem excessive, but it is important to recognize that the wolf essentially balances the books by accounting for the excess 24c. of the Pythagorean comma *and* the 5.5c. subtracted from each of the eleven fifths. Before moving on, remind yourself that every tuning system must always account for the 24c. of the Pythagorean comma and the total amount of cents removed from the fifths.

The bottom line is that in 1/4-syntonic-comma meantone temperament, twelve fifths = seven octaves, with the internal construction designed so that the eight most commonly used thirds at the top of the Circle of Fifths (E♭–G, B♭–D, F–A, C–E, G–B, D–F♯, A–C♯, E–G♯) are pure while the other four thirds are unusable. Don't take my word for it. Check it for yourself by using the cents chart. For example, the third between E♭ and G is a pure 386c. (696.5c. – 310.5c.), and the third between B and D♯ (really E♭) is a nasty 428c. (1510.5c. [310.5c. + 1200c.] – 1082.5c.), not coincidentally a pure third plus the difference between the diatonic semitone and the chromatic semitone (386c. + 42c.). The price for the eight pristine major thirds is that the fifths are somewhat dissonant when compared with pure, but the overall sound of the temperament makes it a bargain.

DIATONIC AND CHROMATIC SEMITONES

Prior to the introduction of accidentals placed at the beginning of a staff to govern all the pitches that appear on its line or space, the first clefs, C and F, were created to indicate the location of the diatonic semitones, specifically, the semitones between B and C or E and F. Without clefs there would be no way of knowing where the semitones are. Diatonic semitones are those in which the two pitches involved bear different letter names. In the solmization system, the two pitches that make up a semitone are enunciated by the syllables *mi* and *fa.* In our example, both B and E are designated as a *mi* and C and F as a *fa, mi* indicating the lower note and *fa* the upper note. *Mi* and *fa* always define a diatonic semitone. In terms of intervals with accidentals, in the diatonic semitone of F♯–G, F♯ is the *mi,* and G is the *fa.* Similarly, in the diatonic semitone, D–E♭, D is the *mi,* and E♭ is the *fa.* Because of this relationship, *mi* came to be used as a general term to indicate a sharp accidental and *fa* a flat accidental. Any sharp or any flat.

The pitch of every course that traverses over a particular fret is either a *mi* or a *fa* at that fret. In other words, depending on the where the fret is located, every note at that fret is either a sharp or a flat note since the same one fret governs all the courses. For instance, on a lute or viol in G, at the 1st fret from the first to sixth courses, the notes from highest to lowest are either A♭, E♭, B♭, G♭, D♭, and A♭ (see diagram 5.9) or G♯, D♯, A♯, F♯, C♯, and G♯ (see diagram 5.10).[11] The painting *Musical Company with Bacchus* by Theodor Rombouts (1597–1637) shows a lute with its frets arranged as in diagram 5.10 with the 1st fret slanted toward the bass side to compensate for sharpening. See plate 8. That all the notes at any perpendicular fret are either a sharp or flat note is both a blessing and a curse. In later chapters we explore how to convert the curse into a blessing.

G	A♭	A	B♭	B	C
D	E♭	E	F	F♯	G
A	B♭	B	C	C♯	D
F	G♭	G	A♭	A	B♭
C	D♭	D	E♭	E	F
G	A♭	A	B♭	B	C

Diagram 5.9. 1/4-comma meantone temperament fretboard notes with 1st fret *fa.*

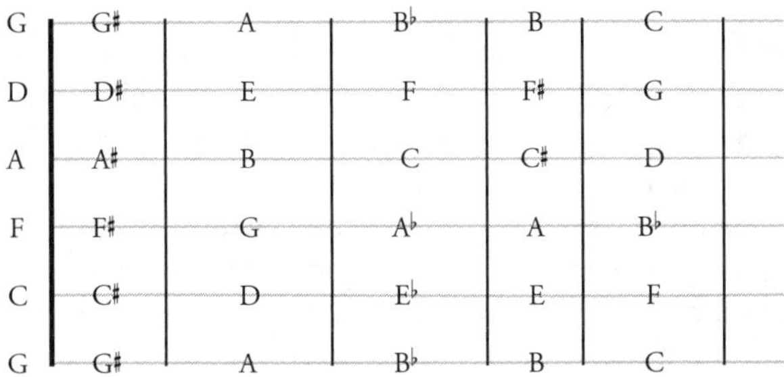

Diagram 5.10. 1/4-comma meantone temperament fretboard notes with 1st fret *mi.*

Depending on the tuning system and whether the fret is a *mi* or a *fa,* a fret is either narrow or wide. Here we are speaking of the fret space rather than the actual fret. For instance, the 2nd fret refers both to the actual 2nd fret, but also to the width of the space between the 1st and 2nd frets. The 3rd fret refers to the space between the 2nd and 3rd frets, and so on. In Pythagorean tuning, the *mi* frets are wide, and the *fa* frets are narrow, but in meantone temperament, it is the exact opposite: the *mi* frets are narrow, and the *fa* frets are wide, as you can see in diagrams 3.1 and 3.2. This provides a convenient visual guide telling us that in meantone temperament *mi* frets with sharp enharmonics are narrow while the *fa* frets with flat enharmonics are wide. In this nomenclature, the B and E in our example above, are not, strictly speaking, sharp notes, just as the C and F are not flat notes. But each is a *mi* or a *fa,* hence both the convenience and accuracy of this ancient classification system. To sum up, *mi* and *fa* refer to the enharmonic designation of the notes at a particular fret, as well as the physical size of the fret relative to its neighbor.

As mentioned above, there are two sizes of semitone in meantone temperaments, diatonic and chromatic, sometimes also referred to as major and minor semitones, respectively. By examining the cents chart, you can see that, contrary to what you might expect, the diatonic semitones (117.5c.) are wider than the chromatic semitones (75.5c.). This is the standard relationship between semitones in meantone temperaments and any of their derivatives. *Fa* frets represent wide diatonic semitones, while narrow chromatic semitones reside at *mi* frets. Returning to our example above, a 1st fret positioned as a *fa* is wide, and all its notes are flat notes or, more precisely, the upper note in a diatonic semitone. So, the intervals between the open strings and the 1st fret locations are diatonic, each interval progressing to different letter name: G–A♭, D–E♭, A–B♭, F–G♭, C–D♭, and G–A♭. When the fret is placed in the narrower *mi* position, the relationship between the open strings and the 1st fret is chromatic, each open string progressing to the sharp version of its name: G–G♯, D–D♯, A–A♯, F–F♯, C–C♯, and G–G♯.

The difference between the sharp and flat enharmonic versions of a note (for example, G♯–A♭) is known as the harmonic diesis, which in 1/4-comma meantone temperament translates into 42c. You may recall that this is also the amount by which three pure thirds fall short of one octave. The wider the harmonic diesis, the less serviceable the temperament is in the tonal areas that approach the region of the Circle of Fifths in which the wolf resides. Additionally, from a purely practical standpoint, the wider the diesis is in cents, the greater the physical distance between *mi* and *fa* locations on the fingerboard, and, therefore, the more difficult it is to substitute or fudge a *mi* for a *fa* and vice versa by slanting a fret because the required slant often exceeds the fret's physical limits. See diagram 5.11, which shows the 1st fret positions of both *mi* and *fa* in 1/4-comma meantone temperament. The harmonic diesis is less of an issue on viols because they have more bows in their quiver, as it were, owing to the ability to adjust the pitch more significantly and easily with left-hand finger placement. Remember that all the notes between the open course and the *mi* fret position are sharp notes, as in diagram 5.10, and all the notes between the open courses and the *fa* position are flat notes as in diagram 5.9. The harmonic diesis' size in cents and corresponding width on the fingerboard diminishes as a function of the decrease in the size of each slice from 1/4 to 1/5 to 1/6, and so on, as the number of comma slices is increased, the syntonic comma, of course, remaining constant. This practical consideration will factor into your choice of temperament. Keep in mind also that the physical width of the harmonic dieses on the fretboard decreases as the frets progress toward the 12th fret, making the use of slanted frets more effective beyond the 2nd fret. This you can see in diagram 3.2. Because the physical distance the harmonic diesis represents is greatest at the 1st fret, often exceeding the fret's physical slanting limit, discussions of tastini and double and split frets are usually, although not necessarily, restricted to the 1st fret.

One of the most striking and counterintuitive features of meantone temperament is that the sharp enharmonic notes are lower than their flat counterparts

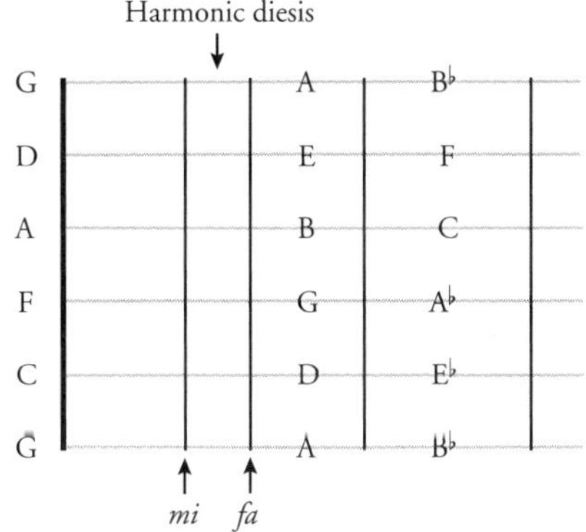

Diagram 5.11. Harmonic diesis in 1/4-comma meantone temperament.

and, correspondingly, the flats are higher than sharp counterparts.[12] The sharp is the upper note in a narrow *mi* semitone, while the flat is the upper note in a wide *fa* semitone. For instance, in the case of F–F♯, the F♯ is the upper note in the slim *mi* chromatic semitone, where the F♯ does not reach as high as it would in equal temperament because the chromatic semitone is narrower than an ET semitone. In the case of A–B♭, B♭ is the upper note of a *fa* diatonic semitone that is wider than an ET semitone resulting in a B♭ that reaches higher than an ET B♭. When you begin to apply meantone temperaments to your instrument, these concepts become immediately apparent visually. For instance, the distance between the nut and the 4th fret on the first string of a viol in D or the second course on a lute in G designated to produces an F♯ is noticeably narrower than were the fret positioned to produce at G♭. It is therefore paramount when playing with singers or instrumentalists on flexible pitched instruments such as violins to explain to them that the sharps are lower than what they're accustomed to, and the flats higher. Again, on our viol in D and lute in G, the distance between the nut and the 4th fret F♯ in 1/4-comma meantone temperament will be narrower than were the 4th fret placed in equal temperament, but for a G♭ will be wider than equal temperament.

In my experience, once singers and instrumentalists realize this, they find it surprisingly easy to match your pitches. This difference is most noticeable at cadences where the leading tone might seem quite low as in musical example 5.2 and audio file 5.3. The F♯ is low, of course, because the size of the interval it makes with the D, a tenth in this case, is narrow. This can be viewed as a question of favoring the quality of the harmony over yielding to the melodic pull toward resolution; however, refusing to yield results in much greater tension and therefore a more satisfying resolution because the distance between the leading tone and its resolution is the wider diatonic semitone. Raising the leading tone in any temperament is, in a sense, surrendering too easily.

Musical Example 5.2. Authentic cadence on G Major.

Initially, pure major thirds in 1/4-comma meantone temperament sound flat, but after you become acclimated to them, major thirds wider than pure sound sharp and unstable because of the beating associated with them. 1/4-comma meantone triads beat considerably less than in equal temperament because the 1/4-comma fifth (696.5c.) beats only slightly faster than the equal-tempered fifth (700c.); the third (386c.), however, does not beat at all compared with the rapidly beating ET third (400c.). With all this attention to the quality of the major third, you may be wondering about the minor third. There's more good news here. As you can see from the cents chart above, it is 310.5c., a mere 5.5c. shy of a pure minor third of 316c., a significant improvement over the ET minor third of 300c., a whopping 16c. narrower than a pure minor third.

The stability of the triads results in much more conclusive cadential motion and significantly greater harmonic security than in equal temperament, which was poorly regarded in most quarters because of its unstable major third. Progressing from chord to chord in 1/4-comma meantone temperament is the

Musical Example 5.3. I–IV–V–I progression in B♭ Major.

Musical Example 5.4. i–iv–V–I progression in G Minor.

aural equivalent of moving from one bright color to another rather than from one shade of gray to another. You can hear this for yourself in audio files 5.4 and 5.5, which are the I–IV–V–I progression in B♭ Major (musical example 5.3) and the i–iv–V–I progression in G Minor in 1/4-comma meantone temperament (musical example 5.4).

ATTENUATED MEANTONE TEMPERAMENTS

As indicated above, musicians and theorists quickly spun off several varieties of meantone temperament with divisions of the comma other than 1/4. Some, such as Zarlino's 2/7-comma meantone temperament introduced in 1558 with its pure 25:24 chromatic semitone, were intended as theoretical exercises, while others, such as the 1/3-comma meantone described by Salinas in 1577 with its pure 6:5 minor thirds and narrower than pure major thirds, are of limited use.[13] Although one can construct a variety of meantone temperaments, for our purposes, we will focus on 1/5-, 1/6-, and 1/8-comma meantone temperaments with a G♯–E♭ wolf. 1/5-comma meantone divides the comma into five slices, each a little narrower than each of the four slices in 1/4-comma meantone; 1/6-comma divides it into six even narrower slices, and so on. Table 5.1 lists the sizes of the perfect fifth, wolf, major thirds, semitones, and harmonic diesis for these temperaments along with 1/4-comma meantone temperament for comparison.

From table 5.1 a number of patterns emerge, which by now, you will realize are quite predictable. As the number of comma divisions increases, the amount that each fifth is narrowed is reduced, leading to increasingly wider fifths, wider good major thirds, and wider chromatic semitones. On the other hand, the size of the wolf is progressively reduced, as are the bad major thirds, the diatonic semitone, and the harmonic diesis. You can see that it's a trade-off. As we progress from 1/4 comma to 1/8 comma, the reduction in the purity of the major third is balanced by a perfect fifth that is closer to pure and bad major thirds that are progressively less wretched. As the difference between the diatonic and chromatic semitones as measured by the size of the harmonic diesis decreases, the color differentiation between tonalities diminishes, but in exchange we gain

Table 5.1.
Size of perfect fifth, wolf fifth, major thirds, semitones, and harmonic diesis in 1/4-, 1/5-, 1/6-, and 1/8-comma meantone temperaments, in cents

Interval	1/4 comma	1/5 comma	1/6 comma	1/8 comma
Perfect fifth	696.5	697.4	698.4	699.25
Wolf fifth	738.5	726.4	717.6	708.25
Good major third	386	390.4	393.6	397
Bad major third	428	419.2	412.8	406
Diatonic semitone	117.5	112	108	103.75
Chromatic semitone	75.5	83.2	88.8	94.75
Harmonic diesis	42	28.8	19.2	9

much greater flexibility in terms of extending the temperament beyond the wolf, because, as you recall, the size of harmonic diesis translates into the physical distance between *mi* and *fa* fret locations; smaller distances allow us to slant our frets more effectively to achieve a wider selection of enharmonic locations, and finger adjustments are increasingly easier and more effective. Diagram 3.2, the fretboard patterns for 1/4-, 1/5-, 1/6-, and 1/8-comma meantone temperaments and equal temperament for comparison, shows this quite clearly. Alternate fret locations are indicated by dashed lines: the *mi* position for the 1st fret and the *fa* position for the 4th fret to illustrate how the harmonic diesis narrows as the frets progress toward the 12th fret and how it narrows as the comma division increases. There can, of course, be alternate locations for any fret. From diagram 3.2 you can also see how fretted instruments have a tremendous advantage over any other class of instrument for the purposes of understanding how one temperament relates to another because you can actually also see how the size of the diatonic and chromatic semitones change according to temperament.

Ultimately, it all comes down to priorities, which are often dictated by the circumstances at hand. In broad strokes, the comma divisions that involve fewer large slices offer better-sounding thirds and more color contrast, whereas the divisions with a larger number of smaller slices offer greater flexibility in a variety of key areas. It also depends on how and what you hear. To your ears, 1/4 comma's pure third may sound so good that you are not bothered by the narrow fifth. But if you are, then you might find 1/5 comma more to your liking. And so on. The following audio files present the cadential progressions in musical examples 5.3 and 5.4 in 1/5-comma meantone temperament (audio files 5.6 and 5.7), 1/6-comma meantone temperament (audio files 5.8 and 5.9), and 1/8-comma meantone temperament (audio files 5.10 and 5.11).

1/5-comma meantone temperament features a pure 16:15 diatonic semitone and concomitant pure 15:8 major seventh. Its cents chart reveals that the major third is only slightly wider than Just, and the perfect fifth is slightly closer to pure than in 1/4 comma:

C	C♯	D	E♭	E	F	F♯	G	G♯	A	B♭	B	C
	83.2	195.2	307.2	390.4	502.4	585.6	697.6	780.8	892.8	1004.8	1088	1200

1/5 comma and its irregular derivatives were favored in France, and, indeed, it works quite well for French music. It retains the clearly etched key colors that characterize 1/4 comma with somewhat greater key flexibility. At the end of this chapter, we examine a method engineered to gauge the relative dissonance levels of each temperament to help us determine what works best given our performance parameters.

1/6-comma meantone is my default temperament and that of a great many early music specialists. It is a practical compromise between 1/4-comma meantone and equal temperament:

C	C♯	D	E♭	E	F	F♯	G	G♯	A	B♭	B	C
	88.8	196.8	304.8	393.6	501.6	590.4	698.4	787.2	895.2	1003.2	1092	1200

Its major thirds, while not quite pure, are noticeably sweeter than equal-tempered thirds; in fact, they are close to halfway between pure and ET thirds. The perfect fifth, considerably closer to pure, beats rather slowly. As Ross Duffin has pointed out, it sports a pure tritone, that is, a pure 45:32 augmented fourth and 65:45 diminished fifth, but more importantly, 1/6-comma meantone temperament strikes a practical balance between vertical harmonic and horizontal melodic concerns particularly in more complicated music of the sort that lutenists often perform.[14] As you have seen, there is bountiful historical evidence that fretted instrument players, particularly of the plucked variety, preferred 1/6 comma or something close to it. Referring to Bruce Haynes's discussion of 1/6-comma meantone temperament in his seminal article "Beyond Temperament: Non-Keyboard Intonation in the 17th and 18th Centuries," Ross Duffin comments:

> Already widely known as Silbermann's temperament (after the organ builder and friend of J. S. Bach), it corresponds to ideals for temperaments given by Telemann, Tosi, Quantz, and Geminiani, among others, and is described by the French theorist Sauveur (1707) as the temperament of "ordinary musicians." The historical evidence presented by Haynes speaks for itself, and is a stunning endorsement. What better temperament to use as a standard for Baroque music than one employed by everyday musicians at the time?[15]

In exchange for the wider-than-pure thirds, 1/6-comma meantone is usable in more keys than 1/4-comma or 1/5-comma meantone. Furthermore, as you can see from diagram 5.12, the distance between *mi* and *fa* fret positions is small

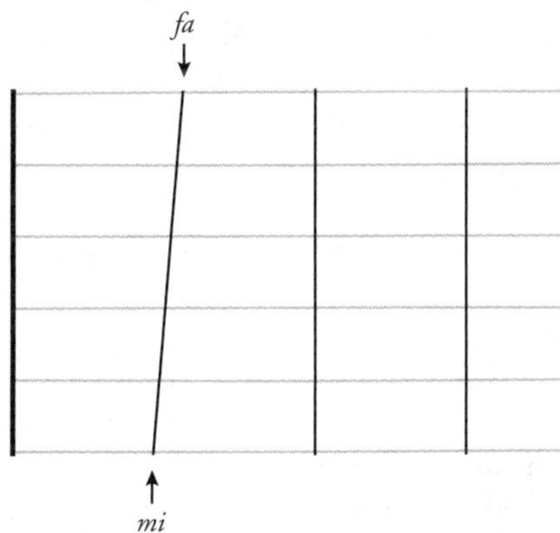

Diagram 5.12. Slanted 1st fret.

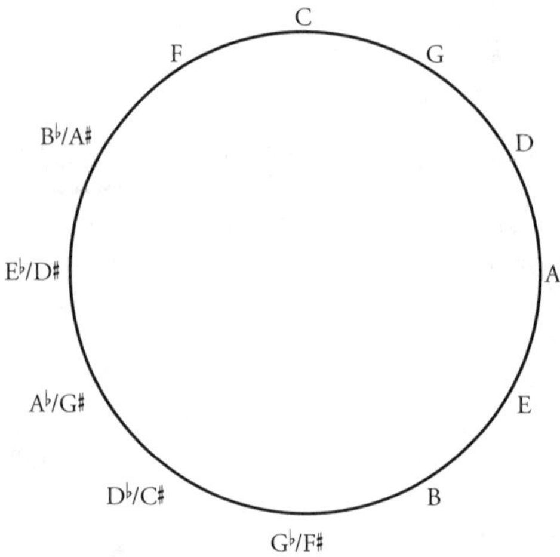

Diagram 5.13. Extended meantone temperament Circle of Fifths.

enough to allow a fret to be slanted enough to execute a *fa* on the higher courses and a *mi* on a lower course simultaneously, even on theorbo, a topic that we will take up more thoroughly in subsequent chapters.

Coupled with the use of tastini, the ability to slant frets more easily and fully in 1/6-comma meantone compared with 1/4- and 1/5-comma meantone significantly extends the enharmonic choices beyond the notes in the Circle of Fifths demarcated by a particular wolf. This capability permits us to have our cake and eat it, too. For instance, we can encompass the enharmonic opposites of the notes that describe the wolf. In other words, we can access both A♭ and G♯, as well as E♭ and D♯, and so on. Whereas normally the wolf functions as a border between sharp and flat notes, extended 1/6-comma meantone dissolves that border, allowing the sharps to continue through from G♯ to D♯ to A♯ clockwise and the flats from A♭ to D♭ to G♭ counterclockwise, and so on. See diagram 5.13. The extended Circle of Fifths, which, of course, is not limited to 1/6-comma meantone, can theoretically extend even beyond these limits. This ability will be discussed further in later chapters.

In chapter 2, we saw that fixed fret instruments with utilitarian fretting arrangements exhibit some intervals approximating 1/8-syntonic-comma meantone temperament. As you can see from its cents chart and diagram 3.2, 1/8-comma meantone is quite close to equal temperament, but nevertheless manages to shade the major third enough to make it an excellent alternative to equal temperament in situations that demand service in a wide variety of keys:

C	C♯	D	E♭	E	F	F♯	G	G♯	A	B♭	B	C
	94.75	198.5	302.25	397	500.75	595.5	699.25	794	897.75	1001.5	1096.25	1200

The diatonic and chromatic semitones differ enough to lend the temperament a wider palette of tonal color than equal temperament, and the small harmonic diesis of 9c. makes slanting the frets very effective, allowing an extensive selection of keys, and left-hand finger shading of pitch is quite easily accomplished on the viol. I have found that 1/8 comma also works quite well for much of the baroque lute repertoire. The thorny problem of temperament on the baroque lute is discussed in greater depth in chapter 7.

MULTIPART DIVISIONS

Various attempts have been made to divide the octave into equal parts in an attempt to optimize the ability to form pure intervals; theoretically, the greater number of divisions, the more precisely the size of the intervals able to be formed. Several of the better-known multipart divisions come close enough to meantone temperaments to be often thought of as equivalents:[16]

1/3c. = 19-part division (3-part whole tone)

1/4c. = 31-part division (5-part whole tone)

1/5c. = 43-part division (7-part whole tone)

1/6c. = 55-part division (9-part whole tone)

Knowledge of this approach is also useful because it helps to explain how theorists and musicians thought of the division of the whole tone into two unequal sections resulting in diatonic and chromatic semitones of differing widths. Note that each division features a whole tone composed of an odd number of parts. In the nineteen-part division, for instance, the diatonic semitone is two parts, and the chromatic semitone one. Together they make up the whole tone of three parts. So in the nineteen-part division, since there are five whole steps and two diatonic semitones within the span of an octave, the whole steps account for fifteen parts (5 × 3 parts) and the diatonic semitones account for four parts (2 × 2 parts), totaling to nineteen. In the thirty-one-part division, the diatonic semitone is three parts, and the chromatic two parts, and so on. As we have seen, one of the problems theorists had with equal temperament was that they did not believe that the whole tone could be divided into equal parts because an equal division of the whole tone, which was thought to be constructed from an odd number of parts, would require a fraction of a comma (1.5, 2.5, 3.5, or 4.5 parts for the examples above), divisions thought to be irrational. Diagram 5.14 illustrates several different scales with octaves divided into multiple parts along with Pythagorean tuning and equal temperament for comparison.[17]

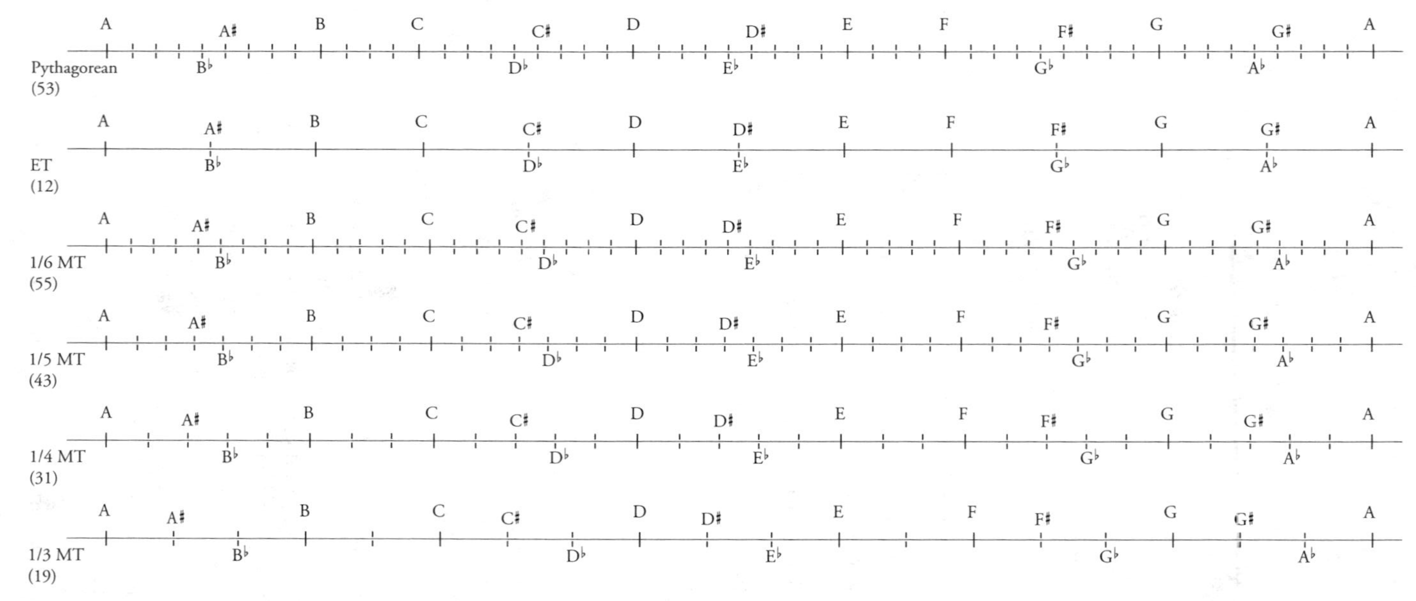

Diagram 5.14. Multipart divisions of the octave in various tuning systems. Courtesy of Richard Carter.

Irregular Temperaments

Although, as we have seen in chapter 2, fretted instrument players arranged their frets in their own unique style of utilitarian irregular temperaments a good century prior to the introduction of irregular temperaments in 1681 by Andreas Werckmeister (1645–1706), irregular temperaments are generally considered to be keyboard temperaments. This is because they were designed with the keyboard in mind and work particularly well on them since once the temperament is set on a keyboard, for the most part, the keyboard player need only be concerned with playing the notes as written. They feature fifths of various dimensions resulting in up to six sizes of semitone and the intervals that are assembled from them, particularly major thirds, which poses no difficulty for solo keyboard music. Irregular temperaments are, however, much more challenging for flexibly pitched instruments such as violins because players must keep track of which intervals are which size and fretted instruments because of the limitations the frets place on the availability of certain notes at each fret. Additionally, irregular keyboard temperaments firmly establish the enharmonic identity of the temperament's pitches, that is, it is D♯ or E♭, and whatever it is, it must serve for the one that it is not, which is not always a bad thing because the pitch is often placed in a compromise position only slightly favoring one enharmonic or the other. These temperaments concern us because we must know how to handle them on those occasions when we are called on to play with keyboard instruments set in such a fashion.

Irregular keyboard temperaments eliminate the wolf in order to render each key serviceable, although to varying degrees. Because the wolf is no longer available to serve as the catchall repository to absorb the excess of the Pythagorean comma and the portions of the syntonic comma meantone temperaments shave off the other fifths, irregular keyboard temperaments must be mathematically precise, and, for this reason, they appealed to music theorists who used the creation of speculative but impractical irregular temperaments as vehicles to display their intellectual prowess, and who also created temperaments to serve the needs of practicing musicians as well.[18] The practical ramification of the elimination of the wolf is that since the Pythagorean comma must be somehow distributed throughout the Circle of Fifths rather than dumped into the wolf, irregular temperaments often reduced the size of several fifths by fractions of the Pythagorean rather than the syntonic comma and set the remaining fifths to pure. Some irregular temperaments also reduced some fifths by 2c., rendering them ET fifths, and some, such as the so-called *tempérament ordinaire* favored in France, even set some fifths wider than pure.[19]

Since irregular keyboard temperaments are functional in every key, they are considered circulating or well-tempered systems. While they confine the best keys to a narrowly focused range, the rest of the keys are considered to be tolerable, whereas in nonextended meantone temperaments, there are keys that are simply unusable. Irregular temperaments were popular in the Baroque era in part because they give each key a distinctly individual tone color as described by such writers as Rousseau, Heinichen, Mattheson, Kirnberger, and others. In general, key areas toward the top of the Circle of Fifths are somewhat tranquil, while those toward the bottom can be quite jarring.

Flexibly pitched instruments and fretted instruments must have found a way to accommodate themselves to the keyboard's penchant for irregular temperaments. Since each fret must serve all the courses that run above it, the precise rendering of irregular keyboard temperaments is difficult on instruments with movable frets without going to absurdly extreme lengths such as multiple tastini for several frets. This might be justified if you have an archlute or theorbo that you can reserve for a specific project, that is, a recording or opera, but for day-to-day performing activities, going to such extraordinary lengths is impractical because changing to or from an irregular keyboard temperament is prohibitively time-consuming on fretted instruments, as we will see when we examine Vallotti's temperament, perhaps the most popular and yet misunderstood of all irregular keyboard temperaments.

Nevertheless, with an understanding of the temperament's basic structure, a fretted instrument player can arrive at a tolerable approximation of an irregular keyboard temperament through a combination of slanted frets, tastini, compromise positions, selective chord shapes, and pushing and pulling, a topic that will be expanded on in later chapters. This is possible because most common irregular keyboard temperaments are derivatives of 1/4-comma, 1/5-comma, and 1/6-comma meantone temperaments combined with pure and occasionally ET and wider than pure fifths. If you know what type of fifth anchors the "spine" or "backbone" of the temperament, you can set your frets to that temperament and be confident that you will be in the neighborhood of the keyboard's temperament at least for the "good" keys, which are those that are going to be used most frequently. This solution is not perfect, but it is practical.

The two best-known systems to feature a 1/4-comma backbone are Werckmeister III (1681 and 1691) and Kirnberger III (1770s). Werckmeister III features four 1/4-Pythagorean-comma fifths, while the rest are pure. Since so many organs were tuned in 1/4-syntonic-comma meantone, to simplify the transition to the new temperament, Werckmeister subsequently adjusted his temperament so that the fifths were reduced by the syntonic instead of the Pythagorean comma, and the extra 2c. were subtracted from one of those fifths.[20] The temperament by Johann Philipp Kirnberger (1721–1783) is quite similar to Werckmeister's modified temperament. Its three fifths of various dimensions result in six sizes of major third, ranging from one pure third of 386c. to two at 408c. The variety of sizes of major third does not cause keyboard players much pause, but it presents significant difficulties for other players trying to match their pitches. The other problem, as you can see, is that there are two major chords with wide

Pythagorean major thirds. While the key that includes these two chords is considered usable, to my ears it is not, except perhaps for dramatic effect.

Based on a 1/5-Pythagorean-comma spine, *tempérament ordinaire* is the term used to refer to a class of irregular keyboard temperaments commonly preferred by eighteenth-century French musicians. In addition to six fifths, each narrowed by one fifth of the Pythagorean comma, three are pure, and two are wider than pure by 2.4c. These are the temperament's general structural details; however, versions of it differ depending on exactly where in the Circle of Fifths each fifth is placed. Usually, the backbone centers toward the top of the Circle of Fifths but can migrate more toward the flat or sharp side. The same holds true for the multiple versions of irregular keyboard temperaments based on 1/4- and 1/6-comma spines. Because *tempérament ordinaire* includes two fifths wider than pure, in addition to its two Pythagorean major thirds, it also has two major thirds even wider than Pythagorean, which calls into question whether *tempérament ordinaire* is truly a circulating class of temperaments. I suggest not. Nevertheless, *tempérament ordinaire* is colorful and does seem quite well suited to eighteenth-century French repertoire as Rameau indicated in his praise of his countrymen's general tuning preference.

In 1724 Johann Georg Neidhardt (ca. 1685–1739) introduced his Circulating Temperament No. 1 in which one fourth of the Pythagorean comma is trimmed from four fifths, four others are ET fifths, and the remaining four are pure. This results in a relatively narrow range of major thirds of 392c. to 404c., although only one third, predictably C–E, is 392c. Eight major thirds are 400c. or greater.[21] Accordingly, it is more truly circulating than the 1/4- and 1/5-comma derivatives.

As in the meantone temperament on which they are based, irregular keyboard temperaments with a 1/6-comma backbone retain a number of major thirds close enough to pure to represent a significant improvement over equal temperament while still permitting a wider range of serviceable keys without losing a key area to the wolf. Today's most popular 1/6-comma-based irregular keyboard temperament was designed by Francesco Antonio Vallotti (1697–1780). Although Vallotti claimed to have devised it in 1728, and it was referred to in 1754 by the violinist Giuseppe Tartini (1692–1770), who worked with Vallotti in Padua, it was not actually published until 1950.[22] His temperament narrows a series of six perfect fifths starting on F by 1/6-Pythagorean comma, with the remaining fifths tuned pure.

Vallotti is often uttered in the same breath as *Young,* as in Vallotti/Young, as if they are the same temperament. They're not. One of the temperaments Thomas Young (1773–1829) devised in 1800, his No. 2, is similar to Vallotti's with the difference that it tempers a series of six fifths by 1/6-Pythagorean comma starting on C rather than F with rest of the fifths pure. Although some consider Young to be a transposition of Vallotti, Young seems to have been totally unaware of Vallotti's temperament, which calls into question whether Vallotti's temperament ever achieved any widespread use beyond the confines of Padua.[23] If not, it is rather ironic that a temperament that is now so commonly used for Baroque music was not even published until the twentieth century and may not have been more than a local temperament. Regardless, given its current widespread use and the fact that many fretted instrument players are under the misconception that they are tuning in Vallotti when they're not, we should linger here to examine it in greater detail. It will also serve as a good example of how irregular keyboard temperaments work in general.

Vallotti's Circle of Fifths (diagram 5.15) shows that the best-sounding keys reside in the environs of C Major with the worse-sounding keys centered around F♯. Its cent chart is as follows:

C	C♯	D	E♭	E	F	F♯	G	G♯	A	B♭	B	C
	94	196	298	392	502	592	698	796	894	1000	1090	1200

Let's see how the two sizes of the fifth cause a variety of sizes of major third. Four fifths of 698c. (F–C–G–D–A) result in a relatively stable F–A major third of 392c. (698c. × 4 = 2792c. – 2400c.). We arrive at the same result for C–E and G–B because they too are composed exclusively of 698c. fifths, but when we introduce a 702c. fifth into the equation to create the D–F♯ major third, things begin to change. Three fifths of 698c. plus one fifth of 702c. (D–A–E–B–F♯) result in a major third of 396c. (698c. × 3 = 2094c. + 702c. = 2796c. – 2400c.). The introduction of another pure fifth into the series (A–E–B–F♯–C♯) yields an ET major third of 400c. for A–C♯ (698c. × 2 = 1396c. + 1404c. [702c. × 2] =

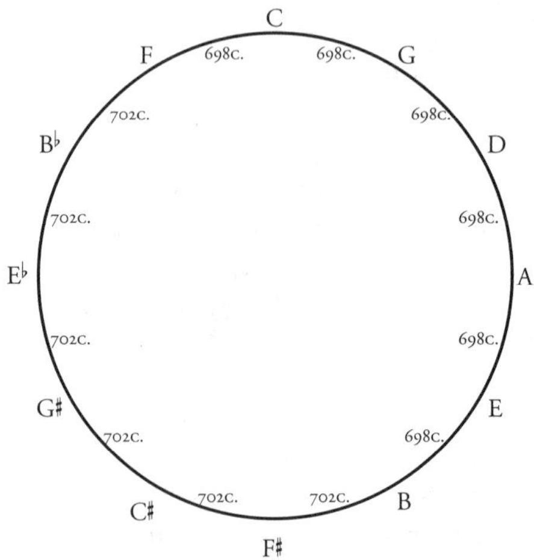

Diagram 5.15. Vallotti temperament Circle of Fifths.

2800c. – 2400c.). From here on, things get progressively worse until we are saddled with three Pythagorean thirds of 408c., which, as you know, is the major third that results from a series of four pure fifths. The ultimate result is a temperament with five sizes of major third (392, 396, 400, 404, and 408 cents), with seven major thirds of 400c. or greater and six sizes of semitone (90, 94, 98, 102, 106, and 110 cents). Again, to my ears, the major chords with 408c. major thirds (B, F♯, and C♯) are unusable despite their pure fifth. You can see what you think by listening to Vallotti's B Major chord in audio file 5.12. The two with 404c. major thirds (E and G♯) are so sour (audio file 5.13 presents the resultant E Major chord) that I question whether Vallotti can truly function as a circulating temperament.[24] I agree wholeheartedly with Ross Duffin's opinion that extended 1/6-comma meantone sounds better, is more flexible, and is more historically accurate than Vallotti.[25]

On a number of occasions I have had the opportunity to perform with superb fretted instrument players who thought they were tuned in Vallotti when they clearly were not. Making such a determination with regard to fretted instruments is quite simple even without hearing a note because irregular keyboard temperaments are impossible to realize on fretted instruments without multiple tastini or a prodigious ability to push and pull notes in tune, which seems to largely be a lost art on lutes and somewhat of a specialized one on viols. In other words, in the absence of extensive pushing and pulling, a fretboard pattern of perpendicular frets without multiple tastini cannot produce irregular keyboard temperaments, although, as mentioned above, by choosing a related meantone temperament, we can get within the ballpark. Diagram 5.16 shows what a fretboard would have to look like to produce Vallotti on an instrument in G, with the standard caveat that these are theoretical fret positions. Note that this pattern is unique to an instrument tuned in G; the pattern required to produce Vallotti on an instrument tuned in A, for instance, would look totally different. This is because in Vallotti, the enharmonic identity of the pitches is specified, and the sizes of the intervals are nonuniform. For example, in an instrument tuned in G, it turns out that all the whole tones between the open string and 2nd fret are 196c. At the 2nd fret on an instrument tuned in A, 4/6

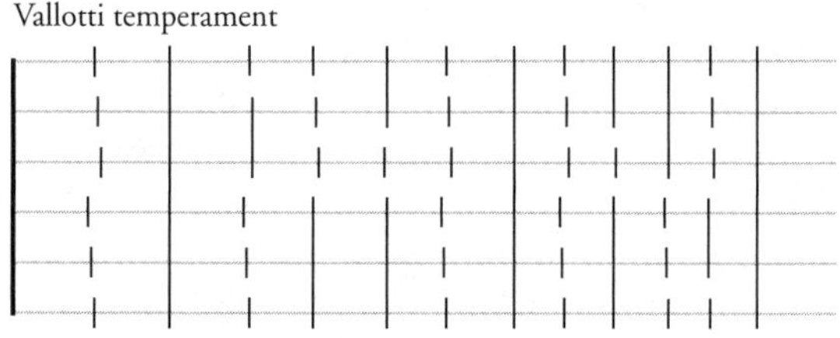

Diagram 5.16. Vallotti temperament fretboard pattern.

courses would be 196c. as all of them are in G, but the E course would require 200c. for the E–F♯, and the B course would require 204c. for the B–C♯. I would imagine that by now, 1/6-comma meantone temperament is starting to look pretty good to you.

Equal Temperament

Throughout most of music history equal temperament was regarded as either a theoretical impossibility or, at best, a temperament of last resort, often reserved for those who valued pragmatism over quality. Although it did not assume its current and largely uncontested status as the one and only temperament for common use until the nineteenth century, its long and controversial history began with its association with Aristotle's pupil, the peripatetic Greek philosopher Aristoxenus (fl. 335 BC). Aristoxenus rejected the Pythagorean conception of musical intervals as flowing from simple numerical proportions, arguing that the quality of intervals should be judged by the senses rather than the intellect. Aristoxenus's stance was regularly challenged by theorists and musicians who correctly recognized that his favoring the ear over the mind seemed to be selective with regard to the major third. As we saw in chapter 1, equal temperament has come to be associated with fretted instruments largely owing to its popularity with amateurs who did not have the discrimination or skills to set or use their frets in the meantone temperaments that prevailed on keyboards and other instruments. We saw how Vincenzo Galilei's publication of a simple and easy method to set frets in equal temperament probably cemented the perception that equal temperament and fretted instruments were inextricably linked.

While Pythagorean tuning and meantone temperaments withdraw the excess 24c. of the Pythagorean comma from only one fifth, the wolf, equal temperament eliminates the wolf and distributes the 24c. throughout the system, but in a much more ecumenical fashion than do irregular temperaments. It does so by tempering each of the twelve fifths by 2c., thereby replacing pure fifths of 702c. with equal-tempered fifths of 700c. See diagram 5.17. The "equal" in equal temperament comes from the fact that all the fifths are tempered by the same amount. Now that the fifths are 700c. rather than 702c., twelve successive fifths do add up to 8400c. (700c. × 12) just as seven successive octaves do (1200c. × 7); rather than overshooting the original C by 24c. twelve pure fifths later, twelve ET fifths return to the exact same starting pitch, adjusted for the correct octave of course. See diagram 5.18.

Aurally, the difference between 702c. and 700c. is minimal, only .3 percent. This adjustment, of course, adds 2c. to every fourth so that it is 500c. rather than a pure 498c. Again, while still relatively insignificant aurally, it is slightly greater at .4 percent. What is significant is that the size of every major third is 400c., every semitone is 100c., and every key sounds alike, and for these reasons, equal temperament was rejected as a viable alternative to unequal temperaments throughout most of the past thousand years. We derive the major

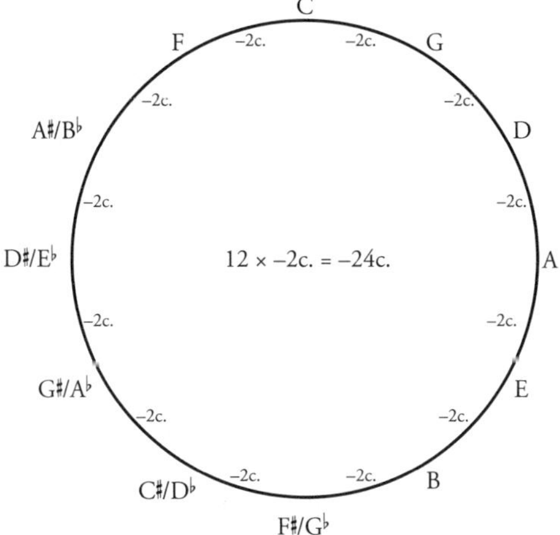

Diagram 5.17. Adjustment of fifths in equal temperament Circle of Fifths.

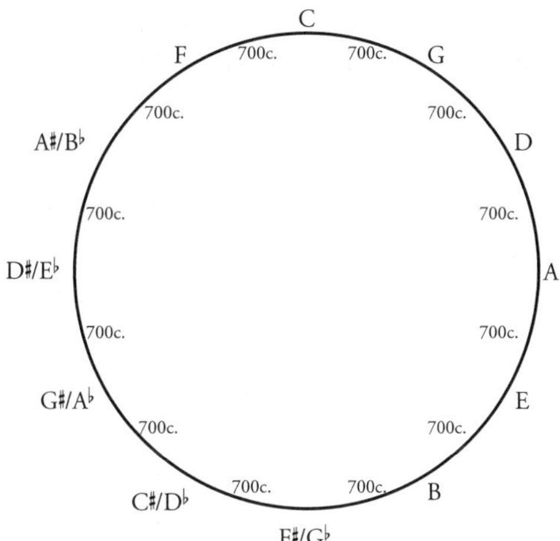

Diagram 5.18. Equal temperament Circle of Fifths.

third of 400c. in the usual fashion by subtracting 2400c. from a series of four fifths (700c. × 4 = 2800c. – 2400c.). While not as strident as a Pythagorean third of 408c., an ET major third is still wide enough to sound rather harsh compared with the various meantone major thirds described above, particularly in music dominated by thirds.

From the cents chart below, you can see that all the semitones are 100c.:

C	C♯/D♭	D	D♯/E♭	E	F	F♯/G♭	G	G♯/A♭	A	A♯/B♭	B	C
	100	200	300	400	500	600	700	800	900	1000	1100	1200

but more important, there are no enharmonic colors. While we are accustomed to considering both the sharp and flat enharmonic versions of the notes between natural notes to be equivalent, that is, D♯ = E♭, we should keep in mind that equal temperament is the only Western tuning system where this is the case. Although equal temperament is equal in the sense that it narrows each fifth by the same amount and makes diatonic and chromatic semitones the same size, as we have seen, it is anything but equal in its impact on the relative purity of every interval except the octave, as you can see by reviewing table 4.1. While a well-tuned equal temperament will get you into the ballpark, only occasionally will it get you into the right section, the fourths and fifths, for example. It will virtually never get you to the right seat. In the case of the thirds and sixths, you must contend with an obstructed view.

After having studied the temperaments that prevailed prior to equal temperament's current popularity, you can see that equal temperament is really quite simple, perhaps even elegant in its symmetry. On paper, that is. But, to give equal temperament its due, because it works as well in one key as another, as Vincenzo Galilei pointed out and guitarists reveled in, it does have the advantage of allowing easier transpositions to more remote keys. And equal temperament is less complicated—not much thinking required to set or use. In a word, it is convenient.

The heart of the matter is that any tuning system is only an arbitrary, man-made configuration designed to compensate for the fact that it is impossible to create a tuning system in which all the intervals are pure. Something must always give. Our challenge is to arrange the intervals so that they best suit our needs by redistributing the Pythagorean comma throughout the Circle of Fifths so that twelve successive fifths arrive at the same pitch as do seven successive octaves. In the end, it is up to each of us to decide our preferred balance between pragmatism and beauty. Dissonance factors can help you weigh your options.

Dissonance Factors

Dissonance factors measure the number of cents from which an interval, chord, or key diverges from pure. For instance, the dissonance factor of an ET major third is 14 since it is 14c. wider than a pure major third; an ET perfect fifth yields 2 since it is 2c. narrower than a pure perfect fifth. When dissonance factors are applied to chords, they add together the dissonance factors for the perfect fifth and the major third, irrespective of whether the values are positive or negative.

Since every major and minor chord consists of a perfect fifth and a major and minor third, albeit in a different order, every ET major or minor chord has a dissonance factor of 16, whereas a 1/4-comma meantone C Major chord has a dissonance factor of 5.5 because the pure major third yields a dissonance factor of 0, while the perfect fifth generates a dissonance factor of 5.5 since it is 5.5c. narrower than pure. Key dissonance factors simply add together the figures of the I, IV, and V or i, iv, and V chords in minor keys. The higher the dissonance factor, the worse the key sounds, or with the glass half full, the lower the dissonance factor, the better the key sounds.

A table such as table 5.2, which compares the key dissonance factors of several of the temperaments we've discussed in this chapter, can illustrate which keys are most consonant (that is, least dissonant) in a particular temperament, and it can also allow you to compare how any chosen key might sound in any temperament.[26] It also confirms a number of observations made throughout this chapter, such as the fact that the closer you get to the wolf, the more out of tune the keys become.

Table 5.2.
Key dissonance factors, in cents

	PT	1/4	1/5	1/6	1/8	ET	Vallotti
C	66	16.5	26.4	33.6	41.25	48	30
G	66	16.5	26.4	33.6	41.25	48	34
D	66	16.5	26.4	33.6	41.25	48	42
A	66	16.5	26.4	33.6	41.25	48	54
E	52	58.5	55.2	52.8	50.25	48	62
B	32	100.5	84.0	72.0	59.25	48	66
F♯	12	142.5	112.8	91.2	68.25	48	66
C♯	28	173.5	132.8	103.2	71.75	48	62
G♯	48	131.5	104.0	84.0	62.75	48	54
E♭	68	89.5	75.2	64.8	53.75	48	42
B♭	66	16.5	26.4	33.6	41.25	48	34
F	66	16.5	26.4	33.6	41.25	48	30
Major key range	56	157.0	106.4	69.6	30.50	0	36
Am	66	16.5	26.4	33.6	41.25	48	42
Em	52	58.5	55.2	52.8	50.25	48	42
Bm	52	58.5	55.2	52.8	50.25	48	42
F♯m	52	58.5	55.2	52.8	50.25	48	46
C♯m	68	89.5	75.2	64.8	53.75	48	50
G♯m	68	89.5	75.2	64.8	53.75	48	54
E♭m	48	131.5	104.0	84.0	62.75	48	54
B♭m	32	100.5	84.0	72.0	59.25	48	54
Fm	32	100.5	84.0	72.0	59.25	48	50
Cm	52	58.5	55.2	52.8	50.25	48	42
Gm	66	16.5	26.4	33.6	41.25	48	38
Dm	66	16.5	26.4	33.6	41.25	48	38
Minor key range	36	115.0	77.6	50.4	21.50	0	16

As you might well imagine, dissonance factors can be used in a variety of fashions depending on what you want to compare. Allocating dissonance factors to the major third and excluding the minor third may seem somewhat arbitrary, but sour major thirds tend to be more offensive than discordant minor thirds, and therefore major thirds take precedence over minor thirds. Moreover, from the fifteenth century on, the raison d'être of temperaments has been primarily to sweeten the major rather than minor thirds. Nonetheless, one could also create a version of the table that adds the dissonance of the minor third to the equation, in which case an ET triad would yield a value of 32 rather than 16 and a key dissonance factor of 96. Of course, if you want to compare major and minor tonalities, the formula applied to each must be the same, and one could also create a dissonance factor table that registers only minor thirds and perfect fifths, and so on. You now have the skills to create whichever version of the table you find most useful.[27]

While dissonance factors are a good place to begin, in determining the suitability of one key over another, they must be considered in concert with other factors since they measure only the component harmonies in a particular key area. And, of course, much of the music we play does not necessarily align itself conveniently into keys. Dissonance factors simply compile harmonies independent of how they interact with each other. For instance, in nonextended meantone temperaments with a G♯–E♭ wolf and Vallotti, in the key of G♯, the D♯ chord is really an E♭ chord, but dissonance factors do not account for the fact that the distance between the roots of each chord, G♯ and E♭, are usually quite far removed from pure, as can be seen in table 5.1. Similarly, in the key of E♭ with a G♯–E♭ wolf, the A♭ chord is really a G♯ chord.

Remember that here we are focusing on simultaneities, and thus dissonance factors do not measure the relative melodic smoothness from semitone to semitone, something the harmonic diesis is better equipped to handle. For instance, because the harmonic diesis is narrower in 1/6- than in 1/4-comma meantone temperament, melodies tend to be smoother in the former than in the latter temperament—another factor that generally recommends 1/6-comma meantone temperament. Also, keep in mind that irregular keyboard temperaments such as Vallotti can have as many as six sizes of semitone. Finally, remember that the table measures nonextended versions of Pythagorean tuning and meantone temperaments; extended versions of these tuning systems, which are generally quite easily accomplished on fretted instruments, can extend the good keys quite well beyond the limits of the wolf. For instance, in extended 1/6- and 1/8-comma meantone temperament with a G♯–E♭ wolf, with a combination of slanted frets and tastini, the key areas of E, B, and E♭ are quite accessible, rendering them with the same key dissonance factors as C Major. With some trickery, A♭ and F♯ can also be made available—more on this in later chapters.

Now, with the caveats aside, let's examine just a few of the many generalities that can be drawn from table 5.2:

- The progression of good to bad keys in Pythagorean tuning is the opposite of meantone temperaments. In other words, as noted above, the key areas actually improve as they approach the wolf, whereas in meantone temperaments they deteriorate as they approach the wolf.
- As meantone temperaments progress from 1/4- to 1/8-comma meantone, the dissonance factor range narrows indicating that the differences among keys are increasingly reduced. The good keys become less consonant while the bad keys become more consonant.
- The dissonance factor range among the minor key areas is significantly narrower than its major counterpart in every tuning system, but there are many fewer good-sounding keys due to the major dominant chord, which is four perfect fifths away from the minor key's relative major key. For example, A Minor's dominant chord, E Major, is four fifths removed from A Minor's relative major, C Major. The ramifications of this become quite evident in E Minor and then even more so in C♯ Minor where the dominant major chords approach the wolf much more quickly than would a dominant minor chord.
- Vallotti's appeal for keyboard temperaments is immediately evident. Without a wolf, it has the narrowest range of dissonance factors of any of the other tuning systems in the table, and half the key areas represent a notable improvement over equal temperament while retaining plenty of key variety. Table 5.2 also illustrates how Vallotti focuses the good key areas in a more narrowly circumscribed region than do meantone temperaments. For keyboard instruments that do not have the ability to extend meantone temperaments, Vallotti and Young and their transpositions provide colorful options for solo repertoire, whereas for instruments such as ours that can extend meantone temperaments, 1/6-comma or one of the other meantone temperaments is a better choice.
- Equal temperament's relentless sameness compared with the table's other tuning systems is manifest.

Table 5.2 can help you determine which temperament works best for you as a default or given the key areas you are likely to encounter at your next performance. You can immediately see that in terms of overall vertical dissonance, the benefits of temperaments such as 1/4-comma meantone easily trump equal temperament and the more attenuated meantone variants as long as the key areas stay within the range of B♭ to A Major along the Circle of Fifths. To the left of B♭ and right of A Major, the benefits of 1/4-comma meantone begin to decline rapidly. And, by now, you know that where this decline begins to occur depends on where you chose to place the wolf in the regular temperaments.

Through experimentation, you can find your own tolerance limits. Mine, for instance, are very simple. As a denizen of the twentieth and twenty-first centuries, I find anything worse than equal temperament's 48 intolerable. From there, I try to work my way from 1/8-comma to 1/4-comma meantone temperament. Most of the time, I can extend 1/6-comma enough to make it a significant improvement over equal temperament, and occasionally I am even able to take advantage of 1/4-comma meantone temperament when the repertoire is key restricted enough, particularly in an ensemble setting. There are times and repertoires though, where I must revert to 1/8-comma meantone and occasionally even equal temperament. For day-to-day use, I think that 1/6-comma meantone temperament provides the best balance between beauty and pragmatism.

PART TWO CONCLUSION

By now you have seen many examples that demonstrate how tuning systems are essentially compromises designed to make the best of the fact that it is impossible to generate a twelve-note scale that fits within an octave in which all intervals are pure. Tuning systems are, in broad strokes, negotiated solutions balancing serviceability in a variety of keys with heightened beauty in fewer key areas. Such decisions involve determining which areas are to be favored at the expense of others, but also which intervals are to be preferred over others, for instance, Pythagorean tuning's choice of rendering the perfect fourths and fifths pure at the expense of the major thirds versus 1/4-comma meantone temperament's selection of the opposite solution of narrowing the perfect fifths and widening the perfect fourths to gain a pure major third.

You are now well familiar with the natural acoustical discrepancies that make tuning systems necessary and compel us to choose one over another, but more important, you now know that you have many options available to you. Armed with an understanding of how tuning systems are constructed, you can weigh those options, considering their advantages and disadvantages relative to your current needs. And you have seen how tuning systems can be classified according to how they generally rearrange the sizes of their intervals to meet their goals, including irregular keyboard temperaments to which we occasionally must accommodate ourselves. You are now equipped to make your own decisions about tuning systems rather than having to rely on recent tradition or the well intentioned, but often misguided, advice about tuning systems that still prevails in many quarters. Having checked and rechecked the math yourself, you can discuss this subject with the confidence that your opinions are backed up with facts rather than myths.

But as we learned in part 1, myths die hard. The only way to be certain that meantone temperaments work and work well on lutes and viols is to see for yourself. Part 3 gets down to the business of understanding the physical and environmental factors that can impact your ability to tune, how to set your open strings and frets in meantone temperaments, strategies to extend those temperaments, and how to manipulate them to your advantage in continuo settings. The final chapter considers the special circumstances that pertain to meantone temperaments on viols.

PART THREE

Practice

PART THREE INTRODUCTION

> For the tuning of the lute one must be very exact; for as there is no perfect harmony in a family, in a city nor in a Commonwealth if there be not an union, a sympathy and good accord, likewise if the lute be not perfectly in tune it is impossible to play well; and instead of a sweet symphony we shall hear nothing but a rude and hurtful cacophony (that is, a disagreeing noise) which discredits the best hands, and turns the truest lessons into a vicious composition and full of faults, against the principles and rules of music. Now one cannot well tune his lute unless it be well strung and have good frets.
>
> —Burwell Lute Tutor

Now the fun begins. After the there and then and this and that, part 3 focuses on the here and now. We now know how tuning systems work and recognize that the notion that fretted instruments were always tuned in equal temperament is at best an overly broad generalization. As usual, the situation on the ground is more complicated than it appears to be. In part 3 you will have the opportunity to apply the perspective and theoretical knowledge you've gained in parts 1 and 2 to immediately improve the quality of your tuning.

CHAPTER SIX

Physical and Environmental Factors

Nothing will improve your ability to tune well more than changing your strings frequently and your frets more frequently. Nearly as important is how well you maintain your pegs and nut, followed by how you attach your strings. By understanding how your strings, frets, bridge, nut, and pegs impact your tuning, you can significantly reduce physical factors that can inadvertently inhibit accurate tuning.[1] How you stop the strings at the frets can also dramatically influence the pitch that is actually produced. Through comprehension of the dynamics of this all-important interaction, discussed in this chapter under the umbrella topic of "sharpening" and throughout the remainder of this book, you can significantly improve your tuning. That you and your entire instrument are subjected to the atmosphere, humidity, and temperature also influences tuning stability while the instrument is at rest or being played. Since atmospheric conditions affect the various components of your instrument in different fashions, their effect will be considered within the discussions of strings, frets, attachment issues, and sharpening rather than separately.

To reiterate, if you do nothing but change your strings and frets early and often, beyond the normal break-in period, you will have a much easier time keeping your instrument in tune. And if you also keep your pegs and nut in good working order, your tuning problems can practically disappear. This small investment in time and effort up front pays enormous dividends over the long run.

Strings

On lutes, the choice of string material usually comes down to the use of various types of gut strings versus synthetic strings such as nylon, Nylgut, carbon fiber, and strings overspun with copper or silver, whereas for viols it is among gut, its variants, and metal strings. Many players choose different materials for different strings. Your choice of string material may also be impacted by your lifestyle. If you keep your instrument in the same place all the time, where the atmospheric humidity is relatively constant, you may find gut to be a superb option; if, however, you travel a great deal with little time for your instrument to become acclimated before you must play, synthetic materials might be more practical for you. It will serve us well to begin with a discussion of gut strings since most of the instruments referred to in chapters 1 and 3 were strung in gut. Beyond that, for the most part, I will restrict the discussion to string issues that affect tuning, primarily how various string materials are affected by sharpening, and on a more positive note in successive chapters, how they impact our ability to adjust the pitch by pushing and pulling. Abundant information on the string choice thicket can be found in the pages of *Early Music,* the *Galpin Society Journal,* the Lute Society's *Lute News,* the *FoMRHI Quarterly,* the various publications generated by the Società del Liuto in Italy, the Viola da Gamba Society, and the Viola da Gamba Society of America over the years, string makers' web pages, and on the websites of prominent luthiers and lutenists.[2]

I recommend that all lutenists (and gambists) follow the famous advice of the late, well-known New York City lute pedagogue Pat O'Brien to at least once in your life string your instrument entirely in gut, if for no other reason than to gain the perspective of knowing the texture and balance our instruments' composers were imagining when they conceived their music. As a natural material, gut's slight imperfections give it a color that enlivens its sound. Instruments fully strung in gut produce a much more treble-dominated texture. The first string sings out of the texture beautifully on both the lute and viol. Overall, gut yields a more unified sound, particularly in chords. On octave-strung bass courses, it is easy to hear the raison d'être for the addition of the octave string, that is, to provide the upper partials suppressed or missing from the thicker fundamental string, giving the composite sound a presence and brightness it would otherwise lack, whereas on synthetic strings, the fundamental and octave produce an interval composed of two discernibly separate pitches.[3] Gut allows for greater dynamic flexibility and speaks faster. It is a complicated but pure sound that resonates better with the wood than do synthetic strings. And in an instant you realize how Renaissance and Baroque lutenists could have played so close to the bridge as depicted in countless historical paintings: it sounds much better on gut than on synthetic strings and gives the player greater dynamic control. A viol strung completely in gut produces a glorious sound that is nothing short of heavenly.

Now that gut strings are available both rectified and varnished, gut no longer deserves much of the bad press it has received over the years, although you will still spend much more time tuning and require greater patience if you string your instrument in gut rather than another material, particularly on lutes.[4] Unless the atmospheric humidity is exceptionally stable and relatively dry, gut basses easily absorb moisture thereby increasing their mass so much so that, as Doni asserted, when fretted, they sharpen to a higher degree than their accompanying octave string.[5] Gut strings also release moisture quickly when conditions are dry and can be very difficult to keep in tune during changes of season. They do not register as well as synthetic strings do on electronic tuners, perhaps because of both their complexity and inconsistency.

On long-necked lutes such as archlutes, theorbos, and tiorbinos, varnished gut works well on the long basses, although Nylgut, carbon fiber, and other materials can be suitable alternatives. Even if you normally string your lute in synthetic materials or travel a great deal and require the greater stability that synthetic strings offer, Paul O'Dette recommends replacing the highest-pitched string with gut for recordings to benefit from its sweeter sound since there is sufficient time between takes to make sure it is precisely in tune, a luxury we do not often have in concerts.[6]

Gut is more sensitive to variations in finger pressure and location, but as our forebears discovered, that disadvantage can be converted to an asset because pushing and pulling to lower or raise the pitch, particularly as you journey from the first to sixth course as the strings become progressively thicker, is much more effective on gut than on synthetic strings. The third course is noticeably easier than second, and from the fourth course to sixth, it is very feasible, particularly on the viol. This suggests that players might have set the frets with this in mind, knowing that they could rely more heavily on pushing and pulling on the lower courses, but less so on the higher courses.

Strings sound most interesting when they are close to, but not perfectly even. Slight imperfections in gut and Nylgut give them a more colorful sound than other materials.[7] Completely cylindrical monofilament strings such as carbon fiber and nylon favor consistent and stable tuning over sonic color. The onset of constant vibrato among unfretted bowed string players during World War I can be attributed to players trying to sweeten the sound of the steel strings they were forced to use because gut strings were in such short supply. Although the copper or silver overspun strings and aforementioned synthetic strings are much more stable than gut, they too can be impacted by changes in humidity, but to a lesser degree. In all cases, the thicker the string, the higher the instrument's action, and the higher up the neck the fret is, the greater will be the tuning challenges when fretted under normal circumstances.

Metal strings, at both low and high tensions, can cause severe tuning difficulties when fretted, and we must be careful to use only as much left-hand finger pressure as required to produce a clear pitch. At low tensions it is very easy to inadvertently slide the string out of its customary track or to press too hard, particularly with scalloped frets, in each case causing the pitch to rise. This, of course, can be turned to your advantage if you need to raise the pitch, but alas, such pitch alterations often occur unintentionally. Under high tension, metal strings are very susceptible to producing pitches higher than intended when fretted, a topic discussed in greater detail below. These same principles apply to other materials as well. The viol's higher tension strings compared with the lute are somewhat of an advantage because their reaction is more consistently predictable, which lends the viol quite well to left-hand tuning adjustments that can be precalculated with reasonable reliability.

One of the many reasons it is advantageous to play in shorter more regular practice sessions than in widely spaced marathons is that, regardless of string material, the more regularly you play your lute or viol, the better it will stay in tune. When strings haven't been played in a while, it can take a little time to revive them; like humans, when they've not been exercised for some time, they become stiff, inflexible, and perhaps a little grouchy. Since gut reacts more severely to irregular contact than do other string materials, players who visit their instruments on a regular basis are more easily able to enjoy gut's benefits.

As strings age, they naturally lose minute bits of material from stretching and being worn away where they are plucked or bowed and where they are most frequently fretted. This loss of material causes the string to become slightly more irregular and therefore more colorful. You may have noticed that your strings sound best after they have been "played in," but that sometime after those golden days they become increasingly difficult to tune. This is when you want to change your strings. The ability to tune well deteriorates because the wearing away of the material has progressed far enough to eventually make the string increasingly false. A string can become false, that is, unable to be tuned, because too much material has worn away at a particular location along the string's length. The constant pressure of pushing a string against a fret can make it false at that location, and strings often break around the first couple of frets where they get the most wear because finger acids break down the string material, making it weak and susceptible to breakage. On the lute, the very thin gut chanterelles can also break at the sweet spot where the string is plucked.

Fretted musical instruments perform best when the humidity and temperature remain constant, the former generally taking precedence over the latter as the Burwell Lute Tutor makes perfectly clear with regard to strings: "They must endure no moisture nor any excessive heat no more than the lute, but they will have a temperate air and place (but of the two the moisture is the worst)."[8] Independently and collectively, humidity and temperature can affect your strings' stability both as your instrument rests in or out of its case and as you tune and play it. Even in its case, leaving your instrument in a sunny spot in your living room or car can cause your strings to go out of tune, a type of "sun damage" that is easily preventable. Turning off your central air conditioning or heating and opening the windows can cause your strings to react extremely as a result of the change in humidity. The effects of such atmospheric variations are accentuated with gut strings because they absorb and dispel moisture more readily than other string materials do. Open gut strings will either rise or lower in pitch while at rest depending on how waterlogged they are. In very humid conditions, when fretted, gut strings can sharpen excessively. Metal and nylon strings, on the other hand, react more to temperature; carbon fiber strings are the most stable. It is useful to note your instrument's tendencies as they relate to your local climate. Always keeping your instrument in its case when not playing it can prevent a good deal of trouble.

Tuning problems are most exasperating, of course, while performing. We are often thrust from a cold dry offstage area into a hot and humid well-lit stage in a concert hall full of people. This sudden change in humidity and temperature can be a recipe for disaster. Having to perform a full-scale tuning while the audience sits waiting for the concert to begin can fluster even the most seasoned performer. Getting your instrument settled into the actual performance space well before the concert begins can give it time to acclimate to its new environment. If at all possible, leave your instrument onstage somewhere instead of bringing it with you to the wings before the concert and between sets unless you are blessed with an instrument that was "tuned at the factory," the phrase musicians use for instruments that never seem to go out of tune.[9] While some presenters prefer that you bring your instrument with you on- and offstage, insisting that you be allowed to leave it on stage or in the dark just behind the curtains is well worth the aggravation given the possible consequences of not doing so. If, on the other hand, the conditions between the wings and the stage are extremely different or you are compelled to leave your instrument offstage, keep it physically close to you because your body becomes part of the equation and can help stabilize it when you start to play. Anything you can do to stack the odds in your favor is well worth the trouble.

Frets

While much of the next couple of chapters involve where to place the frets, here we will pause a moment to consider the frets themselves. Once again, the Burwell Lute Tutor said it best: "The frets must be good and new, and tied very fast."[10] The importance of maintaining your frets in good working order cannot be overemphasized.

Because harder stronger material wears away softer weaker material, gut rather than nylon frets make much more sense for movable frets because every type of string material other than gut itself is harder and stronger than gut. Since it is easier to change frets than strings, especially on the lute, it is always better for the fret material to be softer than the strings. On gut-strung instruments, gut frets are still better than nylon because the harder nylon frets wear away the gut strings forcing them to be changed more frequently than the frets. Frets also wear at different rates at each intersection of fret and string depending on the string material and how often that location is used. As you have probably noticed, the frets get dented or ragged at those intersections, and under copper overspun strings, those intersections turn slightly green as the copper that has worn off the string onto the fret is oxidized.

Van Edwards provides several methods for tying frets, as do purveyors of strings and fret gut; there are also, of course, many internet sources and YouTube videos that demonstrate the same.[11] You will have to change frets more frequently if you use meantone temperaments because moving the frets around and slanting them causes them to expand and lose their elasticity and skate around sooner than does equal temperament—a small price to pay for playing better in tune. In such cases, until the fret can be replaced, little folded bits of paper or matchsticks inserted between the fret and the neck can retighten the fret, and some brave souls even heat the portion of the gut on the back of the neck with a flame from a match or lighter to cause the fret to contract. Worn frets, however, are among the most pernicious causes of tuning problems, even in equal temperament. As the frets wear down, they lose their profile and flatten causing two problems that inevitably result in tuning infelicities. First, as the fret flattens, the string comes into contact with a wider portion of the fret, reducing the precision of the string's contact point on the fret. In other words, one end of the string is securely fastened at the bridge, while the other at the fret is less so. This causes the tone to suffer, reduces pitch identity, or renders the resultant vibrating portion of the string false.[12] Worn frets also cause us to apply greater left-hand finger pressure to compensate for the insecure contact point with the fret, which can easily lead to an unintended rise in pitch and a loss of left-hand dexterity and fluidity. The frets on classical and metal string guitars also eventually wear down as well, but they must have their frets professionally dressed, which involves filing the frets to return them to a more pointed profile. We, on the other hand, just have to change our frets.

As discussed previously, the 1st fret causes the most problems because it is the most difficult to tie snugly. An intriguing option is to use a double fret exclusively for the 1st fret because double frets tend to fit more snugly than single frets. A double fret also offers the option of being split when an alternate enharmonic is required, a technique commonly used by advanced viol players. And as we have seen, it is indeed the 1st fret that is mostly likely to benefit from this technique because it is the fret where enharmonics are most likely to be needed. Research by Tim Watson and Martyn Hodgson indicates that the use of double frets, commonplace on viols, was much more prevalent on plucked instruments than previously thought, a topic discussed in greater detail in chapter 7.[13] Although double frets are much more easily tied on viols and rounded neck lutes, with practice, they can be tied on lutes with flatter necks.

Attachment Issues

Think of the string from its attachment at the tailpiece or bridge through the grooves in the nut to the pegs as a sound delivery system that must be well installed and maintained to function properly. Since all parts of the system are linked through their contact with the string, a defect anywhere in the system can impede both the production of a clear resonant sound and the ability to effectively tune the instrument. We begin our discussion where we begin: by attaching our strings to the tailpiece or bridge.

TAILPIECE AND BRIDGE

You certainly have a method of tying your strings to the tailpiece or bridge that works for you and probably do not give it much thought anymore, yet, by attaching your strings improperly, you can quickly convert a perfectly true string into a false one and thus, unable to be tuned. With regard to false strings, Ganassi wrote that "a bad string can never be tuned as accurately as a good one, and even if the frets are placed in the correct positions, you will never be able to play completely in tune."[14] A false string does not have a consistent diameter throughout its entire sounding length, the irregularity of which disrupts the string's periodic vibration to the order of 10 to 30 cents, particularly upon fretting. In other words, it beats. As Brian Capleton explains, a false string seems to cycle between two pitches; the wider the difference between those two pitches, the more disruptive the falseness.[15] He further explains that the viol bow can even out smaller differences, but, alas, nothing can be done once a false string is struck on a lute.

Many early commentators on musical matters, including Dowland, Agricola, Le Roy, and Mersenne, explained where to purchase the most reliable strings and how to recognize false strings before purchasing them, and, in some cases, how to attempt to rectify the problem should one slip through undetected, but none in a more entertaining fashion than in the Burwell Lute Tutor: "The string must not be full of knots or gouty or rugged, nore be bigger in one place than in another," and later, "Observe the bignesses of them and put no false ones; they become false several ways—if they be old, if they take air, if they be yellow, and (in one word) if they do not come from Rome."[16] Dowland wrote at length about the color and consistency of strings when viewed against the light and recommended various places and times of the year to purchase strings.[17] Fortunately, today this is seldom a problem even with gut strings because of string makers' ability to improve and check the quality of their work through the aid of modern technology. For example, rectified gut strings are much more consistent than unrectified and varnished gut strings even more so. Nevertheless, we should be able to recognize a false string no matter how it occurs.

False strings may be in tune when they are plucked open, but when fretted in certain places can produce a pitch wildly divergent from the pitch that should be produced at that fret. The fretting errors can also be inconsistent along the sounding length of the string, corresponding to where the diameter is wider or narrower than the rest of the string. Sometimes it is just exceedingly difficult to tune the string, or it simply does not sound right. In some cases, the pitch drops precipitously after being plucked. A reliable test to determine if a string is false is to compare the fretted note at the 12th fret with the 12th-fret harmonic. Assuming your 12th fret is set properly, the pitches should be the same. If not, the string is false.

To avoid inadvertently causing a perfectly true string to become false, after tying the string to the bridge, to tighten the knot, instead of grasping the string near the knot on the vibrating portion of the string between the bridge and nut, grasp the string at some point beyond where it would cross the nut; otherwise you can cause the string to become false at the point you pull the string. Grasping it beyond where it would cross the nut allows you to spread the tension across the length of the string rather than at one spot. If, by chance, you do cause the string to become false at the point you have grasped it, no harm is done because the interruption of the string's consistent diameter occurs at a portion of the string that does not vibrate. Should you need to slightly tug on a string while tuning to lower the pitch minutely, do so gently and, if possible, pull the string with several of your fingers at once so as to spread out the tension by not putting too much stress on one location.

When you encounter a false string, however it came to be false, if you are fortunate, the location where the string diameter has been compressed is close to the bridge. If so, you can remove the string and replace it with the ends reversed, a solution suggested as early as ca. 1517 in the *Capirola Lutebook.*[18] The end of the string that was at the bridge is now at the peg, and, if all goes well, the compressed portion is now beyond the nut, where it does not affect the sounding length. Finally, as the Burwell Lute Tutor indicates, strings can become false as they age, just through the normal wear and tear associated with playing. It is therefore more likely that you will encounter false strings on an old set. As mentioned above, you may have noticed that as a set of strings ages beyond a certain point, the strings can become more difficult to tune, forcing you to make all kinds of extreme fret adjustments just to keep the tuning tolerable. At this point, it is time to change your strings. It may be that you only need to change a couple of offenders, and often this can buy you some time between complete changes, but, overall, changing your strings at regular intervals, and your frets even more frequently, are two of the easiest ways to prevent tuning problems.[19]

Finally, on viols, it is crucial that the bridge remain absolutely vertical in its proper position and its feet firmly planted with no space whatsoever between the feet and the soundboard. If the bridge migrates from its location or leans forward toward the nut or backward toward the tailpiece, the vibrating length of the string is altered, rendering all the fret locations inaccurate. To keep the strings from pulling the bridge toward the fingerboard, you can lubricate the string slots with graphite as you do with your nut, as described below. It is much easier to regularly monitor the placement and angle of your bridge than it is to relocate your frets, a topic explored in greater depth in chapter 9.

NUT

You may find it surprising that the configuration and maintenance of the grooves that channel the strings through the nut can have a significant impact on your ability to fine tune. The good news is that maintaining your nut is one of the easiest and quickest things you can do to reduce tuning challenges. Looking down the length of the groove, it should be U-shaped rather than V-shaped. You may need a magnifying glass to see it well enough. A V-shaped groove can break a string as can a groove that rises too steeply from the pegbox to the fingerboard, resulting in too acute of an angle where the vibrating length of the string leaves the nut. If you should find that a string always breaks at that spot, try softening the angle slightly. Many experienced viol players include a set of variously graded files (a needle file set) in their tool kit to address such problems as well as issues with the notches through which the strings traverse at the bridge. Files can work well on lute nuts, too, but since the strings are generally thinner than on viols, it's best to try fine sandpaper before resorting to a file. Any imperfection where the string can catch should be smoothed out.

Assuming that your nut is properly groovy, your main concern with the nut is to keep it lubricated so that the strings can move through their channels smoothly. Overspun strings, whose coils can get stuck on the front edge of the groove, cause the most problems. If the groove is too tight or there is too much friction, the coils can bunch up. When they eventually release, the pitch usually spikes, making it difficult to fine tune. That creak that we've all heard is caused by the string jumping through the nut groove in leaps and starts rather than sliding through smoothly. When this happens, you can tune above and then below the pitch rapidly a few times to mitigate the bunching. The easiest thing you can do, however, is to keep your nut grooves well lubricated. I use graphite either in extra-fine dry powdered tube form, which is usually sold as a lock lubricant, or in the form of pencil lead. While a No. 2 pencil works adequately, since No. 1 pencil lead is finer and softer, it works better. And if the aesthetics of black graphite against a white nut bothers you, you can purchase a white No. 1 or B (soft) pencil at any art supply store. Note that the pencil may be of the soft variety without declaring it; if in doubt, ask the salesperson. Instead of applying graphite to the grooves themselves, applying the graphite to the underside of the string is more effective and lasts longer.[20] Others prefer soap or some other alternate methods to lubricate nut grooves.[21] Whenever you change your strings, you should lubricate your nut, and when you experience fine-tuning problems, simply lubricating the nut groove will often be enough to do the trick.

PEGS

It is well known that wood absorbs atmospheric moisture, causing it to swell. During periods of high humidity, the pegs and the cheeks within which they are fitted expand, inducing the pegs to stick, making it very difficult to turn them with any precision. In dry conditions, the wood contracts relieving the pressure and easing the friction between the peg and its hole. When it is too dry, the pegs may slip. A surprising number of our tuning problems issue from our pegs both because the accuracy of the open string pitch affects the precision of the pitch at every fret and because an incredibly small peg turn can raise or lower the pitch so dramatically, one estimate suggesting that each cent can require as little as a 0.01 mm or 0.2° peg turn.[22]

At home, whenever possible, try to keep your instruments in a room with a relatively constant humidity and temperature. Fifty percent is the museum ideal. Below 40 percent and problems start. In a dry climate or in gas-forced air-heated buildings during the winter, avoid letting it get too hot or dry. It's healthier for both you and your instrument to reduce the temperature. Wear a sweater and keep your instrument in its case, although I wouldn't go as far as Thomas Mace in suggesting you take it to bed with you. While we wouldn't want to give up our central air conditioning and heating, in earlier times, lutes and viols did not have to contend with such extremes within the houses where they resided. In an excessively dry climate where the humidity is normally less than 50 percent, you may need to invest in a room humidifier or have one added to your heating system.[23]

Here, I must caution lutenists on the use of Dampits and guitar humidifiers. Both must be kept away from the pegbox. The greatest potential damage from excessively dry conditions is that the wood shrinks and either pulls the soundboard away from the sides or ribs or that cracks develop in some part of the instrument's body. A Dampit inside a viol or classical guitar effectively protects against this, but lutes, vihuelas, baroque guitars, and so on, do not have that option because their bodies are completely enclosed. In an attempt to maintain an appropriate humidity, players of these instruments sometimes put a Dampit, guitar humidifier, or homemade humidifier such as a sponge in a plastic bag with holes punched in it in their cases. These good intentions can backfire, however, because in lute cases, for instance, the only place available to fit such devices is in the part of the case where the pegbox resides. Placing a humidifying device near the pegbox can cause your pegs to stick, making tuning extremely difficult or impossible—a most insidious self-inflicted wound indeed. In light of how much trouble and expense it is to have our instruments repaired, the costs associated with room or central air humidifiers are well worth it. During the wet season in areas such as the southeastern United States, 24-7 air conditioning can stabilize your instrument quite effectively.

If your pegs become stuck, lightly tap the little end with a small hammer through thick cloth or felt to push the peg out, but hold the opposite end against leg so you can gauge the amount of force you're using. I have always been able to release stuck pegs in this fashion, but if you should encounter a particularly recalcitrant one, you may need to take your instrument to a luthier.

Of course, an ounce of prevention is worth a pound, or in this case, a pounding, of cure. Or in England, several pounds of cure.

To prevent pegs from becoming too tight or loose, apply soap in humid conditions to reduce the friction between the peg and its hole and chalk in dry conditions to increase it. Some players use graphite in a tube to lubricate their pegs, but I find soap to be more effective. And it's cleaner. Instead of treating stuck or loose pegs separately with a lubricant or chalk, many viol players and some lutenists prefer commercially available peg dope or paste.

In order to provide for a fluid turning motion, apply plenty of either to all the portions of the peg that come into contact with the pegbox, particularly the small end. When the small end is not soaped and the portion that goes through the pegbox cheek toward the bulb is, the small end tends to stick, causing the peg to twist away from the nut as the string is brought up to pitch. The larger end of the peg then springs back to the untwisted position when it is released, causing the string to unwind, thereby lowering or flattening the pitch.[24] Be prepared for a breaking in period of a week or two after soaping during which the soaped pegs will slip out of their holes, sometimes suddenly and without warning. This can be alleviated somewhat by applying pressure toward the pegbox as you tune the string up, while applying counterpressure to the opposite side of the pegbox with your free hand so that you do not stress the joint between the pegbox and neck. After soaping a peg, wind and unwind it as many as twenty or thirty times before putting the string on to make sure the soap coats all the surfaces where the peg and pegbox come into contact. If you live in a rather humid climate, I recommend soaping your pegs whenever you change your strings.[25] During excessively dry periods when the pegs tend to slip, applying chalk to the same places prevents slippage. Over a period of time, these compounds can accumulate on your pegs and peg holes to such a degree that further application is futile. When it reaches this stage, simply clean off the entire accumulated old compound with nail polish remover and start from scratch. We would all rather spend our time playing, but this type of maintenance saves you a great deal of time and frustration over the long run.

Finally, superior instruments tend to have fewer tuning problems because their pegs are fitted better and usually made of very hard wood. Your instrument will stay in tune longer and be easier to tune with better pegs. The pegs on some lute models are so small that they are difficult to tune because there is simply not enough peg to get a purchase on. If you are ordering an instrument based on a historical model with small pegs, consider substituting larger pegs. It can make all the difference. And never skimp on peg quality.

How you attach your string to the peg can make tuning easier or more difficult. As for any other project, you need your tools. The standard 5 in. straight hemostatic forceps that can be purchased at a flea market or office or medical supply stores for less than three dollars is a most invaluable tool. I have one packed in each of my lute cases. It can be used both as pliers and as a clamp because of its locking handles. This tool makes both changing strings and replacing frets much easier. The same forceps with a hooked nose is also quite useful; needle-nose pliers, however, can pinch-hit for forceps.

Ideally, the string should run in as straight a line as possible from where it leaves the bridge to the peg hole so that the string does not experience a sharp lateral angle between the nut and the peg hole. Since this can be impossible to avoid for the outer courses, sometimes the peg hole is drilled on the portion of the peg that extends out from the pegbox. When the string leaves the peg hole at an angle, in extreme cases, it can torque the peg sideways enough to cause it to slip.

Tuning is easier if you don't push the peg in all the way until after you've tied the string to the peg; that is, leave it slightly loose while making your knot and performing the initial windings. So that you reduce the amount of excess string that is wound around the peg, pull the string tight after it has gone through the peg hole and press it down on the next peg toward the nut as you make your knot to keep the string taught. The less string wound on the peg, the more easily fine-tuning is possible.[26] It is also advisable to wind the string around the peg neatly so that each new coil of string around the peg snuggly caresses the previous coil such that no peg shows between windings. To ensure precise tuning control, avoid winding the string on top of the coils that are already wound around the peg so that the string is in direct contact with the peg itself as it begins its journey toward the nut. Should you find that there is too much string to do so as you bring it up to pitch, it is better to unwind the string, clip off some of the excess to shorten the length of the string, and start again. To guarantee that your string will never slip from the knot at the peg, after running the string through the peg hole, bring it back under the string and then under itself again to form a self-locking knot. See figure 6.1.

In figure 6.1, notice that the tail of the knot after it has been clipped off points toward the center of the pegbox rather than the cheek. The reason for this is that when the tail touches the cheek, it can sometimes cause a buzz that mimics a loose brace. Note that the tail will point in the same direction that the string left the peg hole when you brought it back under itself; if you bring it to the left of the hole the tail will ultimately end up pointing left, and vice versa. As you approach the narrow end of the pegbox on a lute, you may find that you must point the tail toward the cheek to leave enough room on the peg to wrap the string neatly on the peg without having to overlap coils. In that case, be sure to clip off enough of the tail so that it doesn't rattle against the cheek. Attaching strings to viol pegs is discussed in more detail in chapter 9.

After your initial windings while the peg is still relatively loose, as you approach the correct pitch, push the peg into the pegbox while turning, all the while bracing the outside of the cheek that receives the small end of the peg with your free hand. Once it has gripped the pegbox cheek, that lateral pressure

Figure 6.1. Peg hole knot. Photograph by author.

is no longer necessary. Note how the peg feels as you tighten it: the thicker part of the peg toward the peghead should fit tighter than the narrow end. It is essential that you don't wind string against side of pegbox because the pressure against the cheek can render the peg very difficult to move; it can also cause the peg to fail to grip. In extreme cases, it can cause a peg to either pop out or be jammed inward and possibly even crack the pegbox.[27] To guard against this, place the tip of your forceps between the windings and the cheek. Either clip off the excess string or wind it around itself in the case of gut, but only after you have determined that the string is not false, in case you need to reverse the string to find a portion of its length with a consistent diameter. With regard to a gut string that is your highest course, the first course on most instruments, the third course on a theorbo, you should wind the excess string at the pegbox into a loop around itself because since you can wear away the string at the bridge end where you pluck it, you can clip off the damaged portion and pull through some more from the excess at the pegbox. If, however, you find that the string usually breaks around the 1st fret, you might as well tidy up your instrument and cut off the excess gut and preserve it gently looped in its original packet if you have enough left over to replace a broken string.

Throughout this and the previous chapters, we've lightly touched on the concept of sharpening. We now explore this crucial topic in the depth it merits.

Sharpening

Sometimes referred to as overtension or stretch-sharpening,[28] *sharpening* refers to the process whereby the actual pitch produced by a fretted note is higher or sharper than the pitch that fret's position would produce were it stopped by another bridge at the same height as the originating bridge such as on a monochord. A second bridge the exact same height as the first bridge placed under a string at precisely two-thirds the distance along the sounding length of the string will produce a pure perfect fifth of 702c. (see line a, diagram 6.1), whereas a string stopped at a fret placed at exactly the same point along the string will produce a pitch wider (or higher) than a pure perfect fifth.[29] The reason for this can be explained with simple geometry. If we think of the string as a radius with the point it leaves the bridge as the circle's center point, we see that the same length of string pivoting from that center point (line b) comes into contact with the fingerboard at a position closer to the bridge than where the fret is actually located. In order for the string to reach the additional distance to the fret, it much be stretched. This increased tension causes the pitch to rise because we know that pulling a string tighter raises its pitch. See diagram 6.2. The amount line b has been lengthened is represented by the distance between the arc and the fret. Our forebears were well aware of this phenomenon: in his *Regola Rubertina,* Ganassi wrote that the increased tension resulting from fretting a note necessitates placing the fret a little closer to the nut than one would otherwise.[30]

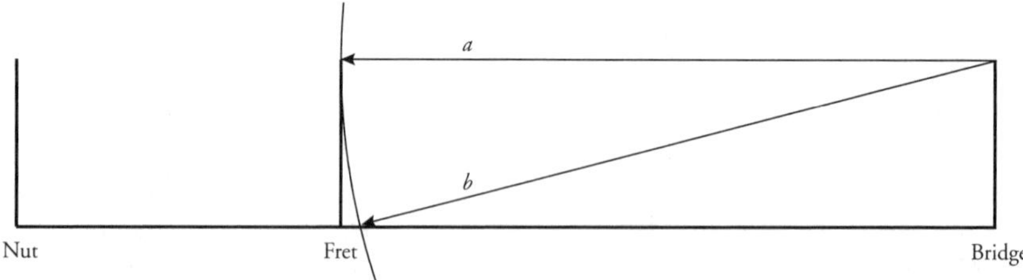

Diagram 6.1. Second bridge added two-thirds the length of the string and where the same length of string would meet the fingerboard.

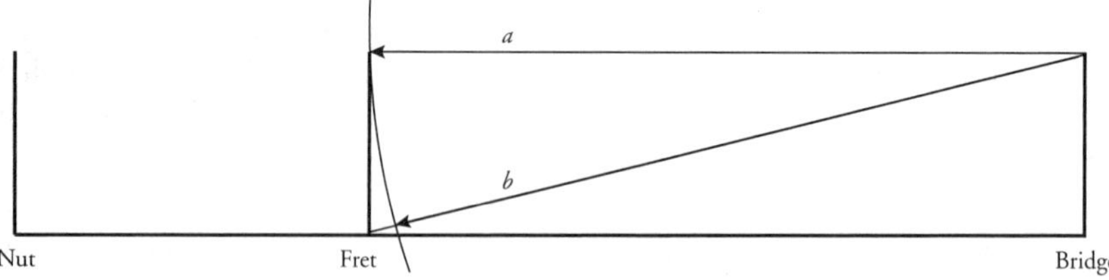

Diagram 6.2. Two thirds of the length of the string stretched to reach the fret.

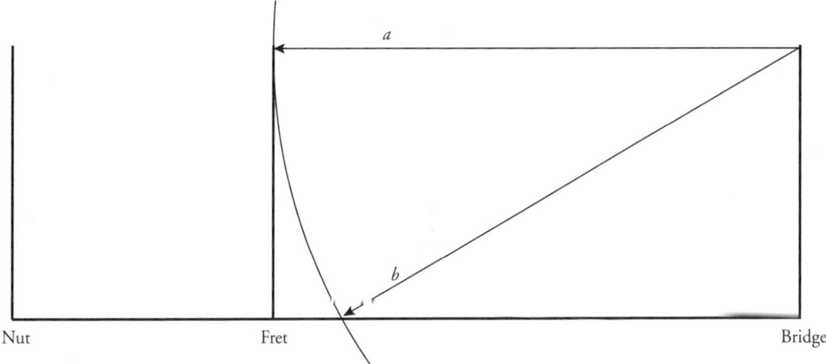

Diagram 6.3. Effect of higher action on sharpening.

As the distance between the fingerboard and bottom surface of the string, that is, the action, increases, so does the sharpening effect, which in part explains why it is so much more of a problem with classical guitars than lutes, since guitars are generally set up with higher action. That the bass strings are actually higher off the fingerboard is another factor that causes them to sharpen more radically than the treble strings.[31] Diagram 6.3 shows how higher action causes the unstretched string to reach the fingerboard farther from the theoretical position than with lower action, necessitating that the string be pulled even tighter to reach the fret. Since the action increases as the string approaches the 12th fret, sharpening also increases proportionately as you go up the neck. The bottom line is that, if you care about tuning and play beyond the first few frets, higher action usually costs more than it's worth.

Sharpening is more pronounced depending on the string material, tension, and thickness, as well as the instrument's action and the height of the frets. In his *A Special Discourse Concerning the Unison,* Galilei wrote that when comparing the pitch of two strings of the same material, length, thickness, and quality stretched over the same length, the pitch should be the same, but should the two strings differ in any one of the aforementioned characteristics, the pitch would not be the same. Furthermore, two strings, one made of gut and the other of some type of metal that produce a unison when played open, will not produce a unison when fretted.[32] He is, of course, referring here to the sharpening effect.

The thicker and stiffer the string and the higher its action, the more pronounced the sharpening effect. Perhaps the most familiar example of this result can be found on the classical guitar where the E Major barré chord at the 7th fret is commonly so hideously sharp even when the frets are set correctly. The third string is usually the thickest and tightest of the guitar's three unwound strings. That string bears the pitch E at the 9th fret, the same pitch as the guitar's first string played open, but because of sharpening, that fingered E is almost always sharp. This is one of the reasons Julian Bream habitually refingered passages in that region to lower fret positions on thinner strings. His action was lower, and he also used thinner strings in order to stay better in tune. The greater power and better tone quality that tighter strings provide comes at the expense of tuning.

While string density does not play as direct a role in the sharpening equation as do thickness, stiffness, and action, since it factors into how thick or thin a string is, it is relevant to this discussion. In order of decreasing density from the most to the least are brass/copper, iron, carbon fiber, gut, Nylgut, and nylon strings.[33] A thinner, denser string can produce the same pitch as a thicker, less dense string. In this scenario, the thinner string will also sharpen less because it is more elastic. So, all other things being equal, a thinner denser string will sharpen less than an equally pitched, less dense, but thicker string. The thinner string's greater elasticity allows it to vibrate more freely than a stiffer string, resulting in a more resonant sound. Overspun metal, demi-filé or gimped gut, and loaded gut strings raise the density without increasing the stiffness, producing a clearer, more resonant, and richer sound than would the same pitch on a stiffer, less dense string. Among the nonmetallic strings, carbon fiber is the densest and most stable by far, but its tone is also the least colorful. As usual, it's a trade-off.

We've not yet mentioned the impact that the size of the frets has on sharpening. All things being equal (temperament excluded, of course), higher, that is, thicker, frets, cause more sharpening than thinner frets because there is more fret to get around, thereby increasing the amount the string must stretch even more, that is, until you move up the neck toward the 12th fret as the angle of the string increases. On the other hand, because they are closer to the bottom surface of the string, fatter frets require less finger pressure to produce a clean note. Less finger pressure usually translates into less sharpening. Excessive left-hand finger pressure, particularly coupled with thicker frets, can cause a fretted note to sharpen because as the finger pushes the string down into the fingerboard, it stretches the string even tighter. This is something that can be used to our advantage; however, more often than not, it happens inadvertently with deleterious effect, particularly on wire-strung instruments and especially those with scalloped frets. Unless we intend to deliberately sharpen a fretted note, if for no other reason than good tuning, and there are many other good reasons, it behooves us to apply only as much finger pressure as necessary for the note to speak cleanly. Food for thought.

We can also cause the pitch to rise if we do not apply finger pressure to the string at a right angle straight into the fretboard. In other words, we unintentionally bend the string as if we were trying to make a "blue" note. When we push the string out of its track by oblique finger pressure, we are actually stretching the string laterally, producing the same action that we saw in diagram 6.3 only viewing it from the top of the fingerboard rather than the side. This is why bent notes on the guitar rise in pitch, albeit with deliberate purpose. Alternatively, on wire-strung instruments such as the cittern, orpharion, and bandora, somewhere between a clear sound and a thud, easing the finger pressure can slightly lower the pitch. On the viol, the pitch can be easily lowered enough to make this technique a reliable utensil in a viol player's tuning toolbox.

On the other hand, literally, strings struck with a great deal of force cause the pitch to spike and then rapidly decline as the sound decays, particularly on bass strings, a phenomenon first described by Mersenne in 1636.[34] You can see this quite easily on an electronic tuner equipped with a needle. The tuning problems excessive force can cause are among the many reasons to avoid striking the strings too vigorously.

Since the amount of sharpening depends on a combination of several factors, mitigating one can compensate for an excess of another. In other words, anything we can do to reduce the opportunity for unintentional sharpening to occur will help us to play better in tune. As you may recall, Galilei's 18:17 rule (the "rule of eighteen") was deemed superior to other methods for deriving an equal temperament fretting scheme because it accounted for sharpening whereas other less successful methods didn't. Some makers tilt the bass side of the bridge and/or nut so that bass courses are slightly longer to compensate for this increased sharpening, a practice recommended by Bermudo in 1555.[35] Classical guitars benefit significantly from compensated saddles, which are essentially six little saddles carved into one. The second string saddle is a little farther back than the first string's, and the third string's is the farthest back, lengthening the string as far as possible within the physical confines of the bridge's available space. This pattern is repeated in similar fashion for the wound fourth through sixth strings.

We have already discussed slanted frets extensively in the previous chapters, but in the next, we explore exactly how to apply them on our instruments. Slanting our frets is one of the very best weapons in our arsenal. It is easy, fast, and effective. As early as 1555, Bermudo recommended slanted frets toward the bass side for vihuelas, and as late as 1851 Charles Delezenne described the progressive slanting of frets to compensate for sharpening on guitars. Ganassi, as well, recommended shading the fret where sharpening occurs toward the nut by the width of the fret to compensate for the increased tension placed on the string by fretting.[36] In all cases, the thicker and stiffer the string and the higher the instrument's action, the greater will be the tuning challenges when fretted under normal circumstances.

This chapter pointed out many steps that we can take to reduce the likelihood of experiencing tuning problems. Armed with an understanding of how physical and environmental factors impact our ability to tune, we can stack the odds in our favor by keeping the humidity and temperature as constant as possible, maintaining our instruments in good working order, and understanding how sharpening affects our tuning. More than anything else, of course, we should change our strings frequently and our frets even more frequently. In chapter 7, we apply our accumulated knowledge toward setting our frets and tuning.

CHAPTER SEVEN

The Zen of Tuning

You would not have made it this far if you didn't recognize how essential good tuning is to our own enjoyment and to that of those who listen to us. An ill-tuned instrument disturbs everyone, audiences and players alike. Playing well requires such attention to both the big picture and minute details that even the slightest distraction caused by tuning problems can be enough to trigger anything from a trivial error to a completely derailed performance. Tuning is preliminary to playing. This may seem obvious, but I wager that, in our haste to commune with our beloved instruments, all of us, including me, have at one time or another just dived in without tuning. I implore you to resist that urge. As Christopher Goodwin points out, echoing Vincenzo Galilei, Mattheson, Mary Burwell's tutor, and many others, it is important to make sure your instrument is in tune prior to beginning to play because "the ear quickly adjusts to a very slightly out-of-tune instrument."[1] And once you are playing, if something seems amiss with your tuning, don't let it go. Neglecting to tune before you play and failing to attend to tuning problems as they arise can become an insidious habit. If you have developed that habit, I suggest that you replace it with a better one, that of correcting every little tuning defect forthwith.

We now turn our attention to acquiring the ability to tune accurately and when necessary, quickly. Once we are assured that our pegs, strings, and frets are in good working order, our next step is to choose a tuning system, a topic we have already discussed at length. Because the Baroque lute is tuned quite differently than other lutes, viols, vihuelas, and guitars, it is discussed separately within this context. We explore a variety of tuning techniques, for the situations we find ourselves in can sometimes dictate our choosing one method over another. In particular, I suggest a procedure for knitting together a tight fabric of unisons and octaves by ear that won't unravel with the slightest untoward tug of any of its constituent threads. By now, you will have grasped that accurate tuning of fretted instruments requires the proper tuning of the open strings and arrangement of the frets accordingly. The two are inextricably and intrinsically intertwined. This discussion addresses the basic arrangement of the frets required to produce your desired tuning, and the use of tastini, double and split frets, slanted frets, compromise fret positions, and pulling and pushing to extend it.

As with anything else worth mastering, learning how to tune well takes practice, focus, and dedication, but in the process we become more intimately acquainted with our instruments and ultimately make better music. There is a certain Zen to tuning that can take some time to master; however, you will find that no matter how poor you think your ears are, you will improve every day if you make it a priority. And you will advance faster if you are able to tune in a quiet, tranquil environment. You may discover that after your initial tuning, your instrument doesn't sound very good. In that case, just tune it again. Depending on atmospheric conditions, the state of your pegs, strings, and frets, and the level of noise and distraction around you, it may take you several times to get it just right. Think of it as progressively fine tuning. After a period of disuse or when you have changed the pitch level or temperament, it can sometimes take several days before your strings settle. In those cases, the pitches will tend to gravitate toward their former levels. Don't become frustrated. This is a natural phenomenon that happens with other instruments as well. New strings also take time to settle down. According to the Burwell Lute Tutor: "If your strings be all new set on, or the most part of them, you must not expect to play upon your lute so soon; but you must tune your lute now and then and let the strings stretch at leisure."[2] Open string exercises and chromatic scales can help your strings settle down quicker.

The Calculus of Temperament Choice

As a practical matter, though, we must all choose a standard everyday default tuning or temperament for each instrument we own depending on how it is used. On the other hand, you might find it convenient to have most of them in the same temperament. The commissioning of a new instrument also requires the selection of an everyday temperament. Because metal frets are fixed and the fret spaces between them are frequently scalloped on citterns, orpharions, bandoras, and similar instruments, you must select the temperament well in advance. And, although we are as of yet unaware of a historical orpharion or bandora sporting tastini, as we saw in chapter 2, some orpharions and bandoras are ordered with tastini. Why not? When commissioning a lute, you must consider the 10th and 11th on-the-body frets, the 12th fret stationed at the same location regardless of the temperament. In virtually every situation involving a meantone temperament, the 10th fret will be a *fa,* and the 11th fret a *mi,* but as you know, how much of a *fa* or *mi* depends on the variety of meantone temperament. The worst that can happen, however, is that your luthier sets them incorrectly, and you simply remove and relocate them.

Now that we have discussed the pros and cons of the various temperaments in the previous chapters, it is time to hear them contextually. Audio files 7.1–7.4 present Dowland's familiar "Tarleton's Riserrectione," musical example 7.1, in 1/4-, 1/6-, and 1/8-comma meantone temperaments as well as in equal temperament for your consideration. Downward pointing arrows in the score indicate prominent major thirds and sixths located lower and thus more

Musical Example 7.1. John Dowland, "Tarleton's Riserrectione."

in tune in meantone temperaments than in equal temperament. These are the locations where the difference between equal and meantone temperaments is most evident.

BAROQUE LUTE

Choosing a temperament for Baroque lute poses special challenges because of its open string tuning of *A d f a d′ f′* and the diversity of music played on it, ranging from the relatively tonal and straightforward French repertoire of the early to mid-seventeenth century to the chromatic adventures we often find in the music of J. S. Bach. At first glance, the Baroque lute's fretboard pitch arrangement appears to prohibit any sort of meantone temperament because the 1st, 3rd, 6th, and 8th frets contain both *mis* and *fas* that would be quite commonly necessary in a given tonality, such as the F♯, E♭, and B♭ at the 1st fret, for instance, in the tonality of G Minor. See diagram 7.1, the Baroque lute fretboard in 1/4-comma meantone temperament with both *mis* and *fas* indicated in italics at the 1st, 3rd, 6th, and 8th frets. In fact, one could not be faulted for envisioning an unwieldy pattern of tastini of one *mi* and two *fas* repeated twice at each of the *mi/fa* frets that might look something like diagram 7.2, although limiting tastini to the 1st fret only is a sensible option. But going to such elaborate extremes to play in a meantone temperament is generally unnecessary because, as François Duprey points out, seventeenth-century composers whose ears were not "polluted by equal temperament" were very well aware of where on their fretboards the good and bad pitches were located in meantone temperaments and worked around them by avoiding them entirely, burying them within big chords, or isolating them such that their harmonic infelicities would cause no offense.[3] When they do appear, "bad" notes are also often strategically placed where a dissonance might serve a musical purpose, such as in a particularly pungent dominant or diminished chord in a remote tonality.

Based on his study of 243 eleven-course French Baroque lute compositions from ca. 1640 to 1710, Duprey concluded that, for the most part, 1/4-comma meantone temperament is not only viable but perfectly apt for most tonalities found within this repertoire. Musical example 7.2, "La Coquette virtuose," a

F♯	G♭	G	G♯	A♭	A	B♭	B	C♭	C	C♯	D♭	D	E♭	E	F
D♯	E♭	E	E♯	F	F♯	G	G♯	A♭	A	A♯	B♭	B	C	C♯	D
A♯	B♭	B	B♯	C	C♯	D	D♯	E♭	E	E♯	F	F♯	G	G♯	A
F♯	G♭	G	G♯	A♭	A	B♭	B	C♭	C	C♯	D♭	D	E♭	E	F
D♯	E♭	E	E♯	F	F♯	G	G♯	A♭	A	A♯	B♭	B	C	C♯	D
A♯	B♭	B	B♯	C	C♯	D	D♯	E♭	E	E♯	F	F♯	G	G♯	A

Diagram 7.1. Baroque lute fretboard in 1/4-comma meantone temperament.

F♯		G	G♯		A	B♭	B		C	C♯		D	E♭	E	F
	E♭	E		F	F♯	G		A♭	A		B♭	B	C	C♯	D
	B♭	B		C	C♯	D		E♭	E		F	F♯	G	G♯	A
F♯		G	G♯		A	B♭	B		C	C♯		D	E♭	E	F
	E♭	E		F	F♯	G		A♭	A		B♭	B	C	C♯	D
	B♭	B		C	C♯	D		E♭	E		F	F♯	G	G♯	A

Diagram 7.2. Baroque lute fretboard in 1/4-comma meantone temperament with tastini.

courante by Denis Gaultier (ca. 1603–1672) in A Major, is recorded as audio file 7.5 in 1/5-comma meantone, which, to my ears, sounds quite arresting—not surprising given the French predilection for 1/5-comma meantone and its related irregular temperaments.[4] Figure 7.1 shows how my frets were arranged for this recording.

Musical Example 7.2. Denis Gaultier, "La Coquette virtuose."

Musical Example 7.2. (*Continued*)

If you restrict yourself to the French eleven-course repertoire Duprey outlines, depending on the diversity of the tonal palette involved, you can probably comfortably set your frets in 1/4-, 1/5-, or 1/6-comma meantone temperament. If, however, your Baroque lute repertoire includes Weiss, some of which actually works rather well in 1/6-comma meantone, and J. S. Bach, you may need to select a more widely serviceable temperament, such as 1/8-comma meantone or even possibly equal temperament. Although I try to avoid it when I can, I find

Figure 7.1. Baroque lute in 1/5-comma meantone temperament set for A Major. Photograph by author.

equal temperament to be more palatable on Baroque lute than on Renaissance lute or even theorbo, perhaps because the excessive beating of equal temperament's wide thirds gets lost in the complexity of the overtones generated by the instrument's expansive range and double courses.

Tuning Modalities

As we saw in chapter 1, throughout most of our instruments' histories our predecessors tuned by ear. They tuned the open strings to each other and set the frets accordingly or set the frets theoretically and then tuned the open strings by matching unisons and/or octaves and then fine-tuned by ear. Another method, still valid as ever, is to simply match open strings and frets with a keyboard that is already in your selected temperament.

While there are many ways to use electronic or digital tuners by themselves or in concert with traditional methods, I have found that after using a tuner to set the open strings and arrange the frets, for subsequent tunings, I can generally either tune the open strings with the tuner or simply tune just the top string with the tuner or some other external reference source and then compare unisons and octaves. On good days, I can tune the open strings to each other and then confirm the tuning with unisons and octaves. Once the frets begin to wear away, it occasionally becomes necessary to use the tuner to revisit their locations.

With electronic tuners, you have the option of matching a pitch generated by the tuner or playing into the tuner, which registers your pitch on a visual meter, allowing you to tune up or down so that the pointer or needle lines up with the desired pitch. The tuning modality we choose is dictated by personal preferences usually based on our strengths and weaknesses or the physical environment in which we find ourselves. For instance, tuning meters are a godsend to those of us who are visually oriented, whereas those of us with very good ears might find it easier and faster to match pitches to an external reference tone.[5] Although we all somehow made do prior to the arrival of visual tuning meters and smartphones, I have found that as the ambient noise around me increases, I am more inclined to tune according to the visual meter. At performances, the visual method can be a lifesaver because often the typical preconcert noise such as other instrumentalists tuning can be so loud that it is nearly impossible to hear a lute well enough to tune. And, prior to and during concerts, our normally adequate tuning ears occasionally desert us. To mitigate these challenges, I try to arrive at the concert venue well before the other players so that I can tune in peace and quiet and allow the lute to become acclimated to the environment, making it much more likely that its tuning will be stable at the downbeat.

Ultimately, it is best to become proficient at all of these tuning methods, the skills gained in each reinforcing the others. Once again, we can profit from the wisdom found in the Burwell Lute Tutor:

> For the tuning of the lute you must begin by the fifth [string]. String it in a pitch proportionable to the lute; then from that string you shall tune all the others by thirds or fourths as the tuning requires (that is, so that you have a musical ear; otherwise you must tune your lute by unisons—stopping several letters as the tuning runneth. That way is good, besides, to try whether your strings are true and to place well your frets). You must use several meanes for the accomplishment of so important a thing as the tuening.[6]

In his own way, Mary Burwell's tutor reiterates the obviously essential notion that tuning requires both the open strings and frets to be tuned to the same temperament. Whether tuning by electronic means or by ear, you must check unisons, octaves, and chords to make sure that everything is in order. Often such a test will reveal a poorly tuned string or a dislocated fret, which can then be easily corrected.

Tuning with Electronic Tuners

Programmable electronic tuners have made fret ratio charts and online fret calculators obsolete because of their ease of use and that they account for the sharpening that these other methods cannot. As you know, I prefer Cleartune for its portability, ease of use, elegant presentation, and ability to program multiple custom temperaments. It is available in iPhone, iPad, and Android versions.[7] Also available in the same formats is PitchLab, an application that rivals and even surpasses Cleartune in some regards for string instruments.[8] All the following references to electronic tuners will refer to the Cleartune interface, although the principles can be applied to any other tuner.

Prior to the advent of Cleartune's smartphone and tablet apps, for more than twenty years, the VioLab "Pitchman" tuner was my constant companion. After all these years, it is still going strong. Prior to Cleartune, the VioLab tuner was the gold standard and still is for those who prefer a multipitch, multitemperament tuner restricted to the tone generation mode.[9] It is particularly popular among viol players. The feature that makes it so valuable for players who prefer a tone-generating tuner is that it has a switch that allows you to select the letter name pitch or its sharp or flat version with the knob selector. For example, in any of the several available meantone temperaments, you have the option of selecting D♭, D natural, or D♯. In other words, you can easily choose whatever wolf you prefer as you go. For players of fretted instruments, this feature is quite useful because after tuning the open strings, you can effortlessly set your frets at a slant by, for instance, matching the 1st fret on a G instrument to A♭ on the first course, but G♯ on the sixth course, essentially giving you the option of extending your temperament to a previously unimaginable precision.

Your main decision will be to choose between the two methods available on most digital electronic tuners, aural or visual, and you may go back and forth between them depending on a number of factors. The aural method in which you match your pitch to the tone generated by the tuner can be very fast and ultimately extremely accurate, but may not be for everyone. When using the pitch generator, make sure to lock in the pitch by selecting the lock icon in the center of the dial. This allows you to select a precise pitch by turning the dial to a specific note. Unlock it and adjust the dial if you're trying to shade a particular pitch in one direction or the other. When you switch to the tone generation mode in Cleartune, the fine tuning cents scale turns into an octave selection scale.

As you can see from the screenshots in appendix 1, Cleartune uses a needle and a pointer in the visual mode. For lutes, particularly with gut strings, the needle needs the most damping the app will allow to keep it from wavering too much. This becomes more of an issue as your strings age. Like other tuners, Cleartune is sometimes unable to register the very lowest pitches, such as the diapasons on a theorbo and can also give false readings, often registering the twelfth, that is, the third note in the harmonic series rather than the fundamental. You can mitigate this somewhat by plucking the strings that go to the second pegbox toward the middle of the strings where they produce a clearer pitch than the more convenient locations either closer to the bridge or nut. Tuning to the mid-string harmonic is another effective way to circumvent a tuner's inability to register the fundamental of the extended neck diapasons. The visual mode registers the pitch your instrument produces with a vertical red line moving across a horizontal scale indicating whether the note is either sharp or flat and by how many cents compared with the nearest note in the temperament to which you have the tuner set as designated by the rotating wheel below. The yellow pointer on the dial turns green when the tuner considers the pitch you are producing to be within ±3c. of being precisely in tune.[10] Although each individual variance is well below the generally accepted human range of 5 to 10c., its composite range of 6c. can become an issue when tuning unison double courses.[11] Let's say that for one string the pointer turns green, but that the pitch is 2–3c. toward the flat side and for the other string it turns green 2–3c. toward the sharp side. While they're both quite close to the true pitch, they can be as far as 6c. apart from each other, which can be noticeable enough to cause problems. I recommend that even if the pointer on the dial turns green, you keep your eye on the cents meter above the dial and do your best to come as close to zero as possible. Turning on the Frequency Display under Options causes a hertz reading to display for each note you play, which can also help you compare the pitches of the two strings of a unison course or any other unison. Note that the vertical red line indicating the precision (in cents, plus or minus) fades as the tone dissipates, signifying that the reading is no longer reliable.

Although its sharp and sensible display is in itself a thing of beauty, Cleartune's greatest glory is its ability to allow you to program custom temperaments, although I have encountered Android versions of the app that do not have this capability. Like other tuners, Cleartune comes equipped with a wide variety of preset temperaments. I strongly recommend, however, that you create your own versions of any temperament that contains a flexible wolf such as Pythagorean tuning or any of the varieties of meantone temperament because tuners do not tell you where the wolf is nor do they produce temperaments that maintain your chosen hertz value for A. Simply follow the directions in appendix 2.

Cleartune does not have the flexibility of VioLab for extended temperaments, but it is easy enough to work around. If, for instance, you want to set a temperament that has the common G♯–E♭ wolf on a lute or viol tuned in G, you run into a problem with the 1st fret because the first course, the course used to set the frets, is usually set to a *fa* or in this case A♭. For this and similar situations, you have three options:

1. Create another custom temperament choosing a different wolf, C♯–A♭, for instance, and use that temperament to set the A♭.
2. Once the open strings are tuned, simply use the second course, D, to derive the fret position for the *fa,* in this case E♭; the A♭ on the first course should be the same distance from the fret as the E♭.
3. Check the following octaves and/or unisons as indicated in diagram 7.3.

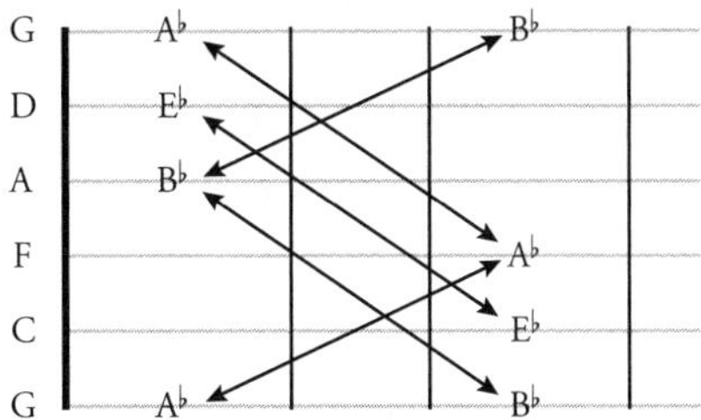

Diagram 7.3. Octave and unison checks for first course 1st fret.

We explore other similar strategies later in this chapter. This may seem like a lot of trouble at first, but once you become accustomed to thinking in terms of *mis* and *fas,* it becomes second nature.

OPEN STRINGS

As you certainly know by now, your goal when tuning the open strings is to tune the open fourths and third to each other properly according to the temperament. Diagram 7.4 shows what that relationship would look like in 1/4-comma meantone temperament. Precise tuning of the open strings that traverse the fingerboard is particularly important because open string tuning errors compound with each fret as you progress toward the 12th fret.

To get a clear reading in the visual mode, damp nearby strings with a combination of your right-hand fingers, the heel of your right hand, the left side of your right-hand thumb, and your left-hand fingers. In the tone generation mode on double courses, I find it easier to tune the upper octave string of octave courses with the tuner, and then tune the fundamental string to it by ear. On the lute, you can often produce a cleaner and more sustained reading on the tuner if you tune with the 12th fret harmonic instead of the open string. Since viols are fretless where the 12th fret would be, you just need to know the

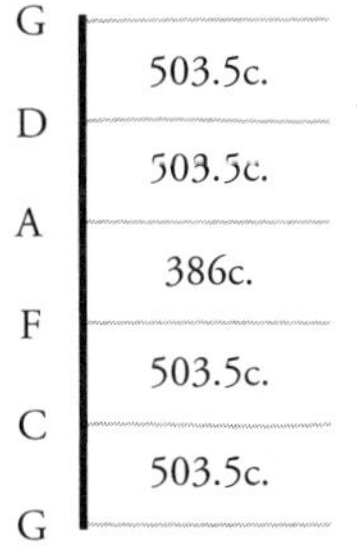

Diagram 7.4. Cents relationship between adjacent courses in 1/4-comma meantone temperament.

location of your string's midpoint—you can always signify it with a discreet pencil mark once you find it.

Finally, there are times when no matter what you do, you cannot get the string spot on because the slightest turn of your peg raises the pitch just too high or brings it too low, sliding past the precise pitch you want. This is more likely an issue when your pegs and nut are out of shape, with gut strings, or even during certain seasons depending on where you are located. If you are not on stage or planning to be so in the imminent future, other than treating your pegs or nut as described in chapter 6, you can unwind your peg until the string is slack and rewind it. This, of course, then necessitates time to allow it to settle in. Quickly turning the peg sharp and flat a few times can also do the trick without a lengthy settling in period. When you need a fine adjustment ever so slightly to the sharp side, pushing on the string between nut and peg sometimes does the trick. On the other hand, when you need a slight adjustment to the flat side, pulling the string out of its track away from your instrument can lower the pitch somewhat, but do be careful to not grasp the string at one location by, for instance, hooking your finger under the string and pulling because, as we have seen, you can make the string go false at that location. Instead, cradle the string among several of your right-hand fingers so that all of the tension for your pulling isn't concentrated on one location along the string.

When using scordatura on the long basses, for instance, retuning from F natural to F♯, the string will tend to return to its original pitch and will gravitate in that direction as it settles in. In our example, when tuning the F natural up to F♯, the string will tend to drop a tad lower than the F♯ when it settles in and vice versa. Since this type of tuning often occurs between pieces while on stage, it is a good idea to memorize how many degrees of peg turn are required to move a semitone, and if you are onstage and don't have time to let it settle in, you can shade it a little in the intended direction to counteract the natural settling effect, that is, tuning it a little past F♯ knowing that it'll drop a little, or when going from F♯ to F natural, a little below F natural because you know it'll elevate slightly. To help the string settle more quickly, you can also initially tune it well past your target pitch and then quickly back to your desired pitch. Continuing with our example, for instance, briefly raising your original F natural up as far as G or beyond and then returning to F♯ can help stabilize the string. If you need to retune between sets during a concert, you can stealthily begin retuning while taking your bow to buy yourself a little more time.

SETTING FRETS: MIND YOUR *mis* AND *fas*

Set your frets first, following the relatively standard patterns described below or by choosing your *mis* and *fas* based on the keys you're going to be playing in, and then afterward refine with tastini, slanted frets, compromise positions, and so on. Keep in mind that because the *mi/fa* identify of perpendicular frets governs each course, just by setting the frets in one arrangement or another already sets us in an extended version of any regular unequal tuning system such as Pythagorean or meantone temperament. Tastini and slanted frets allow us to extend it even further.

Diagram 7.5 shows the most common standard arrangement for fingerboards of instruments tuned in fourths and a major third in meantone and related temperaments in G, A, and D. While these arrangements work for most pitches in the most common keys, some adjustments are obviously required; these will be discussed below. Simply match your fret pitch to either the tone produced by the tuner or to the pointer in the visual mode. On bowed instruments bowing the string too far away from the bridge can make the pitch go flat; it is best to place your bow close by the bridge when tuning and on plucked

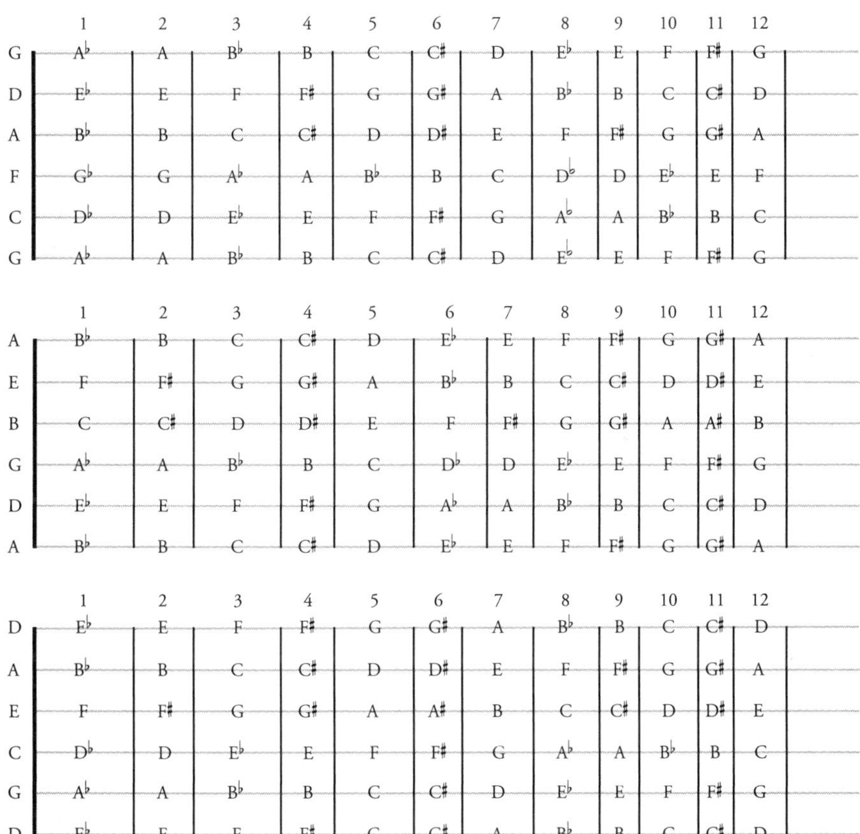

Diagram 7.5. Standard meantone fretboard arrangements for instruments in G, A, and D.

instruments to pluck at the location where you most frequently contact the string. You should bow or pluck at a normal volume.[12]

Set your frets for the first course and then go back and do the same for the lowest fretted course, those in between necessarily relegated to compromise positions when the fret must be slanted to account for sharpening.[13] Because the bass courses sharpen more than the treble courses for the reasons we have seen in chapter 6, any fret wear at all will almost inevitably result in diagonal frets, tilting on the bass side toward the nut. After choosing a default temperament and setting your frets, a tiny unobtrusive pencil mark on the treble side of the fingerboard under the fret can serve as a future location guide, which then facilitates your tuning by ear, which can be very fast once you get the hang of it.[14] On the theorbo, pay special attention to the frets on second string; since it is thicker than the first, it will be subject to more sharpening than the first. Because of its re-entrant tuning, which causes the thickness of the strings to progress from the first to sixth course in a nongraduated order, tuning problems due to sharpening, particularly on the second string, are more difficult to address on the theorbo than on the lute or viol.[15]

Frets in which 4/6 or more of the pitches are "white" or "natural" notes, that is, notes without a flat or a sharp, must almost always remain in the prevailing position that best serves those natural notes. For this reason in G tuning, for instance, the location of frets 2, 3, 4, 5, 7, 9, 10, and, of course, 12, are virtually never variable. In G tuning, the *mi/fa* location of the 6th fret is usually determined by the key signature of the prevailing tonality, flat keys requiring the *fa* position, and sharp keys the *mi* position. The determining pitches are usually the E♭ (D♯) on the third course or the G♯ on the second course, which is often required for V–I cadential formula in A Major or Minor, such as in musical example 7.3, mm. 54–56 in Dowland's "Frog Galliard," in which case the fret must be set as a *mi.* Very rarely are both *mis* and *fas* required at this fret in this

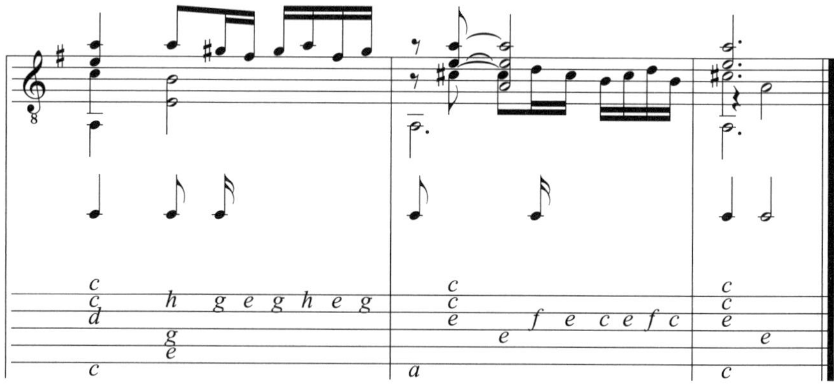

Musical Example 7.3. John Dowland, "Frog Galliard," mm. 54–56.

open string tuning. On instruments in A, the 4th fret is generally more variable than on instruments tuned in G.

Bettina Hoffmann cites Galilei in remarking that on the viol, pitches that fall on frets with *mi/fa* designations the opposite of what are required by the tonality are avoided easily enough because they can be accessed elsewhere since the same pitch can often be found in multiple locations; this, of course, pertains to the lute as well.[16] Frets beyond the 7th are rarely used on the lower courses, so you generally do not need to concern yourself with their *mi/fa* identities, allowing the *mi/fa* designation of the first three courses to prevail. For the occasional piece that ventures into that fingerboard quadrant, it is indeed crucial to check the quality of the intervals involving those locations prior to playing because sharpening issues on upper frets of the lower courses are bound to be severe.

It is always best to think of the tuner as a starting point. You should still check the tuning of your unisons and octaves and, in the case of lutes, the chords you will be playing most frequently. These are all discussed below within the context of tuning by ear.

Creating a Fail-Safe Interlocking Web of Unisons and Octaves by Ear

Tuning by ear is, of course, as old-school as it gets. It can be quite fast and avoids the complication of having to fiddle around with a device once a reference pitch provided by some external source brings one of the strings up to pitch. During a concert, it is much more elegant to tune by ear than with an electronic tuner, and when playing with others it is more important to be in tune with one another than with a tuner. Tuning by ear assumes that you have already properly positioned your frets. Once your fret locations are marked as suggested above, and your frets are in fairly good shape, tuning by ear becomes much more viable. Cultivating the ability to tune your instrument more viscerally gives you the confidence that you can work your way out of any tuning problem that might occur. In a pinch, experienced tuners can even set their frets by ear. As miraculous as all this new technology is, it is still worthwhile to be able to rely on our own ears and wits when necessary. After all, batteries fail, we neglect to recharge our devices, or even forget to bring them with us.

At its most elemental level, tuning by ear involves simply tuning one string to a reference pitch and from that pitch initiating a chain of unisons and octaves to tune the open strings and fine-tune the fret locations. Although the following description assumes starting from the first course, you can really start anywhere; wherever you start, make absolutely sure that the first link in the chain is precise. Should anything sound amiss anywhere along the chain, you need to immediately slow down and double- and cross-check your previous action before making any further adjustment. Otherwise, you run the risk of creating a cascading series of errors, each error compounding the deleterious effects of the previous one. Every step along the way, however, you have the opportunity to set things right, and as you move along from one unison or octave to another, you should constantly go back and check each link in the chain.

SETTING THE REFERENCE PITCH

Most historical sources suggest beginning to tune on one string or another within the context of determining the pitch level, such as the familiar instruction to tune the top string, particularly on the lute, up until just before its breaking point. In the era of pitch levels determined by A in hertz, these instructions are no longer relevant.

The string used to set the pitch level is obviously where the tuning must begin. When tuning by ear, my preference is to begin with the first string, not in deference to the historical precedent just mentioned or even because prior to the advent of electronic tuners, the A = 440 Hz tuning fork pitch was found on the first course, but rather because it is easier to differentiate pitches in the range of the top two courses than on the lower courses.[17] For instance, at a pitch level of A = 440 Hz the average listener's ability to discriminate pitch differences is three times better at the open first course of a lute or viol than it is on the open sixth course.[18] When tuning by ear, you have a better chance of starting off correctly and avoiding compounding errors if you begin with the higher pitched strings. Occasionally, though, it is difficult to get the first string to register on an electronic tuner in the visual mode on Renaissance lute, in which case the tone generation mode is better. The octave string of the lute's sixth course, however, always produces a stable enough tone to register on a tuner. From there, it's an easy enough matter to tune the first course to the octave of the sixth.

One final point about reference pitches. Setting a lute or viol to a particular pitch level is most crucial, of course, when you are rehearsing or performing with other musicians; however, when you are practicing without any upcoming rehearsals or concerts in the near term, you may not want to go to the trouble of tuning your instrument precisely up to pitch. The important thing is that your instrument is tuned to itself. There's often a string or course that seems to never go out of tune. On my eight-course Renaissance lute, that's my seventh course F—practically tuned at the factory, as they say. For a quick tuning without the tuner, I just use that course as my reference pitch, tuning the open fourth course F to the seventh. From there it is an easy matter to initiate the tuning process from the fourth course by comparing unisons and octaves as described below. It may not be absolutely pitch-perfect, but it's usually close enough for the task at hand.

COMPARING PITCHES

There are many approaches to comparing pitches to bring one in accord with another. It is generally easier to start from below and tune up to the reference pitch, although very experienced tuners can lock in on the correct pitch from either direction, much the same way a good batter can connect with pitches from both right- and left-handers. Many musicians compare the note to be tuned with the reference pitch melodically, that is, by playing the notes sequentially, the reference pitch first and then the untuned pitch. It can also help to play them backward, the untuned pitch first. I find it helpful to play them in the following order: untuned string, reference string, slight pause, reference string, untuned string. You may have to perform this sequence several times to make sure you have properly identified which string is lower or higher than the other. Take care to play the pitches you are comparing at the same volume. On lute, notes played with the thumb will sound louder than those played with the index finger. The volume differential can distort your perception of pitch. Similarly, viol players must recognize the volume and sometimes pitch differential between push and pull strokes. Some players find matching the pitches vocally while tuning can clarify the relationship between the two notes since your voice's timbre will be consistent between the two pitches.

Occasionally pitches are so close together that because of the timbre differential between the two strings, you are unable to easily identify the relationship between the two. In these sorts of situations, we sometimes overthink the task. Should you suspect that to be the case, lowering the untuned string and very quickly bringing it up to match the reference string allows your ears to take over before your mind gets in the way.

Other players find it easier to tune harmonically, that is, by playing both pitches simultaneously. This technique is quite useful when you have already tuned one of the strings of a double course and are bringing its partner up to pitch. On small lutes this necessitates bringing the untuned string up to pitch very fast before the tone decays. This technique only works when you are able to free your left hand from having to hold down a fretted note, which is not always possible. A word of caution with regard to tuning harmonically: assiduously avoid the temptation to fret a note with your left hand and reach for the tuning pegs with your right after plucking the notes simultaneously. From the audience's perspective, this method looks extremely awkward because your right arm crosses in front of and obscures your face as your body contorts itself as your right hand reaches for the pegbox.

UNISONS AND OCTAVES

Tuning by comparing unisons and octaves assumes that you have already set your frets, although this method can also guide your fret placement in case you have not set your frets and confirm the accuracy of their locations if you have. The goal of this method is to initiate a series of concordances between the open strings and unisons and octaves, many of which are fretted, starting from the reference pitch string. Fretted notes at the 2nd and 3rd frets, particularly on the higher courses or strings, work quite well because they are less likely to be affected by sharpening. For the same reason, comparing 12th fret harmonics against fretted notes works well, too. As a further check, you can then employ the 4th,

5th, 7th, and 8th frets recommended by Dowland and so many others. Before commencing, make sure that the variable *mi* and *fa* frets line up where they should; this primarily affects frets that accommodate both *mis* and *fas,* such as the 1st, 4th, and 6th frets. With these and the other checks to be described below, you can construct a tuning matrix that practically guarantees your being thoroughly in tune. As with anything else, what follows may at first seem like a lot to do, but once you get comfortable with this series of tuning checks, it is very fast, easy, and effective.

For my initial tuning, once I have brought the first course up to pitch, I usually tune in the following order as represented in musical example 7.4, an approach similar to the one advanced by Gerle.[19] This tactic has several virtues. First, it begins with the open first and sixth course double octaves, which are very easy to hear and require no left-hand activity so that you can tune harmonically if you prefer. On octave courses, I always begin with the octave rather than the fundamental because it is closer to the reference pitch. On a lute with an octave sixth course, for instance, the 12th fret harmonic of the octave string provides a unison with the open first course. After tuning the octave string, I then tune the fundamental to the octave. From there I tune the fourth course to the sixth, which I can check with the first. Once the fourth course is tuned, it's on to the second, and so on. An advantage to this tuning order is that it provides a double check of each course, in most cases, immediately after it has been tuned. This method works on viols as well, although it involves melodic rather than harmonic comparisons. For this reason, viol treatises tend to favor the common 4th and 5th fret unison checks as presented in musical example 7.7. More on this in chapter 9.

After this initial tuning, I usually play a quick succession of chords featuring several open strings since tuning them is our primary goal. The sequence I've settled on for better or worse appears in musical example 7.5. Because I've become so familiar with how these chords sound, it is very easy to quickly identify errant tuning. You may come up with something different that works better for you. Either way, it's important to devise a method that tunes each

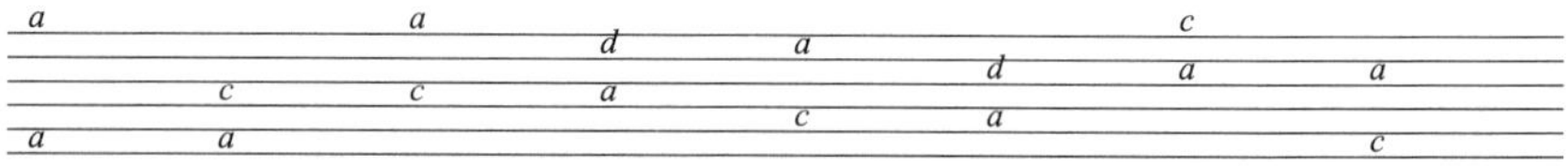

Musical Example 7.4. Octave comparisons at the 2nd and 3rd frets.

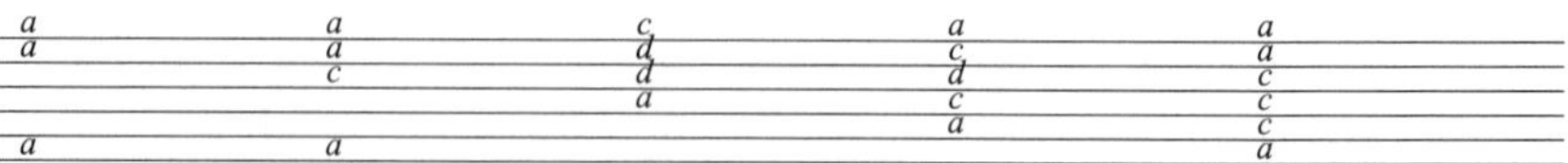

Musical Example 7.5. Quick chord checks involving the 2nd and 3rd frets.

course and concludes with a series of chord confirmations that becomes routine to you.

Once you are sure that your 2nd and 3rd frets are correctly positioned, it's a relatively simple matter to check the rest of them. Before attending to the remaining frets, however, beginning with the second string, comparing the open string 12th fret harmonic with the next highest fretted string is another extremely quick and easy way to confirm the accuracy of your open string tuning; in fact, it is so fast that some players actually begin with this method.[20] As you can see from musical example 7.6, this method tunes each open string in turn.

You may be wondering why I suggest beginning with these methods rather than the ubiquitous 4th and 5th fret method in musical example 7.7 that appears in so many lute and viol books. It is because the 4th and 5th frets frequently require some sort of sharpening adjustment as you approach the lowest courses. Also, on the lute, the timbral difference between the two pitches creating the unison involving an open and fretted string is often significant enough to interfere with your ability to distinguish minute pitch differences.

Following Gerle's lead, John Dowland's famous diagram that appears in his son's *Varietie of Lute Lessons* (1610) and presented here as figure 7.2 augments the 4th and 5th fret comparisons with the following checks as shown in musical example 7.8.[21] After these checks, we have now established or confirmed the locations of the 2nd, 3rd, 4th, 5th, 7th, and 8th frets.

What remains? The 1st fret and its tastino, the 6th fret, and those beyond the 8th fret. We can easily fix the location of the 1st fret by the octave and/or unison checks illustrated in diagram 7.3. Similarly, we can locate the position of the 1st fret tastino by comparing it with the octaves as indicated in diagram 7.6, assuming that the 4th fret is set as a *mi.* Setting the 6th fret as a *mi* is as easy as sliding up the octave relationships between the 1st and 3rd frets as presented in diagram 7.3 to the 4th and 6th frets. If, however, you want the 6th fret to be a *fa,* you can slide the octave relationships in diagram 7.6 up to the 3rd and 6th frets. Most important, you must make sure that when you tune by octaves, you compare *mis* with *mis* and *fas* with *fas.* The inability to understand this relationship is the cause of so many commentators erroneously claiming that

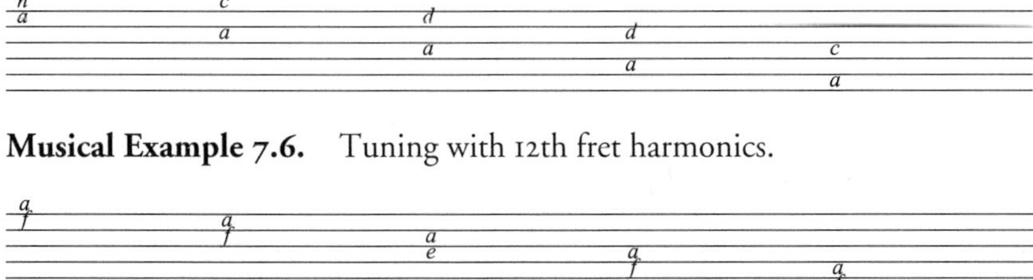

Musical Example 7.6. Tuning with 12th fret harmonics.

Musical Example 7.7. Tuning with the 4th and 5th frets.

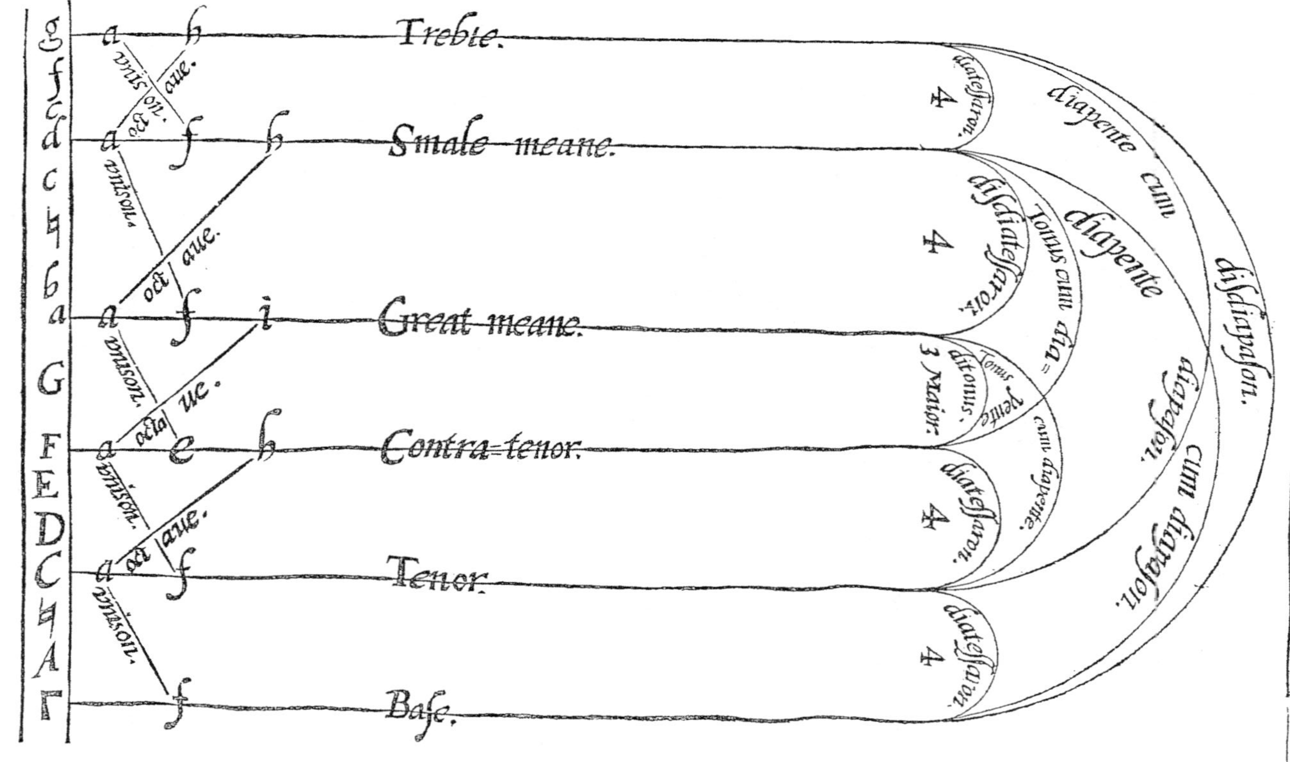

Figure 7.2. John Dowland's tuning chart in Robert Dowland's *Varietie of Lute Lessons.*

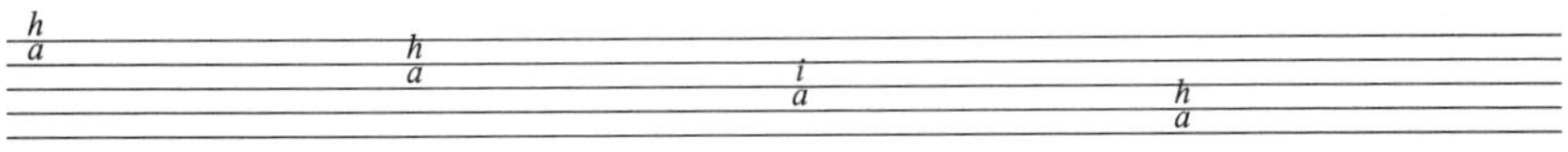

Musical Example 7.8. Dowland's 7th and 8th fret tuning checks.

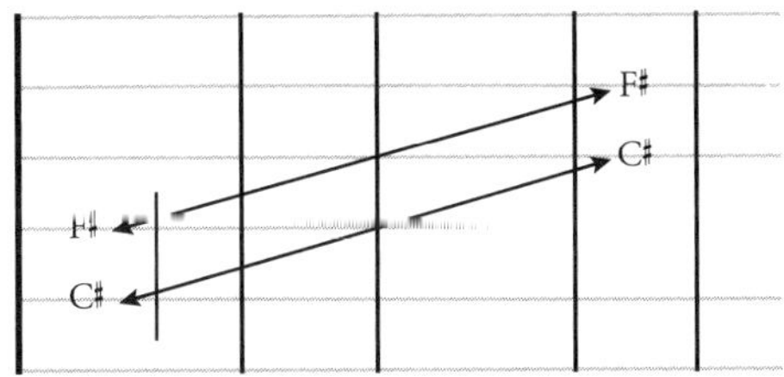

Diagram 7.6. Setting the 1st fret tastino by octaves.

the octaves and unisons in unequal temperaments don't line up. Of course, *mis* don't form octaves with *fas;* they are different pitches.

Finally, after you believe that you have set your frets well, it is advisable to play the basic chords in the tonalities you have on your docket, particularly those involving fretted notes on the lowest courses. As Mary Burwell's tutor mentions and Ganassi repeats multiple times throughout his book, it is important to check, double-check, and cross-check your tuning through a variety of methods. All of this may seem like a great deal of trouble to make sure that you are in tune, but if you create your own routine and do it regularly, all the preceding can take only a few brief minutes.

To your set frets in Pythagorean tuning, simply follow these directions reversing the *mis* and *fas,* but always making sure to compare *mis* against *mis* and *fas* against *fas.*[22] By now you realize that tuning your instrument with 7th fret harmonics can work only in Pythagorean tuning since those harmonics produce pure fifths, which are of course, wider than equal and meantone fifths.[23]

For equal temperament, you can follow the procedures described above, but disregard the *mis* and *fas.* Baroque guitar is almost identical to the lute and viol except that the major third is between the second and third courses rather than the third and fourth. Since the open string pattern repeats itself on the Baroque lute, once one set of A, D, and F courses are tuned following similar procedures easily tailored to the Baroque lute's open string tuning, it is simply a matter of tuning the second set of A, D, F courses to the first.

When tuning to a keyboard, it is best to tune each of your open strings as well as the frets on your highest-sounding course individually to match the keyboard's temperament, which, if you are fortunate, will be set in a regular rather than irregular temperament.

Extending the Pitch Range

We now explore the various methods by which we can expand our palette of available pitches or in theoretical terms, how to extend meantone temperaments. When we choose a particular wolf on a keyboard, we also select a specific default set of pitches, for instance, E♭ rather than D♯ or G♯ rather than A♭. On lutes and viols, however, we can have our cake and eat it, too. The rest of this chapter and much of the next two are dedicated to explaining how that ability is fortunately already baked into our cake; we just need to learn how to take advantage of it. This, however, is a good place to pause to reflect on exactly what we are trying to accomplish. In most situations, we hope to produce a *mi* at a *fa* fret or vice versa; that is, we are attempting to traverse from one side of the harmonic diesis to the other in our given temperament. As you recall, we saw how those widths translate into physical distances on the fretboard.

The distance between the main fret and the tastino, strand of a double or split fret, or the opposite ends of a slanted fret decreases as we progress from 1/4-comma to 1/8-comma meantone. When considering the amount of cents you are able to raise or lower a pitch, you must keep in mind your goal. In 1/4-comma meantone temperament, that is a rather large 42c. Given the circumstances, you may not be able to bridge that gap. On the other hand, the 9c. of the 1/8-comma harmonic diesis is generally quite feasible, and by combining fret location and pulling and pushing, the 19.2c. of 1/6-comma meantone is realistic. Furthermore, there is no law that says that in 1/4-comma meantone temperament, for instance, every major third must be precisely 386c.; some you may be able to only get to 396c. or whatever. You do the best you can and need not worry that the temperament police are ready to pounce. That said, if the music you're playing is chromatic or your pieces travel through a wide variety of tonal areas, an attenuated meantone temperament with a larger number of narrower slices of the comma might be more manageable. As always, it's up to you.

TASTINI

Notwithstanding the historical documentation indicating that the use of tastini may have been limited, they are invaluable assets capable of significantly extending our available pitch range, particularly *mis* on the lower courses of the 1st fret. While I imagine that the majority of lutenists relied instead on slanted, double, or split frets for such purposes, or hid "bad" pitches as Duprey mentions and many others before him, such as Quantz, have advised, there is no reason we should deprive ourselves of the convenience of tastini. The benefits they provide are less singular for the viol because of its ability to shade pitches lower by placing the finger a little closer toward the nut.

In each open string lute tuning, the prevailing *fa* position for the 1st fret should be augmented by at least one *mi* position (tastino) for solo music or several for continuo. For instance, an F♯ at the 1st fret of the fourth course in the G tuning and the G♯ in the A tuning are practically obligatory for much of the solo repertoire. For continuo use, which is discussed in greater detail in chapter 8, a tastino covering the fourth through even seventh courses in open A tuning for theorbo that includes a fretted seventh course in G is most advantageous, particularly for first inversion major chords. Tastini can, of course, be placed anywhere and in great numbers, for instance, to reproduce irregular keyboard temperaments such as Vallotti. This can, of course, be quite unwieldy. In most circumstances, as we have seen, irregular temperaments can be approximated sufficiently without going to such extreme lengths.

Three effective methods for affixing tastini involve tape, glue, or carved-out slots with inserts. I use Scotch tape to attach an old stiff section of fret gut sized the same diameter or slightly wider than the 1st fret to the *mi* position between the nut and *fa* fret. On Renaissance lute, I usually cover only the fourth and sometimes also the fifth courses to get the F♯ and C♯. Admittedly, my method is not the most elegant nor historically authentic, but it is effective. I simply cut the length of fret I need and attach it to a piece of 1/2 in. wide invisible write-on tape or a trimmed piece of matte finish Scotch tape that I slide between the surface of the fretboard and the strings with my forceps and then drop down to the premarked *mi* location I determined by placing a loose fret segment under the string and matching the desired pitch to that produced or measured by my tuner. The trick is to slide the tape just under the strings so that the sticky side does not grip the fretboard until you've reached your desired location. Figure 7.3 shows the taped tastino as it is about to be slid under the fourth course. After the tape is pressed down on either side of the fret, it looks like figure 7.4. On theorbo, sometimes old fret segments are simply not thick enough. While some players use matchsticks or other materials, I've had success with toothpicks, which I sand to the appropriate thickness, affixing the sanded and therefore flattened side to the fingerboard. Figure 7.5 shows the toothpick segment attached to the tape, while figure 7.6 shows how it looks in place. Regardless of the material you use, there is a slim range of thickness that will serve your purpose: it can't be so thick that it buzzes against the unfretted string above it or so thin that when fretted the string buzzes against the *fa* 1st fret. My theorbo tastino covers the fourth through seventh courses: G♯, D♯, A♯, and G♯. Other lutenists attach their tastini with glue, which certainly looks cleaner than my method.

Unquestionably, the best approach is to have a luthier carve out a wide slot between your 1st fret *fa* position and the nut that can receive tastini inserts in a variety of temperaments and lengths such as those created by Maurice Ottiger for Matthias Spaeter's lute. Figures 7.7 and 7.8 show his tastino and flush inserts.

Figure 7.3. Old fret segment tastino prepared for attachment with tape and forceps. Photograph by author.

Figure 7.4. Old fret segment tastino attached with tape. Photograph by author.

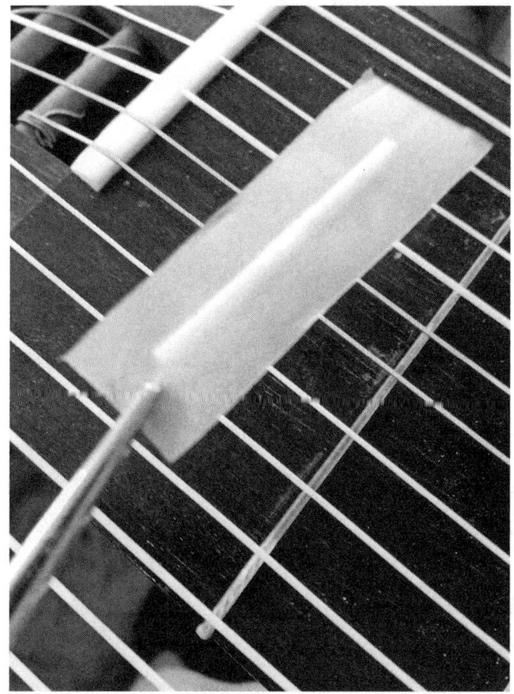

Figure 7.5. Toothpick tastino prepared for attachment with tape and forceps. Photograph by author.

Figure 7.6. Toothpick tastino attached with tape. Photograph by author.

Figure 7.7. Tastino insert. Courtesy of Maurice Ottiger.

Figure 7.8. Flush insert. Courtesy of Maurice Ottiger.

DOUBLE AND SPLIT FRETS

The term *double fret* generally refers to a single strand of fret tied in such a fashion as to present two frets touching each other so as to function as a single fret. It is also sometimes used to refer to two separate frets: one for the *mi* position and one for the *fa.* A split fret is a single strand double fret in which the two frets are separated so that one portion of the strand serves as a *mi* and the other a *fa.*

We associate double and split frets almost exclusively with viols, but there is considerable evidence that lutenists as well used a double fret at least for the 1st fret, not the least of which is Thomas Mace's detailed instructions for tying double frets, although he also describes how to tie single frets as well, as if it were the latest thing, suggesting that at one time double frets may have been quite common. Bermudo discussed placing a double 1st fret, that is, one fret for the *mi* and the other for the *fa,* and Tim Watson's research as cited above is supported by the recommendation in Bartolomeo Lieto Panhormitano's *Dialogo quarto di musica* (Naples, 1559) to split double frets on the vihuela or lute.[24] Moreover, dozens of historical paintings represent double-fretted lutes. Tobias Stimmer's *Portrait of Melchior Neusiedler at the Age of 43,* for instance, clearly shows the great German lutenist (1531–1594) holding a lute where a double 1st fret and single 2nd fret are clearly visible. And as we have seen, Christopher Simpson referred to the use of an additional 1st fret on viols and theorbo more than one hundred years later in 1667. As with tastini, double and split frets are more helpful on instruments with longer string lengths and with temperaments that have a wider harmonic diesis, in both cases, simply because they can provide a wider physical space between *mi* and *fa* positions than can a slanted fret especially in 1/4-comma meantone temperament.

Split frets consisting of a division between the two separate strands of a double fret, however, do indeed work much better on viols than on lutes because double frets are easier to tie on curved than flat fretboards. Split or double frets are practically essential for the bass viol because, as Hoffmann points out, the harmonic diesis at the 1st fret on a bass is approximately 1.5 cm wide, far too great a width for a slanted fret, our next topic of discussion.[25]

SLANTED FRETS

Slanted frets compensate for sharpening and/or provide alternate *mi* or *fa* locations. In either case, the pitches between the outer two courses will normally be imperfect, but are usually close because the increased string length along the slanted fret as it approaches the bass side coincides with the increased thickness of the strings and greater likelihood that compensation for sharpening is required with each lower string except for on the theorbo as noted above because of its re-entrant tuning.[26] When slanting a fret, make sure that the bass portion slanted toward the nut doesn't drag the treble portion with it. After slanting a fret to acquire a particular pitch over the short term, be sure to check the location of the treble portion when you return it to perpendicular because it has probably slipped toward the nut.

Now, let us return to diagram 7.5 to examine how we might employ slanted frets to access accidentals outside of the fret's prevailing enharmonic identity. In each open string tuning, certainly on the lute, tastini are a better option to access sharp notes on the lower courses of the 1st fret, although slanting the fret toward the bass can provide an acceptable alternative, particularly in broader temperaments such as 1/6- or 1/8-comma meantone since the fret does not have to be slanted at an extreme angle to accomplish our goals. In each open string tuning, you must take care to not slant the 1st fret too extremely because *mi* versions of the pitches at the 1st fret of the third course only occur rarely in the case of the G open string tuning (B♭ vs. A♯) and virtually never in the case of the A and D open string tunings (C vs. B♯ and F vs. E♯). Should you have no alternative but to slant the 1st fret, be prepared to raise the pitch of the note on the third course on the fly by some other means as discussed below.

Slanting frets to access *mis* and *fas* at the same fret is an issue particularly with solo repertoire that ranges far and wide harmonically such as that found in Gorzanis's and Galilei's works cited above, which include pieces in all twenty-four key areas. In collections such as these where each individual piece in a major mode tends to be in a tonality that favors the sharp or flat side, assuming a 1st fret tastino, it is usually a matter of choosing the correct *mi/fa* fret positions, a statement that could still certainly apply to the vast majority of music played on fretted instruments. Problems will more likely arise in minor tonalities because the dominant chord is occasionally found in a sharp tonality whereas the other chords are not, for example, in the cases of G Minor and D Minor with their D Major and A Major dominant chords, respectively, which require secure locations for their thirds (F♯ and C♯).

Assuming a tastino for the 1st fret *mis* on the lower courses, in the G tuning, for solo music we occasionally need to access the G♯ on the first course at the 1st fret instead of the A♭, usually when playing in A Minor such as John Dowland's "Semper Dowland Semper Dolens." When playing continuo, it is easy enough to simply choose a location for an E Major chord that doesn't involve the 1st fret. In solo music, slanting the fret in the opposite direction, that is, moving the fret closer to the nut at the first course, can provide that G♯. This is often accomplished coupled with slanting the 3rd fret toward the bass to move the A♭ on the fourth course closer to G♯ and setting your 6th fret as a *mi,* in which case your first few frets would look something like diagram 7.7. In this configuration, you must be prepared to pull the third string 3rd fret C natural up a little bit depending on how much you've slanted the fret. The B♭ at the 3rd fret of the sixth course that shows up quite frequently in "Semper Dowland" requires attention, but once you know that it is an issue, you can be prepared for it. From these examples, you can immediately see why 1/6-comma meantone

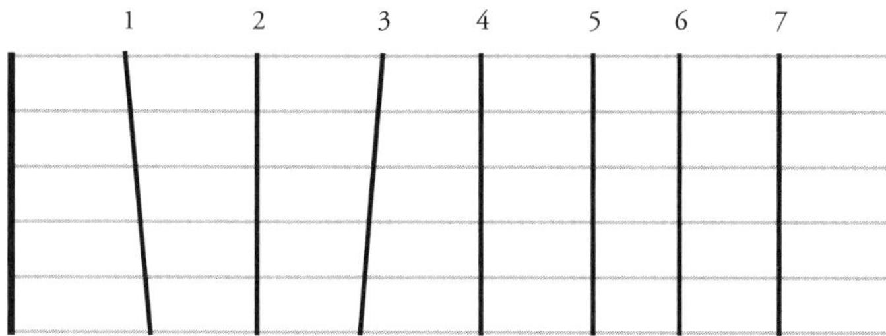

Diagram 7.7. A Minor configuration for instrument in G.

Figure 7.9. Lute with G♯ tastini. Courtesy of John Schneider.

works much better than 1/4-comma meantone if you hope to access additional pitches through slanting frets. Some players use tastini is such situations, which certainly provides a more precise pitch. This approach can work well on a larger instrument such as John Schneider's lute, shown in figure 7.9.

In solo music or lute song tablature accompaniments, we are naturally less inclined to refinger the tablature because the composer has gone to the trouble to specify the exact location on the fingerboard of the notes to be played, although I see no moral cause for such reticence. Self-contained pieces that traverse a wide tonal landscape such as Spinacino's "Recercare I/38" (1507), Castaldi's "Cromatica corrente" (1622), or Kapsberger's famous "Toccata arpeggiata" (1604), which will be examined later, usually require careful fret setting, slanted frets, tastini, compromise positions, and pulling and pushing, or a combination of all of them.[27] We now turn our attention to compromise positions.

COMPROMISE POSITIONS

Keyboards unequipped with split keys and fretted instruments with exclusively perpendicular frets share a similar limitation: one key or fret must stand for either a *mi* or a *fa,* such as D♯/E♭. In the case of frets, that identity prevails for the note sounded on each course at that fret. It is, to be sure, a vexing problem that led some players to accept compromise key pitches or fret positions. And it certainly explains the utility of equal temperament for fixed fret instruments such as the guitar that traverse wide ranges of key areas.

In his approximately 1/6-comma meantone temperament for organ, Arnolt Schlick placed a note halfway between G and A to serve as both G♯ and A♭, and Hans Gerle's approximately 1/6-comma meantone fretting scheme leaves the location of the 4th fret vague: it should be placed somewhere between the 3rd and 5th frets.[28] Both Gerle and Dowland recommend compromise positions for the 6th fret. As we have seen, makers of fixed metal-fret instruments, their players, and presumably Milán and others who recommend sweetening notes by moving just one fret, were not much troubled by the fact that the interval between two nominal pitches might differ from location to location. Compromise fret positions involve either a position halfway between the *mi* and *fa* fret positions or a position slightly shaded toward one or the other of the positions depending on the musical requirements. Compromise fret positions can be an effective strategy when the notes involved are melodically fleeting, for instance, in a scale, and particularly if they are not struck simultaneously with another note. If that note is an octave, unless the compromised note can be raised or lowered to match the octave by other means on the fly, such as pulling and pushing as discussed below, a compromise fret position alone will not work. Compromise positions should be considered an effective stopgap measure or last resort when the circumstances do not permit the forethought required to work around *mi/fa* conflicts through other means.

PULLING AND PUSHING

We have already encountered the observation by many notable music theorists that variations of left-hand finger pressure and location can influence the pitch of the note produced on fretted instruments.[29] Players of unfretted string instruments must constantly make such adjustments, and bending strings is a basic technique in rock and roll and blues guitar, so it shouldn't surprise us that fretted instrument players of the Renaissance and Baroque eras did the same, albeit for slightly different purposes. On viols and the lute in particular, however, it is a sophisticated technique, but one that can pay generous dividends.

Pulling and pushing the strings on fretted instruments doesn't change the length of the string, but rather its tension, which impacts the pitch. Pulling the string toward the nut raises the tension and thus the pitch, while pushing it toward the bridge with the finger jammed right up against the fret yields the opposite effect. To a lesser extent, increasing the pressure on the string with either the left-hand finger right next to the fret can slightly increase the pitch while lessening the left-hand pressure while placing the finger almost on the fret can lower the pitch ever so slightly on viols; as can applying very light left-hand pressure farther away from the fret.[30] This topic is discussed in more detail in chapter 9. We must be particularly careful to not strike too vociferously a note that is either already impacted by sharpening or whose pitch we do not want to raise because, for instance, it might be the third in a major chord.

The effectiveness of pulling and pushing is in part determined by where along the string it is fretted, but also by the thickness of the fret. All other things equal, pulling and pushing is easier and more effective on thicker than thinner frets. Effectiveness is also inversely proportional to the length of the vibrating portion of the string. In other words, the effectiveness of pulling and pushing increases as you progress from the 1st to 12th frets because an increasing percentage of the force applied to the pulling and pushing is exerted on the vibrating portion of the string as it is reduced in length. But the greater ease of pulling and pushing as we move toward the 12th fret also has its perils: it becomes much easier to unintentionally pull the string out of its track laterally thereby unintentionally raising the pitch.[31]

Varying the pitch by pulling and pushing is much more successful on viols and to a slightly lesser degree on single-course lutes such as the theorbo. Beyond its ability to influence the pitch with the bow, the viol has significant advantages over the lute and theorbo in terms of tuning in general and pulling and pushing. Once a note is bowed and a tuning discrepancy is noticed it can be quickly corrected, whereas on the lute, once the note is plucked it begins to rapidly dissipate. On the lute, if it's out of tune, short of quickly dampening the string, there's nothing to be done. The viol's higher action and thicker strings with higher tensions provide the player with much more of an opportunity to adjust the pitch than on plucked instruments. And, while there are, of course, exceptions, such as the lyra viol repertoire and the advanced music of Sainte-Colombe and Marais, the fact that most viol music is single line in contrast to the chordal and contrapuntal repertoire of plucked instruments makes the viol more amenable to pulling and pushing.

While relaxing the left-hand pressure at almost any fret on my theorbo has virtually no effect on the pitch, increasing it with the finger placed right next to the fret can raise the pitch by as much 8–9c. on the thicker courses. Pushing the finger against the fret with significant force toward the bridge lowers the pitch by only about 2–3c. at the 1st fret but by as much as 7–8c. at the 5th fret and on the lower courses. On the lute's first few frets on the thinner strings, I find it nearly impossible or very difficult to lower the pitch by this method. Again, a great deal of pressure is required. Pulling, on the other hand, shows more dramatic results. On the 1st fret of the second string of a theorbo, pulling raises the pitch as much as 15c. while at the 5th fret, it is in the 15–20c. range. On the lower courses, it is not difficult to raise the pitch by as much as 25c. This is good news because, as we have seen, it is more likely that the frets will have to be slanted toward the nut on the bass side both to compensate for sharpening and to provide *mis;* when the occasional *fa* is required, pulling is more than up to the task.

On double-course lutes, we must rely more heavily on fret arrangement, or should we intend to pull and push, since we cannot alter the pitch as substantially as on single-course instruments, pulling and pushing should be used in conjunction with a broader more serviceable temperament or compromise fret positions as discussed previously. Varying the pitch by pulling and pushing works better on gut than synthetic strings, but is particularly successful on wire-strung instruments, especially those with scalloped frets.

Although on the surface this technique seems almost improvised, it actually takes careful forethought and planning. For instance, Elizabeth Liddle tells us that if you intend on raising the pitch with your left-hand fingers, the frets should be placed as low, that is, toward the nut, as practicable.[32] It is also advisable to know in advance which notes you intend to raise ahead of time so that your left-hand finger can anticipate where it needs to be and the amount of pressure to be applied slightly ahead of time so there's no scoop to the note. I mark such notes in my score with ↑ or ↓.

When trying to raise the pitch of a note within a chord, as is usually the case on theorbo, bending the string sideways out of its track is considerably easier than pulling the string, which can be difficult when the other fingers are occupied holding down other chord tones. As the guitarists among us already know, bending the string can alter the pitch as much as a semitone or more as you approach the bridge. For single melodic notes, with very little effort, bending the string out of its track a little and pulling a little simultaneously can yield the same results as a great deal of bending or pulling. Resorting to pulling and bending is most useful in solo compositions, such as Castaldi's "Cromatica corrente" for theorbo, where twelve of the required 4th fret notes are *mis,* whereas only four *fas* are required, all for the E♭ on the third string (mm. 7, 21, 38, and 45). See musical example 7.9. Since *mis* are required on adjacent strings, the only option is to pull or bend the D♯ up to the E♭, which is relatively easy in this case because three of the E♭s are single notes, and one is in a chord that can be easily fingered to facilitate pulling and/or bending the E♭.

The preceding is, of course, not a comprehensive guide; however, you can apply the principles it represents to almost any situation. Although in the vast majority of cases, a 1st fret tastino and frets in the most common *mi/fa* configurations, as illustrated in diagram 7.5, will be all you will ever need. As you are surely beginning to realize, for those exceptional cases, we have a plethora of tools at our disposal, some easier to master than others, but all nevertheless worth knowing about whether we choose to use them or not.

Musical Example 7.9. Bellerofonte Castaldi, "Cromatica corrente."

Musical Example 7.9. (*Continued*)

Beginning in the early sixteenth century, Italian music and the foreign repertoires it influenced began to display increasing chromaticism leading up to the early seventeenth-century experiments of composers such as Castaldi and Girolamo Giovanni Kapsberger (1580–1651). Nevertheless, the vast majority of their music makes no extraordinary claims on our tuning skills. Kapsberger's best-known theorbo solo, "Toccata arpeggiata" from his *Libro primo d'intavolatura di chitarrone (1604),* does, however, require some tuning finesse. Refer to musical example 7.10 and audio file 7.6. As is often the case in this repertoire, a 1st fret tastino is required only once for the G♯ on the fourth string in m. 35. Slanting the 4th fret so that the treble side yields *fas* and the bass side *mis* handily accommodates the four *fas* in mm. 2–3, 28–29, and the one *mi* in m. 48. Since the single *mi* is conveniently fretted with the rather strong first finger, the 4th fret could be slanted less dramatically so that the slant would take the 1st finger note on the sixth string halfway toward the C♯, while pushing the string into the fret could finish the job.

The final difficulty also arises from C♯, but this time, an octave higher, the C♯ on the fourth string at the 6th fret in m. 17. Since there are seven measures that require *fas* for the second and third strings at the 6th fret (mm. 13–15, 25–27, and 29), the 6th fret must be a *fa* and cannot be slanted without compromising the B♭ on the second string and the F natural on the third string. The

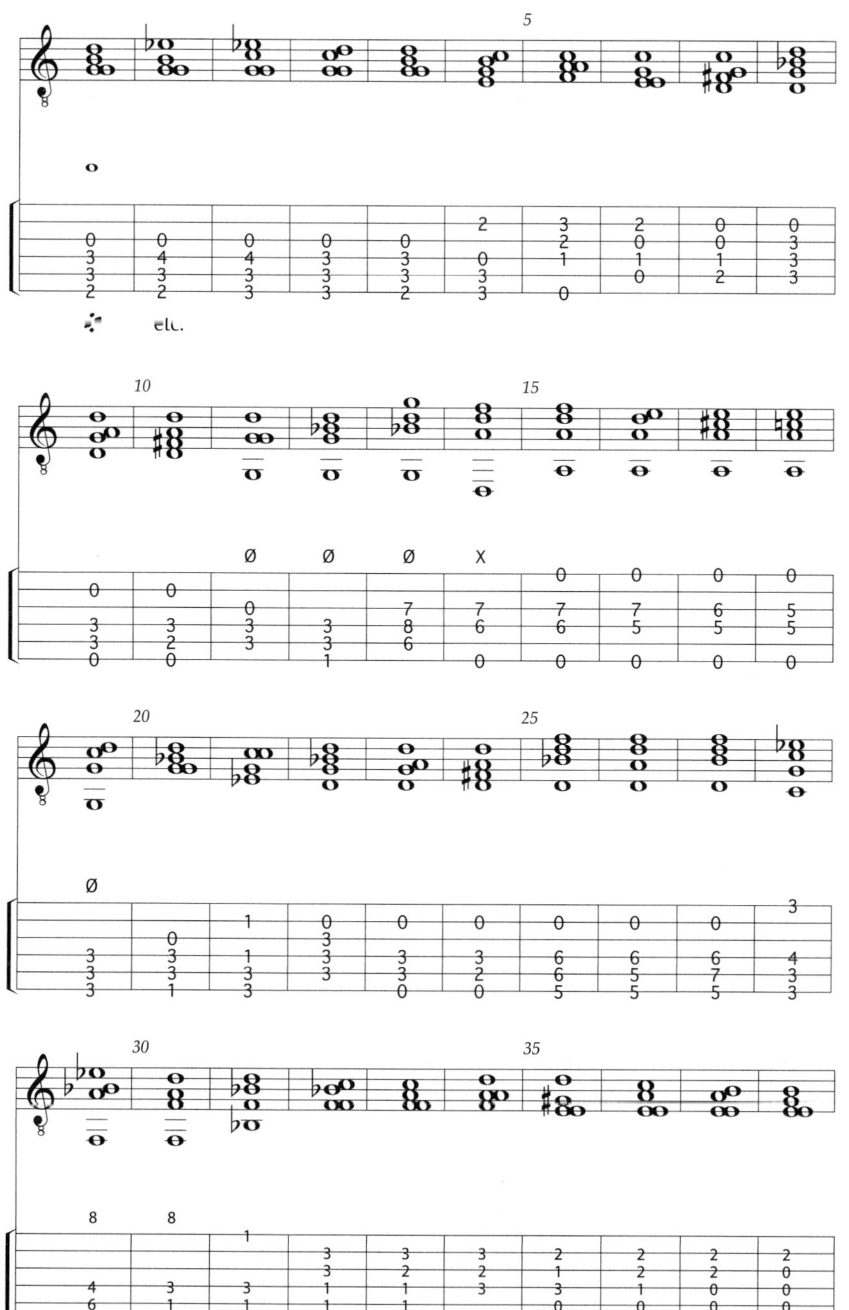

Musical Example 7.10. Girolamo Giovanni Kapsberger, "Toccata arpeggiata."

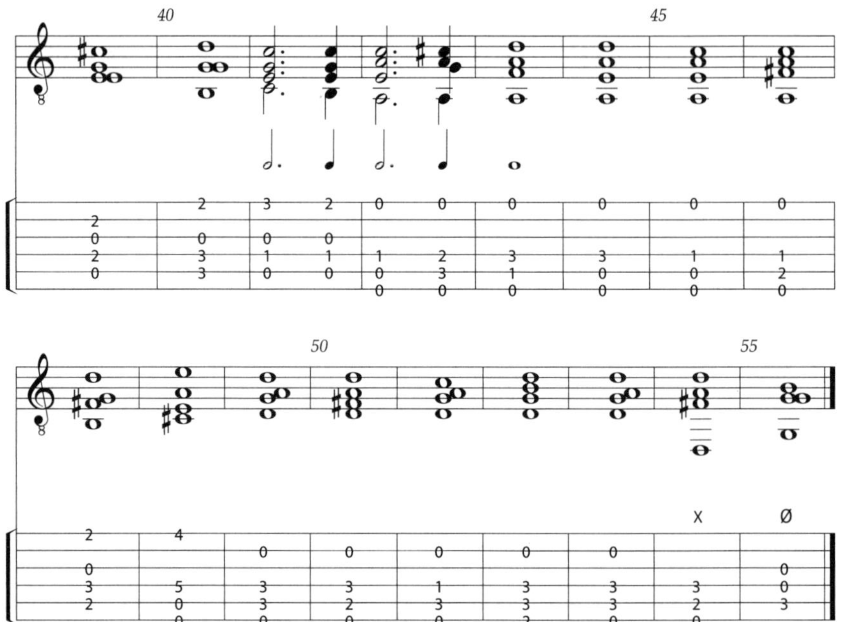

Musical Example 7.10. (*Continued*)

only remaining option to achieve the C♯ is to push the string into the fret to lower the pitch. Fortunately, the second finger that frets this note is more than up to the task, particularly since it is at the 6th fret, where pushing is more easily accomplished than at the lower frets. You can easily check how much pressure is required to bring that pitch down to C♯ by playing it into your tuner in the visual mode or simply comparing it with the C♯ at the 2nd fret of the third string.

Castaldi's response to Kapsberger's "Toccata arpeggiata," his virtuosic "Arpeggiata a mio modo," which traverses the key areas of D, A, E, B, and G Minor and D, C, G, F, E, B, A, and B♭ Major, requires nothing but a 1st fret tastino for the G♯ on the fourth course to accommodate its two fleeting appearances.

This chapter has focused on the basics of tuning using solo lute and theorbo repertoire to demonstrate the various techniques at our disposal to create more precise tuning in whatever system we choose, although the emphasis has been strongly on meantone temperaments. It is now time to consider the subtleties of tuning while playing with others.

CHAPTER EIGHT

Continuo

Perhaps the most common occasion in which fretted instrument players must understand how meantone temperaments function is when realizing a bass line. Because continuo realization requires attention to the *mi/fa* identity of each chord tone, you must know your fingerboard thoroughly and mind your *mis* and *fas.* To be sure, this is an advanced skill but essential for archlute and theorbo players who hope to play in professional or high-caliber amateur ensembles.

Though there is no law against refingering to suit your needs, for intabulated solo and accompanied music such as lute songs, the realization of your chosen temperament is mostly a matter of prearranging the frets the best you can and working within and occasionally around those confines. While providing continuo, however, you have many more options because you can realize a bass line however you choose. Once the frets are set, your decisions pertain to where on the fingerboard you elect to realize the harmony at hand. Here is where your fingerboard knowledge earns its keep—there is simply no substitute for knowing where the notes are. If you do not already know where all the notes can be found for your particular open string tuning, I suggest that you memorize the standard *mi/fa* fret locations for instruments in G and A in meantone temperaments as shown in diagram 7.5. Be particularly conscious of the identity of the pitches at the 4th and 6th frets, but also their alternate *mi/fa* positions, as these are the frets you are most likely to have to move depending on the key you're in. In both open string tunings, you will be best served by a tastino covering the 1st fret *mi* position on the lower three courses or a double or split fret, and in the case of instruments with a fretted seventh course, by a tastino that covers four courses to also provide a *mi* on the seventh course.

By now you know that the *mi/fa* identity of the third defines both major and minor chords, whether the chord is in root position or first or second inversion. This means, of course, that regardless of inversion, you must know which finger in your chord shape plays the third and at which fret that third, rather than its enharmonic partner, is available with the caveat that your favorite chord pattern may not work for a particular chord given the arrangement of your frets. At first this may seem daunting, but once internalized it becomes second nature. When realizing an accompaniment from a bass line, figured or not, rather than a tablature that specifies particular fret locations for each note, you can preplan different locations for chords that use one or the other of the enharmonic versions of the same note. For example, it is a relatively simple matter to plot out one location for a B Major chord placing the D♯ on a *mi* fret and another for an E♭ Major chord with its E♭ on a *fa* fret because, as you know, D♯ and E♭ are not the same pitch in unequal temperaments.

Choosing a Temperament for Ensembles

In ensemble settings, you do not always have a voice in the selection of the prevailing tuning system because, for example, it may be dictated by the musical director, or perhaps the harpsichord or organ is already set in a particular temperament. At the professional level, many ensembles customarily perform in a specific temperament, which could even be an irregular temperament to which you must accommodate yourself as best you can. If you are told that the ensemble is set in "meantone" temperament, remember that for some people this means 1/4-comma meantone temperament, but it could also indicate that your colleagues are unaware that there are varieties of meantone temperament, in which case some clarification would be in order.

Often, however, the ensemble's director and musicians defer to the judgment of the continuo player who knows the most about tuning systems. If you can either tune the keyboard instrument yourself or explain to the tuner what temperament you want and how to use the temperament to an uninitiated keyboard player, you are likely to be able determine the ensemble's temperament. Most often the singers, strings, woodwinds, and brass are happy to adjust themselves to your temperament by ear. You can expedite the process by offering quick hints, such as explaining that in meantone temperaments the flat notes are a little higher than in equal temperament, the sharp notes and leading tones a little lower. On several recordings and in numerous Baroque opera performances, the conductor has allowed me to set the temperament as long as I dealt with the details. In most of these cases, the performance or recording would have been in equal temperament rather than 1/4- or 1/6-comma meantone temperament were I not given leave to influence the decision, which usually would have been no decision at all since equal is the default temperament du jour or, perhaps more accurately, *du siècle.*

On the other hand, you may find yourself in a situation where you must assess whether you will be able to influence the decision and, if so, whether it is worth the trouble or even likely to succeed given the circumstances. Sometimes, alas, it is best for you to keep your counsel and live to play another day in a temperament you prefer. For small chamber ensembles, you must go with the group or convince the group to go with you. And, finally, there are cases when equal temperament is the only option because, for instance, there is simply not enough time to get everyone on board. This can occur when you are a guest performer in an ensemble for a performance that has only one or two rehearsals before the concert or when students or modern instruments are involved. In any event, the more flexible you are, the more valuable you will be to any ensemble.

If you have the option, what temperament should you recommend? As you know by now, 1/6-comma meantone is my personal default choice, but for some repertoires, Monteverdi and Praetorius, for instance, I've set ensembles in 1/4-comma meantone temperament. My Collegium Musicum easily operates in 1/5-comma meantone for French programs, although 1/6 comma meantone is our default temperament, and we have found occasions to use 1/4-comma meantone temperament. Since we often use both a harpsichord and chamber organ on our programs, we can set the wolf on one of the keyboards to favor the sharp keys and the other to favor the flat keys, and even, occasionally, set the various manuals or ranks to extend the temperaments even further. Alison Crum recommends that viol consorts adopt an unequal temperament for "more beautiful harmonic tuning" and finds that 1/6-comma meantone is a good compromise that works well in the keys common to viol consorts.[1]

One last thing. When you are tuning the ensemble, try to get your fretless bowed string players to tune their open strings to the keyboard. Otherwise they will default to their normal procedures, which will inevitably lead to excessively wide fifths between their open strings and the cascading series of tuning problems that naturally issues from these inaccuracies.

Strategies

As a continuo player, you will likely find yourself either with the sole responsibility of realizing the bass line entirely on your own as the only chordal continuo player or in a group with other plucked and/or keyboard players. Most commonly, though, you will be the only plucked continuo player in an ensemble that also includes a harpsichord or a chamber organ. Each situation requires its own strategy.

When you are by yourself, your job is to play all the notes in the chord, if at all possible. This requires studying the score in advance and knowing its requirements well enough that you can set your frets and tastino(i) in a pattern that provides the majority of required pitches according to the key areas you will traverse while preparing to make the kinds of accommodations we discussed in the previous chapter for the pitches that do not fall within the fret arrangement. Assuming a 1st fret tastino, this will most likely involve relocations and/or slanting of the 4th and 6th frets. Quite often you will have the opportunity to adjust your frets between selections, for instance, sliding a *mi* 6th fret up to the *fa* position, but it is crucial that you indicate such directions in your score the same way you would remind yourself to raise your eighth course from

F to F♯. Using the previous example, I would place the following indication just below the last measure of the previous piece and above the first measure of the next one in case I get distracted and don't notice it the first time: VI → *fa* or VI = *fa.* With all that goes on during a concert, it is very easy to overlook shifting a fret, an oversight that the first sour chord involving that fret announces to you and the audience loudly and clearly.

On several occasions when I have found myself as the only plucked continuo player during an oratorio or opera that required my playing constantly throughout, setting my theorbo's lower frets to favor the *mis* and the upper frets to favor the *fas* allowed me to cover the bare necessities. This, of course, means either a lot of jumping around or a profusion of movable barré chords in the upper positions in flat keys—inconvenient, but it gets the job done.

On the other hand, when in doubt, leave it out. In his *Regola di musica* (1657) Giovanni d'Avella suggests avoiding the "incriminating notes" that produce unintended enharmonics, for example, a D♯ when an E♭ is required. Girolamo Diruta's *Il Transilvano* (1622) recommends passing quickly over any unavoidable wrong enharmonics so as to only hint at the intended note, a technique also described by Giovanfrancesco Becattelli (1721) and Pablo Nassare (1724). Johann Joachim Quantz (1752) offers continuo players two methods for handling a *mi* in place of a *fa* or vice versa: (1) simply leave out the offending notes, or (2) place them in the instrument's middle or lower register where they'll be less noticeable.[2] The first bit of advice usually amounts to playing an open fifth when you do not have the proper pitch available for the third, for instance, on the theorbo, in the absence of a 1st fret tastino, omitting the third on the fifth string in the B major chord in musical example 8.1 because without tastino, it is really musical example 8.2. With a 4th fret set as a *fa* and no 1st fret tastino, the second directive suggests refingering musical example 8.3, which is really musical example 8.4, as musical example 8.2 so that the E♭ is less prominent.

When you are fortunate enough to participate in an ensemble with another continuo player, regardless of instrument, and both versions of an enharmonic note are required over a period of time during which neither of you can make any adjustments, it becomes a matter of the strategic distribution of accidentals.

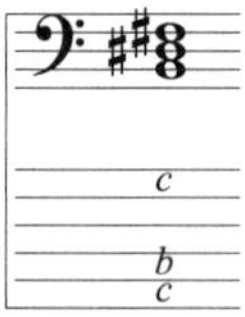

Musical Example 8.1. B Major on theorbo with major third on fifth course.

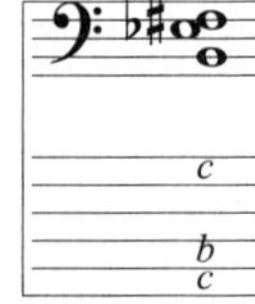

Musical Example 8.2. B Major on theorbo with diminished fourth on fifth course.

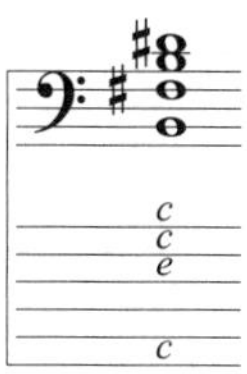

Musical Example 8.3. B Major on theorbo with major third on third course.

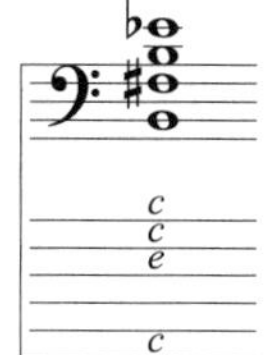

Musical Example 8.4. B Major on theorbo with diminished fourth on third course.

In other words, you agree with the other player who is going to cover which accidentals. Adhering to our familiar example of D♯/E♭, you stipulate that one of you covers the D♯s and the other the E♭s. When a chord appears that contains the pitch that you do not have, you simply play the chord minus the offending pitch. In some situations, you may be able to leave the chord out altogether. This strategy, of course, requires advance score preparation and negotiation. Most of the time, however, there is a suitable chord shape that you can usually find easily enough, particularly on the theorbo.

Lute and Archlute in G

We don't generally think of the lute in its Renaissance six- to eight-course versions as a continuo instrument, but it is often used in exactly that fashion, for example, when accompanying a singer in a lute song for which you have access to nothing but a piano arrangement. While our discussion of continuo on instruments in G will briefly consider the use of the archlute's diapasons, that is, the long bass strings that extend to the second pegbox, our focus will be largely restricted to the first six courses. Rather than showing chord shapes for every possible chord, which Nigel North has already done for us in his *Continuo Playing on the Lute, Archlute, and Theorbo,* a volume that should be on every lutenist's bookshelf, our approach will be to tactically apply your knowledge of tuning systems mostly to shifting movable or sliding chord shapes to the frets that yield the *mis* and *fas* each chord requires.[3] In discussing sliding chord shapes, the clarity of the guitar parlance of classifying a set of movable chords by the lowest course a finger falls on, usually the first finger, will prove beneficial. The course on which the sliding form is based is referred to as the "root," which resides most commonly on the fifth and sixth and occasionally the fourth courses, although, technically, any course could serve as the root course.[4] It often happens that the root of the chord, in music theory terms, that is, the note that carries the letter name of the chord, falls on the course on which the sliding form is based, but, as you will see, it is also possible, for instance, to have a root 5 or 6 sliding shape of a first inversion chord in which the third of the chord happens to be placed on the fifth or sixth course. We will restrict the following discussion to root position and first inversion chords; the rest you can figure out for yourself easily enough.

Fortunately, the common shapes for the I, IV, and V chords in E♭, B♭, F, C, G, and D Major and the i, iv, and V chords in F, C, G, and D Minor land comfortably under the fingers on the first few frets assuming the standard fretboard configuration as presented in diagram 7.5. These require no discussion. The rest of the keys involve chords where the identity of the 4th and 6th frets becomes a factor. As we will see, in most cases, sharp keys require the 4th and 6th frets to be set as *mis* while flat keys require that they be set as *fas*. We first discuss the concept of movable chords, chords with pitches on the lower courses of the 1st fret or its tastino, and first inversion chords before turning our attention to problem chords.

Most chords we consider to be nonsliding shapes are actually sliding shapes that exchange an open course for a note that would be fingered in the sliding shape on a higher fret. For example, the common C Major shape on the lute in musical example 8.5 can be slid up to the 2nd fret to give us the familiar D Major chord in musical example 8.6, where the first finger covers the 2nd fret on the fifth course, which in the C Major chord was realized by the open fifth course. To see the relationship, retaining the same fingering, simply slide the D Major chord back down to the C Major position and notice that your first finger is now free because the nut is stopping the string. This is, then, a classic root 5 movable chord. Back to musical example 8.6, on the archlute you can drop the D covered by your first finger at the fifth course 2nd fret to an octave lower and play it with the appropriate unfretted diapason. You can also delete the note on the first course because it just doubles the A on the fourth course at the octave. This tactic allows you to refinger a tough four-finger chord into the easy three-finger version shown in musical example 8.7 that can be used to reduce the number of left-hand fingers required by one for any chord whose lowest pitch is available on one of the unfretted diapasons. You can even refinger the chord to use your first, second, and third fingers instead of your second, third, and fourth fingers. Much easier. And, of course, the minor version of the chord works in the same fashion, although it is not quite as convenient because it covers three rather than two frets, a topic we discuss further below.

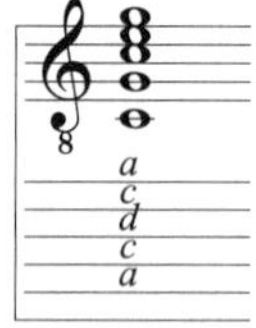

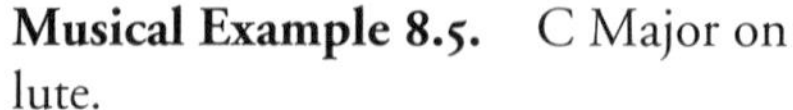

Musical Example 8.5. C Major on lute.

Musical Example 8.6. D Major on lute.

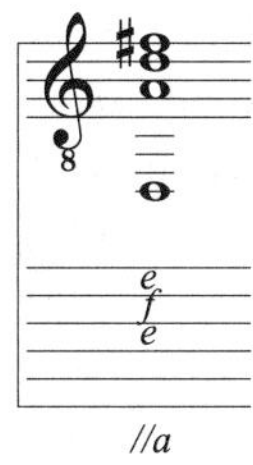

Musical Example 8.7. D Major on lute with root on unfretted diapason.

Musical Example 8.8. First inversion B Major on lute.

But what does this have to do with tuning? Let's say that you are in the key of E Major and you need to play the first inversion B Major chord in musical example 8.8, leading into the tonic major chord. The problem, as you can see, is that in this very common form, the D♯ is placed at the 3rd fret, which must practically always be a *fa* fret. In other words, in this convenient formation, you are actually playing an E♭ rather than a D♯. You can, of course, slant the fret toward the bass side, but on archlute, you can also drop the D♯–E bass motion down an octave to the unfretted diapasons, which can be tuned precisely according to the key you're in. If that first inversion chord is fleeting, however, the difference between the E♭ and D♯ might not be noticed. If, on the other hand, that chord lasts for any length of time, it's best to try to lower it by pushing your first finger into the 3rd fret or slanting it if possible.

Continuing with our exploration of some of the ramifications attached to sliding forms, what if we slide the D Major chord in musical example 8.6 up one more fret to E♭? To make life easy, let's also remove the pitch on the fourth course since it just doubles the note on the first course anyway. This gives us musical example 8.9. Now we've involved the 6th fret. If it happens to be set to *mi,* the E♭ on the third course would actually be a D♯. But here the solution is quite simple since that D♯ disguised as an E♭ doubles the root of the chord at the octave. You really don't need it because the remaining pitches give you the root, third, and fifth of the chord, and you've met your minimal burden with a chord that is actually much easier. See musical example 8.10. The same issue

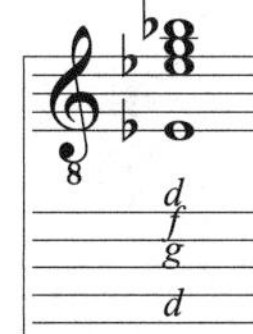

Musical Example 8.9. Four-note E♭ Major on lute.

Musical Example 8.10. Three-note E♭ Major on lute.

would arise using this chord shape for D♭ Major, with the barré at 1st fret since the third course pitch D♭ would fall on the 4th fret where the 4th fret is most commonly set as a *mi.* To slide the formation up to E Major, both the 4th and 6th frets would have to be *mis.* You can see that, here's where knowing your *mis* and *fas* comes in.

As usual, the problems (and solutions) primarily involve the 1st, 4th, and 6th frets. Returning to the 1st fret, diagram 8.1 shows the pitch names at the first few frets for a lute in G including the 1st fret tastino. Five simple and useful chords include the 1st fret tastino: D and A Major, and the first inversions of D, A, and E Major, the last three of which are versatile sliding forms.[5] See musical examples 8.11–8.15.[6] Musical example 8.16 shows an easier and better-sounding version of A Major. As with the root 5 E Major chord mentioned at the end of the last paragraph, to slide the root 6 pattern in musical example 8.16 up to the B Major, both the 4th and 6th frets must be set as *mis.* On the extremely remote chance that you might run into a D♯ Major chord, this same pattern could be slid up to the 8th and 10th frets, both of which would also have to be *mis.* On the other hand, ensuring that the 6th and 8th frets are each positioned as a *fa* sets you up to use the pattern in musical example 8.10 for G♭ Major on the off chance that you encounter it while getting struck by lightning.[7]

Three root position major and three first inversion minor flat key chords are available at the actual 1st fret: A♭, D♭, and G♭ Major (root and third only),

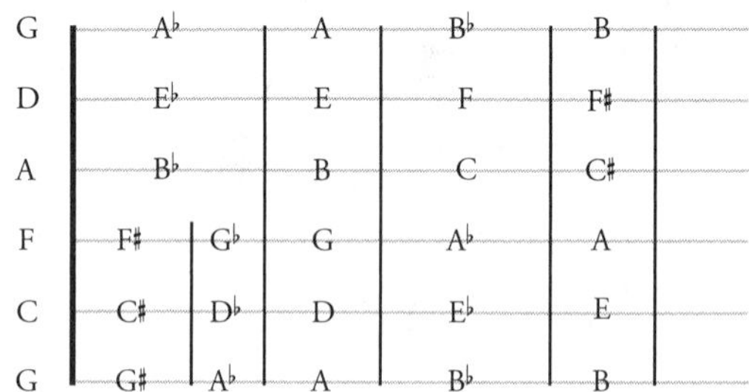

Diagram 8.1. Notes on lute's first four frets, including 1st fret tastino.

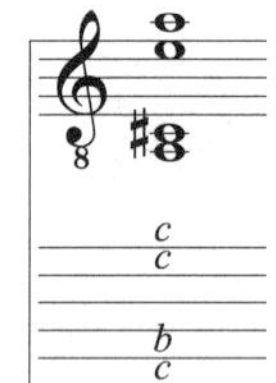

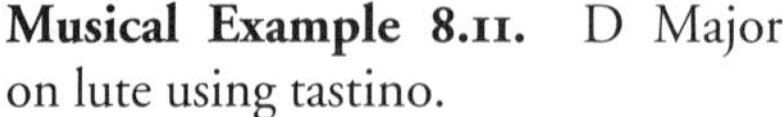

Musical Example 8.11. D Major on lute using tastino.

Musical Example 8.12. A Major on lute using tastino.

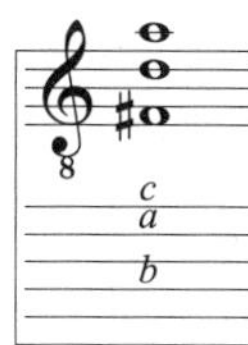

Musical Example 8.13. First inversion D Major on lute using tastino.

Musical Example 8.14. First inversion A Major on lute using tastino.

Musical Example 8.15. First inversion E Major on lute using tastino.

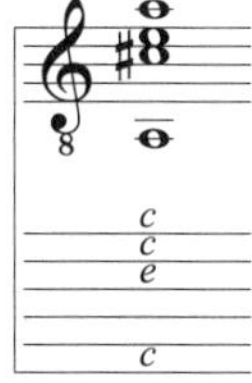

Musical Example 8.16. Preferred A Major on lute.

and F, B♭, and E♭ Minor first inversions, all of which can be used as sliding forms. See musical examples 8.17–8.22. The technical difficulty, of course, is fitting your first finger between the tastino and 1st fret.

Strictly from a meantone tuning standpoint, the fewer frets involved in a chord formation, the more likely you will be able to find a location that works since only two rather than three or four frets need to be in the correct *mi/fa* configuration. For instance, the two-fret root 5 sliding pattern used to produce the first inversion B♭ Major chord in musical example 8.23 will yield more functional chords up the neck than the three-fret sliding pattern in musical example 8.24 will, which requires three frets to line up instead of just two. Since the first finger on the fifth course is so far away from the others, the sliding forms in

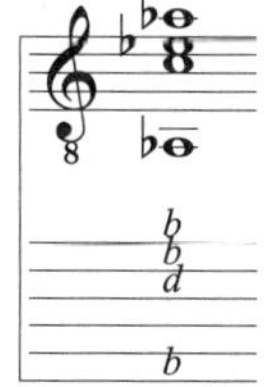

Musical Example 8.17. A♭ Major on lute.

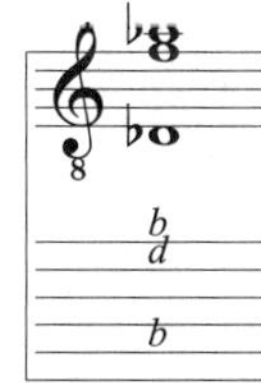

Musical Example 8.18. D♭ Major on lute.

Musical Example 8.19. G♭ Major on lute (root and third only).

Musical Example 8.20. First inversion F Minor on lute.

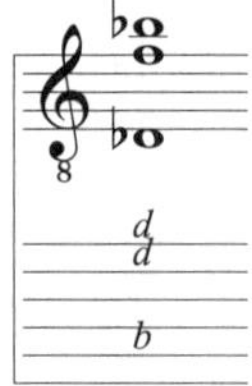

Musical Example 8.21. First inversion B♭ Minor on lute.

Musical Example 8.22. First inversion E♭ Minor on lute.

musical examples 8.15 and 8.23 can take advantage of a slanted fret, for instance, when the first finger is on the 3rd fret for either a first inversion F♯ or B Major chord to convert the chord's third in the bass at the 3rd fret from a *fa* to the requisite *mi,* that is, B♭ to A♯ and E♭ to D♯. You must also be very careful with the common sliding pattern shown in musical example 8.25 because while it works as presented in the example, it can only work slid up the neck if the frets are set accordingly to each chord's requisite *mis* and *fas.* The minor version of this pattern is somewhat more accommodating because, as mentioned above, it only involves two rather than three frets. See musical example 8.26. As always, it's a matter of minding your *mis* and *fas.*

Most of the problem chords naturally appear in rather obscure key areas that we rarely ever encounter. Nevertheless, we should have some idea how to

Musical Example 8.23. Two-fret first inversion B♭ Major on lute.

Musical Example 8.24. Three-fret first inversion B♭ Major on lute.

Musical Example 8.25. Three-fret E♭ Major on lute.

Musical Example 8.26. Two-fret E♭ Minor on lute.

handle them. In the cases of C♯ and F♯ Major, both chords can be formed in patterns we have already discussed thoroughly at the 6th and 8th frets as root 6 and 5 chords, respectively, assuming that those frets are both in the *mi* position. Remember that the third in C♯ Major, E♯, is not the same as F; it is lower, hence the requirement that the 8th fret be moved toward the nut a little into the *mi* position. The F♯ Major chord can be slid up two frets to the 8th and 10th frets to create a G♯ Major if they are both *mis.* Again, remember that its third, B♯ is lower than C. You can see that the main challenge with C♯ and G♯ Major chords is that their thirds are enharmonics of F and C, pitches that are otherwise virtually always stable and immovable *fas.* Substituting the archlute's diapasons for the lowest pitches in difficult chords goes a long way toward mitigating the challenges such chords present. Additionally, chord formations that pair notes on the highest three courses with unfretted diapasons sound particularly glorious on both the archlute and theorbo.

All of this, of course, takes some forethought and planning. Although for concerts I notate every diapason or fret change at the bottom of the last page of the current piece and the top of the first page of the next one, for performances that entail numerous diapason and fret position changes, I also create a diapason and fret choreography. Here is the choreography for theorbo from an Il Furioso concert:

Sonata seconda, "La Cesta"	Ricercata ottava
Preludio decimo	Sonata terza, "La Melana"
Aria di Fiorenza	**8 = F♯**
8 = F	9 = E
9 = E	**10 = D♯**
10 = D	**11 = C♯**
11 = C	12 = B
12 = B	**I = slant to A♯**
IV = mi	IV = mi
VI = fa	**VI = mi**

Toccata quarta Corrente seconda Sonata quinta, "La Clemente" 8 = F♯ 9 = E **10 = D** **11 = C** 12 = B **I = return to perpendicular** IV = mi VI = mi	Sonata no. 3 in G Minor Chaconne in G Minor **8 = F** **9 = E♭** 10 = D 11 = C **12 = B♭** **IV = fa** **VI = fa**

Bold indicates a new diapason or fret identity. I don't bother listing diapasons or frets that don't change in the particular concert. This may seem like a lot of trouble, but with all the natural distractions involved in presenting concerts, it's easy to overlook changing a diapason or adjusting a fret.

Minor chords have their own difficulties and solutions often relating to the fact that the more sonorous minor third is wide compared with the ET minor third. The common root 6 minor form in musical example 8.27 can be slid up to B, C♯, and D Minor without any adjustments, but can also be slid down to A♭ and up to B♭, C, and E♭ Minor provided that the fret on which the third course minor third falls is either pulled up manually or the fret is repositioned to a *fa,* which, of course, is highly unlikely in the case of the A♭ Minor. Similar allowances must be made for the root 5 movable form illustrated in musical example 8.28, where the minor third appears on the second course.

Three minor chords involving the 1st fret tastino require mention. The full form of the root 4 F♯ Minor with the first finger on the tastino is difficult on all but the smallest lutes, but it becomes more manageable as it slides up, always keeping in mind the location of the *mi* and *fa* frets. See musical example 8.29. Dropping the root of this chord an octave lower to an available open string greatly eases the difficulty of this chord by transforming a difficult four-finger chord into an easy three-finger chord. Similarly, this chord shape's major

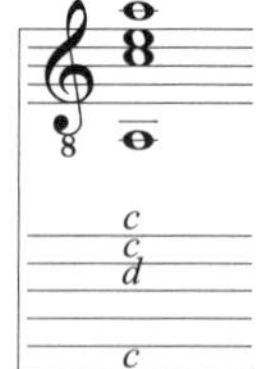

Musical Example 8.27. A Minor on lute.

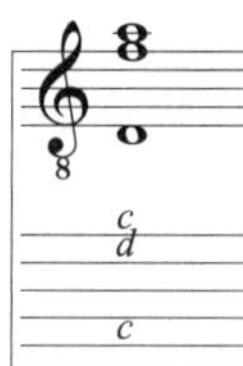

Musical Example 8.28. D Minor on lute.

Musical Example 8.29. F♯ Minor on lute with tastino.

Musical Example 8.30. G Major on lute.

cousin, musical example 8.30, is also amenable to dropping the fourth course note down an octave as in musical example 8.31, a strategy that can be effective on a seven- or eight-course lute, as well as on the archlute. Musical example 8.29's stripped-down version, musical example 8.32, can serve as a suitable alternative when an open string an octave lower than the root is unavailable. G♯ and C♯ Minor can be achieved with the assistance of the tastino on the condition that the 1st fret is slanted toward the treble side to produce a G♯ at the 1st fret of the first course or if the entire 1st fret is relocated to the *mi* position. See musical examples 8.33–8.34.

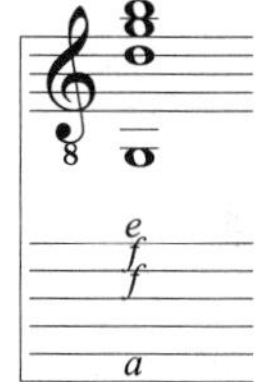

Musical Example 8.31. G Major with root on unfretted course.

Musical Example 8.32. Alternate F♯ Minor on lute with tastino.

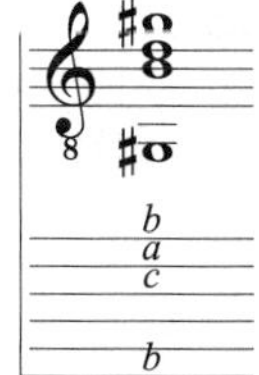

Musical Example 8.33. G♯ Minor with tastino.

Musical Example 8.34. C♯ Minor with tastino.

As exhausting as this all may seem, it is not by any means an exhaustive treatment of the topic, but it should provide you with enough strategic expertise to enable you to solve virtually any tuning challenge involving meantone temperaments on the lute or archlute. We now turn our attention to the theorbo.

Theorbo in A

The theorbo has several advantages over the archlute in terms of its usefulness as a continuo instrument. Chief among them is that its single-string courses make pulling and pushing adjustments more realistic. No advantage, however, is greater than its configuration of the 4th and 6th frets. As it is, the default arrangement of the 4th fret as a *mi* and the 6th as a *fa* as presented in diagram 7.5 permits a wider variety of useful chords without any adjustments whatsoever than does the archlute in its standard configuration in the same diagram with both the 4th and 6th frets as *mis.* Although one could change the archlute's 6th fret to a *fa,* it introduces more problems than it solves. As we experienced in chapter 7, the only regularly recurring problem with setting the 4th fret as a *mi* on the theorbo is the D♯/E♭ on the third course, most often within the context of the C Minor chord illustrated in musical example 8.35. If we do not want to pull up the D♯ to E♭ manually as described in chapter 7, or if we must preserve the 4th fret as a *mi,* we can simply refinger the chord as in musical example 8.36, relocating the E♭ to the first course 6th fret, a *fa.* This shape is also quite useful in forming a B♭ Minor chord when slid toward the nut by two frets, assuming, of course, a *fa* at the 4th fret.

Because there is only one "natural" note on the theorbo's 4th and 6th frets, B and F, respectively, both of which can be conveniently accessed elsewhere courtesy of the theorbo's reentrant tuning, setting the 4th and 6th frets as both *mis* as in diagram 8.2 or both *fas* as in diagram 8.3 provides relatively easy access to distant sharp or flat keys. Referring to diagram 8.2, you can see that F♯ and C♯ Major and G♯ Minor are easily accessed with common sliding forms with fingers on the 4th and 6th frets and an alternate version of G♯ Minor on the 6th and 7th frets as long as the 4th and 6th frets are set as *mis.* See musical examples 8.37–8.40. The F♯ Major form can be slid up two frets to furnish a G♯ Major chord provided that the 8th fret is lowered to its *mi* position. Referring to

Musical Example 8.35. C Minor on theorbo.

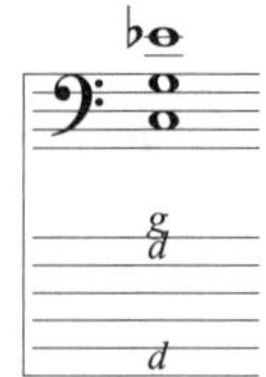

Musical Example 8.36. Alternate C Minor on theorbo.

	1	2	3	4	5	6	7	8	9	10	11	12
A	B♭	B	C	C♯	D	D♯	E	F	F♯	G	G♯	A
E	F	F♯	G	G♯	A	A♯	B	C	C♯	D	D♯	E
B	C	C♯	D	D♯	E	E♯	F♯	G	G♯	A	A♯	B
G	A♭	A	B♭	B	C	C♯	D	E♭	E	F	F♯	G
D	E♭	E	F	F♯	G	G♯	A	B♭	B	C	C♯	D
A	B♭	B	C	C♯	D	D♯	E	F	F♯	G	G♯	A
G	A♭	A	B♭	B	C	C♯	D	E♭	E	F	F♯	G

Diagram 8.2. Theorbo fretboard with 4th and 6th frets set as *mis.*

	1	2	3	4	5	6	7	8	9	10	11	12
A	B♭	B	C	D♭	D	E♭	E	F	F♯	G	G♯	A
E	F	F♯	G	A♭	A	B♭	B	C	C♯	D	D♯	E
B	C	C♯	D	E♭	E	F	F♯	G	G♯	A	A♯	B
G	A♭	A	B♭	C♭	C	D♭	D	E♭	E	F	F♯	G
D	E♭	E	F	G♭	G	A♭	A	B♭	B	C	C♯	D
A	B♭	B	C	D♭	D	E♭	E	F	F♯	G	G♯	A
G	A♭	A	B♭	C♭	C	D♭	D	E♭	E	F	F♯	G

Diagram 8.3. Theorbo fretboard with 4th and 6th frets set as *fas.*

Musical Example 8.37. F♯ Major on theorbo.

Musical Example 8.38. C♯ Major on theorbo.

Musical Example 8.39. G♯ Minor on theorbo.

Musical Example 8.40. Alternate G♯ Minor on theorbo.

diagram 8.3, using the same sliding shapes as in musical examples 8.37–8.38, you can easily access G♭ and D♭ Major at the 4th and 6th frets and E♭ and A♭ Major at the 6th and 8th frets. With the 4th fret set as a *fa,* by using the same pattern as found in musical example 8.11 for the lute (minus the second course), you can easily access the pesky G♭ Major chord on the theorbo since the *fa* transforms the usual F♯ at the 4th fret into a G♭.

Almost any chord can be made easier or more accessible by dropping the lowest note by an octave and placing it on one of the unfretted diapasons. Although Nigel North's book provides a compendium of useful sliding and nonsliding theorbo chord shapes, remember that the shapes he presents assume a theorbo in equal temperament, which means that some of the nonsliding shapes may not work depending on your fret arrangement.[8] For example, the chord given as musical example 8.41 appears to yield a C♯ Major chord, but by now you realize that the "E♯" is really an F since it occurs at the 3rd fret, a *fa.*

Because of the theorbo's reentrant tuning, you must also take care with chords whose third is located on the fourth string, such as in musical example 8.42. Here the lowest-sounding pitch is actually on the second string rather than on the string plucked by the thumb, which we naturally expect to sound the lowest-sounding pitch.

One of the many conveniences of having a fretted seventh course is the first inversion E Major chord shown in musical example 8.43. Since the relationship among the open strings is the same as on the archlute, as you have already seen in several of the previous musical examples, the theorbo uses many of the same chord shapes, their identity up the neck a whole tone higher than on the archlute because of the theorbo's open tuning in A, which also introduces a different set of pitches that can be enlisted to provide the added resonance open strings produce.

As on the archlute, with the addition of a tastino, the 1st fret offers a wealth of possibilities. Referring to diagram 8.4, you can see that in addition to the first inversion E Major chord in musical example 8.43, the 1st fret tastino also provides for standard sliding first inversion F♯ and B Major chords as well. Musical example 8.44 shows yet another G♯ Minor chord, this one making use

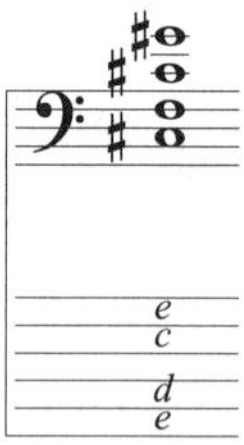

Musical Example 8.41. "C♯ Major" on theorbo.

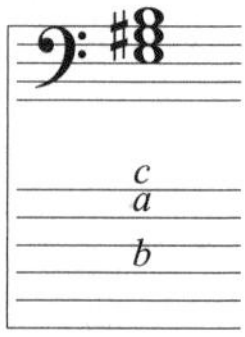

Musical Example 8.42. E Major on theorbo.

Course	Tastino	1st fret	2nd fret	3rd fret	4th fret
A		B♭	B	C	C♯
E		F	F♯	G	G♯
B		C	C♯	D	D♯
G	G♯	A♭	A	B♭	B
D	D♯	E♭	E	F	F♯
A	A♯	B♭	B	C	C♯
G	G♯	A♭	A	B♭	B

Diagram 8.4. Notes on theorbo's first four frets, including 1st fret tastino.

Musical Example 8.43. First inversion E Major on theorbo.

Musical Example 8.44. G♯ Minor on theorbo with tastino.

of the tastino. Even without the tastino, the 1st fret is a godsend to the keys of B Major and Minor in the form of the cadence formula that leads up to them. As you know, the F♯ Major contains an A♯, but the "A♯" at the 3rd fret of the fourth course is really a B♭. Since the rest of the pitches at the 3rd fret are natural notes, it is not generally conducive to enough slanting to offer much help in terms of converting the B♭ into an A♯. Enter the 1st fret, but slanted toward the nut on the treble side, converting the 1st fret of the first course from a B♭ to an A♯. This small adjustment sets the stage for the extremely easy and idiomatic V–i6/4–4–3–i cadence as illustrated in musical example 8.45. Notice that you can keep your second finger on the third string the entire time.

The actual 1st fret is as generous to flat keys as the tastino is to sharp keys. In addition to the standard movable root 5 and 6 forms that begin their journey toward the bridge as E♭ and B♭ Major at the 1st fret, the 1st fret is also home to the first incarnation of a very useful and easy root 7 chord in guise of A♭ Major. See musical example 8.46. This chord shape is particularly useful at the 3rd fret as a B♭ Major chord as an alternative to the common root 6 shape that requires the first finger to thread the needle between the tastino and actual 1st fret. Closely related to this shape is the F Minor in musical example 8.47. Finally, the B♭ and E♭ Minor chords in musical examples 8.48 and 8.49 can be realized at the 1st fret if the minor third in each chord is manually pulled up from its *mi*

Musical Example 8.45. V–i6/4–4–3–i cadence in B Minor on theorbo.

Musical Example 8.46. A♭ Major on theorbo.

Musical Example 8.47. F Minor on theorbo.

Musical Example 8.48. B♭ Minor on theorbo.

Musical Example 8.49. E♭ Minor on theorbo.

form at the 2nd fret. Although this task can be accomplished with the second finger if the first finger provides the barré, it is even easier to pull the 2nd fret note from its normal *mi* to a *fa* if the 1st fret notes are fretted with the first and second fingers, leaving the third finger for the note to be pulled at the 2nd fret, a tactic that can be enlisted to serve many of the chord shapes mentioned above.

We have just scratched the surface of the theorbo's capabilities as a continuo instrument in meantone temperaments. There's no end to its possibilities, and its ability to conform to and even supersede the minimal restrictions meantone temperaments impose on it make it the ideal fretted continuo instrument. While this chapter has been restricted to the archlute and theorbo, the next addresses the unique tuning-related issues pertaining exclusively to the viol.

CHAPTER NINE

Viols

To a lutenist, the control the viol player has over every parameter of sound production is astonishing: its duration, its volume, and its tone quality throughout the length of the note, the connections between notes, and the tuning of each note. Most of the enhanced control of dynamics and articulation can be ascribed to the bow, but it is the left hand in concert with the bow that primarily accounts the viol player's greater ability to tune more precisely once the frets have been set. To a large extent, on plucked instruments, assuming the finger is placed at the correct fret, the note is either good or bad, the latter resulting from either insufficient pressure to keep the string snugly against the fret to produce a clean sound or placing the finger either too far away from or too close to the fret, which produces a buzz or a thud, respectively. Viol players, on the other hand, can turn their use of the bow, stiffer strings, higher action, and preponderance of single note lines to their advantage to perform immediate fine-tuning adjustments as a note sounds.

On the viol, fret position is more of a starting than ending point. According to Richard Carter, fretting patterns are "often referred to by the temperament on which they are based, but it is worth emphasising here that the aim is not to play 'in' any one of these temperaments, but to use fretting based on them as a springboard to good intonation."[1] With the viol, we have arrived at a fretted instrument whose possibilities transcend any particular tuning system.

It is at the same time both easier and more difficult to play in tune on the viol than on the lute. Tuning the viol prior to playing is easier because there are fewer strings, larger tuning pegs, and a louder sustained tone. After the note is bowed, the viol is much more responsive than the lute by virtue of the bow and its higher tension strings, which make left-hand fingering alterations somewhat predictable. On the other hand, because it is impossible to bow notes simultaneously unless they are on adjacent strings, the violist can be compelled to tune using melodic rather than harmonic intervals when tuning to itself, and the scratch of the bow on the lower strings can cause enough noise to prevent a clear tone for the tuner in the visual mode, which can be somewhat mitigated by placing the tuner farther away. Although on the viol an errant note can be quickly corrected, it is quite easy to play out of tune owing to both bowing and left-hand missteps, and its pronounced overtones and the "reedy" quality of its sustained notes cause tuning errors to be much more noticeable on the viol than on the lute.[2] On the lute, a bad note is usually perceived as a nonmusical tone, whereas on the viol that note is out of tune.

While many of the topics covered below have already been touched on previously, this chapter reviews or more fully considers aspects of tuning unique or particularly pertinent to the viol. These include historical evidence of meantone temperaments on the viol, equipment, tuning techniques, tuning a consort, bowing, and left-hand adjustments, as well as how meantone temperaments are realized on both standard and less common viols such as the pardessus, lyra viol, and lirone.

Historical Evidence of Meantone Temperaments on the Viol

From the documentation provided in previous chapters, we can generalize that like the lute, the viol was perceived as wedded to equal temperament by several important theorists, including Mersenne, Vicentino, and Galilei, although the last two also explained how to set frets in meantone temperaments. In most cases, it is unclear whether the authors intended to characterize amateur, professional, or all players. Contrary to the received and oft-repeated "wisdom," many writers who were closer to musical practice than theory, however, saw no reason for viol players not to arrange their movable frets in unequal temperaments in an era when meantone temperaments and later their derivatives were almost universally preferred by players of keyboards and other instruments.[3]

As did lutenists, viol players also regularly performed in professional and high-caliber amateur ensembles that included keyboards tuned in meantone temperaments as they do now. Moreover, we have seen that the fact that the viola da gamba is often accompanied by basso continuo performed on keyboards tuned in meantone temperaments makes it all the more likely that the gamba itself was also tuned in meantone temperaments to match its accompanying instrument. On such occasions, whatever the keyboard temperament, which for the practical reasons discussed earlier takes precedence, some sort of compromise must have been reached to allow them to play together for, according to Penelope Gouk, "Playing in harmony together—keeping time and keeping tune—requires constant negotiation and compromise among the performers."[4] Indeed, as we saw in chapter 1, Banchieri even created a reference guide showing fretted instrument players how to tune their open strings to the keyboard. He was clearly not fooled or cowed by Bardi's comments if he was even aware of them.

While Dowland and the lute maker Venere reported that they and other skilled practitioners set their frets exclusively by ear, the following writers described viol players calculating their fret positions by some other means but perfecting them by ear: Aron (1545), Agricola (1545), Zarlino (1588), John Dowland (1610), Praetorius (1619), Mace (1676), and Danoville (1687). As we will see, Ganassi (1542–1543) emphasized refining fret locations through a series of checks involving unisons and octaves and open and fretted strings. Many of these and other authors also imply that because viol players are so capable of manually adjusting the pitches they produce, where they actually locate their frets matters only so much. Indeed, the evidence conveyed in both historical writings and pictorial reproductions of the viol substantiates the notion that the viol's frets were less likely than the lute to be set in an unequal pattern presumably because it was much easier to refine the pitch by manipulating the string's tension with the left hand.

Shortly after Ganassi's publications, in 1553 the great violist Diego Ortiz wrote how the viol is capable of raising or lowering pitch to match any note produced by the harpsichord. Speaking with the authority of an experienced player and teacher, Ortiz counsels that while this technique is at first challenging, like anything else, it becomes easy with diligent practice.[5] Mark Lindley supplies evidence that 150 years later Marais anticipated that players advanced enough to perform his music would be able to make "significant inflections" in the pitch they produce.[6]

Nevertheless, despite the relative dearth of iconographical representations of viols in meantone temperaments compared with lutes, the aforementioned Voorhout painting and a few others notwithstanding, there is still more than enough evidence that some gamba players did, in fact, set their frets in meantone temperaments to justify our doing the same based on historical precedent. We need look no further than Vincenzo Galilei, equal temperament's most vociferous champion, who in 1584 wrote that *viola d'arco* players who set their frets unequally know well enough how to find alternate fret locations for notes that produce an undesired enharmonic.[7] To Galilei's testimony we can add that of Danckerts, Bottrigari, Della Valle, Cerone, Doni, Valentini, Rousseau, Sauveur, and, by implication, Rameau, all who, like Galilei, acknowledged or simply stated that gamba players were able to or did set their frets in meantone temperaments.

Perhaps the clearest evidence that gamba players set their frets in meantone temperaments is Claude-François Millet de Chales's "common" viola da gamba fretting pattern including the 1st fret tastino shown in figure 1.1. As did de Chales, Doni, Danoville, and Denis too mentioned the use of tastini particularly at the 1st fret. On pages 13–14 of the second edition of *The Division Viol*, Christopher Simpson explains that, contrary to what some others contend, a whole tone cannot be split into two equal semitones, and then he goes on to explain its division into nine commas; he also refers to the use of an additional fret placed between the 1st fret and the nut.[8] Additionally, we have read of gamba players slanting their frets, and there is a surfeit of iconographical evidence documenting this practice. Some authors such as Sauveur also suggested that the violists solve the problem of where to place the *mi* and *fa* frets by recommending compromise positions between the two, a solution we have seen occasionally employed by lutenists and the larger fixed metal-fret wire-strung instruments.

At the highest levels of musical thought and practice, the challenge of realizing meantone temperaments and even the Holy Grail of Just intonation inspired several thinkers, makers, and players to experiment with instruments specially equipped to provide additional enharmonic locations to play more precisely in tune, such as Doni's prepared set of viols, "violone panarmonico," and "viole diarmoniche," Salvetti's "lirone enarmonico," and Salmon's prepared viols. None of them, of course, were practical enough to be of much use for everyday playing.

The unassailable conclusion from the preceding summary of the evidence here and in the previous chapters is that amateur viola da gamba players likely resorted to equal temperament, while through a variety of methods, better players and professionals found a way to make meantone temperaments work on their instruments. We now turn our attention to the features of the viol itself as they pertain to tuning and temperament.

Equipment

In general, the issue of strings is much more straightforward on the viol than on the lute; it largely boils down to a choice between or a combination of some variety of plain or modified gut and overspun strings.[9] Most viol consort music was written well before the invention of overspun strings in the mid-seventeenth century and their widespread adoption in the eighteenth. Contemporary historical string-making techniques have improved to such a degree that gut and gut-based strings provide a reasonable alternative to overspun strings, although Sainte-Colombe, the putative inventor of the seven-string bass, may have intended its lowest string to be overspun. Gut sounds much better, and, because viol strings are thicker and thus at a higher tension than lute strings, it is much easier to work with and more reliable on the viol than on the lute.[10] Overspun strings, on the other hand, are much less pliable than gut for making on-the-fly adjustments on bowed instruments, certainly a consideration for advanced players hoping to alter the pitch with their left-hand fingers. Metal-wound strings also fall quite short of mimicking the sound of gut compared with worn lower-tension copper-wound lute strings and Nylgut, and they tend to rise in pitch between tuning sessions necessitating due vigilance. Nevertheless, as Alison Crum makes perfectly clear, the choice of strings is a highly personal matter.[11]

Gamba players tend not to use the same kind of locking peg knot to keep the string from slipping through the peg as lutenists do, although there is no reason they should not. Instead, they wind one coil around the narrower side of the peg hole before crossing back over toward the peghead for the remaining coils, forming a lock as the string crosses over itself to return to the wider side of the peg. Others abut the first coil against the string as it enters the peg hole when they begin to wind the string around the peg, forming a tight lock of sorts. Some tie a knot larger than the size of the peg hole after the string has gone through the peg to keep it from slipping through, much in the same fashion as they tie a knot on the underside of the tailpiece hole to keep the string from slipping through at that end. Everything else written previously about the pegs as well as the nut pertains to the viol as well as to the lute.

Viol players understand that bridge maintenance is crucial for the instrument's overall structural integrity but are perhaps less aware of the role it plays in accurate tuning. The strings must be able to glide smoothly through the bridge notches just as easily as they slide through the grooves in the nut. Accordingly, the notches should be lubricated just as they are at the nut. If the grooves are so narrow that the string gets stuck in the grooves, fine-tuning becomes impossible, and as the string grips the bridge notch, it tends to pull the bridge along with it toward the nut as the string is tightened to bring it up to pitch. This can tilt the bridge toward the nut so that it is not perfectly vertical and upright, a condition that is easy to spot. Feet that are not flatly seated on the belly quite readily identify a leaning bridge. If you can slide paper between a foot and the top, your bridge is tilted. Aside from the damage that it can cause to the belly, it also reduces the vibrating string length, as illustrated in diagram 9.1, rendering each fret too close to the bridge to yield accurate tuning.[12]

In addition to being lubricated, bridge notches must also be well shaped. The notches must not be so narrow as to grip the string, which is more likely an issue with wider diameter strings and overspun strings because the coils can get stuck in the notch while the core continues to move toward the pegs as the string is tuned up. If the notches are too narrow, carefully use your needle file to ever so slightly widen or flatten the notch, but be very careful not to deepen it. Too much deepening is irreversible and may result in your having to order

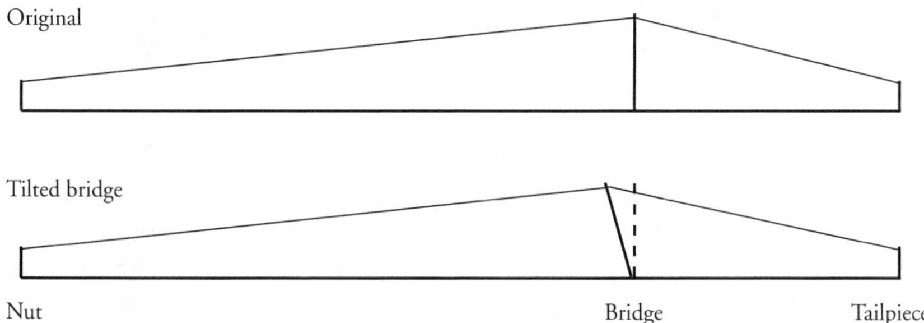

Diagram 9.1. Tilted viol bridge.

a new bridge. If the first two ounces of prevention are lubrication and well-shaped notches, the third is vigilance. Make it a habit to regularly check the verticality of your bridge. If it has tilted, you must stop whatever you are doing and fix it because otherwise, it will only get worse and exacerbate the damage already done.

It is best to return the bridge to its proper position incrementally and patiently. Simply lay the viol flat on your lap face up and place the thumb and index finger of each hand on opposite sides of the bridge immediately adjacent to the left and right sides of the string and pinch that small portion of the bridge back toward the tailpiece. Repeat for each string. It may take several times through the entire procedure to return the bridge to its proper original upright position, but your patience will be rewarded with better tuning and an intact bridge.

Tuning Techniques

Since the intervals between the open strings are the same for viols as they are for lutes, most of the tuning advice in chapter 7 pertains to the viol as well as the lute. Two of the viol's features, however, require additional consideration: its vertical rather than horizontal disposition and the fact that it is bowed.

MECHANICAL ISSUES

Viol pegs are larger than lute pegs, which, on the one hand, makes them easier to grasp, but, on the other, allows them to be wedged into their peg holes much more tightly. It therefore generally takes more physical exertion to turn viol pegs, a difficulty some remedy with a peg turner or conversion to geared pegs. That difficulty is exacerbated by the viol's vertical disposition. Although tuning the lute rarely requires such force, when it does, since it is held horizontally, it is an easy matter to lean the treble side pegs against your left leg as a counterbalance when you push the pegs in from the top, and when pushing the treble side pegs into their holes from the bottom up, the other hand can steady the instrument from the bass side of the pegbox with very little effort.

The viol's vertical disposition necessitates a different approach because the right hand is occupied with bowing. Tenor and bass viols can be somewhat steadied with increased inward pressure from the legs, an assistance unavailable for the treble viol or the pardessus. A common and effective technique for counterbalancing the pegs on the treble side is to press the bass side pegs against your left cheek, chin, or chest while turning them. Tuning the bass side pegs is a little more challenging. It requires wrapping the little finger of your left hand around the opposite side of the pegbox while turning the peg with one, two, or three of your other fingers and your thumb. There are several possible permutations to this technique depending on the size of your hand and instrument. The tighter the peg, the more fingers required to budge it.

One of the many practical gems Ganassi offers viol players is his advice to maintain "constant bowing" while tuning, although, for the most part, that advice would serve us well in almost any situation.[13] Alison Crum advises us to adapt bow speed, pressure, and distance from the bridge to the music we are playing.[14] The same could be said for tuning. It is best to bow as you would normally bow when you play. Although a faster bow speed can raise the pitch ever so slightly, a slow bow speed can reduce the pitch by as much as 10c. Increasing bow pressure can lower the pitch by 20c. or more because the intense pressure on the string restricts its ability to vibrate freely. It is also important to place your bow along the string where you normally position it. Too *tasto,* or close to the fretboard, causes the pitch to drop because there's less tension on the string at that location, resulting in potential pitch decreases of 5–10c. These are all common pitfalls that we must guard against whether tuning or playing.

Absolutely precise tuning also requires you to bow rather than pluck the string because plucking elicits a different pitch than bowing, sometimes lower, sometimes higher. Both because it can be difficult to achieve a tone stable enough to register consistently on a tuning meter in the visual mode particularly on gut strings and because the sustained reference tone produced by such devices as the VioLab tuner and Cleartune are somewhat similar to the viol's tone, many viol players prefer the tone generation rather than visual mode. If you prefer to tune the instrument to itself by plucking, you should still bow the string on which your reference pitch is situated to establish the pitch level. With your reference string securely tuned you can then tune the instrument to itself very quickly by plucking the rest of the strings, particularly when holding the viol horizontally like a lute. This method offers you the opportunity to simultaneously pluck unisons and octaves and to take advantage of the very fast attack plucking affords.

REVIEW OF HISTORICAL APPROACHES TO TUNING

So, how did gamba players tune the instrument to itself? The earliest known viola da gamba tuning diagram is the loose sheet of paper showing a tuning diagram for bass viola da gamba in D added to Antonio da Leno's treatise from the last few years of the fifteenth century conserved at the Biblioteca Marciana in Venice as Lat. 336, col. 1581, and reproduced here as figure 9.1. Later in 1601, on pages 329–330 of his *Della prattica musica vocale, et strumentale,* Scipione Cerreto explains that since the viola da gamba bears the same open string intervals as the lute does, it should be tuned in the same fashion as described earlier on his page 316. Cerreto's tablature tuning diagram for an eight-course lute is reproduced here as figure 9.2 and realized in musical example 9.1. In England as well, the tuning of the viol was related to the lute, in particular by applying the lute's familiar standard for setting the pitch level to the viol as charmingly conveyed by John Playford in 1655: "The *Tuning* by *Notes* or by distances of *Sounds* is thus: the *Treble* being raysed as high as it will conveniently beare without

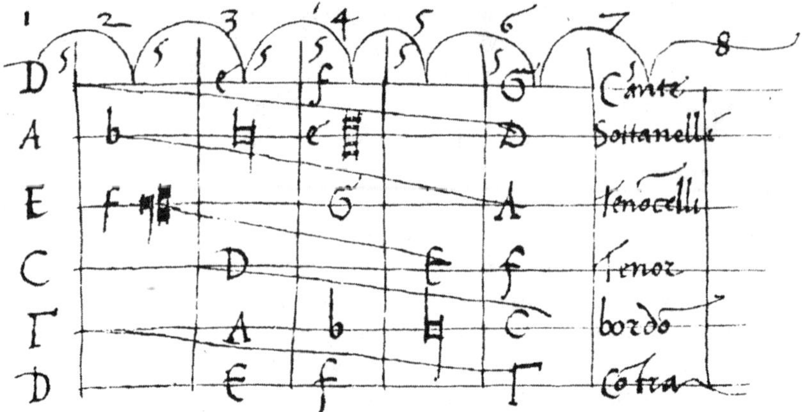

Figure 9.1. Viol tuning chart inserted in Antonio da Leno's treatise (late fifteenth century).

breaking, will then bee *D La Sol Re,*" an instruction first recorded for the viol by Hans Gerle in his *Musica Teutsch* (1532).[15] Playford repeats the same general instructions in his lyra viol books as well.

In his *Lettione seconda* (1543) Ganassi recommended beginning with the lowest string following the same 5th and 4th fret method, as did Leno, Cerreto, and, many years later, Thomas Mace. Compared with the preferred methods described in chapter 7, this method certainly has the advantage of allowing

Figure 9.2. Eight-course lute tablature tuning diagram in Scipione Cerreto's *Della prattica musica vocale, et strumentale* (1601), 316.

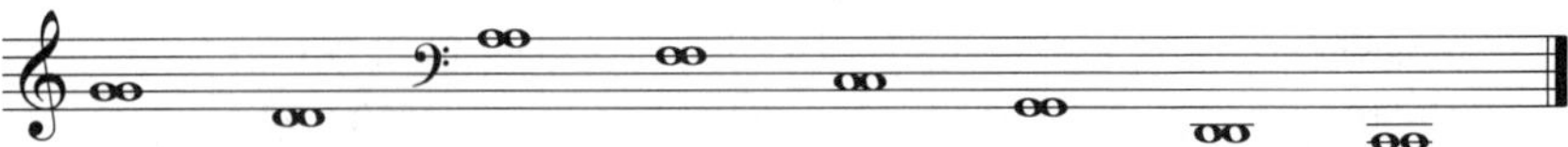

Musical Example 9.1. Eight-course lute tablature tuning diagram in Scipione Cerreto's *Della prattica musica vocale, et strumentale* (1601), 316.

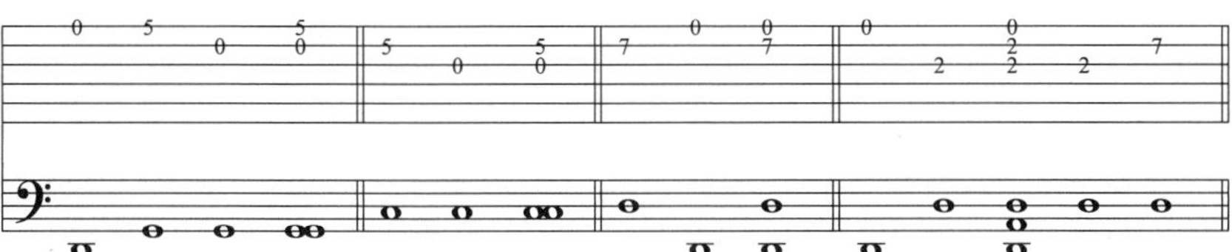

Musical Example 9.2. Tablature viol tuning checks in Sylvestro Ganassi's *Lettione seconda* (1543), n.p.

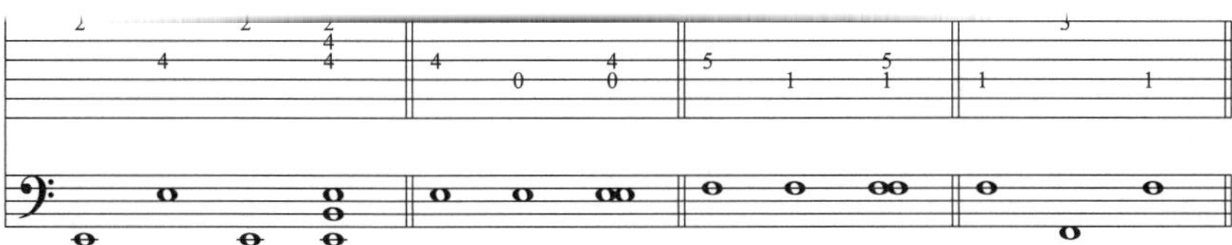

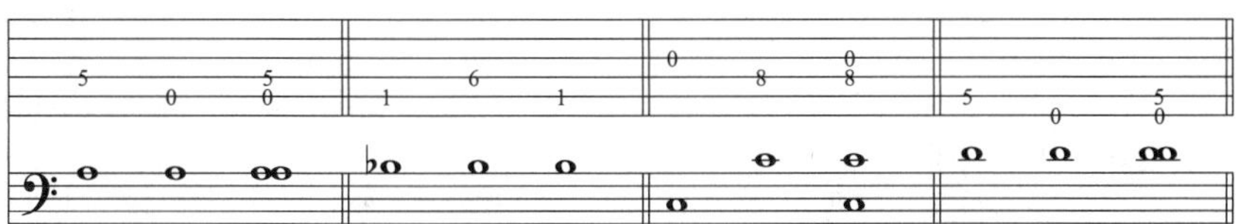

Musical Example 9.3. Tablature viol tuning checks in Sylvestro Ganassi's *Lettione seconda* (1543), n.p.

harmonic or simultaneous tuning with the bow because the unisons are on adjacent strings. Ganassi nevertheless suggests the octave and unison tuning checks shown in tablature. See musical examples 9.2 and 9.3.

To these can be added checking the octave between the 7th fret on the first, second, fourth, and fifth strings and the next lowest open string.[16] Since several octave checks involve nonadjacent strings, Ganassi advises the player to carefully sustain the first note so that it can still be heard while the second is bowed.[17] I have also found Elizabeth Liddle's method of lightly bowing one note while plucking the other with the left hand to be an effective method of tuning harmonically on the viol once the reference string has been established by bowing.[18]

OPEN STRINGS

The problem with tuning the open fourths, or in the case of fretless bowed instruments in open fifths, is that while it is relatively easy to hear a pure fifth or fourth, it is more difficult to hear a tempered one. Many violinists tune pure open fifths rather than equal-tempered fifths, often initiating a cascade of tuning inaccuracies. Some of those who are aware that their fifths must be tempered are able to temper them down to equal temperament's 700c., but that is more difficult than tuning pure fifths. In the case of viols, the fourths must be wide, and in meantone temperaments wider than in equal temperament, making them even more difficult to hear precisely. Frederick Gable points out that when viol players attempt to tune the open fourths, regardless of their intentions, most of the comma is inadvertently placed in the open third, resulting in a tuning system approaching Pythagorean tuning that he entertainingly refers to as the "vile" temperament.[19]

Nonetheless, for those of you who seek a more intimate relationship with your viol, I recommend spending some quality quiet time with its open strings. You may be one of those fortunate souls blessed with the ability to tune your open strings precisely, but even if you are not, it is worthwhile to attempt it to sharpen your tuning sense and to be able to quickly tune your open strings to their approximate pitches. Tuning the open strings does offer you the advantage of being able to compare pitches harmonically since they are on adjacent strings. I would suggest that you devote one of your practice sessions to the following exercise when you do not have an impending rehearsal or concert.

Tune your sixth string to your tuner and then put it away. From there, try to tune the open string a fourth above it by ear. For this exercise, Ganassi's "constant bowing" is crucial. With constant bowing, you may even be able to hear the beats. I suspect that you will immediately discover how hard it is to not tune the open fourths and third pure, giving you a visceral aural appreciation of the attraction of those intervals. If you're listening for beats, try to disregard the sound of your bow on the strings. When you arrive at the pure fourth, the beats will disappear. Assuming you begin with a fifth string pitch that is obviously too low, you will arrive at a beatless pure fourth of 498c. before you reach the wide 500c. fourth of ET or even wider in meantone temperaments. If you are not listening for beats, the pure fourth will still jump out at you with its resonance. But since the fourth needs to be wider, you must keep going. At this point, it is a good idea to begin comparing the sixth string's 5th fret with the open fifth string. Once they are the same, listen to the open strings and try to memorize how the interval between them sounds, comparing it in your mind's ear with how the pure fourth sounded. Now retune the open strings to the pure fourth and try to arrive at the tempered fourth in whatever temperament your frets are set in just by listening to the open strings together. For the open third between C and E on the treble or bass or F and A on the tenor, the same thing will happen: you will arrive at the pure interval and then have to keep going, that is, unless you are in 1/4-comma meantone temperament.

Alternatively, you can begin by tuning the middle major third pure and tune out from there, as a pure major third is also somewhat easy to identify. Remember that it is only pure and beatless in 1/4-comma meantone temperament.

It's a little wider in 1/6 comma, even wider in 1/8 comma, and so on. Either way, when you finish tuning the first and sixth strings, compare them. If they do not form a pure double octave, do not despair; tuning open strings by ear can be very challenging depending on your natural pitch discernment ability or musical training. Go back to the beginning and try again. You can also check the accuracy of your open strings with the tuner. This is not, however, the kind of exercise you should agonize over. Rather, revisit it every once in a while. You will find that, like anything else, it gets easier with practice and that your listening acumen will improve noticeably in every regard.

TUNING METHOD, REFERENCE PITCH, AND TEMPERAMENT

The easiest tuning method, of course, is to follow the instructions provided in chapter 7 for setting your open strings and frets with an electronic tuner. Once your frets are set, it is also quite easy and fast to attain a reference pitch and then tune the rest of the strings to it by any of the various combinations of unisons and octaves as described immediately above or in chapter 7. If you must rely on an A from another instrument or a tuning fork, you will need to start tuning from the open second string on the treble and bass viol (or its "12th fret" harmonic) and the open third string on the tenor or the 2nd fret of the first string.

Finally, to what temperament should you tune? That, of course, is up to you. Throughout this book, I have recommended 1/6-comma meantone temperament because it sounds noticeably better than equal temperament, but the physical distances between the *mi* and *fa* fret positions are small enough that the temperament can be extended quite far beyond the wolf in either direction. In 1/4-comma meantone temperament, that distance is usually so wide that it limits your ability to extend the temperament. For later solo music such as Marais, I recommend something like 1/8-comma meantone or even a slightly shaded equal temperament knowing that individual notes can be inflected when necessary. The *mi/fa* fret arrangement shown in diagram 9.2 should serve the vast

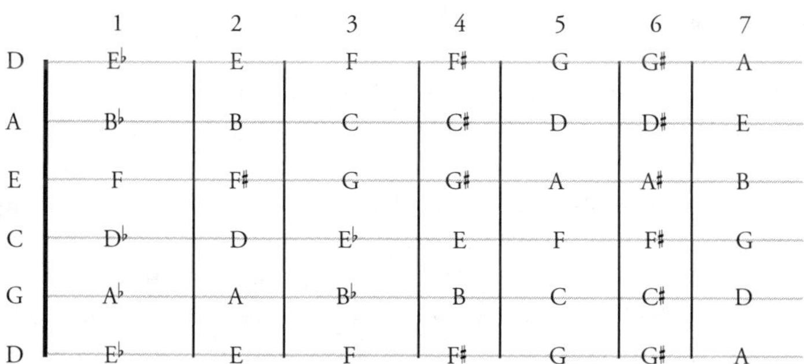

Diagram 9.2. Viol in D pitch locations for most common *mi/fa* fret configuration.

majority of music you will play. With the addition of a 1st fret tastino or split fret or the manipulation of the pitches with your left hand, depending on the size of your instrument, your ability to extend your chosen temperament may be practically limitless.

Tuning the Consort

Throughout virtually the entire history of the lute and viol, some meantone temperament variety or derivative was the standard temperament for keyboard and other fixed pitch instruments. The lute and viol were looked down on and even ridiculed by theorists such as Mersenne because of their misperception, certainly drawn from their exposure to amateur musicians, that lutes and viols were necessarily tuned in equal temperament. As we recall, meantone temperaments were thought of as the best compromise available for instruments that could not approach Just intonation, and equal temperament was deemed the easiest compromise for those who did not have the wherewithal to use meantone temperaments. The very best viol players, however, could aspire to perfectly pure chords regardless of how they set their frets, for instance, in major chords by lowering the major third and raising the perfect fifth to pure by using a combination of the techniques described below.[20]

The issue of temperament for gamba players is most likely to arise when tuning a consort because everyone must tune to the same temperament. Like any good marriage, a viol consort involves a lot of give and take. In a word, compromise. To quote Bottrigari, "It takes a good bit of work to make the Viols, all of which are in one group, accord well together."[21] Given that environment, it is quite often the perfect situation in which to introduce meantone temperaments. We frequently hear uninformed players refer to meantone temperaments as a compromise when in point of fact, equal temperament was considered the compromise of compromises, the compromise of last resort, as it were. This can be the occasion to remind our colleagues that all temperaments are compromises and that equal temperament trades the quality of the thirds, particularly the major third, for broad key serviceability. If, for instance, the consort is not planning on playing pieces that venture into the keys of F♯ Major or B♭ Minor, for instance, there is little advantage to setting the ensemble in equal temperament. In fact, few ensembles benefit more from tuning in meantone temperaments than viol consorts do. I have found the difference to be immediately and stunningly apparent. For instance, after recently upgrading one of our more advanced student viol consorts to 1/6-comma meantone temperament, without the benefit of any explanation of the wherefore and why, one of my undergraduates blurted out: "Where has all the beating gone?" reminding me, of course, of the Pete Seeger song, grateful that with regard to this consort I didn't have to wonder, "When will they ever learn?"[22] May it be that easy for you.

Because we all hear differently, Bottrigari recommended that one person tune the entire consort.[23] Similarly, Alison Crum recommends that whenever possible, one player's instrument should serve as the designated source for the consort's reference pitch, everyone else first tuning their open strings to that person's viol and then frets as necessary.[24] Remember that if you are upgrading to a meantone temperament, you will also have to relocate each viol's frets. Ganassi recommends beginning with the bass viol for the consort's reference pitch, erring on the side of tuning too low rather than too high so that the highest string in the consort is not tuned so high as to break or sound strained.[25] How much easier his life might have been with an iPhone and a digital tuning app. Nevertheless, starting with a precisely tuned treble or bass and tuning the rest of the viols to it in octaves or unisons is still a reasonable approach that, with practice, can be accomplished well and in short order. The only open string on the tenor that must be fretted on the treble or bass to provide a reference pitch is the F, the unison of which can be found at the 1st fret of the third string on the bass and at the 3rd fret on the sixth string on the treble. For the reasons stated above, I do not recommend tuning by fourths or fifths either against open strings or fretted pitches as a matter of course. When the pleasure of tuning the rest of the viols to a reference viol is impractical or time is fleeting, it is best for all the members of the ensemble to tune to the same model of tuner or tuner app calibrated and set up in exactly the same fashion.

Fret and Left-Hand Finger Adjustments

We have already thoroughly discussed problem locations that require some enharmonic adjustment on instruments in G and A.[26] These primarily concern lowering the major third and raising the minor third and secondarily lowering the perfect fourth and raising the perfect fifth toward pure. As you can see, pitch adjustment concerns both understanding the pitch's function within the chord and where it can be found on the instrument, including the *fa/mi* identity prevailing at the location in question according to how the fret is set. With that information well in hand, it is a simple matter to quickly identify the parallel locations on viols in D. As you can see from diagram 9.2, the areas of concern are largely the same as on instruments G and A, except that the profusion of D♯/E♭ locations provides for a slightly more complicated matrix. We have seen in figure 1.1 that de Chales identified the 1st fret of the fourth and fifth strings as the location best suited for a tastino to provide the C♯ and G♯. No surprise there. Although the 1st fret E♭s can be easily converted to D♯s through other means as described below, should the E♭ on the first string be required to serve as a D♯, that pitch can also be located at the 6th fret on the second string if the 6th fret is a *mi*. The use of the 6th fret is most likely to be restricted to the first three strings, so it is an easy matter to simply choose the *mi* or *fa* position, depending on the tonality in play. With a prevailing 1st fret *fa* position, setting the 6th fret as a *mi* can provide a convenient alternate location to the 1st fret's *mi* pitches.[27] For the reason that E and B reside at the 4th fret, it must remain a *mi;* the occasional A♭ can be easily dealt with in isolation. Similarly, should a D♯ or A♯ be required at the 3rd fret, they too would have to be achieved by some means other than manipulation of the fret, as it would certainly need to remain a *fa* because of the Fs, C, and G.

When tastini were used, based on the evidence provided by Galilei, de Chales, Simpson, Doni, Denis, Danoville, and others, it seems likely that they were largely restricted to the 1st fret and sometimes the 4th, although we have had occasion to consider their use at the 3rd as well. Since viol players have many more methods than lutenists to adjust pitch manually and on the fly, the advantage of tastini is not that they enabled gambists to adjust the pitch, but that they allowed them to do it more precisely. It seems likely that while some players used tastini, most were satisfied with double, split, and slanted frets and the manual left-hand manipulations discussed below. Whether single or double, or for the lute or viol, we must remember that the purpose of the frets is primarily "to give an 'open string' sound to stopped notes, and secondarily to provide a guide for the fingers and a starting point for good intonation."[28]

Split and double frets are most effective when the space between the *mi* and *fa* frets is wide enough for a finger to fit between the two frets for the *fa* position. This generally requires a larger viol and usually restricts the use of double and split frets to the lower frets. The viability of double or split frets is also a function of the temperament. As we have discussed previously, the width between the *mi* and *fa* double or split fret positions is determined by the harmonic diesis, which is wider in 1/4-comma meantone than 1/6-comma meantone temperament as shown in figures 9.3 and 9.4, respectively. Double and split frets offer a more sensible solution for music that is highly chromatic or spans a wide variety of tonalities. For a program that requires the occasional *mi* at the 1st fret, splitting the 1st fret for a particular piece as I've seen virtuosi such as Jordi Savall and others do on many occasions, is a most practical solution. Should you intend on splitting a fret, before playing, move the fret toward the nut to loosen it, shift the knot down from edge of the fretboard toward the middle of the neck, and then replace the fret to its proper position. Otherwise the knot will be too close to the fretboard to allow the fret to be split at the sixth or fifth string.

As we can see from diagram 9.2, the most obvious place for a slanted fret is, of course, at the 1st fret on the bass side, and, to a lesser degree, at the 3rd fret. The main difficulty in both cases is that on both the third and sixth strings the enharmonic most likely required at those frets is *fa.* If either fret is to be slanted, it would have to be done so with the forethought that the notes on the third and sixth strings at the 1st fret would have to be raised to *fa* manually. Because the slant is not too far advanced at the third string, adjusting the pitch up to F manually should present little problem. The E♭ on the sixth course is more challenging but not impossible. At the 3rd fret, though, the F is common enough

Figure 9.3. Tenor viol with double frets in 1/4-comma meantone temperament. Courtesy of Richard Carter.

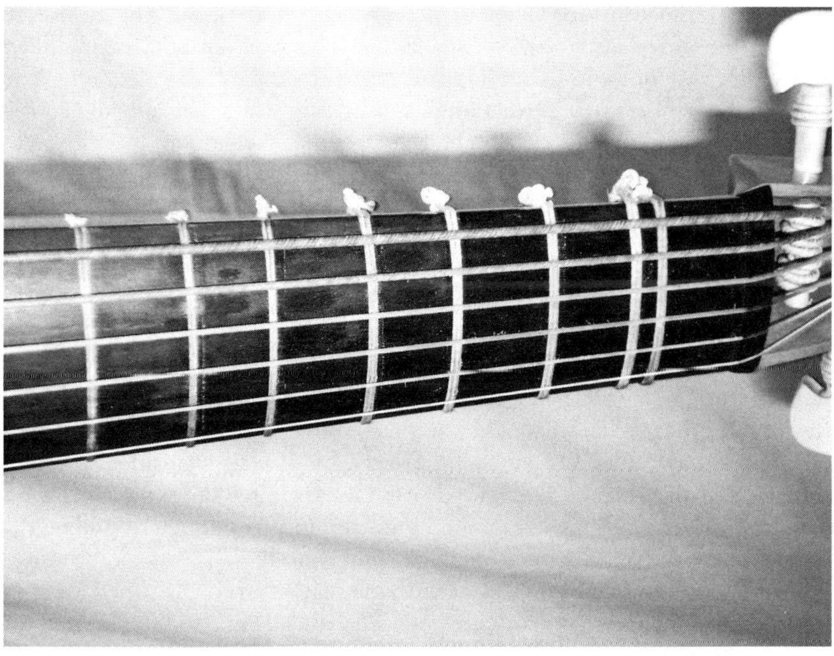

Figure 9.4. Tenor viol with double frets in 1/6-comma meantone temperament. Courtesy of Richard Carter.

that in the unlikely event that one composition should require the A♯, D♯, and F, a better solution is to leave the fret perpendicular and lower the B♭ and E♭ to A♯ and D♯ through other means or to relocate them altogether. A similar strategy could be applied to the 1st fret as well should E♭, G♯, and C♯ be required in the same piece, again, somewhat unlikely. The good thing about a slanted fret is that it is an adjustment that can be made very quickly; some players even choreograph slanting and unslanting within a piece.

At this juncture, it is useful to remind ourselves that the viol player has so many effective methods by which to raise or lower a pitch manually that tastini and double, split, and slanted frets or compromise fret positions do not offer unique solutions, but rather greater convenience. These techniques also tend to affect several strings in a somewhat global and occasionally indiscriminate fashion whereas the left-hand finger adjustments we address shortly can be applied to individual isolated notes without impacting any others. Fret location can also be used in conjunction with left-hand adjustments. For instance, with the foreknowledge that the thickness of your 1st fret allows you to more easily lower and raise the pitch, you can place the fret in a compromise position halfway between the *mi* and *fa* positions, thus requiring less manual effort to attain the pitch you desire.[29]

To a much greater extent on the viol than on the lute, for better or worse, the fret position is a starting rather than ending point in determining which pitch is produced. The irony of the matter is that the technical challenges that can make the viol so vexingly difficult to play in tune can be harnessed to make it play exquisitely in tune. For instance, inadequate left-hand finger pressure can inadvertently cause the pitch to decrease. This may not be desirable when playing the root of a chord, but if it's the major third above, it probably is. The viol's higher tension strings react more consistently and predictably to deliberate finger placement and pressure, and the fact that the viol produces its notes by bowing instead of plucking makes left-hand finger adjustments considerably more effective on the viol than on the lute and more feasible because it enables numerous pitch adjustment techniques that are simply impossible on the lute. Finally, as mentioned previously, left-hand finger adjustments are also more easily accomplished on thicker than thinner frets—yet another feature that accommodates the viol to these purposes.

We can raise the pitch on the viol by pulling the fretted string toward the nut. On my treble viol, by pulling, I can raise the pitch 5–10c. at the first few frets and more as the frets go higher. As on the lute, bending the string sideways is even more effective. On the viol, however, by placing your finger right on top of rather than behind the fret, you can raise the pitch up to 10c. or so with very little effort. This popular method is much more intuitive than pulling the string to raise the pitch because when you pull, your hand is moving in the opposite direction from which we associate higher pitch. Normally, when we want to produce a higher pitch, we move our left hands closer to the bridge. Our natural tendency when we hear a note that is too low is to move our finger a little higher just as would any player of a fretless string instrument. Were we playing the piano we'd naturally think toward the right. On the viol, to produce an E♭ at a *mi* fret we can move the finger from just behind the D♯ fret to a position a little higher on top of the fret toward the direction of the E natural fret, both raising the pitch and maintaining our physical fretboard sense of high and low.

It is much easier to lower the pitch of a note on the viol than on the lute. Simply reducing the bow speed or increasing its pressure on the string can lower the pitch. Advanced players, particularly those with fat frets, can push the finger into the fret at an angle to lower the pitch, much the same as we do on the lute. A much easier technique whose effectiveness increases with the width of the space between the frets is to fret the note farther away from the fret toward the nut, in the middle of the space between the two frets. The closer to the nut, the lower the pitch. For instance, on a C string with the 1st fret set as a *fa,* the note as fretted is D♭. Fretting it closer to the nut can nudge the D♭ *fa* toward a C♯ *mi.* The most common locations for such alterations are shown in diagram 9.3.[30] We can also use this technique to provide a *fa* where a *mi* is normally found by fretting the next higher fret quite low. Referring to diagram 9.3, note how on the third string of the treble viol, for instance, a G♭ can be summoned near the normally F♯ location at the 2nd fret by placing the finger low in the 3rd fret space.

Remember that, as discussed in chapters 5 and 7, with the size of the harmonic diesis in mind, 10–15c. might not be enough to accomplish your goals. An even more potent technique is to lighten the left-hand pressure, which can reduce the pitch by 20c. or more. When applying this technique, we must caution against the natural tendency to also reduce bow pressure and speed. By combining finger location with lighter left-hand pressure, we can reduce the pitch a remarkable 30–50c. We must, however, be aware that playing on top of the fret to raise the pitch and farther behind it to lower the pitch can cause the note to lose clarity, which can be somewhat mitigated by sharper bowing.

In sum, the combination of fret placement and finger manipulation offers the gamba player a tremendous repertoire of pitch adjustment techniques that, directed by a thorough knowledge of temperaments and the fretboard, can be engaged to play spectacularly in tune.

Finally, on occasion, a bass viola da gamba or violone may be called on to provide a bass line in an ensemble situation where the keyboard is set in some irregular temperament such as Vallotti. As discussed in chapter 2 and elsewhere, irregular temperaments can usually be served sufficiently by setting the regular temperament on which they are based in conjunction with left-hand manipulations based on your knowledge of the irregular temperament's features. In her figure 5.b, Elizabeth Liddle shows some of the finger adjustments the gamba player can make to accommodate Vallotti. Her figure 5c shows how several curved split frets can accomplish the same thing, a somewhat enthusiastic and

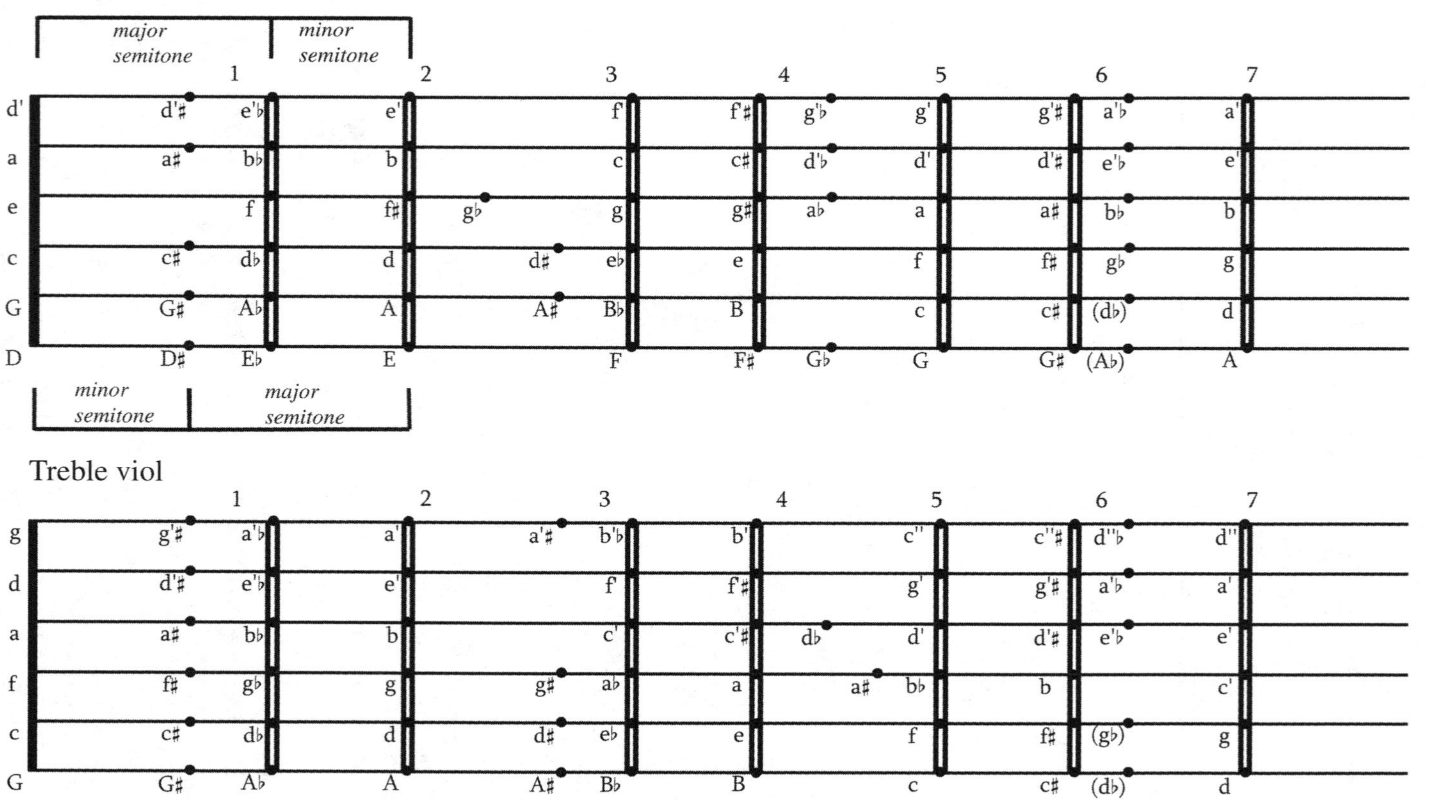

Diagram 9.3. Viol fret space locations providing alternate *mis* and *fas*. Courtesy of Richard Carter.

accommodating solution to a situation that begs for perhaps a different approach: the diplomatic suggestion to switch to a more reasonable regular temperament suited for ensembles.[31] Nevertheless, for the most part, this issue will probably never come up because, according to Carter, irregular temperaments,

> which were mostly developed in the 18th century, are important—but these issues are largely irrelevant to players of consort music. The emphasis placed on them, especially if it takes the form of how much "better" they are than meantone, leads to misunderstanding and confusion for players of bowed strings, for whom intonation, rather than temperament per se, is the real issue, and this is best approached from a slightly different standpoint.[32]

Other Viols

The largest instruments of the viol family are those most likely to have been compelled to tune in meantone temperaments because they were used as bass line continuo instruments in ensembles with a keyboard that would have normally been tuned in some variety of meantone temperament. Their thick frets and wide fret spaces also make left-hand adjustments more effective, the latter also making these large instruments quite suitable for double frets. The instruments in this category include the *violone,* the lowest member of the viol family, tuned in the standard open string interval pattern below the bass viola da gamba in G or an octave lower than the standard bass in D, the great bass in A tuned in the same pattern, and the seven-string bass, a bass viol in D with an added low A.

Several types of viol were tuned in a variety of fashions, among them the *pardessus, lyra viol,* and *lirone.* Open string tunings that repeat the same interval throughout, such as a perfect fourth or fifth, and omit the major third are much more predictable than the standard viol 4–4–3–4–4 open string pattern and are particularly well suited for meantone temperaments.[33] Although many players tune the pardessus in the familiar open string pattern for the sake of ease, other tunings include g–d′–a′–d″–g″ for the five-string pardessus and g–c′–e′–a′–d″–g″ for the six-string instrument, which relocates the third between the fifth and fourth courses. As with the early seventeenth-century French *accords nouveaux* for lute, it is important to know in advance where your *mis* and *fas* are to be found.

While the lyra viol designated a specific type of bass instrument, shorter and with a flatter bridge arch and easier action than the normal bass to facilitate chordal playing, the term is primarily used today to describe a style of playing or repertoire that involves self-accompanied solos or harmonic accompaniments similar to what the lute customarily supplies. Solo lyra viol literature is written in tablature, whose primary raison d'être is to convey chordal or polyphonic music, that is, music that most benefits from efforts to provide more harmonious intonation. The lyra viol could be tuned the same as the standard bass gamba, but at the beginning of the seventeenth century, concurrent with the lute *accords nouveaux,* there were up to sixty different tunings, including one in open fourths and fifths, as we have seen with the pardessus.[34] Since the whole point of special scordatura tunings such as the *accords nouveaux* and lyra viol tunings is to play in a particular tonality with greater ease and more open strings, by their nature, such pieces are rather well suited to unequal temperaments because they tend not to modulate very far and can usually be accommodated quite easily by setting the appropriate *mi* and *fa* frets. Befitting the use of the first string to provide the reference pitch as cited above, lyra viol tunings are customarily presented from the top to the bottom.[35]

For a good two hundred years (1500–1700), the lirone was a popular instrument for accompanying vocal music because of its ethereal sound and ability to provide a sustained chordal accompaniment in a wide variety or tonalities. The several open string tunings all shared a pair of drone strings and nine or more fretted strings tuned in a series of fourths or fifths over a rather flat bridge that facilitated chords of as many as five notes, depending on the tuning, as depicted by Cerreto's tablature in figure 9.5. Erin Headley writes, "An exceptional feature of the lirone's tuning is that it affords pure 3rds in all keys: with flats on one side of the bridge and sharps on the other, it is possible to obtain, for example, pure 3rds in both E♭ and B major chords."[36] Taking the measure of Mersenne's tuning, which is perhaps today's most popular open string lirone tuning, we find confirmation of this very fact as demonstrated in table 9.1, excluding the two G string drones. Furthermore, as Headley points out: "One instrument also shows double frets, so that alternate chord fingerings can be played in tune as well."

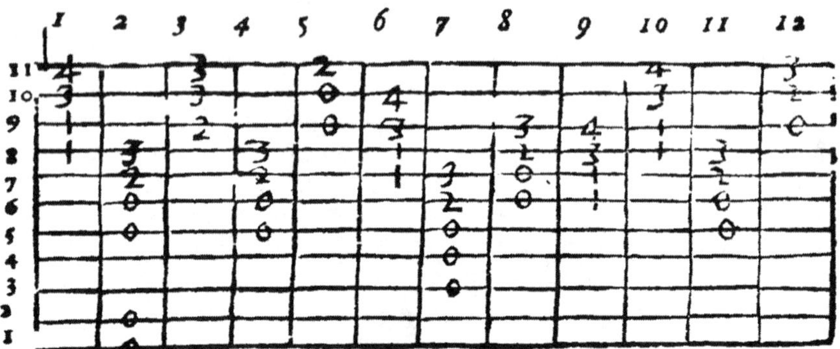

Figure 9.5. Tablature example of lirone chords in Scipione Cerreto's *Della prattica musica vocale, et strumentale* (1601), 325.

Table 9.1.
Mersenne's fretted open string lirone tuning with alternating *fa* and *mi* frets

Open	B♭	F	C	G	D	A	E	B	F♯	C♯	G♯
1st	C♭	G♭	D♭	A♭	E♭	B♭	F	C	G	D	A
2nd	C	G	D	A	E	B	F♯	C♯	G♯	D♯	A♯
3rd	D♭	A♭	E♭	B♭	F	C	G	D	A	E	B
4th	D	A	E	B	F♯	C♯	G♯	D♯	A♯	E♯	B♯
5th	E♭	B♭	F	C	G	D	A	E	B	G♭/F♯	D♭/C♯

Much more so than the lute, the viol's structural features and its use of the bow equip it with a versatile arsenal of techniques that facilitate precise tuning in any regular or even irregular temperament. Moreover, and more important, the viol is the fretted instrument most capable of approaching Just intonation through its ability to effect minute tuning adjustments on any fretted note and to a lesser degree on any open string through deft use of the bow. Ironically, the very features that can make the viol so frustratingly difficult to play in tune are those that bless it with the ability to play so divinely in tune. Were it that all our vices could so easily be transformed into virtues.

Conclusion

SINCE MOST OF US have spent our entire lives encountering only one temperament, it is natural to resist the notion that there may be other legitimate or even better temperaments, but as you have seen, for those of us with movable frets, there are. It is also tempting to think of the history of tuning systems as a linear progression of one temperament giving way to another, when in reality tuning systems often competed with each other, traveling on parallel tracks for as long as centuries at a time.

Pythagorean tuning died hard because of its association with a revered and venerated ancient philosopher. Most scholars obstinately clung to the belief that the path of wisdom laid in following his example until Vincenzo Galilei had the cheek to point out that other respected philosophers, such as Aristoxenus and Ptolemy, disagreed with Pythagoras. Theorists and philosophers stubbornly held on to the dream a workable Just intonation system for fixed pitch instruments in which pure intervals mirrored perfect order in the universe. Men of faith were heavily invested in these ideas for the grander schemes they represented.

Increasingly, the practical superseded the theoretical and conceptual. Meantone temperaments responded to the greater frequency of thirds that were a natural consequence of music in three or more voices by narrowing the fifths to reduce the size of the thirds so that they approached or reached purity. In exchange for this stability, certain keys that were not used anyway were rendered totally inaccessible, but in the spirit of exploration, probably led by lutenists, musicians began to cede increasing amounts of third purity to gain access to a wider range of tonal areas. This we witnessed in our brief examination of the fretting schemes proposed by Gerle and then Dowland. It is likely that their temperaments began with a genuflection to Pythagoras on the way to something more utilitarian and practical based on 1/6-comma meantone temperament or a close relative that could have only been finalized with adjustments by ear and verified by checking octaves and unisons. The arrangement of frets may begin in theory, but it always ends in practice.

By describing a clear, simple, and practical method for setting frets in equal temperament, Vincenzo Galilei set the stage for its eventual hegemony over all other tuning systems. As one of the very first true musical scientists, Vincenzo ushered in an era that increasingly valued the practical over the theoretical; his son Galileo personified the shift in prestige from pure to practical science. None, however, were more practical than the makers of wire-strung instruments, such as Palmer and Rose, whose view of what was practical differed markedly from Vincenzo's as manifested in their creation of utilitarian temperaments, which may offer the most accurate glimpse we have into how fretted instrument players approached temperament on a daily basis. Their instruments embody craft knowledge.

Over the course of this book, we have explored why we need temperaments and delved into how they work. Although anyone can move a fret this way or that following a set of instructions, a chart, or a tuner, until you grasp how tuning systems function, you can never be independent enough to find creative solutions to the unanticipated tuning challenges that inevitably arise throughout the course of a lifetime of playing. You now have a firm command of the various types of tuning systems that can be applied to fretted instruments: Pythagorean tuning, meantone and related irregular temperaments, utilitarian temperaments, and equal temperament. More to the point, though, you can no longer be misled by the all-too-common misguided notion that unequal temperaments cannot work on fretted instruments. You know why they work and how they work.

We have seen how external physical and environmental factors can work for or against us and how to avoid self-imposed limitations. In the end, much of it comes down to following the advice we've seen frequently repeated in historical sources: keep your pegs, strings, and frets in good working order. Change your strings regularly and your frets frequently. The tuning process itself involves choosing a tuning system and method. Fortunately, we now have programmable multitemperament tuners that make tuning in a variety of temperaments quite easy with a modicum of knowledge. It bears repeating that whatever tuning system and method we choose, in all cases, the open strings and frets must be tuned to the same tuning system. Most of the time, just tuning your open strings and setting your frets will be enough to accommodate the majority of the pitches you require; however, for those cases where this proves to be insufficient, we have many arrows in our quiver: slanted frets, tastini, double and split frets, compromise positions, and pulling and pushing. We also learned to how to construct a foolproof network of unisons and octaves by ear.

The successful application of unequal temperaments in ensemble situations depends on specific strategies to ensure that all the required pitches are covered in one way or another. Because the archlute and particularly the theorbo are capable of realizing extended meantone temperaments, whereas keyboards, save for those rare instruments equipped with split keys, are not, they can provide the continuo team with much wider coverage than can a keyboard alone. Earlier we explained how you can't always get what you want in terms of temperament, but, with the viol, you might indeed get what you need, for it is the fretted instrument most capable of approaching Just intonation.

If, despite all the evidence presented here, you still believe that equal temperament has always been irrevocably linked to fretted instruments, don't let your view of the past get in the way of your future. Equal temperament may be the most practical temperament, but for many repertoires it is more practical than necessary, and, I think, more practical than it's worth. However you choose to arrange your frets, stay tuned.

Appendix 1: Hertz in Cleartune

In Cleartune, under "Options," you must have the Temperament Key set to the default C. For this experiment, A4 calibration should be at 440 and temperament set to Equal Temperament. Select the pitch pipe icon on the right side of the screen. This modality allows you to see the pitches in hertz. Click the little lock icon in the center of the dial to allow the dial to precisely lock into your selected pitch. Turn the dial to A and press the circle with the "4" in it. See figure A1.1 Press the on/off button in the middle to hear the pitch. Now select the circle with the "3" in it to produce the A an octave lower. As you can see in figure A1.2 and hear when you press the on/off icon, the sound produced is one octave lower at 220.0 Hz. Now return to A = 440 Hz by reselecting the circle with the "4" in it. Turn the dial to A♭, and you will see that it registers 415.3 Hz and listen to it. Now turn the dial back to A. Next return to the settings and change the A4 Calibration to 415. The A now reads 415.0 Hz and sounds a semitone lower than the A = 440 Hz, roughly the equivalent of the A♭ in 440 Hz.[1] See figure A1.3 While you are there, turn the dial to B♭, and you will see that it measures at 439.7 Hz, very nearly the 440 Hz with which we started.[2]

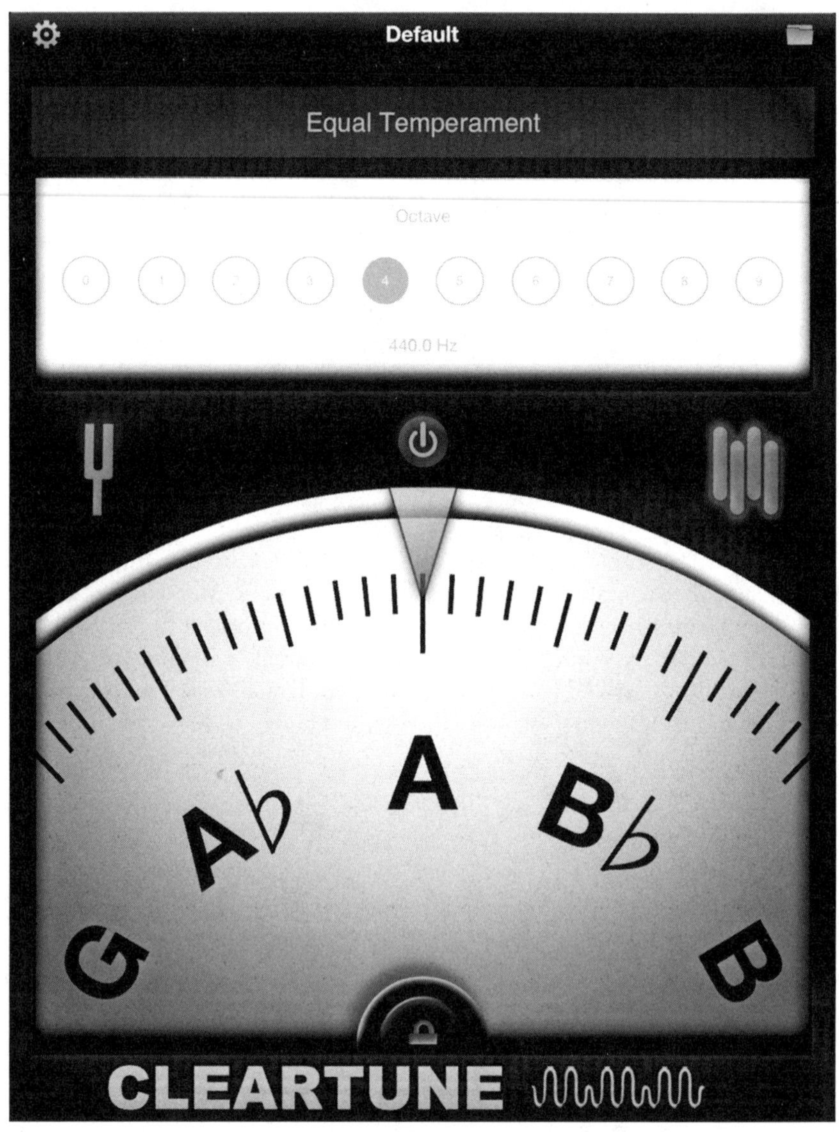

Figure A1.1. Cleartune screenshot: A = 440 Hz.

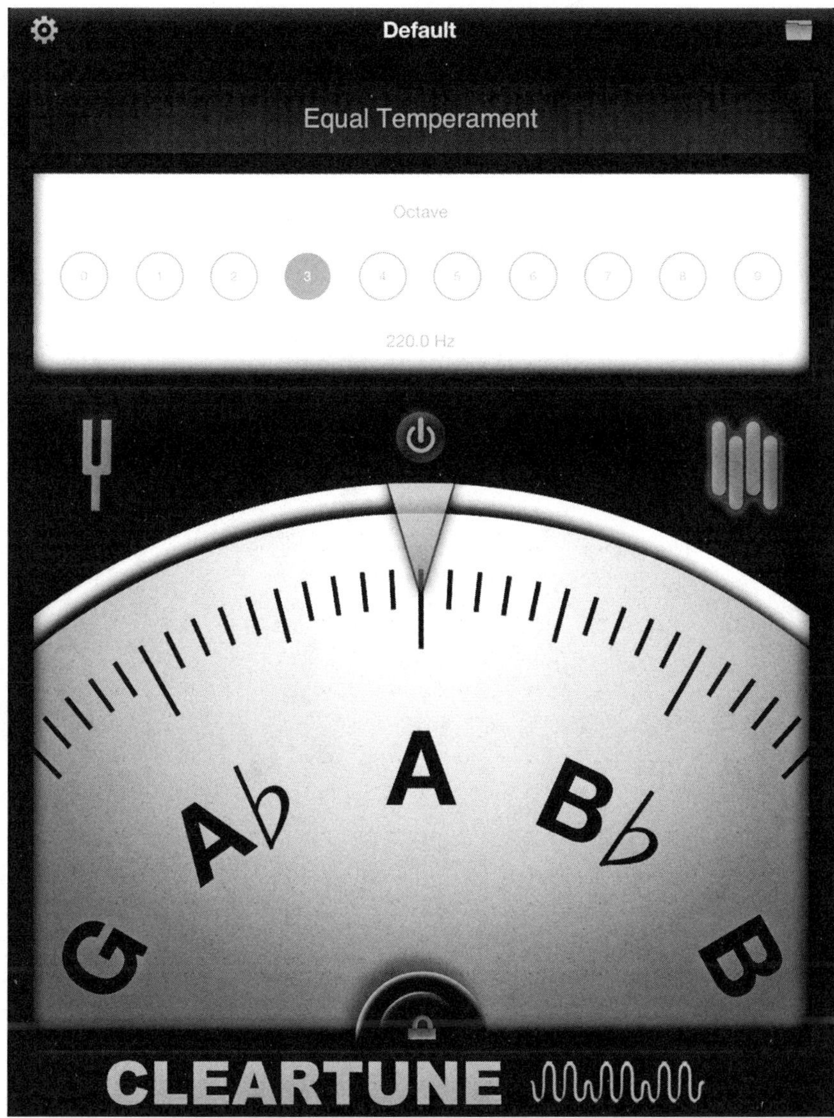

Figure A1.2. Cleartune screenshot: A = 220 Hz.

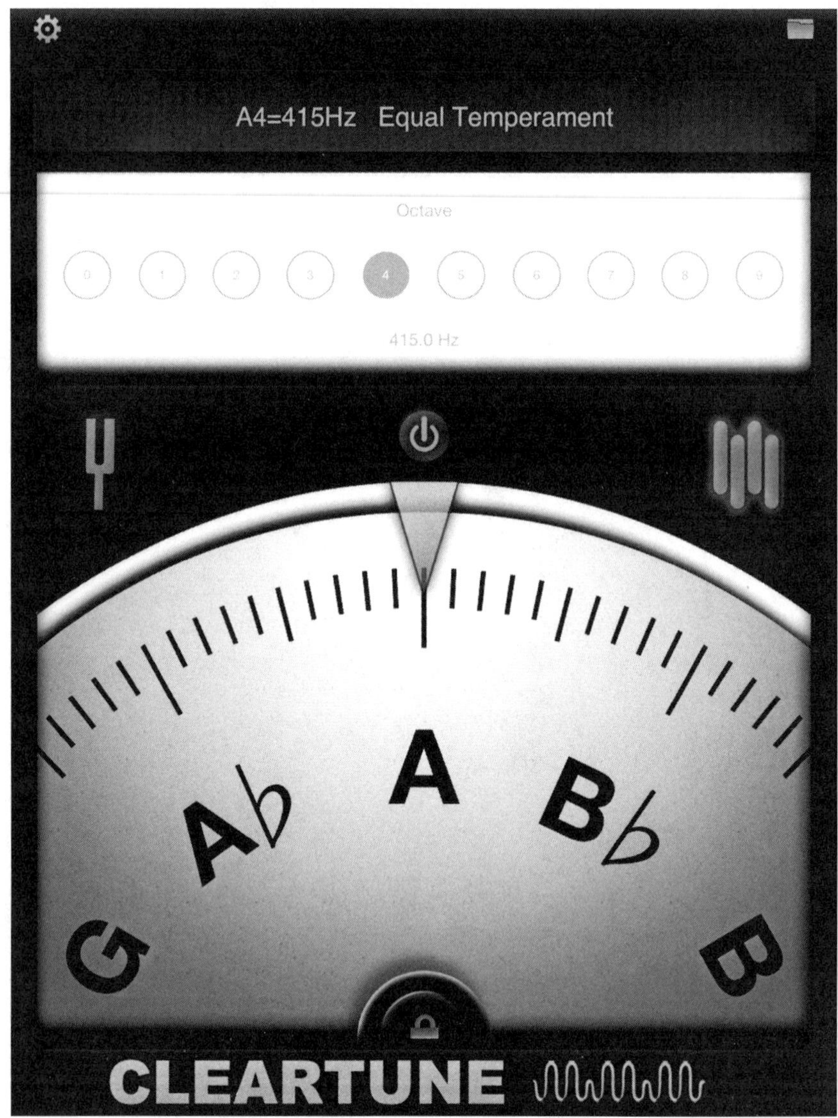

Figure A1.3. Cleartune screenshot: A = 415 Hz.

Appendix 2: Equal Temperament Offset Charts

Cleartune and other tuning apps come equipped with a variety of preset temperaments; however, I get better results by creating my own version of the temperaments I regularly use. Tuning apps such as Cleartune provide users with the ability to create custom temperaments by inputting the difference in cents between each pitch you want and its corresponding value in equal temperament.[1] Just like a normal cents chart, the size of the interval is determined from the starting pitch, which is preset to C. If the interval between the cents chart's starting pitch and the pitch being set is wider than the corresponding ET pitch, the offset is a positive number. To create a fifth of 702c. rather than a 700c. (ET) fifth, you would enter 2 in the field next to G, since 702c. is 2c. wider than the corresponding ET value. If it is less, it is a negative number. For a 498c. fourth in the F field, you would enter −2, since 498c. is 2c. narrower than an ET fourth of 500c.

While it is easier to think of temperaments with cents charts starting on C, and Cleartune and other tuners begin their cents chart templates on C (with the exception of PitchLab), the cents chart from which you derive your values must start on A because we use A as our tuning standard.[2] Otherwise, your A will diverge 2–3 Hz from the your pitch standard as represented in the A4 calibration box because the cents chart overrides the tuner's A calibration, and some of the other pitches will be even farther off owing to the effect of compounding. This is easy enough to check for yourself by simply comparing the hertz figures for the same temperament with C as the 0 value and A as the 0 value. Just as everyone agrees that octaves must be pure, we also agree that, for better or worse, our As must agree, and we go from there. With one exception, wolves in the following charts are placed between the G♯ and E♭; however, you can place them wherever you like by recalculating the cents chart accordingly.

To begin, select Cleartune Settings, which will automatically bring up the Options menu. It should look something like figure A2.1. It's important that the Transposition and Temperament Key both be set to C. Select Temperament to navigate to the Temperament menu. There you will find several categories: Custom, Equal Temperament, Strings, Pythagorean/Just, Meantone, Well Tempered, and French in Cleartune. Whatever temperament you are currently using will be selected with a checkmark. See figure A2.2. To access Cleartune's Custom Temperament Window, select Edit, which then becomes a plus sign. Select the plus sign, which takes you to the Add Temperament window. See figure A2.3. From here, you simply name the temperament and enter the appropriate plus/minus numbers in the boxes. Don't be concerned that the Cent Offset chart in the window begins on C rather than A. Simply transfer the offsets from the cents charts below, which give both the cents chart in A and the offsets that you can enter into the Cent Offset fields of the Edit Temperament window.

Because you cannot change how the pitches are labeled in the Cleartune custom temperament list,[3] you must remember that A♭ may actually be G♯ rather than A♭, and E♭ may actually be D♯, and so on, depending on where you've placed the wolf. To accommodate Cleartune's field limitation to one decimal place, you must round any offsets with two decimal places to one decimal place. You can do it yourself, or Cleartune will do it for you. Your completed ET Offset Chart should look something like figure A2.4. The figure in the A field out of the picture is 0.0.

This appendix provides the ET offset tuning charts for most of the regular temperaments discussed in this book. You can, of course, create your own ET offset tuning charts for any temperament you desire by following the examples below, but make sure you start on A rather than C. For your convenience, the offsets with A set to 0.0 are also transcribed into a chart beginning on C so that your chart matches what you see on your tuner for easier transcription. Notice that, as would be expected, in the meantone temperaments the *mis* (sharp notes and B and E) always have a negative number and the *fas* (flat notes and C and F) always have a positive number because, as you know, compared with equal temperament, in meantone temperaments the *mis* are lower and the *fas* are higher. The offset charts are also useful because they demonstrate how all the minus and plus values on either side of the tritone between A and D♯ (augmented fourth) and A and E♭ (diminished fifth) balance each other out.

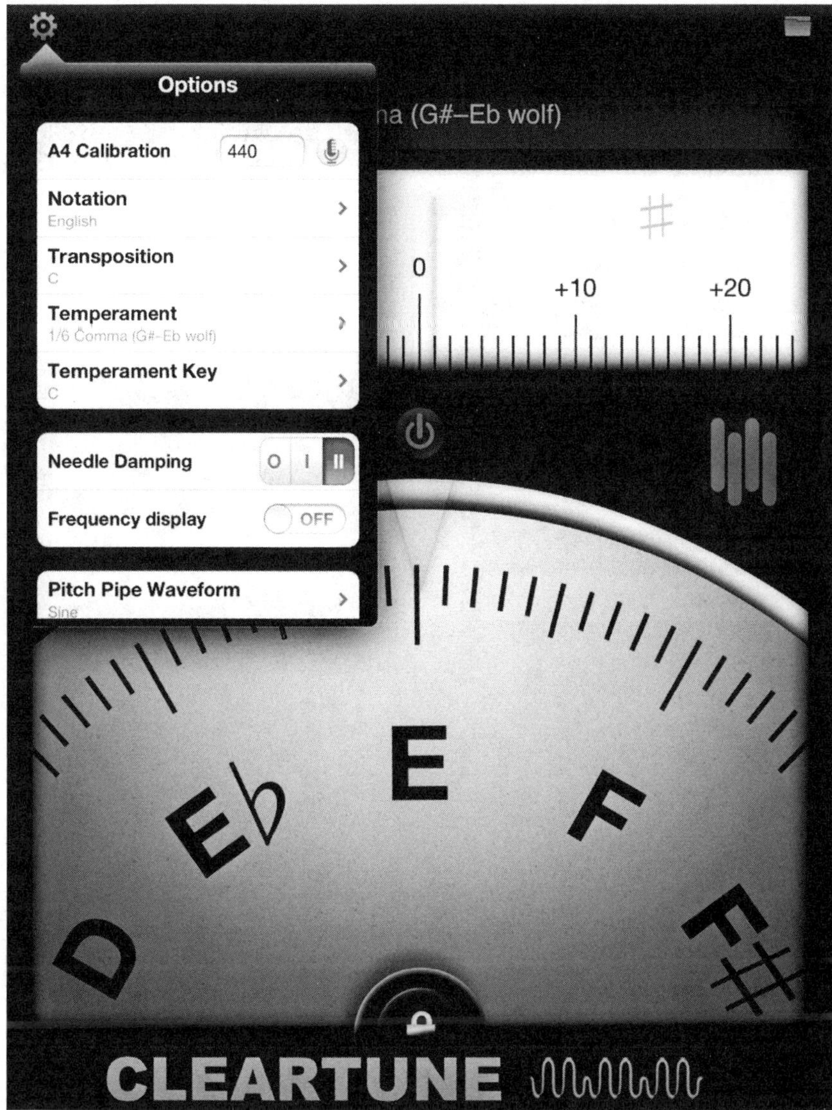

Figure A2.1. Cleartune screenshot: Options.

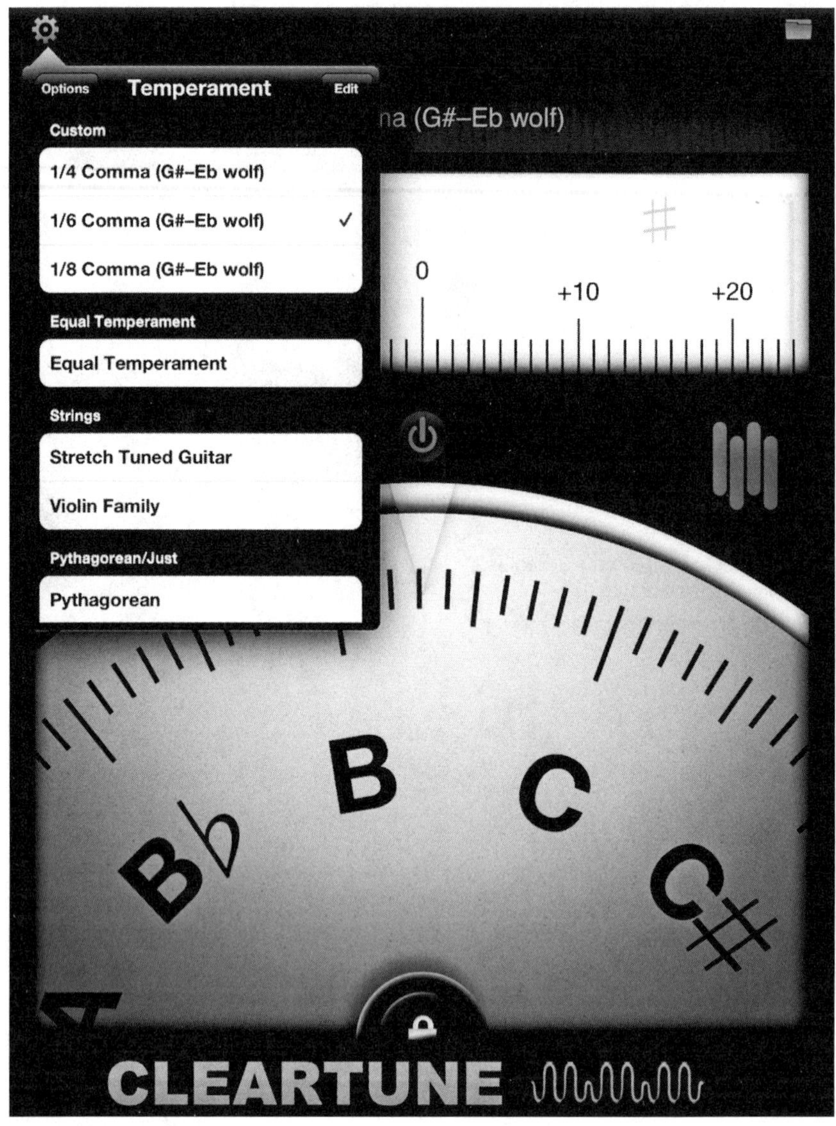

Figure A2.2. Cleartune screenshot: Temperament.

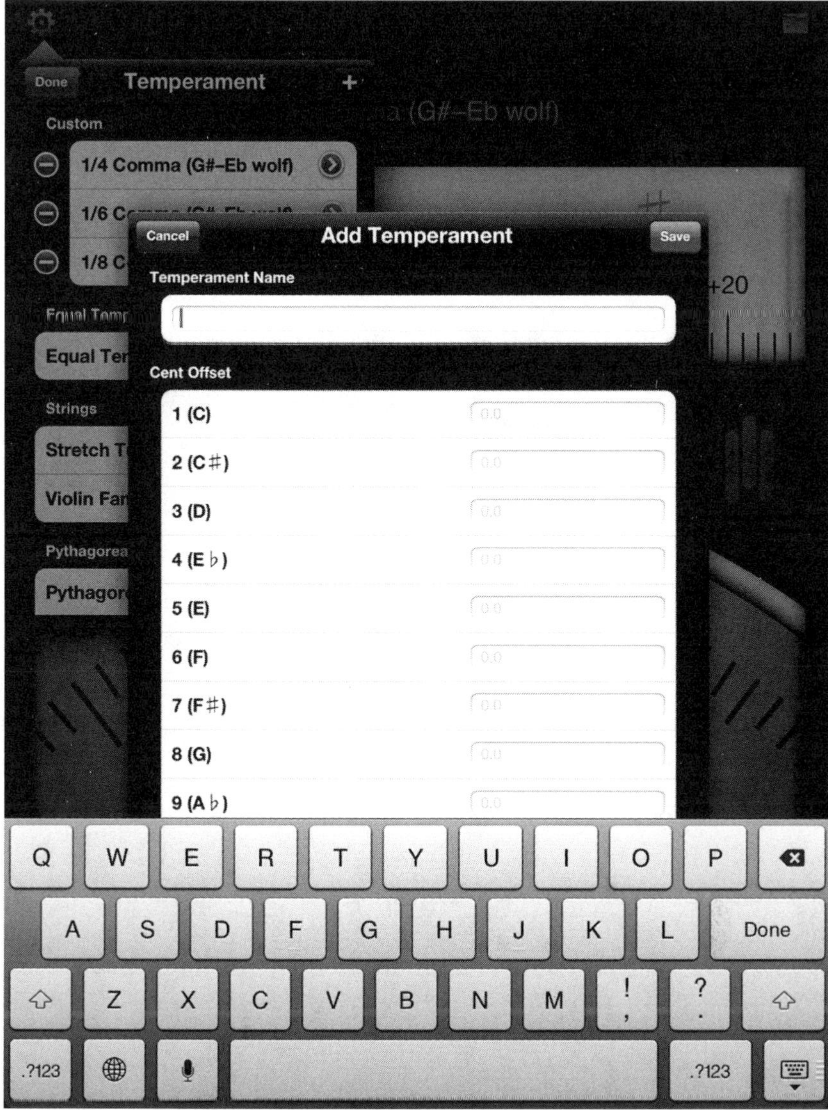

Figure A2.3. Cleartune screenshot: Add Temperament.

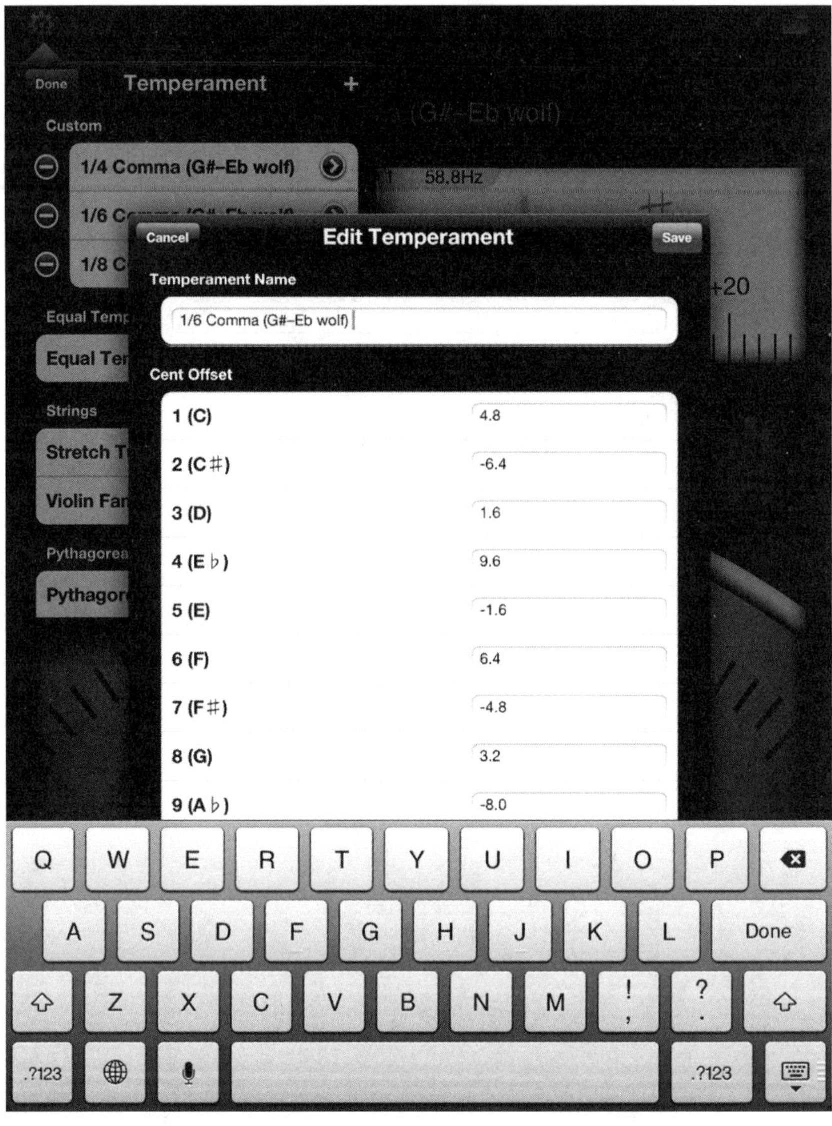

Figure A2.4. Cleartune screenshot: Edit Temperament.

Chart A2.1.
Pythagorean tuning (G♯–E♭ wolf)

A	B♭	3	C	C♯	D	E♭	E	F	F♯	G	G♯	A
	90	204	294	408	498	588	702	792	906	996	1110	1200
	–10	4	–6	8	–2	–12	2	–8	6	–4	10	0.0

C	C♯	D	E♭	E	F	F♯	G	G♯	A	B♭	B
–6	8	–2	–12	2	–8	6	–4	10	0.0	–10	4

Chart A2.2.
1/4-comma meantone (G♯–E♭ wolf)

A	B♭	B	C	C♯	D	E♭	E	F	F♯	G	G♯	A
	117.5	193	310.5	386	503.5	621	696.5	814	889.5	1007	1082.5	1200
	17.5	–7.0	10.5	–14.0	3.5	21.0	–3.5	14.0	–10.5	7.0	–17.5	0.0

C	C♯	D	E♭	E	F	F♯	G	G♯	A	B♭	B
10.5	–14.0	3.5	21.0	–3.5	14.0	–10.5	7.0	–17.5	0.0	17.5	–7.0

Chart A2.3.
1/5-comma meantone (G♯–E♭ wolf)

A	B♭	B	C	C♯	D	E♭	E	F	F♯	G	G♯	A
	112	195.2	307.2	390.4	502.4	614.4	697.6	809.6	892.8	1004.8	1088	1200
	12.0	-4.8	7.2	-9.6	2.4	14.4	-2.4	9.6	-7.2	4.8	-12.0	0.0

C	C♯	D	E♭	E	F	F♯	G	G♯	A	B♭	B
7.2	-9.6	2.4	14.4	-2.4	9.6	-7.2	4.8	-12.0	0.0	12.0	-4.8

Chart A2.4.
1/6-comma meantone (G♯–E♭ wolf)

A	B♭	B	C	C♯	D	E♭	E	F	F♯	G	G♯	A
	108	196.8	304.8	393.6	501.6	609.6	698.4	806.4	895.2	1003.2	1092	1200
	8.0	-3.2	4.8	-6.4	1.6	9.6	-1.6	6.4	-4.8	3.2	-8.0	0.0

C	C♯	D	E♭	E	F	F♯	G	G♯	A	B♭	B
4.8	-6.4	1.6	9.6	-1.6	6.4	-4.8	3.2	-8.0	0.0	8.0	-3.2

Chart A2.5.
1/6-comma meantone (A♯–F wolf)

A	A♯	B	C	C♯	D	D♯	E	F	F♯	G	G♯	A
	88.8	196.8	304.8	393.6	501.6	590.4	698.4	806.4	895.2	1003.2	1092	1200
	-1.2	-3.2	4.8	-6.4	1.6	-9.6	-1.6	6.4	-4.8	3.2	-8.0	0.0

C	C♯	D	D♯	E	F	F♯	G	G♯	A	A♯	B
4.8	-6.4	1.6	-9.6	-1.6	6.4	-4.8	3.2	-8.0	0.0	-1.2	-3.2

Chart A2.6.
1/7-comma meantone (G♯–E♭ wolf)

A	B♭	B	C	C♯	D	E♭	E	F	F♯	G	G♯	A
	105.7	197 72	303.42	395.44	501.14	606.84	698.9	804.56	896.58	1002.28	1094.3	1200
	5.7	-2 28	3.42	-4.56	1.14	6.84	-1.1	4.56	-3.42	2.28	-5.7	0.0

C	C♯	D	E♭	E	F	F♯	G	G♯	A	B♭	B
3.42	-4.56	1.14	6.84	-1.1	4.56	-3.42	2.28	-5.7	0.0	5.7	-2.28

Chart A2.7.

1/8-comma meantone (G♯–E♭ wolf)

A	B♭	B	C	C♯	D	E♭	E	F	F♯	G	G♯	A
	103.75	198.5	302.25	397	500.75	604.5	699.25	803	897.75	1001.5	1096.25	1200
	3.75	–1.5	2.25	–3	0.75	4.5	–0.75	3	–2.25	1.5	–3.75	0.0

C	C♯	D	E♭	E	F	F♯	G	G♯	A	B♭	B
2.25	–3	0.75	4.5	–0.75	3	–2.25	1.5	–3.75	0.0	3.75	–1.5

Notes

INTRODUCTION

1. My thanks to Pascale Boquet and Miriam Escudero for this information.

2. Special thanks to Arthur Ness for giving me a copy of the book long after it had gone out of print.

3. My thanks to Paul O'Dette for providing this narrative.

4. Wollenberg, 1, 3–4.

5. Such rounding can eventually become an issue when these numbers are compounded, but since we are concerned only with matters at hand, it will not impact our study.

1. PRECEDENT

1. In 1984, Lindley was not as sanguine: "One would like to imagine that the most sensitive and adroit players of the lute or viol might accommodate their intonation to meantone for a more euphonious ensemble when accompanied by keyboard instruments. We should not be too optimistic about this, however." Lindley, *Lutes, Viols and Temperaments,* 43–44. On the contrary, I think we have every reason to be optimistic, especially with regard to ensemble situations where lutenists can easily choose chord voicings that accommodate themselves to the minimal restrictions that a meantone fretting arrangement imposes. This practical topic is discussed in detail in chapter 8.

2. Personal conversations and in public forums.

1. HISTORICAL PERFORMANCE, THOUGHT, AND PERSPECTIVE

1. Barbieri, "Conflitti," 123; Nuti, 40; A. Smith, 47–51.

2. See Gary R. Boye's extensive list of sources that specify lute or guitar as members of the continuo collective at http://applications.library.appstate.edu/music/lute/continuo.html#d1610.

3. Nuti, 10–12, 41–46. Patrizio Barbieri adds that a parallel argument could be made with regard to the harp, which was typically tuned in meantone temperaments and often paired with the lute or theorbo either as members of a continuo band or in the case of the canzonas found in the manuscript Mus. 156 Biblioteca Nazionale di Roma of the compositions of Stefano Landi and Filippo Nicoletti, as individual voices in polyphonic compositions that sometimes include sections in unison. Barbieri, "Conflitti," 143.

4. Nuti, 34–38. Among the many examples of composers whose works specify lutes with keyboard are Carlo Mannelli (1682), Giovanni Pietro Franchi (1685), Antonio Luigi Baldassini (1691), Antonio Veracini (1692 and 1696), Ippolito Boccaletti (1692), Giovanni Maria Ruggieri (1693), John Ravenscroft (1695), and Petro Migali (1696). See Barbieri, "Conflitti," 143n52.

5. Nuti, 37.
6. Marais, 190–191.
7. Fabris, 18–22.
8. Day, 21.
9. Mace, 40.
10. Castaldi, 3–4.
11. Fabris, 16.
12. Poulton and Crawford.
13. Gouk, 73.
14. Lindley, *Lutes, Viols and Temperaments,* 81–83. For more on Dowland's fretting recommendations, see Mitchell.
15. For an extended discussion of the sixteenth- and seventeenth-century conception of the terms *nature, science,* and *art,* particularly in England, see Gouk.
16. Bermudo, 79.
17. Dowland, 15.
18. Barbieri, "Conflitti," 129. Artusi remarked that Venere also told him that in "ancient times" frets were positioned by chance and without any system, but also that some lute makers used the 18:17 geometrical method espoused by Galilei. Fabris, 28n20.
19. Lindley, *Lutes, Viols and Temperaments,* 5; Bermudo, 115.
20. Bottrigari, 22.
21. Praetorius, 68.
22. Dowland, 15; Le Roy, 51.
23. Ganassi, 91.
24. For more on this subject, see Gouk, 74.
25. For a description of the lure that Pythagorean tuning must have held over those with a theoretical bent of mind, see Reeve.
26. Bermudo, xx.
27. Griffiths, "Vihuela," 172.
28. Fabris, 31–32. That Lieto intends the resultant tuning to yield a meantone temperament is obvious from his discussion of the various sizes of the frets.
29. Margerum, 22–40.
30. Mersenne, *Harmonie universelle,* pt. II, "Livre second des instruments a chordes," 52.
31. The reasons for this futility are explained in detail in part 2.
32. For an explanation of how Just intonation can be approximated in a cappella vocal music, see Duffin, "Just Intonation."
33. Walker, "Some Aspects of the Musical Theory," 36.
34. No fixed fret instrument can be completely "Just," but a guitar with extra frets can furnish additional pitch choices that dramatically improve the purity of many of the intervals, much in the same fashion as do extended meantone temperaments on lutes and viols as described in later chapters. Contemporary guitarists who have made great strides in this arena, now referred to as microtonal guitar, include John Schneider, Turkish classical guitarist Tolgahan Çoğulu, and Neil Haverstick. For a thorough introduction to the world of microtonal guitar, see John Schneider's article "Just Guitar," which can be easily accessed at www.microstick.net/ under "Articles." See also his *Contemporary Guitar.* For more information on Tolgahan Çoğulu's microtonal guitar, including videos, see www.tolgahancogulu.com/en/?page_id=4. Videos of Neil Haver-

stick playing his twenty-two-fret guitar can be found at www.broadlandsmedia.com /microstick/videos/.

35. Duffin, "Tuning and Temperament," 281; Barbour, 26. For a detailed explanation of meantone and related irregular temperaments, see chapter 5.

36. O'Dette, 7.

37. Agricola, 114.

38. Banchieri, 43.

39. Barbieri, "Conflitti," 135–136.

40. For greater detail on Valentini's work, see Fabris, 39–41, to which this discussion is indebted. The translations are Fabris's.

41. Lindley, *Lutes, Viols and Temperaments,* 44–48.

42. Since Doni had little faith in the ability to adjust pitches with the left hand, in his view, if the frets are set unequally, they could only produce unequal intervals.

43. Lindley, *Lutes, Viols and Temperaments,* 51–58.

44. Milán, 299 and 317; Gásser, 156–157.

45. Gásser, 157.

46. For the viol in D substitute the major third E–G♯ and the open strings C–E. For an explanation of cents, see chapter 4.

47. Remember that the directions cited instructing the player to move one fret in isolation say nothing about retuning the open strings.

48. All diagrams of fretboard patterns are precisely measured to scale based on the theoretical fret positions of a 40 cm instrument and then reduced by a uniform amount to fit on the page. They present the view from the perspective of a lute player looking down at the fretboard while playing, with the first course at the top of the diagram.

49. Lindley, *Lutes, Viols and Temperaments,* 50.

50. Ibid., 52.

51. Bermudo, 115.

52. Fabris, 32.

53. Barbieri, "Conflitti," 136.

54. Lusitano, 22–23. My thanks to Stewart Carter for alerting me to this passage and Philippe Canguilhem and Margaret Murata for their help in translating Lusitano's awkward comingling of Spanish and Italian. The instruments in the final sentence certainly refer to those such as Vicentino's *arcicembalo,* designed to perform in microtones.

55. Or *fas* at a *mi* fret in Pythagorean tuning.

56. Kirnbauer, 49–50.

57. Galilei, *Fronimo,* 102–103.

58. *Sharpening* refers to the process whereby the actual pitch produced by a fretted note is sharper than the pitch that fret's position would theoretically produce were it not subjected to factors such the instrument's action, the string's physical features, humidity, and so on. See chapter 6 for an in-depth discussion of sharpening.

59. Barbieri, "Conflitti," 137; Barbieri, *Enharmonic,* 40–41.

60. Barbieri, *Enharmonic,* 41–42; Barbieri, "L'Accordatura strumentale in Toscana," 230.

61. Denis, 12.

62. Simpson, *Compendium of Practical Music,* 51–52.

63. Ibid., 54.

64. Barbieri, "Conflitti," 133, 138–139.

65. Duffin, *How Equal Temperament Ruined Harmony,* 47; Barbieri, *Enharmonic,* 125.

66. Barbieri, "Conflitti," 131–134; Barbieri, "L'Accordatura strumentale in Toscana," 212–214.

67. As Christian Meyer points out, when considering a utilitarian temperament, we must evaluate the intervals between not only the open string and fretted notes but also between different courses, as well as those between one fret and another on the same string. Meyer, 125. Meyer also points out that in utilitarian temperaments, that is, those in which all nominal intervals are not necessarily the same size, different tuning methods such as comparing octaves or the familiar 5th fret/4th fret method yield diverse results.

68. For a detailed explanation of equal temperament, see chapter 5.

69. Hoffmann, 92.

70. My thanks to Monica Hall for this citation and all related information regarding the Baroque guitar.

71. Gásser, 157.

72. Lindley, *Lutes, Viols and Temperaments,* 19.

73. Galilei, *Dialogue,* 121–122 (49–50 in the facsimile).

74. The 18:17 method generates 99c. semitones, resulting in a progression from the 1st fret of 99c., 198c., 297c., 396c., and so on. On paper, this makes it appear that the major third at the 4th fret is slightly narrower than equal and that the fifth at the 7th fret is an exceedingly narrow 693c., yet because this method accounts for sharpening, the aural results, are accurate within 1–2c. and fractions of a millimeter when compared with the equal temperament produced by a digital electronic tuner.

75. Mersenne, *Harmonie universelle,* pt. II, "Nouvelles observations physiques et mathématiques," 20; Hoffmann, 86–87.

76. Cited in Lindley, *Lutes, Viols and Temperaments,* 45.

77. Chua cites Weber, *The Rational and Social Foundations of Music,* ed. and trans. Don Martindale, Johannes Riedel, and Gertrude Neuwirth (Carbondale: Southern Illinois University Press, 1958), 102–103.

78. Chua, 21.

79. Lindley, *Lutes, Viols and Temperaments,* 19.

80. Duffin, "Tuning and Temperament," 284.

81. Palisca, "Mathematics and Geometry," 238.

82. Palisca, "Was Galileo's Father an Experimental Scientist," 143–144; Palisca, *Florentine Camerata,* 163, 171; and Palisca, "Mathematics and Geometry," 245. See also Drake, "Renaissance Music and Experimental Science," 488, 497–499; Brown and Lascelle, 175. Galileo's study of Aristoxenus certainly reinforced the principles he learned at his father's workbench. According to Didymus, Aristoxenus emphasized that only sense perception can verify the theoretical concepts the mind creates. Palisca, quoted in Galilei, *Dialogue,* 77n113.

83. Their rancorous dispute was titanic enough for Marin Mersenne to summarize it in Proposition III of the "First Book of String Instruments" in his *Harmonie universelle* (1637) some fifty years later and Doni in 1640. For further detail on Galilei's feud with Zarlino, see Palisca's introduction to Galilei's *Dialogue,* xvii–lv; Palisca, *Florentine Camerata,* 152–163; Walker, "Some Aspects," 33–43; Korrick, 129–130; Moyer, 141; and Narvey. In addition to these sources, for more on Galilei's inconsistencies, see also Chua, 29.

84. Palisca, *Florentine Camerata,* 199–203. We can draw a similar comparison between the harpsichord and the modern piano, which, like the lute, seems to soften the harshness of equal temperament. Although many gamba players these days still string their instruments in gut, most lutenists do not. Nevertheless, today's synthetic strings such as Nylgut, for instance, can come close to mimicking gut's finer qualities without its inconveniences.

85. Moyer, 133. I might add that "classify" is not the same as "hear." Bibby refers to this phenomenon as "cultural conditioning." Bibby, 27. With regard to equal temperament's most offensive interval, its wide major third, Galilei may have been considering the effect of the "draw," the phenomenon where the pitch of a note seems to drop at the end of its duration as the energy that keeps the string vibrating becomes spent, thus causing the pitch to drop as the string returns to its original quiet state. It is most noticeable when the same interval is restruck after a long duration—it often sounds higher when restruck. Since the sound decays rather rapidly on plucked instruments, there is some merit to Galilei's opinion that equal temperament's bitter thirds are somewhat mitigated by the lute's idiosyncrasies.

86. Galilei, *Fronimo,* 155. Galilei added several additional compositions to part 1 and thirty pages to part 2 of the 1584 edition of *Fronimo* that were not in the first edition (1568). These include additional and replaced compositions and, most notably, an extensive discussion of temperaments on the lute, from which I draw heavily in the following pages.

87. Those familiar with Galilei's writings will certainly recognize that his criticizing something and then going on to explain how it should really be done is a common thread throughout the fabric of his publishing career. Perhaps the most noteworthy example of this predilection is his vilification of vocal polyphony in favor of monodic delivery in the prefaces of each of the several versions of his two extensive treatises devoted to a highly competent and thorough explanation of the rules of counterpoint, a topic he also covered broadly in *Fronimo.* Walker, *Studies,* 18.

88. An opinion also advanced by Orlando Cristoforetti in his introduction to the facsimile edition of Galilei's *Libro d'intavolatura di liuto,* n.p.

89. For a detailed analysis of the letter and its contents, see Palisca, *Florentine Camerata,* 78–89.

90. Bardi, 290; Palisca, *Florentine Camerata,* 81–84.

91. Galilei conforms well to Gouk's characterization of "upwardly mobile artisans . . . aspiring to liberal status." Gouk, 74.

92. Here Bardi means to say that the sizes of the intervals other than the octave differ on instruments tuned in equal and meantone temperaments.

93. Bardi, 297.

94. Cited in Nuti, 42.

2. SURVIVING FIXED METAL-FRET INSTRUMENTS

1. Nordstrom, 5–6, 40–42.
2. For a history of the consort through 1910, see Harwood, "Six Several Instruments."
3. Segerman, "Instruments of the Consort," 43–44.
4. Harwood, *Wire Strings at Helmingham Hall,* 22.

5. Forrester, "Wood and Wire," 12; conversations with Paul O'Dette.
6. Goodwin, ". . . and What Makes a Good Cittern?," 15.
7. Forrester, "Wood and Wire," 12.
8. For a comprehensive survey of cittern fret patterns, see Grijp.
9. Among the factors that make it difficult to tune the cittern are its wire strings, double and triple courses, and friction tuning pegs, a small rotation of which on low string tension wire-strung instruments produces a large pitch differential. See Harwood, *Wire Strings at Helmingham Hall,* 16.
10. Goodwin, ". . . and What Makes a Good Cittern?," 14. This advantage can inadvertently become a disadvantage because it is quite easy to press the fingers too forcefully into the fretboard, thereby unintentionally raising the pitch.
11. Harwood, *Wire Strings at Helmingham Hall,* 14; Segerman and Abbott, "On the Palmer Orpharion," 52. A further complication is that striking the strings too violently with the plectrum can also cause the pitch to temporarily spike.
12. Gill, "Orpharion and Bandora," 21.
13. Nordstrom, 10.
14. Segerman and Abbott, "On the Palmer Orpharion," 50.
15. Segerman, "Orpharion News," 25.
16. My thanks to Andreas Schlegel and Peter Forrester for sharing illustrations and their assessment of this instrument with me.
17. Because the Palmer orpharion's bridge, frets, and nut are in a fan pattern with the bass courses longer than the treble courses, while the Rose instrument has a parallel bridge, frets, and nut and may possibly be a bandora, it is easy to generalize that the fan arrangement was peculiar to the orpharion, but not the bandora. In fact, the fan pattern was a later modification that impacted both orpharions and bandoras although no bandora of this design has survived. The purpose of the fan pattern was probably threefold: to facilitate additional bass courses; to improve the clarity of the basses through the use of the thinner strings the increased length permitted, and, related to this, to reduce the excessive sharpening that would occur on the thicker shorter wire-strung bass strings compared with the same pitches on longer thinner strings.
18. Goodwin, ". . . and What Makes a Good Cittern?," 15; Forrester, "Wood and Wire," 12. For a detailed report on the Palmer and Rose instruments, see Coakley, "Orpharion and Cittern Fret Analysis."
19. Martin, *Report and Drawing Notes.*
20. The fret positions are supplied by Martin's report and confirmed by luthier Ray Nurse's tracing of the Palmer fretboard, which he generously shared with me. Determining the original position of the saddle at the lowest course is much more problematic because of the pronounced sharpening effect, but much less relevant because we determine an instrument's theoretical temperament by measuring the fret distances on the first course, which is least affected by sharpening.
21. At 599.1 mm, the Rose instrument's 12th fret is 298.7 mm from the nut, leaving 300.4 mm between the 12th fret and the bridge, resulting in an excess of 1.7 mm of compensation (300.4 – 298.7 = 1.7). Applying the same ratio of the Palmer orpharion's *mensur* results in approx. 1.5 mm in compensation.
22. According to Joël Dugot, former restorer at the Musée de la Musique in Paris, the wedges also facilitate the removal and replacement of worn frets. My thanks to Pascale Boquet for sharing this information with me.

23. Personal correspondence with Peter Forrester.

24. See, for instance, Duffin, *Equal Temperament,* 130n; Duffin, *Baroque Ensemble Tuning.*

25. In personal correspondence, luthier Peter Forrester points out that he adds tastini for the 1st and occasionally the 4th and 6th frets on bandoras according to his customers' wishes.

26. Similar to the purpose of the very first two staff lines when there were only two: to identify the *mi/fa* pairs between B and C and E and F, and then, later, the first two clefs C and F, which were also chosen to signify the location of the *mi/fa* pairs.

27. For step-by-step instructions explaining how to convert cents to fretting ratios and vice versa, see Dolata, "Making Cents Out of Fretting Ratios."

28. Harwood, *Wire Strings at Helmingham Hall,* 26.

29. My thanks to Darryl Martin and Peter Forrester for this information.

3. FRETTING PATTERN ICONOGRAPHY

1. Heck, 25.

2. Katritzky, 68.

3. Watson, "Dei pericoli," 7.

4. The dashed lines indicate alternate *mi* positions at *fa* frets in the meantone temperaments and alternate *fa* positions at *mi* frets in Pythagorean tuning.

5. My thanks to Tim Watson for pointing this out to me, as well as for his observations regarding the arrangement of the upper frets in the discussion that follows.

6. When in hot, humid climates, moving into a dehumidified air-conditioned environment reduces the sharpening effect just as moving out of a dehumidified air-conditioned environment increases it.

7. Barbieri, *Enharmonic,* 40–41; Watson, "The Lute and the Case for Double Frets," 45.

8. Kerala Snyder makes the case that Buxtehude is in fact the gamba player. Snyder, 109–112.

9. As Vries reminds us, "Images that refer to reality can be schematized beyond recognition, can aim at *trompe-l'oeil* effects, or anything in between." Vries, 52.

10. That is, other than diatonic citterns, which omit certain frets in part to facilitate left-hand fingering.

11. Again, the culprit here could also be sharpening, a phenomenon magnified by the use of gut strings. Even with Nylgut and copper-wound strings, once frets become worn, a casual observer could not be faulted for perceiving a perfectly workable fret arrangement as totally chaotic.

12. Andreas Schlegel and Joachim Lüdtke point out that "in Robert Fludd's second volume of his *Utriusque cosmi maioris scilicet et minoris metaphysica, physica atque technica historia, the Tractatus secundus: De naturae simia seu technica macrocosmi historia in partes undecim divisa,* Oppenheim 1618, on pages 226 and 233 of Pars II Liber sextus, there are depictions of a lute and an orpharion, which seem to show alternate frets closely positioned to each other, but as these details are neither explained in the book's text, nor are found for instance in the schematic representations of the lute's stringing and the position of notes on the lute's neck on page 227f., they are probably caused by a lack of realistic clarity in the pictures—the lute, e.g., has neither saddle nor tuning

pegs, and both instruments are shown with their parts looking in different directions." Schlegel and Lüdtke, 386n21. Furthermore, what appear to be split frets are mostly placed in nonsensical locations where they would serve no purpose whatsoever.

13. Brown and Lascelle, 3–5.

14. Watson, "Dei pericoli," 8, 15. On page 7, Watson comments that the inaccuracy of the depiction of lutes in paintings that are otherwise precise in all other respects has always evoked in him a visual unease that is comparable to that he experiences when he tries to listen to a poorly tuned lute.

15. In a trenchant remark about the values of works of art with regard to fretting patterns, Louis Peter Grijp states, "Of course most mistakes were made by artists who depicted instruments which they did not know much about, or who simply were not interested in details." Grijp, 63.

16. Forrester, "Violas, Vihuelas, and Iconography," 60–63.

17. For a detailed study of this painting, see Watson, "Dei pericoli," 14–16; for a close comparison of two versions of this painting, see Ferraris, *Caravaggio e Baschenis,* 7–10.

18. Watson, "Dei pericoli."

19. My thanks to Tim Watson for drawing my attention to the 1st fret placement of this painting.

20. See Pavan, 13–15; Slim, 2:1–8; and Carlone, "Portrait of a Lutenist at the Museo Civico of Como." My thanks to Franco Pavan for his kind assistance with regard to this painting. The image presented here is of the original painting that hangs in the museum rather than the reversed and touched-up version more commonly reproduced.

21. For greater detail on Giulio and his younger brothers Antonio and Vincenzo and their possible influence on Caravaggio, see Povoledo, 41ff.

22. This too was noted by Carlone ("Portrait of a Lutenist at the Museo Civico of Como," 95), who referred to "the extreme fidelity of the image of the lute itself," which reveals "a close observation from life on the part of the artist."

23. Tim Watson in personal correspondence. Watson also explains how similar problems afflict Caravaggio's *The Musicians.* See plate 7.

24. Graham-Dixon, 271, 302.

25. Ferraris, *Caravaggio e Baschenis,* 2–3, 10.

26. Watson, "Dei pericoli," 15–16, 20. Camiz cites Libin's opinion that "Caravaggio's instruments, even when copied from real models, are not painted with photographic accuracy." Camiz, 222. I might add that were it possible, "photographic accuracy" is still not a photograph nor does it carry its evidentiary value.

27. Camiz, 222.

28. Ferraris, *Caravaggio e Baschenis,* 13, 15; Coelho, 174–177.

29. Coelho, 175.

30. Ferraris, *Caravaggio e Baschenis,* 15.

31. Coelho, 176. Ferraris, *Caravaggio e Baschenis,* 13. For a detailed list of the instruments Baschenis owned, see Ferraris, *Caravaggio e Baschenis,* 12. Note that the painting's title refers to Ottavio's brother who appears in another of the triptych's panels.

32. It is no surprise that, as we have seen, much more progress has been made with regard to cittern fretting patterns since the frets are permanently fixed. Grijp's article could serve as a valuable model in this regard.

33. Grijp, 63.

11. THEORY

1. I recommend beginning with Lloyd; Donahue; and Duffin, *Equal Temperament.*

4. INSIDE THE NUMBERS

1. Introduced by Alexander Ellis in 1885, the cent has become the standard unit with which to measure the width of intervals. One cent constitutes 1/100th of an equal-tempered semitone, which is composed of 100 cents. An octave consists of 1200c.

2. These values are extracted from the "Table of Intervals in Cents" in Duffin, *Equal Temperament,* 163, however, they are rounded to avoid decimals.

3. While the shape will be the same on guitar, the major third will be a minor third lower: D–F♯. On a viol in D, the interval will be C–E. All musical examples will assume a six-course lute or viol in G unless otherwise indicated.

4. Playing an interval melodically means plucking or bowing each note in succession from lowest to highest or highest to lowest. Harmonic execution of an interval means playing both pitches simultaneously.

5. Here's where the guitar's different arrangement of open fourths and thirds begins to break down our experiments because its major third is between the third and second courses rather than the fourth and third courses as on the lute and viol. (A course is either a pair of strings tuned as a unison or an octave and played as if they were one string or a single string on a plucked instrument set up with primarily double courses. Some citterns include a triple course.) You can, however, achieve the same results by relocating the interval shape to the fourth and third courses to yield a major third of F–A. On the viol in D, the original shape on the third and second string generates the major third G–B.

6. A harmonic is produced by very lightly touching but not depressing the string at one of its nodal points with the left hand while plucking or bowing it with the right. Harmonics are most easily produced at the 12th, 7th, and 5th frets in that order. As we see in chapter 7, 12th fret harmonics can be used to quickly tune a fretted instrument.

7. Since I use Cleartune, all such examples will be from that app. The Cleartune tuner is available for iPhone, iPad, iPod touch, and Android at www.bitcount.com/. Screen shots in this book come from my iPad version.

8. This discussion is particularly indebted to Donahue, 10–17, whose tables are reproduced here, and Taylor, 19–20.

9. Taylor, 32. Other factors as well affect our perception of timbre, such as in this case, where the string is bowed or plucked with the right hand.

10. Note that the rounding decimal places in hertz sometimes results in values that are not mathematically precise in terms of the ratios between the two pitches that comprise an interval, but for our purposes, they are more than close enough. As you work through these tables and we transition from concerning ourselves with pitches to intervals, you will begin to appreciate how much simpler it is to think in terms of cents rather than hertz.

11. Padgham, 14.

12. Klickstein, "Pain-Free Tuning," 25n3.

13. My thanks to Federico Bonacossa for providing all the artificially generated audio files in this chapter.

14. For more detail on this matter, see Padgham, 26–28.

15. Shepherd, 8.

16. Most of us have grown up believing that enharmonic notes are equivalent, that is, E♭ is the same as D♯, because we have known no tuning system other than equal temperament, in which these equivalents exist for what we consider to be accidentals. In Pythagorean and meantone tuning systems, you must choose one or the other, and in irregular temperaments the tuning system's designer, that is, Kirnberger, Vallotti, and others, has chosen for you. As we will see, however, there are occasions when for practical reasons ET intervals can play a role within unequal regular and irregular temperaments. For the present purposes, as we consider the Circle of Fifths, we will maintain consistent enharmonic identity, counting fifths from C as sharps and fourths from C as flats. Because octaves are inviolable, and we are starting with C hoping to close the circle on C, our goal is to make B♯ = C. Although there are occasional exceptions, as the lower members of diatonic semitones, E♯ and B♯ are generally required to serve as F and C, which is one of the other problems that temperaments generally resolve.

17. For a more precise reckoning without rounding, see Padgham, 24–26.

18. If the Pythagorean comma is the amount by which twelve pure fifths exceed seven octaves, it follows that since the fourth is the inversion of the fifth (1200c. – 702c. = 498c.), twelve successive pure fourths (12 × 498c. = 5976c.) should fall short of five octaves (6000c.) by the same amount, 24c., and they do: 6000c. – 5976c. = 24c.

19. It is a good idea to be able to create a cents chart with a variety of starting pitches. Although it has no impact whatsoever on the sizes of the intervals, assuming that the wolf remains in the same location, creating a cents chart on a different starting pitch is a good way to check your math. The sizes of the intervals should be exactly the same in any given tuning system, regardless of the starting pitch, although the absolute pitch of some of the notes may differ. Since C is the easiest to grasp and also the most common starting pitch for cents charts, we'll use C in the main text, but as explained in appendix 2, to ensure that your instrument is at the correct pitch level, you need to be able to write out a cents chart in A if you plan to create your own ET offset cents chart since A rather than C serves as the international pitch standard.

20. You also don't want to get used to the chromatic semitone being the larger of the two. The reverse is much more common.

21. This section on ratios and fractions is indebted to Harkleroad, 21–29.

22. "Impure" and "unjust" carry too many extramusical connotations to be effective terms no matter how precise or proper they might be.

5. TOUR THROUGH TUNING SYSTEMS

1. While tempered fifths are usually narrowed, there are tuning systems such as *tempérament ordinaire* that widen them.

2. As we have seen, the difference between a Pythagorean chromatic semitone and a pure chromatic semitone is the Pythagorean comma.

3. Duffin, "Tuning," 545; Carter, 3n4.

4. Duffin, "Tuning and Temperament," 281.

5. My thanks to Nuria Torres for generously sharing her work on Arnaut with me.

6. This, of course, assumes that we base our temperament on C. As Arnaut did with Pythagorean tuning, we can also rotate the wolf to a different location, which then correspondingly concentrates the good keys elsewhere.

7. Duffin, "Tuning and Temperament," 282.

8. The term *syntonic* specifies that the comma that is divided is the syntonic comma of 22c. rather than the ditonic or Pythagorean comma of 24c. since there are some temperaments that divide the latter rather than former of these two commas. As you become more familiar with the concept, the "syntonic" will be dropped with the understanding that it is implied when referring to meantone temperaments unless otherwise noted.

9. In continuo playing, keyboard players sometimes place one accidental in one octave or on one manual and the other in another octave or manual.

10. Many authors report that the "mean" in meantone stems from the fact that the whole tone or major second (193c.) is exactly half the size of the pure third. Since the whole tone is also exactly half the size of the major third in Pythagorean tuning and equal temperament, I find Herb Myers's explanation that the temperament's name is derived from the fact that its major second is the average between the Just 10:9 minor tone of 182.4c. and the Just 9:8 major tone of 203.9c. more compelling. See Myers, 370. It is quite unfortunate that when used as an adjective, nowadays, the word *mean* has a negative meaning; in this context it is anything but. Musicians attuned to the beauties of meantone temperaments sometimes jokingly consider equal temperament to be equally mean in every key because the thirds sound just as bad in one key as in another.

11. Remember that the issue of *mi* and *fa* frets pertains to every fret. In many cases, such as the 2nd and 5th frets, the fret is always a *mi* or a *fa* because of the identity of the pitches that happen to reside at that fret.

12. This terminology has the benefit of corresponding fret position to pitch. "Higher" and "lower" refer to both the distance of the fret from the nut and pitch: the farther the fret is from the nut, the higher the pitch generated at that fret and vice versa.

13. See Karp, 18.

14. Duffin, *Equal Temperament,* 72.

15. Duffin, "Why I Hate Vallotti," 4.

16. For further information, see Duffin, *Equal Temperament,* 55ff. Note that the parts were historically referred to as "commas," a nomenclature that can sometimes cause confusion because, as we have seen, the term *comma* was used to indicate several different discrepancies or small intervals.

17. In this graphic, 1/6-comma meantone divides the Pythagorean comma, while 1/5-, 1/4-, and 1/3-comma meantone temperaments divide the syntonic comma. Note that equal temperament divides the octave into twelve parts; it could theoretically be divided into an infinite number of parts, for instance, 24, 36, 48, or 144, and so on. The graphic is not designed to precisely illustrate relative interval widths across the tuning systems, although the division of each scale into multiple parts does approximate those relationships.

18. Several of these theorists also created ET schemes that were exclusively theoretical but were rejected for practical use on the grounds that they destroyed key color.

19. Not to be confused with the regular ordinary temperament referred to by Haynes and Duffin above.

20. Donahue, 26. For a straightforward and clear explanation of the design principles of these and other commonly known irregular keyboard temperaments, see Dona-

hue's *A Guide to Musical Temperament,* and for an encyclopedic treatment of temperaments in general, see Jorgensen's *Tuning the Historical Temperaments by Ear.*

21. Donahue, 29–30.

22. Duffin, "Why I Hate Vallotti." See Duffin's article for greater detail on Vallotti and Young than this space allows.

23. Notwithstanding the fact that these two temperaments were devised independently, that each is a transposition of the other tells us that it or they can be transposed anywhere. For instance, the 1/6-comma backbone could start on E♭, in which case B♭ would be the best key area and E would be the worst. In such cases, the temperament could then be legitimately referred to as Transposed Vallotti or Young.

24. I arrived at these and other judgments regarding the efficacy of irregular keyboard temperaments key areas in consort with my graduate students at Florida International University during our seminars on tuning during which we listened to each of these temperaments and experimented with a wide variety of keys and compositional types on a harpsichord and chamber organ set to each of the temperaments discussed in this chapter.

25. For entertaining descriptions of the problems associated with Vallotti, see Duffin, "Why I Hate Vallotti"; Hammer.

26. Your ability to create a cents chart for any temperament provides you with the requisite skills to create a dissonance factor table for any temperament.

27. In *The Well-Tempered Organ,* Charles Padgham supplies each key with figures for accumulated errors for that key's major and harmonic minor scale, focusing on the horizontal rather than vertical aspect. Padgham, 44–97.

6. PHYSICAL AND ENVIRONMENTAL FACTORS

1. Resources for viola da gamba care and maintenance can be found at the Viola da Gamba Society of America's web page on viol care: http://vdgsa.org/pgs/violcare.html; see also John Catch's booklets *The Care of Your Viol* and *Fitting Up Your Viol,* available for purchase from the Viola da Gamba Society at www.vdgs.org.uk/misc.html. Helpful maintenance hints also abound throughout Alison Crum's *The Viol Rules.* For the lute, David Van Edwards's booklet *The Care of Your Lute* can be purchased through the Lute Society at www.lutesociety.org/pages/catalogue#n.

2. Linda Sayce's web page provides basic information on gut strings: www.theorbo.com/Writings/Gutstrings.htm; Arto Wikla's String Calculator page expands the treatment to include other materials: http://www.cs.helsinki.fi/u/wikla/mus/NewScalc/. The Lute Society's "Lute Stringing" page provides preliminary information: www.lutesociety.org/pages/lute-stringing. For the viol, see the "strings" section of the web pages and booklets cited in note 1 and also pp. 120–121 in *The Viol Rules.* The websites of Aquila USA (www.aquilausa.com/Default.html), Savarez (www.savarez.fr/anglais/index.html), and luthier Daniel Larson (www.gamutmusic.com) furnish a great deal of basic information as well.

3. Mason, 20. In personal conversations, Boston Catlines string purveyor and fretted instrument player Chris Henriksen has pointed out that although the research on historical string-making techniques in recent years has led us closer to an understanding of how historical gut bass strings may have been produced, we still do not have

a solid knowledge of what they sounded like, particularly on the lower courses of single neck Renaissance lutes, although he and a number of luthiers I queried on this matter all agree that they probably sounded better than the current modern versions suggest.

4. Gut's instability compared with metal was commonly accepted knowledge in the sixteenth and seventeenth centuries. See, for instance, Bottrigari, 14.

5. Barbieri, *Enharmonic,* 40–41.

6. Personal conversations with Paul O'Dette.

7. Extreme imperfections, however, cause a string to become false, a topic discussed later in this chapter.

8. Dart, 15. Warm air is able to hold more moisture than cold air, but for the atmosphere to be humid there must be a source of moisture such as a large body of water or a weather system. That is why the wet season in the tropics occurs during the warmer time of year even though there is still abundant moisture available in the dry season. On the other hand, during the winter in northern climes, the humidity tends to be lower, a situation exacerbated by indoor heating systems that dry out the interior atmosphere.

9. An A-frame guitar stand that allows you to keep your instrument on stage works splendidly for all but the very largest lutes and viols.

10. Dart, 15.

11. Van Edwards, *Care of Your Lute,* 18–26; www.vanedwards.co.uk/fretknot.htm; from Daniel Larson's web page: www.gamutmusic.com/tying-lute-frets/ for single frets, and www.gamutmusic.com/tying-viol-frets/ for double frets.

12. This, in fact, is a common cause of false harpsichord strings, that is, the string's loss of firm contact with either the bridge or nut pins. See Kottick, 127–128.

13. See Watson, "The Lute and the Case for Double Frets"; Hodgson.

14. Ganassi, 57.

15. Capleton, 57.

16. Dart, 15–16.

17. Dowland, *Varietie of Lute Lessons,* 13–14.

18. Capirola, 3v–4r.

19. I second Gordon Gregory's advice to "go home tonight and fit a new set of strings, it will be the best thing you can do to improve your lute's tuning and sound!" Gregory, 11.

20. L. D. Brown, 3.

21. Gregory recommends polishing the grooves by pulling an old string over the slot (Gregory, 11); Van Edwards recommends the same but with a dab of Brasso added to the string (Van Edwards, *Care of Your Lute,* 4–5).

22. Coakley, "Tuning Temperaments for Lutes," 12.

23. Van Edwards, *Care of Your Lute,* 1–2.

24. Lundberg, 212.

25. Lundberg also recommends tuning the strings a half step low for the first few hours to reduce the breaking-in period for new strings and to help the lute "find its voice" (ibid., 212).

26. Ibid., 68.

27. L. D. Brown, 2. Both Gregory and Van Edwards, on the other hand, recommend that the string just touch or kiss the side of the pegbox to keep the peg from

slipping, but caution against jamming the string against the side of the pegbox. Gregory, 12; Van Edwards, *Care of Your Lute,* 4. In my experience, touching or kissing the pegbox can easily slide into jamming, and, for this reason, I recommend no contact between the string and pegbox.

28. See Gómez and Bustamante, 11–13. For detailed and precise mathematical explanations of the physics behind sharpening, see Coakley, "Orpharion and Cittern Analysis," 59–68, 111.

29. The height of the bridge in this and the following figure are heightened disproportionately in order to make the different endpoints of lines a and b more clearly discernable than would a scale drawing able to fit on this page.

30. Ganassi, 58.

31. L. D. Brown, 4.

32. Palisca, *Florentine Camerata,* 199–206.

33. Sharpening is generally more of an issue with gut and Nylgut when the humidity is high because they absorb moisture more readily than the other materials do.

34. Segerman, "Some Theory," 28.

35. L. D. Brown, 5; Barbieri, "Inharmonicity," 407–408; Bermudo, 120–121. Bermudo points out that because the knots with which they are tied on to the bridge are thicker, the actual sounding length of the bass strings is shorter. This is because the string's vibrating length begins not at the bridge, but at the leading edge of the knot, which can reduce the string's length by 1–3 mm.

36. Bermudo, 112–113; Barbieri, "Inharmonicity," 408, 410.

7. THE ZEN OF TUNING

1. Goodwin, "Review of the VioLab 'Pitchman,'" 18.

2. Dart, 17.

3. Duprey, 43. Keep in mind that to Renaissance and Baroque ears, equal temperament was full of offensive dissonances to the extent that for the keyboard parallel to the music under discussion, equal temperament was hardly considered an option, a view all the more potent since keyboards were limited to a greater extent than fretted instruments and unable to extend meantone temperaments unless they were fitted with split keys.

4. "La Coquette virtuose" also works perfectly well in 1/4-comma and, of course, 1/6-comma meantone temperaments.

5. Vincenzo Galilei's son, the great astronomer Galileo Galilei, recognizing that he was able to hear more precisely than he was able to see, was known to have contrived experimental methods that relied more on his sense of sound than of sight.

6. Dart, 17.

7. Available at www.bitcount.com/cleartune/index.html and the App Store.

8. My thanks to Alison Crum for alerting me to PitchLab and its developer Karl Morton for providing me with detailed information regarding his app. While Cleartune is a superb all-purpose tuning app, PitchLab is specifically geared toward string instruments and outperforms Cleartune in terms of custom programmability. Though the basic app is free, with the purchase of the upgrade, $2.99 at this writing, users can create custom-made temperaments catered to any type of stringed instrument. Equal temperament offset charts begin on A and are quickly and easily crafted by adjusting ET

offsets with up and down arrows. No currently available electronic tuner offers as many options or such a wide array of tuning modalities for stringed instruments as PitchLab.

9. Unfortunately, the VioLab "Pitchman" is no longer in production as of 2015, though units are available on the secondary market. For a detailed review as it pertains to lute, see Goodwin, "Review of the VioLab 'Pitchman.'"

10. My thanks to Matt Finn and Brad Vargo at Bitcount for this and other information with regard to their application.

11. I have, however, had students who could consistently identify pitch variances within 2c.

12. My thanks to Alison Crum for pointing this out in personal conversation. Force of attack is much more of an issue for wire-strung instruments such as the cittern and those that are strummed such as the baroque or four-course guitar.

13. L. D. Brown, 5.

14. You mark the treble side because it is much more likely to remain constant than the bass side, which, as we have seen, is subject to the variegated effects of sharpening to a greater extent.

15. In such cases, choosing a second string with less tension than you may otherwise prefer can mitigate the sharpening effect somewhat.

16. Hoffmann, 83.

17. Elizabeth Liddle points out: "because low notes have lower frequencies than high notes, beats will be slower for a given amount of difference between two low notes than between two high notes. This may be a reason why an out-of-tune treble viol sounds more unpleasant than an out-of-tune bass." Liddle, 155. This is also why it is easier to discern pitch differences more easily with higher than lower pitches.

18. Seashore, 59–60.

19. Meyer, 122–123. Gerle's other method focuses on unisons, including those with the bass courses' octave strings.

20. My thanks to Clare Callahan for showing me this method.

21. Silbiger, 39.

22. For a method of tuning the lute (or viol) in Pythagorean tuning by using harmonics, refer to Joseph Baldassare's articles listed in the bibliography.

23. For more detail on this topic, see Dolata, "Secret of Tuning by Harmonics."

24. Bermudo, 115–116; Corona-Alcalde, 33.

25. Hoffmann, 90.

26. In his chapter 82, Bermudo warns against slanted frets: "With all urgency, I beseech that the serious player heed two points. The first [is] that some players hope to fix the abovementioned faults by putting the frets where the said faults occur at an angle, taking them out of line. . . . This is not a solution but a cover-up as can be seen in the above examples. Take a fret where there is a fault . . . and you will find that, by slanting the fret, it does not hit any string in the right place." Bermudo, 112–113. Bermudo, was, of course, correct to a degree, but once again, in his desire for theoretical precision, as a nonplayer, his view of the forest has been obscured by the trees, except in the case of isolated octaves played against notes at a slanted fret, which must be checked for accuracy.

27. Regarding Spinacino's "Recercare I/38," see Griffiths, "Spinacino's Twelve-Tone Experiment."

28. Lindley, *Lutes, Viols and Temperaments,* 58–60.
29. Duffin, "Tuning and Temperament," 283; Bermudo, 108, 115–116; Praetorius, 68.
30. Liddle, 162; personal conversations with José Vázquez.
31. Taylor, 17.
32. Liddle, 163–164.

8. CONTINUO

1. Crum, 130.
2. Barbieri, "Conflitti," 144.
3. For sliding and nonsliding chord shapes for lutes in G, see North, 102–104, 119–131.
4. For a basic primer in music theory as it pertains to continuo specifically on fretted instruments, see North, 27–54. See musical examples 8.25–8.26 for examples of root 5 chords where the third finger is on the fifth course.
5. The first two are also sliding forms if the open course is excluded. Chords that are technically possible but that sound muddy or can be achieved more conveniently elsewhere are not included.
6. The open third course can be added to musical examples 8.11 and 8.12, although first inversion chords are better left to three notes only.
7. Joking aside, there are pieces such as the Chaconne in G Minor often attributed to Tommaso Vitali that contain a surfeit of G♭ Major chords or first inversion E♭ Minor chords.
8. North, 177–193.

9. VIOLS

1. Carter, 27.
2. Gable, 22, who also adds, "When it's good, it's very good. When it's bad, it's horrid!"
3. Ibid., 23.
4. Gouk, 116.
5. Ortiz, 26.
6. Lindley, *Lutes, Viols and Temperaments,* 37–42.
7. Galilei, *Fronimo,* 104.
8. Simpson, *Division Viol,* 13–14. Simpson as well as Galilei and Dowland are examples of superb practitioners attempting to gain admission into the more prestigious company of natural philosophers through the inclusion of significant theoretical exegeses in their works.
9. My thanks to Daniel Larson and Chris Henriksen for their advice on such matters.
10. To mitigate the stiffness of thicker plain or gimped gut strings, which can make them initially difficult to tune, gamba players can increase the suppleness of these strings by tuning them up to pitch and then rapidly winding the peg to and fro twenty to thirty times.
11. Crum, 120.

12. Ganassi, however, recommends relocating the bridge either higher or lower as a means of changing the overall pitch of the instrument. Ganassi, 15.

13. Ibid., 61.

14. Crum, 23.

15. See Playford, 44; see also Silbiger, 39, who characterizes this instruction as "a common if risky admonition!"

16. Carter, 29.

17. Ganassi, 62.

18. Liddle, 163.

19. Gable, 25–26.

20. Mark Lindley states that every first-rate consort he has heard concerns itself with trying to "cultivate justly intoned chords," an opinion echoed by Paul O'Dette in personal conversations. See Lindley, *Lutes, Viols and Temperaments,* 93.

21. Cited by Gable, 38.

22. "Where Have All the Flowers Gone?" by Pete Seeger repeats the refrain "When will they ever learn?"

23. Bottrigari, 14–16.

24. Crum, 129–130.

25. Ganassi, 15. Ganassi assumes that the bass viol will be pitched on the low side.

26. Gable points out that for those accustomed to thinking in A, a tenor viol tuned in that open string configuration can immediately solve many of the tuning issues associated with sharp tonalities. Gable, 36.

27. Carter, 29.

28. Ibid., 24.

29. Gable, 35.

30. Note that the Arabic numerals indicate where ET frets would be placed and that it omits B♯, E♯, C♭, and F♭. Diagram 9.3 was originally designed to show where the frets would need to be placed to generate the pitches indicated between the frets; however, it also happens to show the approximate locations between the frets where the fingers can be placed to produce those pitches in the absence of a fret or tastino.

31. Liddle, 159.

32. Carter, 24.

33. Hoffmann, 89.

34. Ibid., 87.

35. My thanks to Richard Carter for many of the finer points regarding the lyra viol.

36. Headley.

APPENDIX I

1. You can change whether your dial reads A♭ or G♯ under Options > Notation. "English" gives you Cleartune presets; "English (♭)" makes all the accidentals flat, and "English (♯)" makes all the accidentals sharp. I prefer to create my own set of sharps and flats under "Custom" by selecting "Edit" and choosing their identity based on where I place the wolf, a concept explained in chapter 4.

2. As you can see, because they measure vibrations per second, hertz do not conveniently translate into an equivalent number of units between all half steps. For

instance, at A = 415 Hz, the difference between ET semitones A♭–A is 23.3 Hz, A–B♭ 24.7 Hz, and B♭–B 26.1 Hz. For this reason hertz are somewhat cumbersome compared with cents when evaluating musical intervals.

APPENDIX 2

1. Anachronistic, clumsy, and prone to error, equal temperament offset charts are unfortunately the only currently available method to create custom temperaments in electronic tuners.

2. The other option, of course, would be to change the international reference pitch to C, an improvement unlikely to occur in the near future given the difficulties of finally arriving at the international standard of A = 440 Hz, often ignored by symphony orchestras as it is. See Haynes, *History of Performing Pitch.*

3. "Notation" only affects the pitch wheel.

Bibliography

Agricola, Martin. *The "Musica instrumentalis deudsch" of Martin Agricola: A Treatise on Musical Instruments, 1529 and 1545.* Translated and edited by William E. Hettrick. Cambridge: Cambridge University Press, 1994.

Annoni, Maria Therese. "Tuning, Temperament and Pedagogy for the Vihuela in Juan Bermudo's 'Declaración de Instrumentos Musicales' (1555)." Ph.D. diss., Ohio State University, 1989.

Backus, John. *The Acoustical Foundations of Music.* New York: Norton, 1969.

Bailes, Anthony. "The Lute 1600–1645: A Review." *Lute News* 63 (September 2002): 5–10.

Baldassare, Joseph A. "Playing the Lute of Mediaeval Europe, Part 2." *Lute News* 70 (July 2004): 14–19.

——. "Playing the Lute of Mediaeval Europe, Part 3." *Lute News* 72 (December 2004): 21–28.

Banchieri, Adriano. *L'Organo suonarino* (1611). Bologna: Forni, 1969.

Barbieri, Patrizio. "Conflitti di intonazione tra cembalo, liuto e archi nel 'concerto' italiano del Seicento." In *Studi Corelliani,* edited by Pierluigi Petrobelli and Gloria Staffieri, 4:123–153. Florence: Olschki, 1990.

——. *Enharmonic Instruments and Music 1470–1900.* Latina, Italy: Levante, 2008.

——. "The Inharmonicity of Musical String Instruments (1543–1993): With an Unpublished Memoir by J.-B. Mercadier (1784)." *Studi Musicali* 27, no. 2 (1998): 383–419.

——. "L'Accordatura strumentale in Toscana: Proposte e contrasti da V. Galilei a Cristofori (c. 1580–1730)." In *Musicologia Humana: Studies in Honor of Warren and Ursula Kirkendale,* edited by Siegfried Gmeinwieser, David Hiley, and Jörg Riedlbauer, 209–232. Florence: Olschki, 1994.

Barbour, J. Murray. *Tunings and Temperament: A Historical Survey.* East Lansing: Michigan State College Press, 1953.

Bardi, Giovanni de'. "Discourse on Ancient Music and Good Singing." In *Source Readings in Music History: From Classical Antiquity through the Romantic Era,* edited by Oliver Strunk, 290–301. New York: Norton, 1950.

Benade, Arthur H. *Fundamentals of Musical Acoustics.* New York: Oxford University Press, 1976.

Benson, David J. *Music: A Mathematical Offering.* Cambridge: Cambridge University Press, 2007.

Bermudo Juan. "'On Playing the Vihuela,' from *Declaración de instrumentos musicales* (Osuna, 1555). Dawn Astrid Espinosa, trans. and commentary." *Journal of the Lute Society of America* 28–29 (1995–1996): 1–139.

Bibby, Neil. "Tuning and Temperament: Closing the Spiral." In *Music and Mathematics: From Pythagoras to Fractals,* edited by John Fauvel, Raymond Flood, and Robin Wilson, 12–27. Oxford: Oxford University Press, 2003.

Blackwood, Easley. *The Structure of Recognizable Diatonic Tunings.* Princeton, NJ: Princeton University Press, 1985.

Bodig, Richard D. "Silvestro Ganassi's *Regola Rubertina* Revelations and Questions." *Journal of the Viola da Gamba Society of America* 14 (December 1977): 61–70.

Borgir, Tharald. *The Performance of the Basso Continuo in Italian Baroque Music.* Ann Arbor: UMI Research Press, 1987.

Bottrigari, Ercole. *Il Desiderio: Or, Concerning the Playing Together of Various Musical Instruments.* Translated by Carol MacClintock. Musicological Studies and Documents 9. Rome: American Institute of Musicology, 1962.

Bream, Julian. "How to Write for the Guitar." *The Score and IMA Magazine* 19 (March 1957): 19–26.

Bromberg, Carla, and Ana Maria Alfonso-Goldfarb. "Vincenzo Galilei and Music: Some Socio-cultural and Acoustical Discussions." *Circumscribere* 6 (2009): 1–11.

Brown, Howard Mayer, and Joan Lascelle. *Musical Iconography: A Manual for Cataloguing Musical Subjects in Western Art before 1800.* Cambridge, MA: Harvard University Press, 1972.

Brown, Lawrence D. "Stringed Instrument Care for Lutes, Viols and Related Instruments." *Continuo* (May 1984): 2–5.

Browne, Charles. "Review of the Peterson VSAM II Virtual Strobe Tuner, Sound Generator and Metronome." *Lute News* 74 (July 2005): 16–17.

Buetens, Stanley. "The Instructions of Alessandro Piccinini." *Journal of the Lute Society of America* 2 (1969): 6–17.

———. "On Fretting a Lute." *Journal of the Lute Society of America* 3 (1970): 53–63.

Camiz, Franca Trinchieri. "Music and Painting in Cardinal del Monte's Household." *Metropolitan Museum Journal* 26 (1991): 213–226.

Canguilhem, Philippe. *Fronimo de Vincenzo Galilei.* Paris: Minerve, 2001.

Capirola, Vincenzo. *Compositione di meser Vincenzo Capirola.* 1517.

Capleton, Brian. "Carl Friedrich Abel, a Gainsborough Painting, and Viol Temperament: Some Evidence and Enigmas." *Consort* 59 (Summer 2003): 51–74.

Carlone, Mariagrazia. "Lutes, Archlutes, Theorboes in Iconography." *Music in Art* 30, no. 1–2 (2005): 75–87.

———. "Portrait of a Lutenist at the Museo Civico of Como: An Inquiry." In *Art and Music in the Early Modern Period: Essays in Honor of Franca Trinchieri Camiz,* edited by Katherine A. McIver, 91–99. Aldershot, UK: Ashgate, 2003.

———. "Portraits of Lutenists." *Music in Art* 29, no. 1–2 (2004): 64–76.

Carter, Richard. "Unequal Fretting on Viols and Better Intonation in Consort: Some Background Information and Practical Tips." *The Viol* 20 (Autumn 2010): 24–32. Corrected version sent with *The Viol* 21 (Winter 2010–2011).

Castaldi, Bellerofonte. *Capricci (1622), Part 1: Duos for Theorbo and Tiorbino, Sonatas for Theorbo.* Edited by David Dolata. Recent Researches in the Music of the Baroque Era 142. Middleton, WI: A-R Editions, 2006.

Chua, David K. "Vincenzo Galilei, Modernity and the Division of Nature." In *Music Theory and Natural Order: From the Renaissance to the Twentieth Century,* edited by Suzannah Clark and Alex Rehding, 17–29. Cambridge: Cambridge University Press, 2001.

Coakley, Chris. "Dowland's Lute Tuning and Other Ancient Methods, Including Gerle's." *Fellowship of Makers and Researchers of Historical Instruments Quarterly* 123 (2013): 16–43.

———. “Orpharion and Cittern Fret Analysis and Other Ancient Tunings, Including Baroque Lutes.” *Fellowship of Makers and Researchers of Historical Instruments Quarterly* 123 (2013): 44–111.

———. “Tuning Temperaments for Lutes.” *Fellowship of Makers and Researchers of Historical Instruments Quarterly* 109 (2008): 5–22.

Coelho, Victor. “The Baroque Guitar: Players, Paintings, Patrons, and the Public.” In *The World of Baroque Music: New Perspectives,* edited by George B. Stauffer, 169–184. Bloomington: Indiana University Press, 2006.

Corona-Alcalde, Antonio. “‘You Will Raise Your 4th Fret’: An Equivocal Instruction by Luis Milan?” *Galpin Society Journal* 44 (March 1991): 2–45.

Covey-Crump, Roger. “Pythagoras at the Forge: Tunings in Early Music.” In *Companion to Medieval and Renaissance Music,* edited by Tess Knighton and David Fallows, 317–326. Berkeley: University of California Press, 1992.

Crum, Alison. *The Viol Rules: A Notebook.* Oxford: Author, 2009.

Damiani, Andrea. “Temperament.” In *Method for Renaissance Lute,* translated by Doc Rossi, 190–192. Bologna: Ut Orpheus, 1999.

Dart, Thurston. “Miss Mary Burwell’s Instruction Book for the Lute.” *Galpin Society Journal* 11 (May 1958): 3–62.

Day, T. “Teachers’ Craft Knowledge: A Constant in Times of Change?” *Irish Educational Studies* 24, no. 1 (March 2005): 21–30.

Denis, Jean. *Traité de l’accord de l’espinette.* New York: Da Capo, 1969.

Dolata, David. “Bellerofonte Castaldi (1580–1649) of Modena: Musician, Poet, and Adventurer.” *Acta Musicologica* 79, no. 1 (2007): 85–111.

———. “Castaldi’s Practice Room: Onomatopoeic Echoes.” *Fellowship of Makers and Researchers of Historical Instruments Quarterly* 121 (2012): 30–34.

———. “An Introduction to Tunings and Temperaments, Part 1.” *Lute Society of America Quarterly* 28, no. 2–3 (May–August 1993): 30–31.

———. “An Introduction to Tunings and Temperaments, Part 2.” *Lute Society of America Quarterly* 29, no. 1 (February 1994): 20–23.

———. “Lute Tuning with Harmonics: A Square Peg in a Round Hole.” *Lute Society of America Quarterly* 27, no. 1 (February 1993): 7–9.

———. “Lute Tuning with Meantone Temperaments.” *Lute Society of America Quarterly* 27, no. 1 (February 1993): 12–15.

———. “Making Cents out of Fretting Ratios and Vice Versa.” *Fellowship of Makers and Researchers of Historical Instruments Quarterly* 124 (2013): 16–24.

———. “The Secret of Tuning by Harmonics.” *Soundboard* 19, no. 4 (Spring 1993): 27–37.

———. “Tunings and Temperaments: Theory in the Service of Practice.” *Lute Society of America Quarterly* 30, no. 1 (February 1995): 26–29.

Dombois, Eugen. “Correct and Easy Fret Placement.” *Journal of the Lute Society of America* 6 (1973): 30–33.

———. “Lute Temperament in Hans Gerle (1532)—A Comment from the Author.” *Journal of the Lute Society* 22, no. 2 (1982): 3–14, 89.

———. “Varieties of Meantone Temperament Realized on the Lute.” *Journal of the Lute Society of America* 7 (1974): 82–89.

Donahue, Thomas. *A Guide to Musical Temperament.* Lanham, MD: Scarecrow, 2005.

Dowland, Robert. *Varietie of Lute Lessons* (1610). London: Schott, 1958.

Drake, Stillman. *Galileo at Work: His Scientific Biography.* Chicago: Chicago University Press, 1970.

——. "Music and Philosophy in Early Modern Science." In *Music and Science in the Age of Galileo,* edited by Victor Coelho, 3–16. Dordrecht: Kluwer, 1992.

——. "Renaissance Music and Experimental Science." *Journal of the History of Ideas* 31, no. 4 (1970): 483–500.

Duffin, Ross W. *Baroque Ensemble Tuning in Extended 1/6 Syntonic Comma Meantone.* http://musicserver.case.edu/~rwd/BaroqueTemp/Default.html. Accessed July 25, 2014.

——. *How Equal Temperament Ruined Harmony (and Why You Should Care).* New York: Norton, 2007.

——. "Just Intonation in Renaissance Theory and Practice." *Music Theory Online* 12, no. 3 (October 2006). Accessed July 25, 2014.

——. "Tuning." In *A Performer's Guide to Medieval Music,* edited by Ross Duffin, 545–562. Bloomington: Indiana University Press, 2000.

——. "Tuning and Temperament." In *A Performer's Guide to Renaissance Music,* edited by Jeffery Kite-Powell, 279–289. 2nd ed. Bloomington: Indiana University Press, 2007.

——."Why I Hate Vallotti (or Is It Young?)." *Early Music Historical Performance Online* 1 (2000). Accessed July 25, 2014.

Duprey, François. "Peut-on jouer les tablatures de luth baroque au XVIIe siècle française en tempérament mésotonique?" *Tablature* 17 (2002): 43–50.

Dürer, Albrecht. *Treatise on Mensuration with the Compass and Ruler in Lines, Planes, and Whole Bodies.* Nuremberg, 1525.

Edwards, David Van. *The Care of Your Lute.* Lute Society Booklets 6. Guildford, UK: Lute Society, 1998.

——. "The English Theorbo, the 12-Course Lute, and Thomas Mace's 'Lute Dyphone.'" *Lute News* 40, no. 9 (December 1996): 7–8.

Fabris, Dinko. "Lute Tablature Instructions in Italy: A Survey of the *Regole* from 1507 to 1759." In *Performance on Lute, Guitar and Vihuela: Historical Practice and Modern Interpretation,* edited by Victor Anand Coelho, 16–46. Cambridge: Cambridge University Press, 1997.

Ferraris, Giorgio. *Caravaggio e Baschenis: Due rappresentazioni della stessa musica.* Florence: Società del Liuto, 2011.

——. "Il Musico ritrovato: Francesco da Milano in un ritratto di Giulio Campi? *Resconto del convegno di Como.*" *Bollettino della Società Italiana del Liuto* 13, no. 3 (July 1994): 13.

Forrester, Peter. "Some Notes on Cittern Fingerboards and Stringing." *Fellowship of Makers and Researchers of Historical Instruments Quarterly* 32 (1983): 19–22.

——. "Violas, Vihuelas, and Iconography." *Fellowship of Makers and Researchers of Historical Instruments Quarterly* 44 (1986): 60–63.

——. "Wood and Wire: Cittern Building." *Lute News* 75 (October 2005): 6–14.

Freis, Wolfgang. "Perfecting the Perfect Instrument: Fray Juan Bermudo on the Tuning and Temperament of the Vihuela de Mano." *Early Music* 23 (1995): 421–436.

Gable, Frederick K. "Possibilities for Mean-Tone Temperament Playing on Viols." *Journal of the Viola da Gamba Society of America* 16 (December 1979): 22–39.

Galilei, Vincenzo. *Dialogue on Ancient and Modern Music* (1581). Translated by Claude Palisca. New Haven, CT: Yale University Press, 2003.

——. *Fronimo* (1584). Translated by Carol MacClintock. Neuhausen, Germany: American Institute of Musicology, 1985.

——. *Il Fronimo* (Firenze, 1584). Bibliotheca Musica Bononiensis 2, no. 22. Bologna: Arnaldo Forni, 1988.

——. *Libro d'intavolatura di liuto* (Firenze, 1584). Monumenta Musicae Revocata 11. Florence: Scelte, 1992.

Galpin, Francis. *Old English Instruments of Music, Their History and Character.* London: Methuen, 1911.

Gammie, Ian. "*Ganassi: Regola Rubertina (1542), Lettione Seconda (1543):* A Synopsis of the Text Relating to the Viol." *Chelys* 8 (1978–1979): 23–30.

Ganassi, Sylvestro. *Regola Rubertina* (Venice, 1542 and 1543). Berlin: Robert Lienau, 1977.

Gásser, Luis. *Luis Milán on Sixteenth-Century Performance Practice.* Bloomington: Indiana University Press, 1996.

Gill, Donald. "James Talbot's Manuscript: V: Plucked Strings—The Wire-Strung Fretted Instruments and the Guitar." *Galpin Society Journal* 15 (1962): 60–69.

——. "The Orpharion and Bandora." *Galpin Society Journal* 13 (1960): 14–25.

——. "An Orpharion by John Rose." *Journal of the Lute Society* 2 (1960): 33–39.

Gingerich, Owen. "Kepler, Galilei, and the Harmony of the World." In *Music and Science in the Age of Galileo,* edited by Victor Coelho, 45–63. Dordrecht: Kluwer, 1992.

Gómez, Francisco Fernández del Castillo, and Felipe Orduña Bustamante. "Factors Involved in Classical Guitar Tuning." *Soundboard* 29, no. 1 (Summer 2002): 5–16.

Goodwin, Christopher. ". . . and What Makes a Good Cittern?" *Lute News* 57 (April 2001): 14–15.

——. "Review of the VioLab 'Pitchman.'" *Lute News* 74 (July 2005): 17–18.

Gouk, Penelope. *Music, Science, and Natural Magic in Seventeenth-Century England.* New Haven, CT: Yale University Press, 1999.

Graham-Dixon, Andrew. *Caravaggio: A Life Sacred and Profane.* New York: Norton, 2010.

Gregory, Gordon. "Tuning Lutes." *Lute News* 79 (October 2006): 11–14.

Griffiths, John. "Spinacino's Twelve-Tone Experiment." *Journal of the Lute Society of America* 44 (2011): 47–76.

——. "The Vihuela: Performance Practice, Style, and Context." In *Performance on Lute, Guitar and Vihuela: Historical Practice and Modern Interpretation,* edited by Victor Anand Coelho, 158–179. Cambridge: Cambridge University Press, 1997.

Grijp, Louis Peter. "Fret Patterns of the Cittern." *Galpin Society Journal* 34 (March 1981): 62–97.

Hammer, Stephen. "Toward a Sensible Tuning System of Baroque Orchestras." *Early Music America* 16, no. 3 (Fall 2010): 66–68.

Harkleroad, Leon. *The Math behind the Music.* Cambridge: Cambridge University Press, 2006.

Hartig, Andrew. "The Wire Connection: A Brief Survey of Plucked Wire-Strung Instruments, 15th–18th Centuries—Part One." *Lute Society of America Quarterly* 44, no. 3 (Fall 2009): 42–43.

——. "The Wire Connection: A Brief Survey of Plucked Wire-Strung Instruments, 15th–18th Centuries—Part Two." *Lute Society of America Quarterly* 44, no. 4 (Winter 2009): 56–59.

——. "The Wire Connection: A Brief Survey of Plucked Wire-Strung Instruments, 15th–18th Centuries—Part Three." *Lute Society of America Quarterly* 45, no. 2 (Summer 2010): 31–34.

——. "The Wire Connection: A Brief Survey of Plucked Wire-Strung Instruments, 15th–18th Centuries—Part Four." *Lute Society of America Quarterly* 46, no. 1 (Spring 2011): 33–38.

——. "The Wire Connection: Some Myths and Misconceptions about Wire-Strung Instruments." *Lute Society of America Quarterly* 44, no. 2 (Spring 2009): 32, 41, and 56.

Harwood, Ian. "'Six Several Instruments': Aspects of the English Consort and Its Music." *Lute News* 62 (June 2002): 6–15.

——. *Wire Strings at Helmingham Hall: An Instrument and a Music Book.* Lute Society Booklets 10. Guildford, UK: Lute Society, 2005.

Haynes, Bruce. "Beyond Temperament: Non-keyboard Intonation in the 17th and 18th Centuries." *Early Music* 19, no. 3 (August 1991): 357–382.

——. *A History of Performing Pitch: The Story of "A."* Lanham, MD: Scarecrow, 2002.

Headley, Erin. S.v. "Lirone." *Grove Music Online.* www.oxfordmusiconline.com. Accessed January 20, 2014.

Heck, Thomas F. "The Evolving Meanings of Iconology and Iconography: Toward Some *Descriptive* Definitions." In *Picturing Performance: The Iconography of the Performing Arts in Concept and Practice,* edited by Thomas F. Heck, 7–41. Rochester, NY: University of Rochester Press, 1999.

Hodgson, Martyn. "Early Evidence for the Use of Double Frets and a List of Their Advantages over Single Frets." *Fellowship of Makers and Researchers of Historical Instruments Quarterly* 122 (October 2012): 21–22.

Hoffmann, Bettina. *La Viola da gamba.* Organologia 2, Collana diretta da Renato Meucci. Palermo, Italy: L'Epos, 2010.

Jacobson, Bernard. *Conductors on Conducting.* Frenchtown, NJ: Columbia, 1979.

James, Jamie. *The Music of the Spheres: Music Science and the Natural Order of the Universe.* London: Little, Brown, 1993.

Jorgensen, Owen. *Tuning the Historical Temperaments by Ear: A Manual of Eighty-Nine Methods for Tuning Fifty-One Scales on the Harpsichord, Piano, and Other Keyboard Instruments.* Marquette: Northern Michigan University Press, 1977.

Kapsberger, Girolamo Giovanni. *Libro primo d'intavolatura di chitarrone* (1604). Archivum Musicum, Collana di testi rari, 46. Florence: Scelte, 1982.

Karp, Cary. "The Meantone." *Fellowship of Makers and Researchers of Historical Instruments Quarterly* 32 (1983): 17–19.

Katritzky, M. A. "Performing-Arts Iconography: Traditions, Techniques, and Trends." In *Picturing Performance: The Iconography of the Performing Arts in Concept and Practice,* edited by Thomas F. Heck, 68–90. Rochester, NY: University of Rochester Press, 1999.

Kirnbauer, Martin. "'Wherein the Most Complete Harmony Was Heard': The Viola da Gamba in Chromatic and Enharmonic Music in Seventeenth-Century Rome." In *The Italian Viola da Gamba: Proceedings of the International Symposium on the*

Italian Viola da Gamba, edited by Susan Orlando, 35–52. Solignac, France: Ensemble Baroque de Limoges, 2002.

Klickstein, Gerald. "Pain-Free Tuning." *Soundboard* 28, no. 2 (Fall 2001): 21–25.

——. *Tuning the Guitar by Ear.* Pacific, MO: Mel Bay, 1996.

Kolb, Richard. "What Do Lute Players Really Need to Know about Temperament?" *Lute Society of America Quarterly* 44, no. 2 (Spring 2009): 15–20.

Korrick, Leslie. "Vincenzo Galilei's Re-vision of Renaissance Tuning: Trading on Nature and Art." In *The Sounds and Sights of Performance in Early Music: Essays in Honour of Timothy J. McGhee,* edited by Maureen Epp and Brian E. Power, 123–154. Aldershot, UK: Ashgate, 2009.

Kottick, Edward L. *The Harpsichord Owner's Guide.* Chapel Hill: University of North Carolina Press, 1987.

Langley, Anna, and Gordon Gregory. "Initial Impressions of the New Korg OT12 Multi-temperament 'Orchestral Tuner.'" *Lute News* 57 (April 2001): 16–17.

Le Roy, Adrian. *Les Instructions pour le luth* (1574). Corpus des luthistes français. Paris: Centre National de la Recherche Scientifique, 1977.

Lehman, Bradley. "Bach's Extraordinary Temperament: Our Rosetta Stone I." *Early Music* 33, no. 1 (February 2005): 3–23.

——. "Bach's Extraordinary Temperament: Our Rosetta Stone II." *Early Music* 33, no. 2 (May 2005): 211–231.

Liddle, Elizabeth. "Tuning." Appendix I in *Playing the Viol,* by Alison Crum, 155–164. Oxford: Oxford University Press, 1989.

Lindley, Mark. "An Exceptional G-Sharp in Milan." *Fellowship of Makers and Researchers of Historical Instruments Quarterly* 42 (1986): 69.

——. "Luis Milan and Meantone Temperament." *Journal of the Lute Society of America* 11 (1978): 45–62.

——. *Lutes, Viols and Temperaments.* Cambridge: Cambridge University Press, 1984.

——. S.v. "Temperaments." *Grove Music Online.* www.oxfordmusiconline.com. Accessed July 25, 2014.

——."Tuning and Intonation." In *Performance Practices: Music after 1600,* edited by Howard Mayer Brown and Stanley Sadie, 169–185. New York: Norton, 1989.

Lloyd, Llewellyn. *Intervals, Scales, and Temperaments.* London: MacDonald, 1963.

Loy, Gareth. *Musimathics: The Mathematical Foundations of Music.* Vol. 1. Cambridge, MA: MIT Press, 2006.

Lundberg, Robert. *Historical Lute Construction.* Tacoma, WA: Guild of American Luthiers, 2002.

Lusitano, Vicente. *Introduttione facilissima, et novissima, di canto fermo, figurato, contraponto semplice, et in concerto, con regole generali par far fughe differenti sopra il canto fermo, a 2, 3, et 4 voci, et compositioni, proportioni, generi. s. diatonico, cromatico, enarmonico.* Venice: Francesco Rampazetto, 1561.

Mace, Thomas. *Musick's Monument.* London: T. Radcliffe and N. Thompson, 1676.

Macioce, Stefania, and Enrico De Pascale, eds. *La Musica al tempo di Caravaggio.* Rome: Gangemi, 2010.

Marais, Marin. *The Instrumental Works.* Vol. 1: *Pièces à une et à deux violes (1686–1689).* Edited by John Hsu. New York: Broude Brothers, 1980.

Margerum, Alice. "Early Ud Fretting Systems Described by Al-Kindi." *Fellowship of Makers and Researchers of Historical Instruments Quarterly* 105 (2001): 22–40.

Martin, Darryl. "The Palmer Orpharion: A Re-evaluation." www.darryl-martin.co.uk/palmer.htm. Accessed July 25, 2014.

——. *Report and Drawing Notes on the Orpharion Francis Palmer, London, 1617.* Copenhagen: Musikmuseet, Musikhistorisk Museum and Carl Claudius' Samling, 2007.

Mason, Kevin. "The Chitarrone and Its Repertoire in Early Seventeenth-Century Italy." Ph.D. diss., Washington University, 1983.

Mersenne, Marin. *Harmonie universelle.* Pt. 1. Paris: Cramoisy, 1636.

——. *Harmonie universelle.* Pt. 2. Paris: Ballard, 1637.

Meyer, Christian. "Observations pour une analyse des tempéraments des instruments à cordes pincées: Le Luth de Hans Gerle (1532)." *Revue de Musicologie* 71, no. 1–2 (1985): 119–141.

Milán, Luis. *El Maestro.* Edited, translated, and transcribed by Charles Jacobs. University Park: Pennsylvania State University Press, 1971.

Mitchell, David. "Fretting and Tuning the Lute." In *John Dowland: His Life and Works,* edited by Diana Poulton, 456–465. Berkeley: University of California Press, 1972.

Monson, Craig. "Songs of Shakespeare's England." In *The World of Baroque Music: New Perspectives,* edited by George B. Stauffer, 1–24. Bloomington: Indiana University Press, 2006.

Moyer, Ann E. "Music, Mathematics, and Aesthetics." In *Music and Mathematics in Late Medieval and Early Modern Europe,* edited by Philippe Vendrix, 111–146. Turnhout, Belgium: Brepols, 2008.

Myers, Herbert. "Tuning and Temperament." In *A Performer's Guide to Seventeenth-Century Music,* edited by Jeffery Kite-Powell, 368–374. 2nd ed. Bloomington: Indiana University Press, 2012.

Narvey, Benjamin. "The Differing Temperaments of Gioseffo Zarlino and Vincenzo Galilei: An Exploration of 16th Century Tuning Systems and World Views." *Lute News* 64 (December 2002): 19–21.

Nelson, David K. "An Interview with Pinchas Zukerman." *Fanfare* 14 (March–April 1991): 20–39.

Nordstrom, Lyle. *The Bandora: Its Music and Sources.* Sterling Heights, MI: Harmonie Park Press, 1992.

North, Nigel. *Continuo Playing on the Lute, Archlute and Theorbo.* Bloomington: Indiana University Press, 1987.

Nuti, Giulia. *The Performance of Italian Basso Continuo: Style in Keyboard Accompaniment in the Seventeenth and Eighteenth Centuries.* Aldershot, UK: Ashgate, 2007.

O'Dette, Paul. Notes to Paul O'Dette, *Marco dall'Aquila: Pieces for Lute* (2010), CD. Harmonia Mundi HMU 907548.

Ortiz, Diego. *Trattado de glosas: Libro segundo.* Rome: Valerio e Luis Dorico, 1553.

Otterstedt, Annette. "The Compatibility of the Viol Consort with the Organ in the Early Seventeenth Century." *Chelys* 25 (1996): 32–52.

——. *The Viol: History of an Instrument.* Translated by Hans Reiners. Kassel, Germany: Bärenreiter, 2002.

Padgham, Charles A. *The Well-Tempered Organ.* Oxford: Positif, 1986.

Palisca, Claude V. *The Florentine Camerata.* New Haven, CT: Yale University Press, 1989.

——. *The Florentine Camerata: Documentary Studies and Translations.* New Haven, CT: Yale University Press, 1989.

———. "Mathematics and Geometry in Galilei's *Dialogo* of 1581." In *Music and Mathematics in Late Medieval and Early Modern Europe,* edited by Philippe Vendrix, 235–252. Turnhout, Belgium: Brepols, 2008.

———. "Was Galileo's Father an Experimental Scientist?" In *Music and Science in the Age of Galileo,* edited by Victor Coelho, 143–151. Dordrecht: Kluwer, 1992.

Pavan, Franco. "Francesco Canova da Milano (1497–1543): Ipotesi di identificazione del ritratto di liutista della Pinacoteca Civica di Como." *Bollettino della Società Italiana del Liuto* 15, no. 1 (January 1995): 13–15.

Pirrotta, Nino. "Temperaments and Tendencies in the Florentine Camerata." *Musical Quarterly* 40 (1954): 169–189.

Playford, John. *An Introduction to the Skill of Musick.* London, 1655.

Pohlmann, Ernst. *Laute, Theorbe, Chitarrone: Die Lauten-Instrumente, ihre Musik und Literatur von 1500 bis zur Gegenwart.* 5th ed. Bremen, Germany: Eres, 1982.

Pollens, Stewart. "A Viola da Gamba Temperament Preserved by Antonio Stradivari." *Eighteenth-Century Music* 3, no. 1 (2006): 125–132.

Poulton, Diana. *John Dowland.* 2nd ed. Berkeley: University of California Press, 1982.

Poulton, Diana, and Tim Crawford. S.v. "Lute: Technique." *Grove Music Online.* www.oxfordmusiconline.com. Accessed January 20, 2014.

Povoledo, Elisabetta Angela. "Caravaggio's Early Works and the Tradition of Lombard Realism." Master's thesis, McGill University, 1988.

Powers, Katherine. "Music-Making Angels in Renaissance Painting: Symbolism and Reality." *Music in Art* 29, no. 1–2 (2004): 52–63.

Praetorius, Michael. *Syntagma musicum II: De organographia.* Translated and edited by David Z. Crookes. Oxford: Clarendon, 1986.

Rasch, Rudolf. "Tuning and Temperament." In *The Cambridge History of Western Music Theory,* edited by Thomas Christensen, 193–222. Cambridge: Cambridge University Press, 2002.

Reeve, John. "A Mid-Sixteenth-Century French Guide to Fret Placement." *The Lute* 43 (2003): 44–62.

Robiczek, Bonnie. "A Method for Tuning the Lute." *Lute Society of America Newsletter* 16, no. 1 (1981); reprinted in *Lute Society of America Quarterly* 28, no. 2–3 (May–August 1993): 28–29.

Schlegel, Andreas, and Joachim Lüdtke. *The Lute in Europe 2.* Menziken, Switzerland: Lute Corner, 2011.

Schneider, John. *The Contemporary Guitar.* 2nd ed. Lanham, MD: Scarecrow, 2015.

———. "Just Guitar." *Guitar International* 6 (April–June 2004): 42–50.

Seashore, Carl E. *Psychology of Music.* New York: Dover, 1967.

Segerman, Ephraim. "Fingerboard Shapes and Graded Frets." *Fellowship of Makers and Researchers of Historical Instruments Quarterly* 71 (1993): 40–43.

———. "The Instruments of the Consort." *Fellowship of Makers and Researchers of Historical Instruments Quarterly* 82 (1996): 43–49.

———. "A Note on Meantone Temperaments." *Fellowship of Makers and Researchers of Historical Instruments Quarterly* 31 (1983): 52–54.

———. "On Medieval and Early Renaissance Tunings and Fretting Patterns." *Fellowship of Makers and Researchers of Historical Instruments Quarterly* 9 (1977): 62–66.

———. "Orpharion News." *Fellowship of Makers and Researchers of Historical Instruments Quarterly* 27 (1982): 25–28.

——. "A Reminder on the Principles of Scholarly Choice." *Fellowship of Makers and Researchers of Historical Instruments Quarterly* 52 (1988): 25–26.

——. "Some Theory on Pitch Instability, Inharmonicity and Lowest Pitch Limits." *Fellowship of Makers and Researchers of Historical Instruments Quarterly* 104 (2001): 28–29.

——. "Stress and Equilibrium Moisture Content in Gut and Wood." *Fellowship of Makers and Researchers of Historical Instruments Quarterly* 104 (2001): 39–40.

Segerman, Ephraim, and Djilda Abbott. "On the Palmer Orpharion." *Fellowship of Makers and Researchers of Historical Instruments Quarterly* 3 (1976): 48–56.

——. "A Reasoned and Practical Approach to Mean-Tone Fretting." *Fellowship of Makers and Researchers of Historical Instruments Quarterly* 9 (1977): 54–61.

Segerman, Ephraim, Djilda Abbott, and Pete Spencer. "Fret Distances from the Nut for Every Fret above the Open String." *Fellowship of Makers and Researchers of Historical Instruments Quarterly* 14 (1979): 32–36.

Shepherd, Martin. "The Well-Tempered Lute." *Lute News* 41 (March 1997): 8–10.

Silbiger, Alexander. "The First Viol Tutor: Hans Gerle's *Musica Teutsch.*" *Viola da Gamba Society of America* 6 (November 1969): 34–48.

Simpson, Christopher. *A Compendium of Practical Music in Five Parts.* Edited by Phillip J. Lord. Reprinted from the Second Edition of 1667. Oxford: Basil Blackwell, 1970.

——. *The Division Viol.* London: Godbid, 1665.

Slim, H. Colin. "Some Possible Likenesses of Francesco Canova da Milano (1497–1543)." In *Painting Music in the Sixteenth Century: Essays in Iconography,* 2:1–8. Variorum Collected Studies Series 727. Aldershot, UK: Ashgate, 2002.

Smith, Anne. *The Performance of 16th-Century Music: Learning from the Theorists.* New York: Oxford, 2011.

Smith, Douglas Alton. "Baron and Weiss contra Mattheson: In Defense of the Lute." *Journal of the Lute Society of America* 6 (1973): 48–62.

——. *A History of the Lute from Antiquity to the Renaissance.* Lexington, VA: Lute Society of America, 2002.

Snyder, Kerala J. *Dieterich Buxtehude: Organist in Lübeck.* Rev. ed. Rochester, NY: University of Rochester Press, 2007.

Southwell, Gary. *The Panormo Guitar and Its Makers.* London: London College of Furniture, 1983.

Spencer, Robert. "How to Hold a Lute: Historical Evidence from Paintings." *Early Music* 3, no. 4 (October 1975): 352–354.

Strauch, Werner von. *Handbuch der Stimmungen und Temperaturen ein praktischer Leitfaden für die Spieler von Bund- und Tasteninstrumenten.* Berlin: Pape, 2009.

Taylor, John. *Tone Production on the Classical Guitar.* Higher Diploma in Musical Instrument Technology. London: Musical New Services, 1978.

Teplow, Deborah A. *Performance Practice and Technique in Marin Marais' Pièces de viole.* Ann Arbor: UMI Research Press, 1986.

Tittle, Martin B. *A Performer's Guide through Historical Keyboard Tunings.* Ann Arbor, MI: Anderson, 1978.

Tourin, Peter. "A Quick and Easy Method for Tuning a Consort." *Viola da Gamba Society of America News* 21, no. 3 (September 1984): 13–14.

Tyler, James, and Paul Sparks. *The Guitar and Its Music: From the Renaissance to the Classical Era.* Oxford: Oxford University Press, 2002.

Veroli, Claudio di. *Unequal Temperaments: Theory, History and Practice.* Rev. 2nd ed. Self-published e-book, 2009.

Vries, Lyckle de. "Iconography and Iconology in Art History: Panofsky's Prescriptive Definitions and Some Art-Historical Responses to Them." In *Picturing Performance: The Iconography of the Performing Arts in Concept and Practice,* edited by Thomas F. Heck, 42–64. Rochester, NY: University of Rochester Press, 1999.

Walker, Daniel P. "Some Aspects of the Musical Theory of Vincenzo Galilei and Galileo Galilei." *Proceedings of the Royal Musical Association* 100 (1973–1974): 33–47.

——. *Studies in Musical Science in the Late Renaissance.* London: Warburg Institute, 1978.

Watson, Tim. "Dei pericoli nell'avere fiducia nell'iconografia, ovvero: Possiamo consolarci che, se il liuto è così difficile da suonare è ancora difficile da dipingere. Un viaggio attraverso i comuni errori geometrici nelle raffigurazioni pittoriche del liuto." *Il Liuto: Rivista della Società del Liuto* 2 (2011): 7–20.

——."The Lute and the Case for Double Frets." *Fellowship of Makers and Researchers of Historical Instruments Quarterly* 121 (2012): 39–46.

Wollenberg, Susan. "Music and Mathematics: An Overview." In *Music and Mathematics: From Pythagoras to Fractals,* edited by John Fauvel, Raymond Flood, and Robin Wilson, 1–9. Oxford: Oxford University Press, 2003.

Woodfield, Ian. *The Early History of the Viol.* Cambridge: Cambridge University Press, 1984.

Young, Crawford. "Lute, Gittern, and Citole." In *A Performer's Guide to Medieval Music,* edited by Ross Duffin, 355–375. Bloomington: Indiana University Press, 2000.

Index

Page numbers in italics refer to illustrations.

DAVID DOLATA is Professor of Musicology at Florida International University in Miami. The *Bulletin de la Société Française de Luth* has referred to him as a "gentleman de la Renaissance" for his activities as a performer and scholar. As a lutenist, he has appeared at such venues as the Glimmerglass Opera, the Florida Grand Opera, the Northwest Bach Festival, and the Miami Bach Society, and on recordings for BBC, Koch International, and Toccata Classics. He codirects Il Furioso with Victor Coelho and maintains a long-standing affiliation with Boston University's Center for Early Music Studies. His research on early seventeenth-century Italian lute music has been published in *Recent Researches in the Music of the Baroque Era, Early Music, Acta Musicologica, Grove Music Online,* and the *Grove Dictionary of Musical Instruments.* David Dolata has served as visiting research professor at the Centre d'Études Supérieures de la Renaissance at the Université François-Rabelais de Tours–CNRS, where he remains a Chercheur Associé and coedits the Centre's tablature-related publications with John Griffiths and Philippe Vendrix. He has been tuning in meantone temperaments for more than twenty-five years.